Digital Accounting:
The Effects of the Internet and ERP on Accounting

Ashutosh Deshmukh
Pennsylvania State University – Erie, USA

IRM Press
Publisher of innovative scholarly and professional information technology titles in the cyberage
Hershey • London • Melbourne • Singapore

Acquisitions Editor: Michelle Potter
Development Editor: Kristin Roth
Senior Managing Editor: Amanda Appicello
Managing Editor: Jennifer Neidig
Copy Editor: Julie LeBlanc
Typesetter: Sharon Berger
Cover Design: Lisa Tosheff
Printed at: Integrated Book Technology

Published in the United States of America by
IRM Press (an imprint of Idea Group Inc.)
701 E. Chocolate Avenue, Suite 200
Hershey PA 17033-1240
Tel: 717-533-8845
Fax: 717-533-8661
E-mail: cust@idea-group.com
Web site: http://www.irm-press.com

and in the United Kingdom by
IRM Press (an imprint of Idea Group Inc.)
3 Henrietta Street
Covent Garden
London WC2E 8LU
Tel: 44 20 72400856
Fax: 44 20 7379 0609
Web site: http://www.eurospanonline.com

Library of Congress Cataloging-in-Publication Data

Deshmukh, Ashutosh, 1959-
Digital accounting : the effects of the Internet and ERP on accounting / Ashutosh Deshmukh.
p. cm.
Summary: "This book provides a foundation in digital accounting by covering fundamental topics such as accounting software, XBRL (eXtensible Business Reporting Language), and EDI"--Provided by publisher.
Includes bibliographical references and index.
ISBN 1-59140-738-9 (hardcover) -- ISBN 1-59140-739-7 (softcover) -- ISBN 1-59140-740-0 (ebook)
1. Accounting--Software. 2. XBRL (Document markup language) 3. Electronic data interchange. 4. Internet--Economic aspects. 5. Business planning. I. Title.
HF5679.D47 2005
657'.0285'5--dc22

2005022460

British Cataloguing in Publication Data
A Cataloguing in Publication record for this book is available from the British Library.

Dedication

This book is dedicated to Hema, my wife, for her unrelenting support through many ups and downs that led to the publication of this book.

Digital Accounting: The Effects of the Internet and ERP on Accounting

Table of Contents

Preface

Accounting and information technology have been constant companions since the days of tabulating machines. Accounting — an art and science of financial information — has evolved in tandem with information technology. The distinctions between the accounting message and information technology medium are blurring faster and faster. The advent of the Internet and enterprise resource planning (ERP) has not only continued but accelerated the trend. The rise and fall of the e-revolution has been spectacular; however, the promised work goes on. The changes are fast and furious, even in the e-bust period. This book is an attempt to capture these changes in accounting workflows, internal controls, and tools due to the e-age, e-era, and e-confusion!

What is Digital Accounting?

The term *digital* refers to digits or numbers; however, in the computer science lexicon, this term refers to the representation of the information in 0s and 1s, which can be read, written and stored using machines. The prefix "e" refers to *electronic*, meaning the use of electricity in powering machines such as computers. Digital accounting, or e-accounting, as a corresponding analog, refers to the representation of accounting information in the digital format, which can then be electronically manipulated and transmitted. Digital accounting does not have a standard definition, but merely refers to the changes in accounting due to computing and networking technologies. The term *digital accounting* is used in this book to capture the changes in the accounting cycles, processes, and functions due to the Internet and ERP systems. The primary focus is on accounting, and the secondary focus is on related finance functions. The level of coverage in financial functions is primarily restricted to intra-business, and topics such as Web-based stock investments and portfolio management are excluded.

The terminology, jargon, and lingo spawned by the computer era are unprecedented, and the title and the subject matter of the book has been debated and questioned repeatedly. In covering various topics, I have erred on the side of caution. I have covered a number of technologies and topics that may only be peripherally related to the main theme of the book. This book is still version 1.0, and I am sure topics will be found that escaped me. I welcome your comments and criticisms.

What Makes This Book Different?

Integrating e-commerce/e-business in the accounting literature has been a challenge. Neither the pervasive effects of e-commerce on internal and external accounting processes are clearly articulated nor a conceptual approach for handling these changes has been formulated. There is no consensus in the coverage of underlying networking technologies, changes in accounting software, and new xRM (relationship management) tools.

This book, though by no means definitive, presents a way to understand these developments. This book provides a foundation in digital accounting by covering developments in accounting software, Web-based financial reporting languages and Electronic data interchange (EDI). Then the effects of the Internet and ERP on accounting are classified and presented for each accounting cycle. Such an approach in handling the e-developments in the accounting context allows us a comprehensive examination of the changes in the established accounting cycle framework.

Chapter I expands on this theme and provides a framework for developments in accounting due to the Internet and ERP. This chapter also deals with the description and history of digital accounting. The next three chapters are the foundations of digital accounting. These chapters cover the evolution of accounting software, XML (eXtensible Markup Language) and XBRL (eXtensible Business Reporting Language), and EDI, respectively. Accounting software is no longer accounting software, but is being sold even by mid-level vendors as business software. Accounting software not only integrates the internal functions but comes pre-packaged with a number of e-commerce/e-business functionalities. XML directly affects data transfer and data analysis. The most famous XML-based language for accountants is XBRL. XBRL is discussed in-depth to get a better understanding of changes in financial reporting. EDI, the forerunner of e-commerce, is not dead but is going strong and is getting adopted for XML and the Internet. A large installed base and heavy monetary investment characterize EDI; this important technology needs to be properly understood by accountants. I believe an in-depth understanding of these three areas is necessary to understand the effects of the Internet and ERP on accounting and finance functions.

The next four chapters focus on chronicling and analyzing digital developments in the context of accounting cycles. Chapter V deals with the revenue cycle. Here, Web-based sales orders, effects of customer relationship management (CRM) software on sales orders and accounting data, online credit approvals and its connection with the accounting system, Web-based tracking of goods and its implications for accounting, electronic invoice/bill presentment and payment, electronic payment mechanisms, and online automated receivables management are discussed. Chapter VI deals with the expenditure cycle. Topics such as Web-based purchase orders, electronic procurement of goods and services, and consequent posting and payment activities are discussed here. These activities are increasingly handled by supplier relationship management

(SRM) and e-procurement tools, which are extensively covered with an emphasis on accounting processes. Additionally, the areas of procurement cards, online management of expenses and payroll, and online travel centers are covered. Chapter VII deals with the conversion cycle. The focus in this chapter is not on production activities but on supply chain management. The production function is now part of an extended collaborative enterprise in many organizations. Cost accounting is not merely assessing product costs but also striving to identify and optimize costs across the supply chain. Basic principles of supply chain management, software tools for supply chain management, and changes in cost accounting are covered here. Finally, Chapter VIII considers the general ledger cycle. This chapter discusses the evolution of the general ledger and financial reporting. First, managerial and information technology tools for Web-enabled virtual close of the books are discussed. The rest of the chapter primarily focuses on reporting software, business intelligence tools, executive dashboards, enterprise portals and its interaction with accounting data. I have primarily used SAP tools to illustrate the functionalities; however, these are supplemented with the latest software tools from other vendors.

Chapter IX deals with the role of digital accounting in financial and strategic management. Developments such as financial supply chain and corporate performance management that integrate e-developments in comprehensive managerial philosophies are covered. Finally, Chapter X discusses controls, security, and audit in the online-networked world. This chapter first presents a conceptual framework for internal controls in the online world. Then, various standard control techniques are discussed. The new Web-based anti-fraud and anti-money laundering software is also covered. The discussion of privacy and assurance issues concludes the chapter and rounds off the book.

To Whom is This Book Addressed?

This book provides a broad introduction to the effects of the Internet and ERP on accounting workflows, processes and controls. Specifically, this book is useful to practicing accountants and auditors who want to familiarize themselves with the latest developments in this area. This book can be used as a supplement in introductory accounting information systems or auditing courses. The accounting cycle approach will fit perfectly with current approaches of teaching accounting information systems. The book can also be used as a stand-alone book in advanced accounting information systems or e-commerce course at the undergraduate or graduate level. If you wish to use this book for classroom purposes, an end-of-chapter questions and solutions manual is available on request from the author.

Ash Deshmukh
Associate Professor of Accounting & Information Systems
Department of Accounting
Sam and Irene Black School of Business
Pennsylvania State University—Erie

Acknowledgments

I wish to thank the team — Mehdi Khosrow-Pour, Jan Travers, and Michele Rossi at Idea Group Inc. — who made the publication of this book possible by accepting my proposal. My special thanks to Kristin Roth and Amanda Appicello for guiding me through the maze of publication requirements. This book benefited due to the comments made by several experts: Neal Hannon (University of Hartford) and Kinsun Tam (University at Albany) provided insightful comments on the XML/XBRL chapter. Also, Somnath Bhattacharya (Florida Atlantic University), Jeffrey Romine (Truman State University), Ido Millet (Pennsylvania State University – Erie), and two anonymous reviewers provided many helpful comments. I also wish to thank corporations that allowed me to use their products and screen shots from their Web sites for illustrative purposes. Finally, I am grateful to Altova Corporation for providing me with the XML Spy software. All errors are my responsibility.

Chapter I

A Framework for Digital Accounting

Digital Accounting, E-Accounting, and the E-Thing

The term *digital* refers to digits or numbers; however, in the computer science lexicon this term refers to the representation of information in 0s and 1s, which can be read, written and stored using machines. The prefix "e" refers to *electronic*, meaning use of electricity in powering machines such as computers. Digital accounting, or e-accounting, as a corresponding analog, refers to the representation of accounting information in the digital format, which then can be electronically manipulated and transmitted. Digital accounting does not have a standard definition but merely refers to the changes in accounting due to computing and networking technologies.

Accounting, the art and science of measuring business performance, has evolved with business, more so with information technology. Punch cards and mainframes, databases and data warehouses, personal computers and productivity software, specialized accounting software and Enterprise Resource Planning (ERP) systems, Local Area Networks (LANs) and Wide Area Networks (WANs), among other things, have left their mark on accounting theory and practice. For example, data-entry mechanisms, data storage and processing mechanisms, end reports, internal controls, audit trails and skill sets for accountants have been in continual flux for the past several decades.

Roots of Digital Accounting

Accounting is sometimes called a *lagging science*, meaning accounting is reactive — it reacts to developments in business and technology. Interestingly, accounting was initially on the cutting edge of the Information Technology revolution. The roots of digital accounting can be traced to the depression era and World War II. Tax regulation, at the time, was becoming complex, and World War II introduced a variety of logistical and data management problems. The details of financial transactions and physical location of goods could not be reliably handled, even with the armies of clerks. This work was boring, paid poorly and demanded a high degree of accuracy. Welcome the tabulating machines. As many know, Mr. Watson, the CEO of IBM, remarked that world might not need more than five computers. Tabulating machines soon evolved, and the new technology found newer and wider applications, undreamt even by its wildest proponents.

In the late 1950s and early 1960s, the mega corporations of the day began to handle data that rivaled government requirements. This data could not be handled manually, let alone cost effectively. Accounting and financial information, due to its repetitive nature and heavy volume, became a prime candidate for automation. Initial investments in information technology, though the term was not yet invented, were controlled by accounting and finance departments. The mechanization of accounting and finance information expanded the power of Chief Financial Officers (CFOs) and controllers by enabling them to influence operational and strategic decisions. The financial justification of investments was not an issue, since financial executives endorsed the investments. However, as the tabulating installations turned into data processing centers, the technology became too complex to be controlled by accountants. Data processing managers started handling the data processing center and the Data Processing Management Association (DPMA) was born. The automation of accounting and financial data had begun, and soon developed an irreversible momentum.

Accounting and e-commerce also met decades ago. The development of Electronic Data Interchange (EDI) and Electronic Fund Transfer (EFT) can be said to be the beginnings of the digital exchange of accounting information among trading partners. EDI and EFT both involve exchange of data electronically and sound very similar to e-commerce. The conceptual roots of EDI can be traced back to the Berlin Airlift in the late 1940s. During the Berlin Airlift, consignments of various goods and materials arrived with manifests in different languages, different numbers of copies and differing formats, among other things. To overcome problems caused by such documents, a *standard* manifest was designed. This standard manifest could be transmitted via telephone, telex or radio. Thousands of tons of cargo per day were tracked using these manifests. The United States (U.S.) army logistics officers who designed the scheme later implemented it in the corporate world. EDI is based on the idea of this standard manifest. EDI uses a standardized format for documents that can be transmitted, read and processed electronically. The standardized formats of these documents are controlled by various industry standards and trade associations. Initially, EDI was used to transfer purchasing and selling documents. Later on, EDI was used to handle financial transactions such as payment and collection activities.

EDI, if properly implemented, can streamline supply chain management, reduce labor costs and errors, increase processing speed and accelerate cash flows. The primary problems with EDI are: (a) the formats are highly structured and sometimes proprietary; (b) the structure of the data format limits the amount of information in the EDI messages; (c) specialized software that is expensive to install and maintain is required; and (d) it offers few financial benefits to suppliers. Currently, only 6% of the estimated 10 million businesses in the U.S. are EDI capable. Large corporations, banks and transportation companies have invested and continue to refine EDI technology; many large corporations — for example, Wal-Mart — will not do business with a supplier unless the supplier is EDI capable.

EFT, on the other hand, can be traced back to wire transfers pioneered by Western Union in 1871. Money could be delivered at one location and then transferred to another location using telegraph; the third party with appropriate identification then could collect those funds at that location. As the development of electronic networks reached a critical mass, the banking industry started using these networks to transfer money. The primary purposes of EFT were to lower banking costs, speed up clearing of checks, and control errors and fraud. Eventually, the capabilities of EFT were combined with EDI, and Financial EDI (FEDI) was born. FEDI formats are now capable of handling payment and collection activities in the business world.

The Internet and Digital Accounting

The advent of the Internet and e-commerce/e-business has continued and in many ways accelerated the trend.[1] The Internet and e-commerce not only promised to change intra- and inter-business processes but also challenged the very foundations of established business practices. All business areas, accounting and finance included, came under intense scrutiny as dot com businesses mushroomed. The rise and fall of the e-revolution had been spectacular and breathtaking. The hype and hysteria surrounding these new technologies have been replaced with more realistic appraisal of their costs and benefits. The changes and constants in accounting probably can be better analyzed from this vantage point.

A brief historical perspective for the Internet and e-commerce will equip us better to appreciate the evolution of digital accounting. The Internet is a collection of interconnected computer networks. These connections span the world, creating a computing space used for a variety of activities such as business, entertainment, communication and so on. The Internet has no hub, is not owned by any corporation or government, but is sustained by the efforts of individuals, corporations and governments. The specific information transmission protocols developed for the Internet allow information to flow over different communication mediums, different software and hardware platforms, and even different languages. Information on the Internet courses through various conduits such as optical fibers, telephone lines, satellite transmissions and microwave emissions, to name a few.

Exhibit 1. Structure of the Internet

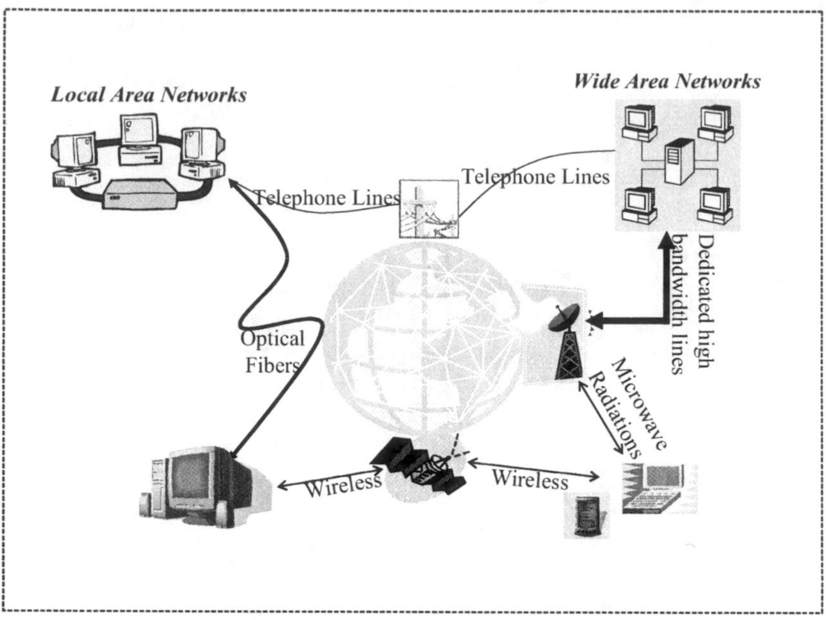

Exhibit 2. Tele-marketing, t-tailing, or e-tailing?

Think of the vast potential of the market — total population of 10 million, about 12 cities having population greater than 200,000 and an annual national income of $10 billion. Dreams are made up of this stuff? This is the U.S. of the 1880s.

Richard was an agent of a railway station in North Redwood, Minn., having plenty of spare time on hand. A Chicago company shipped gold-filled watches to a local jeweler, but the jeweler had never ordered those watches. Richard obtained the shipment of watches and used a *telegraph* to contact railroad operators and employees to sell the batch.

Richard made a nice profit. He soon started R. Sears Watch Company, a predecessor to today's *Sears, Roebuck and Co.*

The development of the Internet is not a 1990s activity; the roots of the Internet go far deeper. The technological foundations of the Internet were laid in the 19th century. The development of the Telegraph (communicating as dots and dashes), Transatlantic Cable (as a communication medium) and Telephone all contributed to the development of the Internet. The development of the Advanced Research Projects Agency Network (ARPANET) in the late 1960s heralded the era of interconnected computers. The primary objective of ARPANET was to develop a network that would provide numerous alternate network paths to the ultimate destination. The packet switching mechanism for data transfer was the key. This mechanism split data into different packets and routed it to the destination using different network paths. Thus, if one part of the network was down an alternate network path could be taken, and data flow remained unbroken.

In the 1970s, however, ARPANET was primarily used by academics and research agencies for the exchange of information. E-mail, File Transfer Protocols (FTP), newsgroups and remote computer connection protocols, among other things, were developed to facilitate free-flow of information. The National Science Foundation (NSF) built a backbone (56 KB) that was primitive by today's standards, but it was a start. In the 1980s, the NSF took off commercial restrictions for the use of NSFNet, which was by then a primary backbone for carrying Internet messages.

Exhibit 3. Timeline for the Internet

1836	Telegraph
1858-'66	Transatlantic Cable
1876	Telephone
1962-'68	Packet switching networks developed.
1969	• ARPANET. Department of Defense (DOD) establishes nodes at UCLA, Stanford Research Institute and University of Utah. The objective is research into networking. • The idea of Electronic Data Interchange begins to emerge from various industry initiatives.
1971	Individuals go online for the first time. E-mail invented.
1972	E-mail goes international (Norway and England). Telnet protocol specified.
1976-'79	• E-mail takes off, newsgroups are born, and UNIX platform is employed. Interactive games make appearance. • Electronic Data Interchange and Electronic Fund Transfer continue to grow.
1982	Transmission Control Protocol/Internet Protocol (TCP/IP) for the network invented. This leads to the definition of an internet as a connected set of networks using TCP/IP protocol.
1986	NSF creates NSFNet, a backbone with 56KB speed. Cleveland FreeNet comes online and offers free Internet access.
1988-'90	NSF lifts commercial restriction on the Internet. The Internet continues to grow; businesses go online.
1991	Tools such as Gopher (developed by University of Minnesota) and WAIS to index and access information on the Internet become available.
1991-'92	Birth of the WWW. The graphical, hyperlinked interface to the Internet is developed by (Centre Européen de Recherche Nucléaire (CERN). The WWW allowed multimedia to come to the Internet; WWW has now become synonymous with the Internet.
1993	The United Nations and U.S. White House come online. Mosaic, the WWW browsing software, released, making net surfing popular. Businesses and media begin to understand the potential of the Internet.
1994-'96	The commercialization of the Internet begins in earnest. Microsoft enters the fray, Internet Explorer and Netscape battle for supremacy.
1996-'99	• The golden days of the Internet. Bandwidth explodes, along with the number of users of the Internet. Experts herald the arrival of the e-revolution and promise to change the world. Dot com stock values reach sky high. • The arrival of Internet2 and NGI.
2000-'02	The dot com revolution crashes. Terrorism, corporate mis-governance, dubious business practices and creative accounting destroy stock values.
≥ 2004	• Will the Internet deliver on its promised revolution? • Is it just one more tool in the toolkit of businesses? • What will be global effects of the Internet? • What do you think?

The 1990s witnessed an explosion in the personal, business and government uses of the Internet. This field was characterized by numerous buzzwords, fast-changing technical specifications, continual new releases of software, new Web programming languages, numerous standard-setting industry associations, and emergence of new alliances and ventures promising new and improved management methods. Information became obsolete by the time it saw virtual or real daylight. Telecom companies rushed in to build the bandwidth and backbones, new Internet Service Providers (ISPs) and Web sites mushroomed, and the Internet grew rich in information content. To mine the information riches of the Internet, various tools were invented. Tools such as Wide Area Information Services (WAIS), Archie (short for archives), Gopher and scores of others were used to index and then to access information. The World Wide Web (WWW) is a graphical, hyperlinked, multimedia part of the Internet that spread rapidly and became synonymous with the Internet. Mosaic was the first browser used to browse the contents of the WWW. Mosaic grew into Netscape and Microsoft introduced its competing version — Internet Explorer. The earlier tools for file transfer, newsgroup reading, chat, e-mail and so forth are now integrated in these browsers and almost transparent to the end user. The functionality of browsers continues to grow with every new version.

The potential applications of the Internet are vast; however, bandwidth limitations may limit the development of data-hungry applications. The Internet2 is an initiative led by universities and backed by the industry and government. Next Generation Internet (NGI) is a parallel effort by the U.S. federal government. The idea behind both initiatives is to develop high-bandwidth networks that will enable advanced applications such as real-time video broadcast, digital libraries, virtual laboratories, distance-independent learning, tele-immersion and national security applications. The Internet2 and NGI initiatives aim to bring these new technologies to businesses and individuals to spur new advances in Internet applications. The Internet thus continues to evolve in exciting directions.

The use of the Internet by businesses gave rise to e-commerce. The complexity of this area is characterized by multiple definitions, a profusion of jargon and diversity of opinions. Academics and practitioners have defined e-commerce, e-business, e-tailing and i-commerce; different types of e-commerce such as Business-to-Consumer (B2C) and Business-to-Business (B2B); online vs. off-line business models; and so on. E-commerce alone has several definitions. The effects of the Internet on business are so pervasive that such diversity is understandable. For example, communication infrastructure, business processes, delivery of products and services, managerial philosophies and organizational structure are subject to change due to the influence of the Internet.

For our purposes, the understanding of what e-commerce does is more critical than a specific term or definition. The three common threads that run through the definitions of e-commerce (and e-business) can be summarized as follows:

- Electronic networks or the Internet is used as a communications medium for the exchange of business information
- Provides capability to sell and deliver products or services on the Internet
- Uses the networks and digital information to redesign inter- and intra-business processes and workflows.

Exhibit 4. The effects of the Internet and e-commerce on business

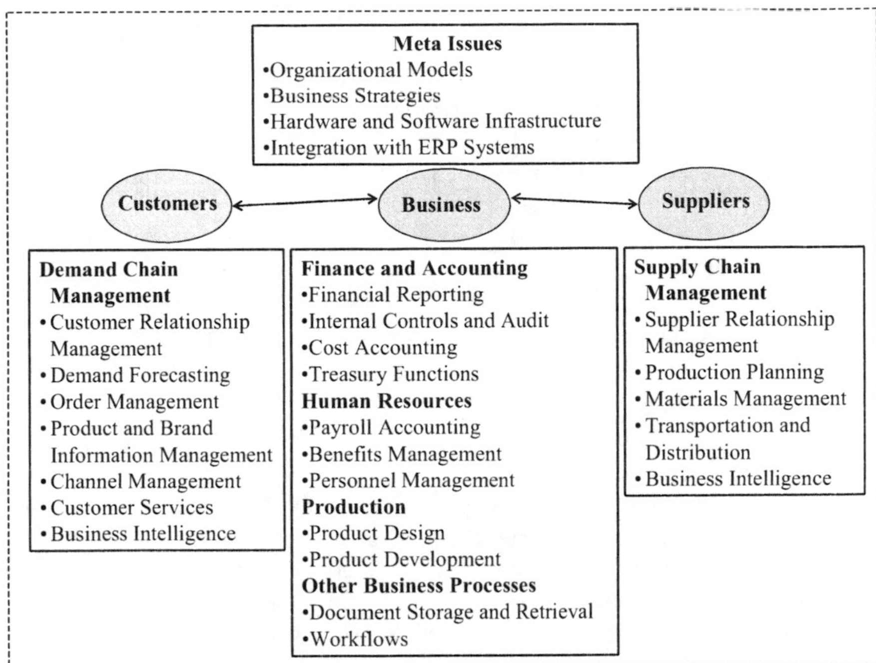

The effects of e-commerce, as can be seen, cut across various industries; industry intermediaries; and, the ultimate, consumers; and also within the industry itself. E-commerce is more of an umbrella term that refers to all areas of business affected by use of the Internet and not merely selling and buying activities.

The initial effect of e-commerce was on front-end business processes, especially sales and marketing in retail and consumer products segments (sometimes referred to as e-tailing). The B2C segment connects directly with retail consumers. E-commerce marketing efforts first spawned business Web sites, or electronic storefronts. These Web sites provided information about businesses and could be interactive. Such Web sites enabled sales of products and services by providing catalogs for products, information about products and helpful advice, and also had mechanisms for electronic payments. This phase of e-commerce was characterized by a wave of B2C Web sites, some of which became very successful, though only a few (such as Amazon.com and eBay) survive today.

The B2C e-commerce area became crowded very quickly, and the problems with running profitable Web sites were apparent by the late 1990s. B2B e-commerce was proclaimed as the next big step in the evolution of e-commerce. Organizations understood that e-commerce is a pervasive concept and will affect the demand chain (demand forecasting, delivery of products to customers and cash collections, customer profitability analysis, best ways of delivery, etc.), supply chain (production planning, purchasing of raw materials and services and consequent payments, inventory management, transportation and distribution, etc.), internal business processes, technology applications and business models, among other things.

As B2B e-commerce took off, there was a proliferation of Web portals, exchanges, online auctions and community e-marketplaces that provided a centralized place on the Internet for buying and selling of products. The prime purpose of portals, exchanges or e-marketplaces was to facilitate business activities. The products offered in the B2B commerce catered to vertical industries (markets for raw materials to finished goods) or horizontal industries (cross-industry buying and selling activities). And the selling methods involved either negotiations between the seller and buyer or auctions. The selling of products for one organization is buying for another; thus, purchasing, production and logistics activities also got tied in. The illustrative models of e-commerce are listed in Exhibit 5. This listing is not exhaustive, there is considerable overlap in the models and the definitions are neither clear-cut nor universally accepted; however, these models give an idea about the diversity of e-commerce practices.

The Internet also transformed internal business processes. For example, purchasing departments can employ online auctions in real time to reduce costs, employees can use e-procurement software to order supplies from their desktops, customers can configure products online, engineers can collaborate on product development across the world, travel and operating expenses can be managed online and goods in transit can be monitored over the Internet.

Exhibit 5. Illustrative models of e-commerce

B2C	Selling of products or services to the ultimate consumer.
B2B	Selling of products or services within businesses. Following are some models of B2B commerce.
B2B Web Sites	These Web sites are similar to mini-trade exhibits. They contain information about the company, allow customers to conduct business by providing catalogs, order forms and payment mechanisms; and provide self-service abilities to the customers and suppliers by allowing access to internal back-office systems.
B2B Exchanges	Here, multiple suppliers list their products so a company can shop for a desired product, request and participate in bids, or simply explore various purchasing options.
B2B Vertical Portals	These provide information about a particular industry, product listings, discussion groups and other Web sites of interest, among other things. These sites may provide capabilities of B2B exchanges.
B2B Brokering Sites	These sites serve as a broker between a buyer and a seller.
B2B Information Sites	These include trade and industry associations, industry standard organizations, and any other sites that offer information pertinent to a particular industry.
B2G	Selling of products or services to federal, state or local governments.
C2C	Selling of products or services within consumers.
C2B	Selling of products or services by consumers to businesses.

Exhibit 6. Accounting – A lagging science?

IT'S MARCH 3RD IN SHIPPING. IT'S MARCH 3RD IN SALES. TOO BAD IT'S JANUARY 3RD IN FINANCE **SAP Advertisement, *Business Week*, December 9, 2002**

E-commerce in general and B2B commerce in particular continue to evolve. The general mood that dot com companies will overwhelm established industrial behemoths had dissipated. Talk about disruptive technologies, new organizational models, virtual corporations and other exotic concepts have been replaced with more sober assessments of the effects of the Internet. The majority of the corporations have strategies for leveraging the Internet and e-commerce. These technologies will continue to transform the business landscape; however, the extent and depth of these changes is open for speculation. Initial estimates of B2B commerce in the U.S. were forecasted to be approximately $1 to $3 trillion by 2003/2004. The final numbers did not match these estimates. The general slowdown of business coupled with the stock market crash has put a big question mark on the estimates, in this area.

As changes sweep through business, can accounting be left behind? The early days of dot com companies are replete with horror stories. Businesses got overwhelmed because back-office systems were unable to process the flood of orders pouring through the Web. What an interesting way to get into trouble! Consequently, the accounting information system (as a subsystem of the enterprise information system) was tinkered, reengineered, Web enabled and customer oriented, giving rise to a host of new developments.

The effects of the Internet on accounting are described via different terms in the literature; for example, financial electronic commerce, e-finance and e-accounting. There has been one conference, the *Financial Electronic Commerce Conference*, and the presentations in the conference did not explicitly define or describe the term. However, the subject matter presented in the conference mainly dealt with accounting and finance. The term e-finance industry does appear in the literature. This term refers to major traditional finance industries such as banking, brokerage and insurance that have become net centric. On the other hand, the e-finance term has also been used to delineate changes in the accounting/finance functions due to the Internet. This terminological confusion is very common in the e-commerce arena. The effects on accounting due to the Internet, shorn of technical jargon, can be described, on the lines of the description of the e-commerce term, as follows.

- Electronic networks or the Internet is used as a communications medium for the exchange of accounting and financial information
- Accounting and finance functionality that supports capability to sell and deliver products or services on the Internet
- Uses the networks and digital information to redesign accounting and finance processes and workflows

Developments in computers and networks have now affected virtually every area in accounting. Take revenue cycle, for example. Sales orders can arrive on the Web through EDI, B2B or B2C storefronts, Customer Relationship Management software or automated sales force. In cases of sales orders that need credit decisions in few minutes, Web-based credit services offer automation of the entire credit approval process. Web-enabled Warehouse Management Systems (WMSs) partially or completely automate picking and packing of goods and products. Shipments can be tracked or monitored using the Internet. The billing function can be handled as Electronic Bill Presentment and Payment (EBPP) or e-billing and/or by FEDI. Online receivable services can automate the entire receivables process. Payments can be made using credit cards, procurement cards, electronic checks or digital cash in addition to traditional methods. New software tools and accounting processes have emerged to implement and handle these changes.

Costs and Benefits of Digital Accounting

The problems inherent in measuring benefits of Information Technology or e-commerce also are present in the cost/benefit analysis of digital accounting. A general listing of costs and benefits is easy; however, quantification with a reasonable degree of accuracy is difficult. The costs are quite readily apparent and can be quantified to a certain extent. However, the quantification of benefits remains elusive. How do you put dollar numbers on a Web-based download of bank statement and automatic bank reconciliation by an ERP system?

Let us take a conceptual look at costs and benefits.

Benefits

- Faster cycle times — these include credit approvals, payments and collections, posting of transactions, closing of the books, generation of reports and more time available for higher-level analysis
- Broader geographic reach
- Continuous service availability, 24/7 access, and more satisfied internal and external customers
- Reduced error rates – that means fewer transactions with errors as well as fewer errors
- Reduced accounting staff and improved productivity
- Better cash management – efficient payments and effective collections
- Cost savings in mail, paper and storage of paper
- Improved audit trails and security.

Costs

- Investments required in computer hardware and software
- Initial need for expensive consultants
- Costs involved in systems, processes, processing of information and report generation changes
- Continual training or retraining needs and/or requirements for personnel with specialized skills
- User resistance
- Careful attention needs to be paid to security, control and audit requirements for financial transactions during the initial configuration. If the initial configuration of the system is not correct or the integration with ERP software or legacy systems is faulty, then there are recurring costs and fewer benefits from the implementation.

Exhibit 7. The Church of Jesus Christ of Latter-Day Saints: A case study of cost-effective payments

The Church of Jesus Christ of Latter-Day Saints (Church) had thousands of vendors and vendor payments were done as follows: 5% by procurement cards, 80% by check and 15% by EFT. In 1997, the Church had decentralized payment structure, redundant payment systems, DOS EDI translator and old check printing software. The Church wanted to minimize the number of payments, lower cost per payment, eliminate process redundancy and improve vendor satisfaction. The primary drivers for change were: a new PeopleSoft Accounts Payable (AP) system, increasing number of vendors and existing banks moving to mandatory electronic payments.

The Church analyzed hard costs (such as bank charges and office supplies) and soft costs (such as processing minutes and filing) for checks ($2.06 per check), EDI payments ($0.84 per transaction) and EFT ($0.37 per transaction). A decision to shift vendors from paper checks to EFT was done; the EDI option, though viable, was not pursued, since 90% of the vendors were not EDI capable. The vendors were offered incentives to move to the EFT system, and by 1999, the number of vendors receiving payments moved from 700 to 7,500. The conversion rate was approximately 25% of the vendors. The projected payback period in 1999 was 17 months, and IRR for the next 4 years was 39%.

The implementation of EFT achieved the objectives of lower costs payments and reduction in manual processes. However, the Church was concerned with vendor satisfaction. To address this issue they needed a mechanism that would provide vendors details of the payment. The Church designed the Electronic Remittance Delivery System (ERADS) based on the PeopleSoft system. This system uses connected e-mail and fax servers to issue payments details. The Church reported that the system was running fine, with little manual intervention. The Church continues to improve the payment process.

Exhibit 8. Chapters and contents

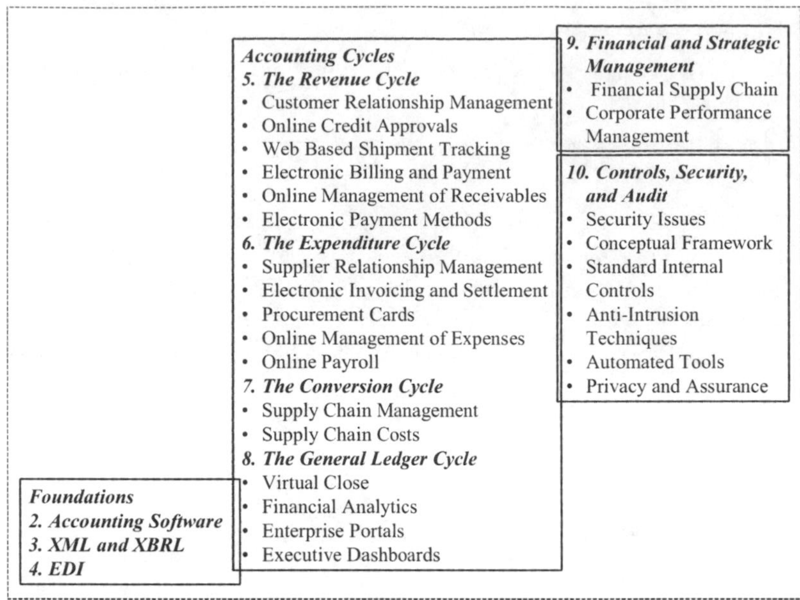

The costs and benefits of digital accounting decisions are intimately linked with targeted accounting processes, the information technology used and the knowledge needs for the proposed solution; as such, each decision is unique. For example, factors such as current document volume per period, percentage of digital documents, current cycle times and error rates, current transactions costs, security and control issues, and nature of accounting software or legacy systems all need to be considered in implementing new technologies and solutions. There is no silver bullet or a standard template for such decisions.

Structure of the Book

The changes and new developments in digital accounting are comprehensively covered in the coming chapters. This book focuses on capturing changes in the accounting cycles, processes and functions due to computing and networking technologies. A classification of these e-changes in the context of accounting cycles provides us with a framework that can be used for present as well as future developments in accounting. The primary focus is on accounting, and a secondary focus is on related finance functions. The level of coverage in financial functions is primarily restricted to intra-business finance functions; topics such as Web-based stock investments and portfolio management are excluded.

The next three chapters deal with the topics of Accounting Software, eXtensible Business Reporting Language (XBRL) and EDI, which should serve as foundations for the study of digital accounting. Then the accounting cycles — revenue, expenditure, conversion and general ledger — and the resulting changes are investigated. The next chapter explores the effects of digital accounting on financial and strategic management. This chapter also covers new concepts such as financial supply chain and corporate performance management. Finally, control, security and audit issues in the online world are explored.

Summary

This chapter sets the tone for chronicling and analyzing developments in accounting due to the Internet and ERP. The origins of storage and exchange of accounting information in digital format go back to mainframes, EDI and EFT, all of which are decades old. EDI and EFT both involve electronic exchange of data over networks. EDI is used by most major corporations, who have invested heavily in this technology. EFT is used by banks in moving funds, and EDI-enabled EFT is referred to as Financial EDI. Digital accounting has gone beyond EDI and EFT, and now encompasses all accounting cycles.

A brief history of the Internet and WWW is provided to get a better understanding of its effects. The business effects of the Internet/WWW are reflected in a terminological explosion. To simplify matters, the term e-commerce is used and defined, and the description is comprehensive enough to capture major inter- and intra-organizational effects of the Internet. This definition of e-commerce is extended to accounting and finance. Next, a conceptual discussion of costs and benefits of digital accounting is provided. The quantification of benefits is a difficult issue and is still being researched. Finally, the structure of the book is discussed.

References

Clarke, R. (1998). *Electronic data interchange (EDI): An introduction.* The Australian National University. Retrieved May 10, 2003, from www.anu.edu.au/people/Roger.Clarke/EC/EDIIntro.html/

Cohn, M., & Bellone, R. (1997, January). Looking back: History of accounting software. *Accounting Technology,* 19-36.

Fogarty, K. (2002, June). E-future lies in the back office. *Computerworld, 17*, 36.

Glover, S., Liddle, S., & Prawitt, D. (2001). *E-business: Principles and strategies for accountants.* Upper Saddle River, NJ: Prentice Hall.

Greenstein, M., & Vasarhelyi, M. (2002). *Electronic commerce: Security, risk, management, and control.* New York: McGraw-Hill Irwin.

Hayes, M. (2002, June 17). E-business loses momentum. *InformationWeek*, 52-55.

Hill, N., & Ferguson, D. (1989, March). Electronic data interchange: A definition and perspective. *EDI Forum: The Journal of Electronic Interchange,* 5-12.

History of the Internet. (2003). Net Valley. Retrieved May 8, 2003, from www.netvalley.com/archives/mirrors/davemarsh-timeline-1.htm

Internet2. (2002). Internet2. Retrieved May 8, 2003, from *www.internet2.edu/*

Kalakota, R., & Whinston, A.B. (1996). *Frontiers of electronic commerce.* Reading, MA: Addison-Wesley.

Leiner, B., Cerf, V., Clark, D., Kahn, R., Kleinrock, L., Lynch, D., Postel, R., Roberts, L., & Wolff, S. (2002). *A brief history of the Internet.* Internet Society. Retrieved May 8, 2003, from www.isoc.org/internet/history/brief.shtml/

Levinsohn, A. (2001, April). The wild, wired world of e-finance. *Strategic Finance,* 26-32.

Macola Software (2001). *Macola's electronic data interchange white paper* (Progression Series 7.5). Exact America. Retrieved December 9, 2002, from http://exactamerica.com/macola/

McKie, S. (1998). *The accounting software handbook.* Loveland: Duke Communications International.

Napier, A., Judd, P., Rivers, O., & Wagner, S. (2001). *Creating a winning e-business.* Boston, MA: Course Technology: Thomson Learning.

Rayport, J., & Jaworski, B. (2001). *E-commerce.* New York: McGraw Hill.

Schneider, P., & Perry, J. (2001). *Electronic commerce* (2nd ed.). Boston: Course Technology: Thomson Learning.

Sears history. (2002). Sears and Gurunet. Retrieved January 23, 2003, from www.sears.com/ and www.gurunet.com/

Stultz, R. (2001). *Demystifying EDI.* Plano, TX: Wordware Publishing.

Turban, E., Lee, J., King, D., & Chung, H. (2000). *Electronic commerce: A managerial perspective.* Upper Saddle River, NJ: Prentice Hall.

Tynan, D. (2003). 1996-'99: The Internet Era. *InfoWorld, 25*(49), 50.

Williams, J. (2000). Developing the most cost effective FEC strategy: A case study by The Church of Jesus Christ of Latter-Day Saints. In the *Proceedings of the Financial Electronic Commerce Conference*, April 2-5, Chicago.

Endnote

[1] This chapter (and the rest of this book) uses the terms e-commerce and e-business interchangeably.

Chapter II

The Evolution of Accounting Software

History of Accounting Software

In the late 1950s and early 1960s, mega corporations of the day began to handle data that rivaled government requirements. This data could not be handled manually, let alone cost-effectively. Accounting and financial information, due to its repetitive nature and heavy volume, became a prime candidate for automation. Initial accounting programs were written for mainframe computers, not surprisingly, since IBM and its Big Irons ruled the computer world. Early mainframe computers were large, due to the ferrite core memory, and cumbersome. The processing intelligence was centralized in the mainframe. Mainframes served a large number of users, and data was processed in a batch mode. Users submitted data using dumb terminals and jobs were processed based on the length of the queue and priority of the jobs. Mainframes provided a high level of security and reliability. Minicomputers, pioneered by the Digital Equipment Corporation, had similar capabilities but were smaller and less powerful. Currently, distinctions between mainframes and minis are very blurred, and for our purposes make very little practical difference.

Exhibit 1. Hardware/software cycles

Approximate Time Period	Computer Type	Characteristics of Accounting Software
1960–'75 1975–'85	The Mainframe The Minicomputer	• Centralized intelligence; dumb terminals; and batch processing mode; no Graphical User Interface (GUI) support • Flat files or indexed file organization • Hierarchical or network databases • High transaction processing capacity • Large number of users supported
1980–'90	The Microcomputer Local Area Networks	• Shared intelligence across network • File sharing architecture • Indexed file organization • Limited transaction processing capacity • Limited users supported
1988–'95	The Client-Server Local Area Networks Wide Area Networks	• Mixture of mainframe, mini and PCs supported • Shared intelligence across network • Client-server architecture • Relational database systems • Databases can be centralized or decentralized • High transaction processing capacity • Large number of users supported
>1995	The Client-Server Local Area Networks Wide Area Networks The Browser-Server The Internet and WWW	• Mixture of mainframe, mini and PCs supported • Shared intelligence across network or centralized intelligence • Client-server architecture and browser-server architecture • Relational databases, multidimensional databases, object-oriented databases • Databases can be centralized or decentralized • Flexible transaction processing capacity • Large number of users; support for world-wide users

Early accounting software on mainframe- or minicomputer-type systems was written in programming languages such as COBOL, Assembler, FORTRAN and RPG. Data were stored in flat files with fixed formats or indexed file organization structures of the mainframe. Later on, if the database was used, it was a hierarchical or network type. These accounting packages were usually developed by programmers within the company to solve particular problems. These home-grown packages were sometimes adapted and taken to market by the enterprising programmers. As the demands on these systems grew, programs were modified and updated. Generally, there was no life-cycle plan for systems modification, maintenance and update. The resulting systems were rigid, inflexible, unscalable but critical.

Some of these systems still run in the business world and in governments, and are now called *legacy systems*. This term does not have a standard definition, but refers to computer systems based on old hardware and software technology — primarily mainframe-based and powered by second- and third-generation software languages. The term *old* is a relative term, and with time every system has potential to become a legacy system. The Internet had made some systems developed in the 1990s obsolete and even those could be termed as legacy systems. Many businesses are heavily invested in legacy systems and do not have financial wherewithal to reengineer these systems. Legacy systems run mission critical applications, excel in heavy-duty transaction processing, and any system disruptions can have disastrous consequences. On the other hand,

Exhibit 2. File/database management systems

Data Organization Method	Brief Explanation
• Flat files	• Data is contained in only one table
• Indexed structure	• Data can be accessed sequentially or randomly by using an index of records
• Virtual Storage Access Method (VSAM)	• Data is accessed using inverted index (called *B+tree*); file management system used on IBM mainframes; used for legacy databases
• Hierarchical databases	• Hierarchically arranged data – tree structure
• Network databases	• Similar to hierarchical; however, unlike hierarchical databases, child tables can have more than one parent, thus supporting many-to-many relationships
• Relational databases	• Data stored in collection of tables that follows mathematical rules
• Client-server databases	• Database server runs 24/7 to handle requests coming through the clients; mostly relational
• Multidimensional databases	• DBMS organized around group of records that share common field value; rapidly provides values at each intersection; useful for complex, user-driven, ad-hoc queries
• Object-oriented databases	• Supports modeling and creation of data as objects; useful in multi-media environment
• Object-relational databases	• Relational database systems with added object capabilities
• Data warehouse	• Collection of wide variety of data to support management decisions; useful in presenting a picture of business at a point in time
• Data marts	• Database(s) or subsets of a database that focus on particular department or subject

continuance of legacy systems may result in operations and service-related failures; maintenance of these systems is expensive, since mainframe programmers and mainframe parts are more expensive than PC programmers and PC parts; and the applications are more difficult to modify. Not all legacy systems need to be changed; however, in due time changes in legacy systems are bound to accelerate.

Primarily, two approaches to address legacy systems exist. First, an organization migrates to an entirely new software and/or hardware platform— generally by utilizing a new software package. This can be a phased introduction or a big bang approach, where all systems are changed in one shot. Spectacular successes and failures in both of these techniques have been recorded. The second option is to modernize the existing legacy system — restructure, reengineer, refurbish, rejuvenate or rearchitect the legacy system. Different techniques used in these modernization methods are— rewrite the old code in a new language, transport the existing business knowledge to current hardware platforms, extend the legacy system by adding Web front-end and query facilities, or some combination of these techniques.

Lord Corporation provides an interesting story of migration vs. modernization of legacy systems. Lord is a 75-year-old, approximately $400 million multinational corporation. They offer high-tech mechanical and chemical products to aerospace, transportation and chemical industries. Lord had a heavy investment in legacy systems. They used ASK MANMAN in the DEC/VAX environment for the mechanical division and Infinium and

Exhibit 3. Lord's legacy system

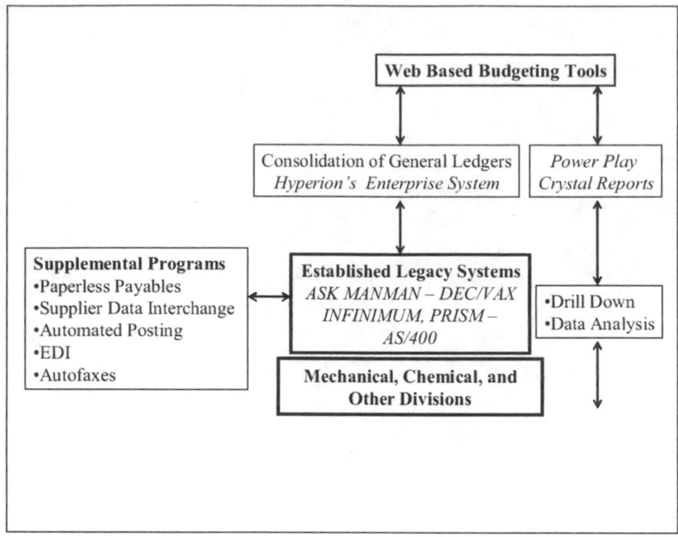

Prism in the AS/400 environment for the chemical division. The transaction processing capacity of these systems was deemed adequate; however, a major problem was inflexibility of the system and consequent inability of the company to extract and analyze data.

Lord made an ambitious effort to modernize the legacy system. The legacy system was enhanced in phases to increase capabilities. Some examples are:

- **Paperless payables:** The mechanical products division wrote a program in FORTRAN that created payment vouchers from receiving a report and purchase order. This program interacted with the ASK MANMAN system and saved Lord $100,000 in the introductory year.
- **Supplier data interchange:** This add-on program enabled the suppliers of the mechanical division to tap into databases and determine material requirements, access data on quality problems and view payment information.
- **Automated posting of travel and procurement expenses:** This add-on program enabled periodic posting of travel and procurement expenses to the legacy system ledgers.
- **EDI with customers:** Data in the legacy system was restructured. This restructured data was exported to EDI mailboxes and from there to customers.
- **Autofaxes:** This program collected information from the legacy database and automatically faxed shipments and other ancillary information to customers.

Disparate general ledgers in the legacy system for various departments were consolidated by using Hyperion's Enterprise system. Reporting tools such as Cognos' Power Play and Crystal Reports were used for drill down and data slicing and dicing. Intranet Workflow software was used to redesign accounts receivable, accounts payable and purchase order approval workflows. The budget process was streamlined using Web-based tools developed in-house.

These improvements enabled Lord Corporation to considerably extend the life of its legacy systems. Not only was the life extended, but data extraction and analysis capabilities were also enhanced. However, problems with legacy systems were deep rooted ,and every solution created new problems. Lord, after overcoming Y2K challenges and an intense evaluation of its systems, decided to scrap the legacy system and replace it with SAP R/3. As this experience shows, the migration vs. modification decision is neither easy nor inexpensive.

In the 1980s, microcomputers arrived on the scene — computing for the proletariat. Personal Computers (PCs) were a major paradigm shift; the high priests of information technology lost their stranglehold on the technology, now anyone and everyone could understand and utilize Information Technology. The individual PCs soon got connected, giving rise to PC networks. The earlier networks were LANs. LANs served users in a confined geographical area, such as a building, campus or corporate headquarters. Earlier LANs were based on Novell Netware, IBM PC Network or Microsoft LAN manager, and used the file sharing architecture. Generally, one powerful computer served as a file server, and other networked computers interacted with this server. The file server would download files from the shared location to the user's desktop, and the user would process data and upload it to the server.

Accounting data were generally stored using an indexed sequential access file structure or Pervasive Software's Btrieve engine. Btrieve is a transactional database engine. This engine can handle heavy transaction loads, speedily access data and update data. Data are maintained in tables; however, Btrieve does not maintain information about the tables, validate input data or format information. These functions are generally performed by the application, and to that extent Btrieve differs from relational databases. Btrieve is still an engine of choice for low-level accounting software, though the trend is unmistakably toward relational databases. In fact, Btrieve has introduced Pervasive Structured Query Language (SQL), a relational database engine. The initial PC file-sharing architecture could not support a large number of users, transfer data quickly and handle heavy transaction processing.

The majority of initial accounting systems in the PC environment were single-user systems, but some of the programs could use file-sharing server architecture and served the multi-user environment. Many of these systems shipped on floppies and could be run from a floppy disk drive. *Simply Accounting* in 1985 could be run — the entire program, including the data — from *one* floppy disk. The hard disk space was expensive — at one time, $1,000 a megabyte — and few businesses could afford it. Programming languages such as Basic, Pascal and dBase II, to mention a few, were used. Operating systems such as Disk Operating System (DOS), Apple and Control Program for Microprocessors (CP/M) were used by earlier PCs. As DOS became the de facto operating system in the microcomputer arena, the majority of the programs were either written for DOS or ported over to DOS.

DOS was soon replaced by the Windows architecture that enabled GUI; and the ensuing Windows versions provided advanced networking capabilities. The GUI for accounting applications had become a reality.

Quite a few accountants misunderstood GUI and the Windows environment. The GUI is not merely use of colors or graphs on-screen. In the absence of Windows, earlier accounting programs built their own versions of interfaces; thus, input/output screens were not standardized, valuable programming resources were spent and the user learning curve was steep.

Windows allowed accounting software programmers to build cheap, consistent and standardized interfaces. Programmers could now focus on improving functionality of the product, and users did not have as steep of a learning curve. Accounting systems and documents are hierarchical in nature; for example, a chart of accounts or financial statements. The GUI enabled efficient navigation of the accounting environment. The What You See Is What You Get (WYSIWYG) features allowed for exact duplication of paper documents, making entries easier. And perhaps most importantly, internal controls could be built right onto the screen, minimizing input errors. The Windows environment facilitated sophisticated data extraction, analysis and presentation functions, which traditionally had been an Achilles' heel for legacy systems. The dynamic links and object embedding and linking in Windows also enabled interoperability of different software products. These features and its new avatars are now so standardized that it is hard for a new generation to think about text- and cursor-based entries.

Concurrent with the rise of Microsoft's Windows operating system, the client-server environment also shot to prominence. The file-sharing architecture of the original PC era was quickly replaced by the client-server environment. The client-server architecture is not based on a vendor-specific platform. A server is defined as a provider of services, and a client is a requester of services. In this environment, one or more computers — mainframe, mini or PC — function as a server, which contains centralized files. A client can be any computer that requests services of the server, generally through the network. The clients can be *thick*, meaning they are powerful and offer local processing, or *thin*, meaning they merely operate as data display devices.

The file server is now replaced by the Relational Database Management System (RDBMS) server. Instead of sharing the entire file, only the query and response to the query is shared. Queries are generally posed using some form of SQL. In this environment, applications can run on both the server and the client. This scalable and flexible architecture handled large numbers of users and transferred heavy loads of data speedily. Additionally, in the client-server environment, exchange of information is generally handled via GUI.

Technically, the client-server environment is characterized by three layers: presentation, application and database. The presentation layer is at the client level, and its main function is to download, upload and display data. If the client has sufficient processing power, then data processing can also be done locally. Application and database layers are maintained at the server level. The application layer handles business rules and logic for processing data and performs other ancillary functions such as data validation, error

Exhibit 4. Client-server architecture[1]

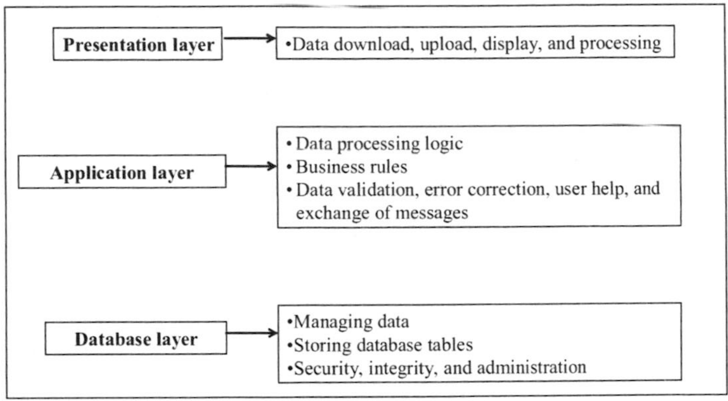

corrections, data retrieval and user help, among other things. In the context of an accounting system, financial transactions will be processed at this level. The database layer essentially performs standard database functions, such as data storage, security, backups and administration.

In the two-tier client-server architecture, application logic is run on the client and/or server computer. The accounting application can now run on the client side (if the client is powerful enough – *thick client*) or on the server side (if the client is not powerful enough – *thin client*) depending on the program. In the three-tier client-server architecture, the application layer is run on the application server and the database layer is run on the database server. The application server handles business rules and processing logic and eases demands on the presentation clients and database servers. The application server simplifies the system by queuing messages, scheduling transactions and assigning priorities to different transactions. In this situation, accounting software will run on application servers and, if the need arises, processing logic can be run on the client or database server. The transaction database will be stored on the database server. Users can be managed more effectively, since user queries first hit the application server and thereafter are passed on to the database.

If the database is licensed only for 50 users, then the application server will only submit queries in batches of 50. This architecture is speedier, scalable and secure compared to the two-tier architecture, but requires more hardware and increases the complexity of the system. In the N-tier architecture, the application layer consists of more than one server and allows different processes to run on different application servers in that layer. For example, one server can handle AR, a second one can handle AP and a third one can handle financial reports. This architecture is more powerful than two- and three-tier, but is also more complex and expensive.

The client-server environment forced accounting software developers to either develop accounting programs from scratch or rewrite existing applications. The client-server architecture enabled use of GUI as a front end for data extraction, analysis and

Exhibit 5. Different configurations in the client-server architecture

Two-Tier	Three -Tier	N-Tier
Presentation layer	Presentation layer	Presentation layer
↕	↕	↕
Application layer	Application layer	Application layer
Database layer	↕	*Application sub layers 1,2,3....n*
	Database layer	↕
		Database layer

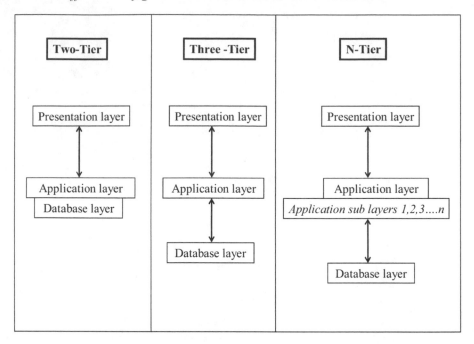

presentation. The back end usually consisted of RDBMS, which ran on a powerful computer. Accounting transactions could now be processed in a distributive processing environment. The separation of database from application enabled accounting software developers to focus on accounting programs, thereby avoiding maintenance of proprietary databases. Accounting programs could quickly adapt to changes in databases and new developments in databases, such as multi-media and object-oriented databases, without extensive rewriting of programs.

Not all accounting systems use power of relational databases. Accounting software can use a proprietary front end to: connect to a relational database instead of re-writing the accounting application, enforce referential integrity in the application and not in the database, and ignore the replication and distributed processing functionalities of the database. A few accounting systems are written from scratch to use the power of databases such as Microsoft's SQL server and the client-server architecture — for example, MAS 500 by Best Software (now Sage Software). In any case, the majority of these accounting applications can now run on LANs or WANs (which serve a wide geographic area such as state or a county) and can serve hundreds of users. Generalized accounting software or packaged accounting software really took off with the advent of the PC and client-server environment. The majority of today's accounting software companies such as Intuit, Peachtree, Great Plains, Exact Macola and Best Software were born during the early 1980s.

Exhibit 6. Browser-server and client-server architecture

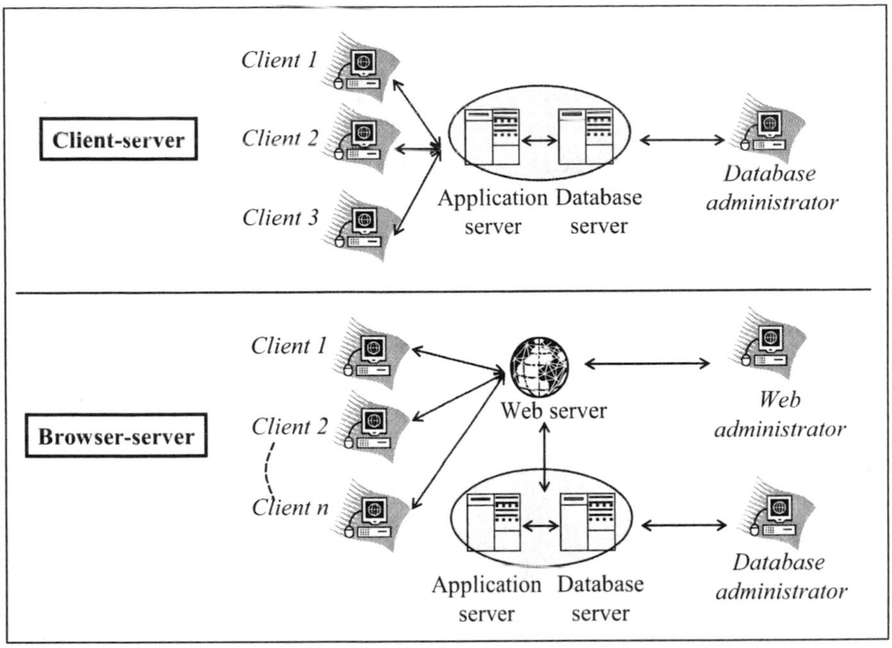

The next paradigm shift occurred with the rise of the Internet and WWW. The functionality of accounting software expanded to accommodate e-commerce capabilities. This gave rise to browser-server architecture (for details of the origin of this term see www.browsersoft.com/about.shtml/), which is essentially an extension of the client-server environment. The server can be accessed over the Internet by a graphical browser and data can be downloaded and uploaded. The server that can be accessed over the Internet is called a Web server. This Web server sits between the application and database layer and the clients. The Web server handles incoming and outgoing messages using various Internet protocols, and application and database servers perform standard functions. In other words, the Web server provides Web-related services.

Generally, Web servers can provide various Internet-related services such as FTP, e-mail and telnet in addition to Web-related services. These services are provided via numbered ports. A port is essentially a pathway into and out of the computer or network devices. For example, a PC has ports for the keyboard, mouse, modem and printer. Different ports or different pathways on the server provide different services. Some of the well-known ports are port 21 for FTP, port 25 for e-mail and port 80 for Web-related services. As a security precaution, servers will allow outside connections only to the designated ports. If there are no restrictions, then the client can connect to any port on the server using the Internet. Once a connection to the port is established, Internet protocols will be used to access various services.

Exhibit 7. Internet-related services and port numbers

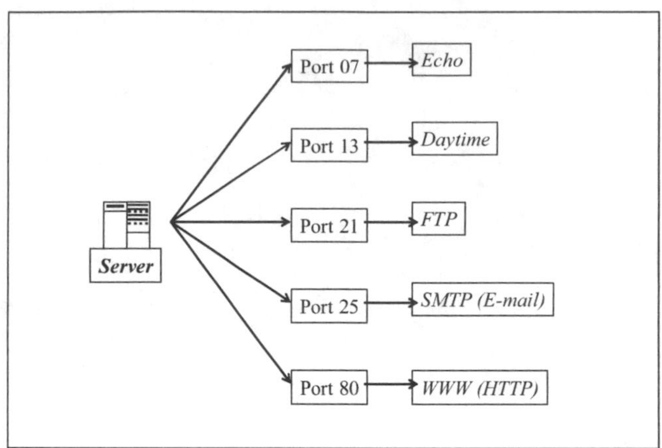

The browser-server architecture enabled a variety of e-commerce features. Web stores can be established on the Internet, and customers have 24/7 access to these stores. The customers and suppliers can, with appropriate authority, log on to the company network and use self-service features. Thus, the demand and supply chains remain perpetually connected and can communicate in real time. Employees can access company databases for information, tap into bulletin boards, and enter travel and other expenses when on the road; the list is endless.

SAP R/3 has been designed for the client-server environment and can be used to illustrate both client-server and browser-server environments. SAP R/3 is an ERP system. The term ERP was coined by Gartner Group in the early 1990s. ERP systems offer enterprise-wide applications by connecting differing functional systems such as accounting, finance, production, human resources, and sales and distribution. ERP systems in essence integrate all departments and functions across the organization, using a suite of commercial software packages. ERP systems, to reiterate, use RDBMS or a data warehouse to store immense amounts data, are based on client-server and its successor architectures, and allow user interaction through GUI. SAP R/3, and Oracle are leading vendors of ERP packages.

A very simplistic representation of the SAP R/3 system is shown in Exhibit 8. This is a conceptual representation of the system and is independent of the version. The databases supported at the database server level include IBM DB2, Oracle, Informix and Microsoft SQL server. SAP stores master data, transaction data and metadata that describe the database structure at the database server. The Advanced Business Application Programming (ABAP) language can be used to define and manipulate such stored data. Application servers can run on various operating systems such as Uniplexed Information and Computing System (UNIX), its variations, Virtual Memory System (VMS) and Windows New Technology (NT), and its successors. Business logic runs on

Exhibit 8. SAP R/3 implementation of client-server architecture

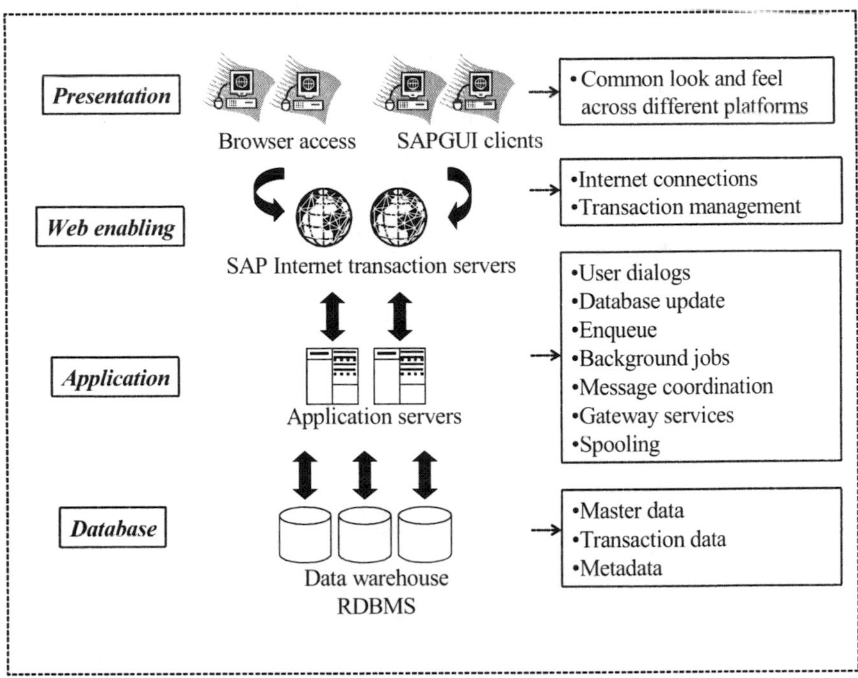

application servers, and these servers also perform basic services: the user dialogs service processes user inputs using business logic; database updates service updates the database after the transaction is complete; enqueue service controls business objects by generating, holding and releasing locks; background jobs service completes transaction processing; message coordination service controls to and fro movement of data; gateways service controls communication between SAP R/3 and the external systems; and spooling service controls printing. Since database, application and presentation layers can and generally run on different systems, the application layer supports various networks and network protocols.

The SAP Internet Transaction Server (ITS) is a Web server. The primary function of SAP ITS is to establish communication between the Internet and the SAP R/3 system, a difficult task given the technical differences. This server converts the SAPGUI interface into HTML, enabling Internet and intranet (a private network that generally can only be accessed by authorized persons, such as the employees of a company) users to access and use the SAP R/3 system. SAP ITS is a cornerstone for *mySAP.com* service that provides a multitude of Web functionalities. The presentation layer contains SAP GUI, which is an interface operated by users to access data, launch applications and display data. This GUI provides a consistent look and feel across different platforms. The SAP R/3 system is very complex; however, the preceding brief description provides us with a cutting-edge example of a client-server/browser-server implementation of accounting software.

ASPs (Application Service Providers) use browser-server architecture to develop a whole new way of delivering accounting software. ASPs deploy, host and manage a software application from a centralized facility, allow access to this software over the Internet and charge fees for access. This is a general definition; however, in the dynamic world of computing one encounters a wide band of services under the rubric of ASPs. These services can range from purely HTML- (or a variant) based, which allow the user to enter data and display reports by using merely a browser and the Internet connection, to application(s) hosted and managed by the ASP in its entirety, which make the client-side computer function as a dumb terminal, but the user can see all screens as if the applications are installed locally.

A problem for many small- and medium-sized businesses is the management of accounting software, which consumes vital resources. The installation, configuration, upgrade, maintenance, security and backup requirements can be onerous for small businesses. The needed expertise is scarce and/or expensive. The lower-level accounting software may come with a weak database engine, or some required features may have to be sacrificed. ASPs offer Web-based accounting software as a cost-effective solution for small- and medium-sized businesses. Oracle was the first company to introduce Web-based accounting software, named Netledger, in 1998. Netledger started slowly and lacked many necessary capabilities; for example, the early version only had standard accounting modules and a payroll module. Netledger has considerably changed and added more capabilities in its later versions. Oracle offered various products such as Oracle Small Business Suite, NetLedger, NetCRM, NetSuite and NetLedger Advanced Accounting. The database engine used was the Oracle database, a powerful database for small- or medium-sized businesses. Oracle took responsibility for upgrade, maintenance, backup and security (including the Internet security) of the software. However, in 2004, NetSuite separated from Oracle and has become an independent company.

Small-business accounting software vendors are not standing still, either. QuickBooks has introduced an online version to compete with NetLedger, Microsoft has its own online Finance Manager, and Peachtree has introduced ePeachtree, a pure online product. Peachtree has another version for online accounting — it has added a Web module called Peachtree Web Accounting to its flagship product, Peachtree Complete Accounting. Data and the main program reside on the user's computer; however, the Web module can be used to push data to the Web. The Web-based data can be accessed by online users, with proper authorization and authentication, for processing and running reports. At predefined synchronization intervals, the Web data and the desk data are synchronized, creating a unified version of data. ACCPAC (published by Best Software) offers ACCPAC online service as a Web-based accounting package for mid-sized businesses. SAP offers a limited number of modules in an online mode at *mySAP.com*. The functionality of online products continues to increase and presents a viable alternative to in-house accounting software.

The current generation of accounting software is enabled for standalone computers, many variants of a client-server environment, browser-server architecture or Internet delivery. Accounting software is written for a variety of operating systems and networks, uses a variety of programming languages and supports a range of databases. The dominant operating system is Windows NT and its successive generations; other supported operating systems are Linux (opens source version of UNIX), variations of UNIX and Novell Netware. Few accounting systems are also available on the Macintosh and IBM Operating System 2 (OS/2) platform. The databases at the core of accounting systems primarily consist of Btrieve, Pervasive SQL, Microsoft SQL, Microsoft Access, Informix, IBM DB2 and Oracle — most of these are relational databases. Programming languages such as Visual Basic, Visual FoxPro, C, C^{++}, JAVA and other object-oriented or Web-based languages are used in writing accounting software.

What Constitutes Accounting Software?

The term *accounting software* denotes software that handles accounting and perhaps finance functions. The traditional view of classifying accounting software is by the size of businesses served by the accounting software. Initial offerings of accounting software packages were and (often times) now are aimed at a certain-size business. The size of the business is mostly measured by revenue and considerations such as number of employees or volume of transactions. The market starts at the lowest level of home/ small office and extends to billion-dollar multinational and multi-product companies. The functionalities, databases, operating systems and capabilities of accounting software vary at each level.

The broad segments within the market are as follows: home/small, small, medium, large and multinational corporations – an accounting software market space. The approximate revenue range is less than $1 million, $1 to $25 million, $25 to $250 million, $250 to $350 million and greater than $500 million for each segment, respectively. These distinctions are, of course, arbitrary; however, useful for our purposes. There have been hundreds of accounting software companies. Some major players in each segment are shown in Exhibit 9. Most of these companies have existed for more than a decade, have a substantial installed base and have provided proven solutions.

Accounting software aimed at each segment has different characteristics. At the lowest level, accounting software offers standard accounting modules such as order entry, payroll, general ledger and financials; it generally runs on a standalone system or supports few users; and a database is embedded in the software. The cost is low and the software can be bought off the shelf. Accounting software that serves the mid-size market can provide a full financial suite and advanced industry-specific modules, and offer e-commerce solutions. This software can support multiple users, operate on multiple operating systems and come with an embedded database or work with any existing relational database products. The software is expensive and is generally sold by Value Added Resellers (VARs). VARs specialize in a particular software package and serve as consultants during installation and operation of the system. The ERP packages at the high end are extremely expensive — a software cost of millions of dollars being merely a drop in the bucket compared to extensive consulting, training, reengineering of workflows and restructuring of organizations costs — and require armies of consultants and multiple years to install and make operational.

Exhibit 9. Major accounting software vendors

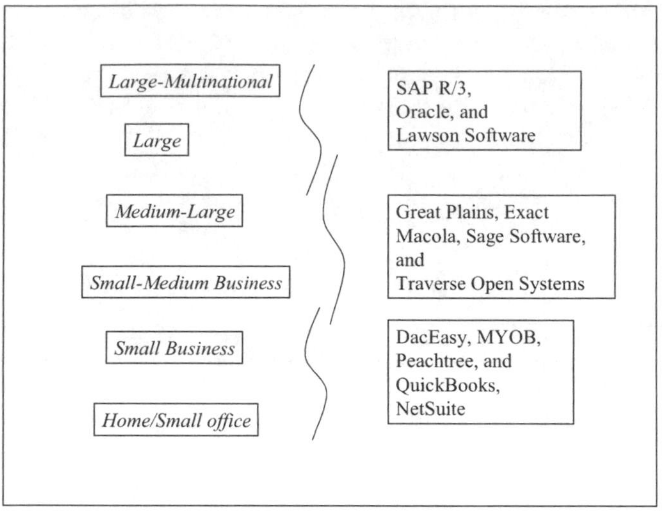

Within broad categories of low-, mid- and high-end accounting; there can be other distinctions. The Web site *www.accountingsoftwareverticals.com/* provided the following classification: *Vertical Accounting*, where accounting solutions are geared toward a particular industry; *Add-On products*, which perform certain specialized functions and can work with existing accounting packages or in a standalone mode, and *Horizontal Accounting*, which provides accounting solutions for a wide range of industries. This accounting software discussion so far has been in the context of *Horizontal Accounting* solutions, which is a dominant pattern in the accounting software industry.

Many accounting software packages are aimed at certain industries or types of businesses. The following discussion of these software packages does not strictly follow the definition of *Vertical Accounting*, though it uses the general concept. For example, programs such as Exact Macola offer a historical focus on manufacturing; CAP Automation and Cougar Mountain software are geared to point-of-sale retail environments; and there are programs specifically written for service industries. Due to special information needs, industry segments such as insurance, construction, property management, and law and accounting practices require specialized accounting packages. Then there are numerous packages aimed at the non-profit sector, which obviously has different reporting and analysis requirements. Packages — *Add-On* products — generally focus on a special accounting function. For example, there are packages that specialize in fixed assets management, payroll, time and billing, and tax preparation. As accounting software gets increasingly integrated, a trend fueled by SAP, the majority of add-on product vendors either get acquired or develop alliances.

The accounting software market is also segmented by countries. Languages, financial reporting rules, auditing requirements, tax code, and business laws and regulations are different in each country. Many high-end accounting software vendors have built multi-language, multi-tax code and multi-currency support in their software so multinational companies can coordinate their operations in various countries and regions. There also are specialized companies that serve specific national markets. For example, several accounting software packages cater to the new European Union and deal with the Euro currency.

The traditional market-size view gives us a good understanding of the markets and market strategies of accounting software vendors. These markets are dynamic in nature, and as companies become successful in one segment, they try to branch upstream, downstream or both. The product functionalities and product offerings of accounting software are also continually changing. The installed base remains a good indicator of the long-term survival of accounting software vendors and, as such, software vendors continuously struggle to seize market share. Accounting software companies also offer products to different segments to ensure that as customers grow (or occasionally shrink) they can seamlessly move from one software product to another within the same family.

As business demands on accounting software grow, new functionalities are continuously added in accounting software. The mantra of this new age is *comprehensive functionality*. No matter what functional area the software catered to, vendors cannot survive unless they offer a reasonably integrated package to their core constituency of customers. Hundreds of business software vendors now offer accounting and finance

Exhibit 10. Competition in various segments

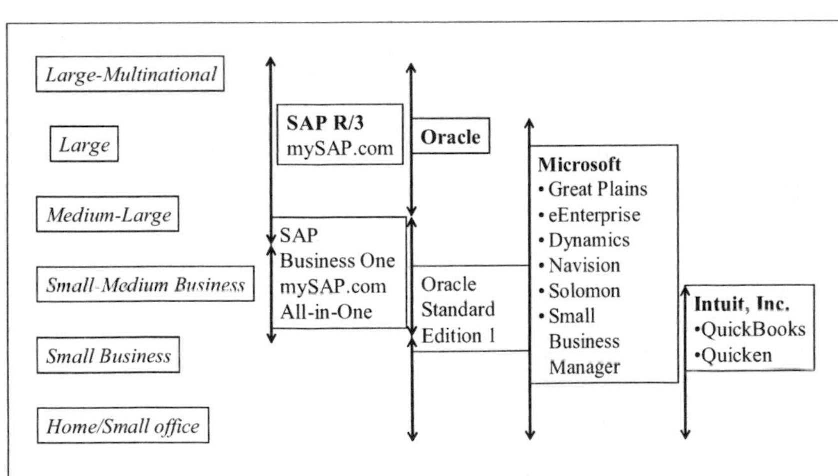

functionalities. The major players in every market and industry segment now offer integrated solutions, and the role of stand-alone product vendors is slowly but surely diminishing. The terminology and alphabet soup of new capabilities become more fantastic, and one wonders what do vendors mean by the term accounting software? The answer is that traditional accounting software no longer exists.

High-end ERP vendors such as SAP R/3 never claimed to be accounting software vendors, though SAP has one of the best accounting and finance modules. This trend has filtered down to mid-size vendors. The majority of mid-sized accounting vendors claimed that their systems were in fact ERP systems. In the late 1990s, markets zoomed beyond ERP and into e-commerce and the resulting inter- and intra-business integration. Accounting software vendors, keeping up with the times, added new e-functionalities. ERP claims were modified to describe this new face of accounting software. Following are some descriptions of accounting software picked up from the Web sites of the traditional mid-sized accounting software vendors:

- **Microsoft Great Plains (www.microsoft.com/BusinessSolutions/):** Microsoft Business Solutions–Great Plains offers integrated capabilities for financial management, distribution, manufacturing, project accounting, human resource management, field service management and business analytics.
- **Sage Software (www.bestsoftware.com/):** MAS 500 boasts integrated solutions that automate all areas of business management, including CRM, accounting and financials, project accounting, distribution, manufacturing, human resources and more.
- **Macola (www.exactamerica.com/Macola):** Macola ES is the only ERP solution designed for the mid market with native Business Process Management (BPM) capabilities, including powerful exception management tools.

The accounting function, as a trend of our times, is getting submerged in the greater business information system. Today's accounting software contains accounting modules and a plethora of business modules, even at the low end of the accounting software spectrum. Accounting modules depict traditional journals and ledger; however, accounting data now resides in relational databases. The database or data warehouse may consist not only of financial information but also non-financial information.

A standard structure for accounting software is shown in the Exhibit 11. Accounting modules are at the core of the business information system, since accounting is still the language of business. The accounting modules are supplemented and/or complemented by various functional modules, such as production planning and control, inventory order processing, project management and warehouse management. The inter-organizational transactions are managed using specialized modules such as supply chain management, supplier relationship management and customer relationship management. The primary database of an organization now consists of financial and non-financial information, often times a data warehouse with which all functional modules interact. The e-commerce modules can be physically separated or integrated with the software; however, they

Exhibit 11. Structure of accounting/business software

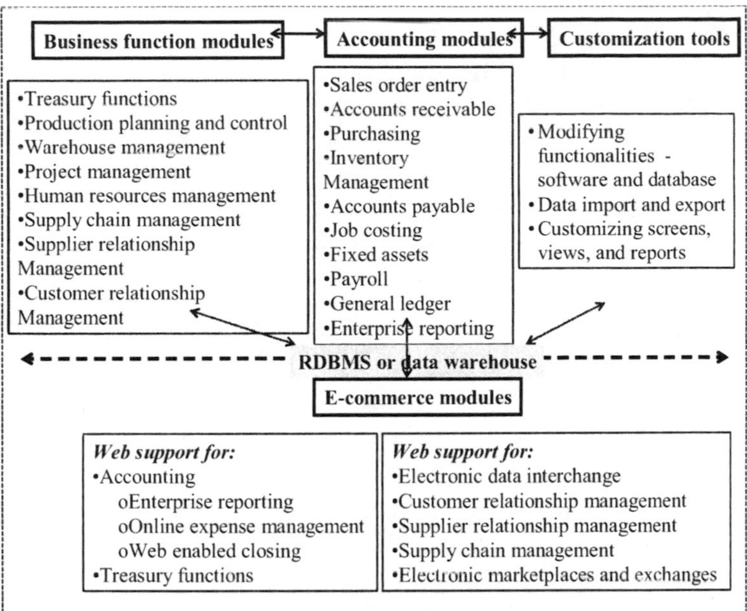

enable various inter- and intra-organizational Web-based processes. A general structure of accounting/business software is outlined below.

- **Accounting modules:** The core accounting modules perform standard accounting jobs; for example, order entry and billing, accounts receivable, accounts payable, inventory, payroll, fixed assets, job costing and general ledger. In addition to these core modules can exist other accounting-related modules, such as bank reconciliation, foreign currency managers, time and billing, and travel expense management, among other things. These modules are sometimes standard and sometimes sold separately. Software almost always includes a separate module called *system manager* (or a similar term) that provides common services to all accounting modules — for example, searching data across all applications. Accounting modules are often supplemented with treasury modules that manage cash, working capital, derivatives, investments in bond and stock markets, and foreign exchange and interest rate risk exposure.
- **Business function modules:** These modules run the entire gamut, from functional areas to supply-and-demand chain management. The functional modules can be manufacturing related, such as material requirements planning, capacity requirements planning, production scheduling or warehouse management. Demand chain management may include modules like sales forecasting, customer relationship management or sales force automation; and supply chain management modules can

consist of supplier relationship management and inventory forecasting and management modules. The business function modules may also contain industry specific modules — for example, modules for non-profit companies.

- **E-commerce modules:** E-commerce modules vary, from support for traditional EDI to Web-based executive dashboards/enterprise portals, which provide vital business information to executives/employees in a user-friendly format. Almost every accounting cycle has seen emergence of different types of e-functionalities.
- **Third-party add-on products:** Add-on products can vary from vendor to vendor. Some accounting software products offer a comprehensive set of accounting modules and do not need add-on products. Few accounting vendors offer core modules and have an open architecture for the software, and generally third-party developers can easily develop add-on products purchased separately. Additionally, standard modules on specific software can be add-on product for other accounting software, due to each product's market focus. The common add-on products are fixed assets modules; reporting modules such as F9, Crystal Reports or FRx; and e-commerce-related modules.
- **Customization tools:** Customization tools add or improve functionality of the software; import and export data; and customize forms, screen views and reports. In earlier days, many software companies shared the program code with customers. The trend now is to provide 4th Generation Programming Languages (4GL) tools, such as Visual Basic or Visual Basic for Applications-based tools, which allow extension of accounting software sometimes without tampering with the program code.

The evolution of accounting software marches on. Accounting software is now part of integrated business software, business information system and business solutions, and no doubt there are even more exotic terms on the horizon. Accounting software analyzes financial and non-financial information, interacts with powerful reporting tools, is enhanced by Web-based processes, and of course fulfills the basic requirements of financial reporting in accordance with Generally Accepted Accounting Principles (GAAP). The requirements of the Sarbanes-Oxley Act 2002 make it even more imperative for accountants and auditors to have a deeper understanding of the continuously evolving and changing accounting systems.

Looking Ahead

Directions for the evolution of accounting software and the accounting software industry remain unpredictable, which of course is true for all predictions. In any case, here they are! The high-end accounting/business software market is becoming, and the trend will continue, supportive of what can be called multi-enterprise collaboration, which was described as collaborative commerce (c-commerce) in the late 1990s. The ERP infrastructure is now a foundation for the applications that connect suppliers, customers, employees and other stakeholders in a giant web of information. Gartner Group has already coined a term ERP II and AMR Research Group has offered Enterprise Commerce Applications (ECM) as an alternative for these types of applications. The terminology continues to be confusing, and each software vendor and consultant defines identical or similar things with different labels.

Basically, ERP II and ECM functionalities include e-commerce and Internet applications. These applications also cover what is called xRM categories; for example, Customer Relationship Management (CRM), Supplier Relationship Management (SRM), Supply Chain Management (SCM), Partner Relationship Management (PRM) and Employee Relationship Management (ERM). There is an endless debate about what these terms mean, and different definitions and interpretations are offered by vendors, consultants and academicians. The explanations provided here use commonly accepted definitions and provide general understanding of the terms.

CRM integrates customer-centric efforts such as marketing campaigns, call centers, help desks, sales force automation and customer analytics (such as most profitable customers). SRM and SCM handle managing sourcing of raw materials, production, inventory and logistics; additionally, these also improve collaboration with suppliers, manage risk and analyze supplier profitability. PRM deals with efficient management of relationships between sellers and indirect channels, such as dealers, agents, VARs, wholesalers and distributors. ERM focuses on employee education, performance analysis, incentive effects, workforce analytics and additional tasks, such as recruitment, time and expense reporting, and employee self-service. A new field called Demand Chain Management (DCM) that encompasses customer demand and consequent activities, and intersects with CRM, SRM and SCM, is also sometimes offered as a separate module.

Analytical abilities of accounting/business software are also being enhanced. Earlier business intelligence applications generally collected and analyzed data from customer and supplier databases, manufacturing and marketing activities, personnel data and financial data to generate reports in the desired format for the end user. Some of these tools were not user-friendly nor fully exploited. Now, enterprise portals and executive dashboards that are Web- and GUI-based, provide various user-friendly tools and can be accessed remotely are being developed and deployed. These portals and dashboards can be utilized to view information in a numerical or visual format, drill down to obtain further information, and analyze information and data using embedded analytical tools.

These preceding management issues are not new— these are as old as business itself. A number of independent software vendors have products in these areas that are decade(s) old. The novelty is that these products are getting integrated and, on the base provided by ERPs, can now offer powerful capabilities. The extent of integration of these tools and consequent effectiveness is a matter of debate, and different software vendors have strengths in different areas. Different businesses have deployed these technologies with varied results. What seems certain is that seamless integration of these functionalities remains the Holy Grail for software vendors.

These high-end developments will continue to filter down the hierarchy, faster and quicker than ever before. Accounting software vendors are merging and consolidating to acquire new markets and new capabilities. The accounting software industry still remains in a fragmented state— many accounting software vendors are competing for the same mid-sized market. As such, powerful industry players such as SAP, Oracle and Microsoft are moving upstream and downstream in the accounting software market. The million-dollar question, of course, is what is the comparative effectiveness and efficiency of these tools offered by various companies? The answer is illusive and remains open for further research and experimentation.

At the lower end of the accounting software, movement toward relational databases and client-server architecture is expected. The use of relational database capabilities by accounting software varies widely; however, more accounting programs have begun to exploit power of relational databases. The use of Web-based accounting software is a continuing experiment. Web-based offerings are developing a clientele; the extent of penetration in the market is not clear. Web-based systems, though, are going to be part of the accounting software landscape, and in due course, most of the accounting software vendors will offer some type of Web-based access, entry and reporting capabilities.

These speculations for the future are based on experts' thinking and trends observed in the past. Accounting software is not required to follow any of these directions. Though unlikely, niche software players or garage developers could change the face of the industry. Coming developments, whatever they may be, will certainly test our ability to learn, understand and employ new technologies.

Summary

Accounting was the first functional area to get automated and feel the effects of Information Technology. Accounting software has become more sophisticated over the last several decades, and now it forms the core of business information systems. Accounting software based on older mainframe technologies is often referred to as legacy systems. Accounting software changed with the advent of PCs and client-server and browser-server environments. Today's accounting software is GUI-based, user-friendly and accessible from remote places. RDBMS is at the core of these accounting systems, which provides flexible and scalable accounting systems that can serve hundreds or thousands of users. Most of these software suites now look similar and provide comprehensive functionalities; however, these suites have different strengths and weaknesses.

Accounting software no longer exists at mid-size and higher-ends. Instead, we have accounting/business software, integrated business information systems, or ERP systems with accounting and finance modules. Accounting modules interact with other functional modules and also with entities outside the organization. In the future, the functionality of high-end software will include increasingly powerful capabilities for intra- and inter-organizational collaboration. The trend is toward integration of different functions in one software package. The present high-end functionality should filter down to mid-sized accounting software, a process that has already begun. Lower-end accounting software will use the full power of RDBMS and be written or re-written to take advantage of the client-server environment. E-commerce developments have added new capabilities to existing software. Accounting workflows and processes in every accounting cycle have changed due to these features.

References

Alderson, A., & Shah, H. (1999). *Understanding legacy systems through viewpoints and events*. The University of York, UK. Retrieved June 8, 2003, from www-users.cs.york.ac.uk/~kimble/teaching/mis/Legacy_Systems.doc/

Anonymous. (2002, June). The future of WMS. *Material Handling Management,* 3-12.

Basile, A., Papa, L., & Johnston, R. (2002, August). Leading low-end accounting software. *CPA Journal,* 41-49.

Bourne, T. (1997, October). Helping to tackle the legacy systems problem. *Management Accounting,* 24-25.

Carlton, C. (1999a). How to select the right accounting software. *Journal of Accountancy, August,* 67-75.

Carlton, C. (1999b, September). How to select the right accounting software. *Journal of Accountancy,* 31-37.

Carlton, C. (1999c, October). How to select the right accounting software. *Journal of Accountancy,* 61-68.

Carlton, C. (2002a). *Customizing accounting software.* Retrieved June 15, 2003, from www.accountingsoftwareadvisor.com/

Carlton, C. (2002b). *Guide to accounting software modules.* Retrieved June 15, 2003, from www.accountingsoftwareadvisor.com/

Carlton, C. (2002c). *History of Web-based accounting software.* Retrieved June 15, 2003, from www.accountingsoftwareadvisor.com/

Carlton, C. (2002d). *History of Web-based accounting*. Retrieved June 15, 2003, from www.accountingsoftwareadvisor.com/

Carnegie Mellon Software Engineering Institute. (2003). Client-server software architectures – An overview. *Software Technology Review.* Retrieved June 16, 2003, from www.sei.cmu.edu/str/descriptions/

Cohn, M. (1994, December). Accounting technology: The first decade. *Accounting Technology*, 12-23.

Cohn, M., & Bellone, R. (1997, January). Looking back: History of accounting software. *Accounting Technology,* 19-36.

Courteny, H.M., Prachyl, C.L., & Glandon, T. (1998, March). Guide to accounting software. *Journal of Accountancy,* 44-46.

Darrow, B. (2003). Once more into the fray: Microsoft to take on Intuit. *CRN*, *8*(1074), 6.

Deshmukh, A., & Romine, J. (2002, November). Accounting software and e-business. *CPA Journal*, 52-54.

Enterprise information portals and executive dashboards. (2002). Information Builders. Retrieved June 17, 2003, from www.informationbuilders.com/

Ericson, J. (2001). *Measuring supplier performance*. Line 56. Retrieved December 8, 2002, from www.line56.com/articles/

Ericson, J. (2002a). *Is ERM a contender*. Line 56. Retrieved December 8, 2002, from www.line56.com/articles/

Ericson, J. (2002b). *The partner channel*. Line 56. Retrieved December 8, 2002, from www.line56.com/articles/

ERP II: The next source of competitive edge or just another acronym. (2003). Centerline ERP. Retrieved May 8, 2004, from www.centerlineerp.com/press/ERPII.htm

Gilmore, D., & Tompkins, J. (2003). *WMS footprint expands into supply chain*. IDY Systems. Retrieved May 8, 2004, from www.idysystems.com/reader/2000_05/rw10500/rw10500.htm/

Glick, B. (2000). *JD Edwards bets the farm on ERP II*. VNU Network. Retrieved December 8, 2003, from www.vnunet.com/Analysis/1113214/

Gumaer, R. (1999, September). Beyond ERP and MRP II. *IIE Solutions*, 32-36.

Harrington, A. (2001). *Gartner touts ERP II vision*. VNU Network. Retrieved December 8, 2003, from www.vnunet.com/Analysis/1115981/

Hedtke, J. (1998, May). Classy small biz accounting software. *Accounting Technology*, 37-44.

Hedtke, J. (2001, May). The best of the disk and the Web. *Accounting Technology*, 40-43.

Hibbard, J. (2002). A field day. *Red Herring*. Retrieved December 8, 2003, from www.redherring.com/

Jones, R.A. (2002, May). Spotlight on midlevel ERP software. *Journal of Accountancy*, 24-47.

Koch, C. (2002). The ABCs of ERP. *CIO*. Retrieved December 8, 2003, from www.cio.com/research/erp/edit/erpbasics.html

Lobaugh, J., & Deshmukh, A. (2000, September). Supplementing legacy financial systems by integrating high-end technology. *Strategic Finance*, 52-60.

McCausland, R. (1999, September). SQL database shoot-out. *Accounting Technology*, 54-60.

McCausland, R. (2002, August). Distribution software: ROI is king. *Accounting Technology*, 50-54.

McCausland, R. (2004). ERP for the masses? *Accounting Technology*, *20*(4), 14-20.

McCullough, D. (1999). *A white paper on: The North American market for Warehouse Management Systems (WMS), software and systems integration services*. Venture Development Corporation. Retrieved December 8, 2003, from www.vdc-corp.com/

McKie, S. (1998). *The accounting software handbook*. Loveland: Duke Communications International.

McNaurlin, B.C., & Sprague, R.H. (2004). *Information systems management in practice*. Upper Saddle River, NJ: Pearson Prentice Hall.

Mello, A. (2001). *Battle of the labels: ERP II vs. ECM.* ZDNet. Retrieved December 8, 2003, from www.zdnet.com.au/news/business/0,39023166,20260789,00.htm

Pervasive Software Inc. (2002). *Differences in programming: Btrieve's way of thinking.* Retrieved December 10, 2003, from www.pervasive.com/

Robinson, P. (2001). *ERP survival guide.* BPIC. Retrieved December 10, 2003, from www.bpic.co.uk/erp.htm/

Rogers, A. (2002). ERP startup targets smaller manufacturers. *CRN.* Retrieved December 10, 2003, from www.crn.com/

SAP history. (2001). SAP. Retrieved December 10, 2003, from www.sap.com/

Schroeder, J. (1999). *Enterprise portals: A new business intelligence paradigm.* DM Review. Retrieved December 10, 2003, from www.dmreview.com/master.cfm/

Scott, R. (1999, December). J.D. Edwards counts on midmarket history. *Accounting Technology*, 58.

Scott, R. (2002, June). Squeezing the mid-range. *Accounting Technology*, 6.

Stimpson, J. (2002, September). Mid-level accounting software takes off. *Practical Accountant*, 42-45.

Trunk, C. (2002, July). Putting more "M" into WMS. *Material Handling Management*, 45-57.

Vendor information: Microsoft Great Plains. (2002). Microsoft. Retrieved May 10, 2004, from www.microsoft.com/BusinessSolutions/GreatPlains/Default.aspx/

Endnote

1 Exhibits 4 and 5 are adapted from McKie, S. (1998). *The accounting software handbook.* Loveland: Duke Communications International.

Appendix A: A Checklist for E-commerce Features

This appendix provides a list of e-commerce features that intersect with accounting and finance. The exact nature of intersection is discussed in later chapters. Listed features are available on most accounting software packages aimed at mid-sized or large businesses. This list is illustrative and not exhaustive.

Revenue Cycle

Web Storefronts – B2B and/or B2C

- Web site creation tools; offers support for third party storefronts; have preferred partners for creating or hosting Web sites
- Produces ready-to-publish Web catalogs; can represent product items in more than one category in an online catalog; links photographs with products
- Price and product changes automatically flow to the Web
- Ability to create shopping carts and forms
- Supports EDI – automatically confirms, fills and ships customer orders; generates support documents at each step of the process
- Real-time connectivity with back-end office processing

Customer Relationship Management Tools

- Clickstream analysis
- Customer intelligence
- Sales intelligence
- Support for sales force automation
- Online promotions and targeting

Sales Order

- Retrieves orders from the Web in all formats
- Supports remote data entry via Web; online confirmation of orders for immediate verification by customers; e-mail acknowledgement of the order
- Accepts new customers

Customer Self-Service

- Order entry, order tracking, links to tracking pages of courier services
- Product price and product availability
- Product configurators to customize products

- Ability to view billing and payment information, purchases and returns chronologically, by order or by item
- Drill-down capabilities
- Chat facilities with sales people

Credit Approval

- Web-based credit check and credit approvals
- Automatic credit check and approval
- Automatic credit card validation
- Ability to check on established credit limit

Billing and Collections

- E-mail invoicing
- Electronic bill presentment
- Ability to handle multi-format payments; for example, letters of credit, bills of exchange, electronic fund transfers, credit cards, digital cash and so forth

Services

- Capability to create and track service request
- Ability to integrate call centers and e-mail requests with back-end office processing
- Access to company knowledge bases
- Real-time information on orders, shipping and payment information
- Ability to create collaborative platforms or forums
- Online technical support

Expenditure and Conversion Cycles

EDI

- Integrated EDI solution – electronically sends and receives purchase orders and payments
- Can handle various EDI standards
- EDI solution pre-mapped to each trading partner's standards
- Links to third-party translators and mapping software applications
- Interfaces with EDI and fax software
- Bar code interface

Supply Chain Management

Supplier Relationship Management/E-Procurement

- Supports multiple standards for security and data communication
- Support for sourcing
- Support for online negotiation
- Support for catalog development and hosting
- Support for auctions
- Support for customization and automation according to trading agreements, workflows and business rules

Vendor Self-Service

- Get information on request for quotation or proposals, purchase order revision, receipt or return of goods and payments
- Performance metrics for quality and delivery
- Inventory requirements available through EDI or Internet posting
- Drill-down capabilities
- Chat facilities with purchase people

Expenditures

- Online forms for claiming travel and entertainment expenses
- Online management of expense reimbursements
- Online payroll
- Online time sheets
- Support for online travel centers

Product Development

- Online design and development tools
- Sharing of product design over the Internet
- Virtual testing and collaboration
- Integration or interface with Computer Aided Design/Computer Aided Manufacturing (CAD/CAM) software

Human Resources

- Access to personal files, job performance and company policies
- Access to 401K funds

- Internal bulletin boards for jobs and other projects
- Support for online payroll services

General Ledger Cycle and Financial Reporting

- Support for enterprise portals and executive dashboards
- Web-enabled closing of the books
- Web-based planning and budgeting
- Printing of financial reports to Web publishable format, allowing report generation via Web queries and distributing reports via e-mail
- Supports global tax code requirements
- Supports multiple exchange rates
- Supports multiple languages

These changes are illustrative and not exhaustive; however, the description is fairly comprehensive. But even this checklist fails to capture sweeping changes covered later on. A number of new software tools and new accounting processes have emerged to implement and handle these changes. A classification of these e-changes in the context of accounting cycles provides us with a framework that can be used for classifying the present as well as future developments in accounting.

Chapter III

The XML-Based Web Languages and Accounting

XML: What's in it for Accountants?[1]

The Internet spins a vast web of information across the globe. Data and information flow freely — available to anyone for learning, understanding and analysis. Organizations can cooperate across departments, regions and countries. ERP II and ECM herald the era of intra- and inter-business collaboration. Sounds wonderful – what is the problem? The problem is as old as mainframe vs. PC and Windows vs. Macintosh. Data can move freely but are not standardized. Data streams have no universal meanings; consequently, data are not understood by all systems, analyzed easily, translated across different languages and human readable, among other things. Specialized hardware and software is needed for data decoding, and if the required tools are not available, then you are out of luck. This problem is not only confined to the Internet. A great deal of money (by one estimate, almost 20% of the U.S. gross national product) is spent on generating new information, and more than 90% of this information is in documents, not in databases. Businesses in the U.S. produce approximately 100 billion documents per year. This information is stored in various formats across a range of computer systems. These disparate storage formats cause severe problems in accessing, searching and distributing this information.

Any solution (a combination of information technology products and services) that manages information across diverse software and hardware platforms must address a few key requirements. First, these solutions should be transparent to users. The technical details should not be handled by users. Second, users should be able to save data and information in the desired format; for example, databases, text files or proprietary formats. Third, a solution must intelligently retrieve data and information. This solution should be knowledgeable regarding meaning of the information itself. Finally, such solution should be capable of providing the desired output — print, screen, Web or CD/DVD format.

eXtensible Markup Language (XML) has been designed to meet these requirements. Needless to say, XML will not solve all information management problems, and certainly not in a short time. XML is the first step, but has been hailed as a revolutionary advance in data transfer and information identification on the Internet. XML has developed tremendous momentum in the last few years. The majority of key software vendors is involved in XML standard-setting forums and products, and is actively promoting XML gospel. Microsoft CEO Ballmer says: "*You could say we've put 100 percent of our resources into it. We've taken an approach that incorporates XML into everything we do. I'd say we're betting the company on XML.*" The future seems promising, but only time can tell.

XML has applications in a wide range of areas; for example, sciences, mathematics, music, religion and, of course, business. XML and various XML-based languages are affecting different business areas, such as e-procurement, e-commerce, EDI, electronic payment systems, financial data transfer and derivatives, to mention a few. XML influence is also felt across different areas; for example, there are XML applications in accounting, finance, advertising and manufacturing. XBRL, an application of XML, is an electronic format for simplifying the flow of financial statements, performance reports, accounting records and other financial information between software programs. XBRL International explains XBRL as the accounting industry's method to take standard business reporting data and transform it into the digital world of bits and bytes. Financial data consists of financial statements, cost accounting data and tax information; prior to XBRL, there was no standard way to transfer, analyze and understand this data. XBRL is designed to standardize financial data transfer and enable preparation and publication of that information in a desired format. XBRL is finding worldwide acceptance and is backed by major businesses, accounting institutes and governmental agencies worldwide. See the most current member list at *www.xbrl.org/*.

As XML and XBRL make inroads in accounting software and internal and external accounting reports, and affect information transfer across businesses, it is necessary to understand the mechanics of these languages. A required depth of understanding, of course, depends on whether one wants to be involved in developing standards, preparing and/or programming reports, or simply using the language. However, whatever your role, you must understand these new developments.

Exhibit 1. Timeline for markup languages

Year	Developments
1940s	• Concept of hyperlinks–use of a markup in a document to point to another page or file; creating hypertext
1960s	• Procedural markups for text processing–Text and RTFs (Rich Text Files) • W. Tunnicliffe, President of Composition Committee of GCA (Graphic Communication Association) forwards the idea of separating content from formatting of a document • GCA Gencode (Generic Coding) Committee advocates the use of descriptive over procedural markups • In 1969 at IBM, Charles Goldfarb and his colleagues Mosher and Lorie create a markup language called GML (initials of three creators, also Generalized Markup Language), by 1980, 90% of documents at IBM are in GML
1978	• ANSI (American National Standards Institute) forms *The Computer Languages for the Processing of Text Committee*
1980s	• First working draft of SGML (Standard Generalized Markup Language) • Department of Defense and IRS use SGML • Text processing becomes Word processing; software specific formatting procedural markups • WYSIWIG (What You See Is What You Get) features–Markups go under the hood
1990s	• Advent of WWW (World Wide Web) o HTTP (Hyper Text Transfer Protocol)–based on hyperlinks and hypertext o HTML (Hyper Text Markup Language)–an application of SGML o URL – Uniform Resource Locator • HTML and its successor versions continue to become more powerful though ultimately found inadequate for tasks of the information management on the web
Mid 1990s	• XML, a less complex version of SGML, is formulated o W3C makes XML recommendation in 1998
> 2000	• XML evolution marches on

History of Markup Languages

SGML is one of the first standardized markup languages. Most of today's markup languages, including XML, have descended from SGML. What are these markup languages? To understand markup languages, we have to first understand *markups*. Markups (also referred to as *tags*) are notations in a document that are not *content*. The term content refers to information contained in the document; for example, financial data, product specifications, news, catalogs and contracts, among other things. Markups can be any sequence of characters or symbols inserted in the document to provide information concerning formatting, printing, appearance or, most importantly, providing information about the content. Markups are not unique to electronic documents; for example, headings, punctuation and paragraphs provide information about the content of a paper document and help human readers navigate the document. Also, markups such as annotations, wavy underlines or special symbols have been used to guide the printer or compositor. Markups for electronic documents perform a similar function by providing information about content, format, printing and processing of a document.

Markups can be of two types — procedural and descriptive (also known as generic markups). Procedural markups specify how to process the text and primarily deal with the formatting and presentation of the document (not with the content). These are software specific; for example, formatting markups, codes or tags used by Word or WordPerfect. "Move right margin by ¼ inch," "skip the line" and "go to new page" are some instances of procedural markups used by word processing software. Since procedural markups do not contain information regarding content and are proprietary, they cannot be communicated between software packages and operating systems. Organizations store *content* in various formats across various departments and computer systems: word processor files, spreadsheet files, database files, text files and image files, to mention a few. These formats mostly use procedural markups and do not talk to each other, causing difficulties in content management.

Descriptive markups, on the other hand, contain information about the logical structure of text and content in the document. The basic premise behind descriptive markups is to keep content separate from style of the document. Descriptive markups can help identify elements of the document structure, such as chapter, section or a table of contents. For example, descriptive markup *<para>* tells us that either the following item is a paragraph or it is the end of the previous paragraph. These markups can also be used for presentation of content in different data formats such as HTML, Portable Document Format (PDF), relational data tables and so forth. Additionally, descriptive markups are human and machine-readable and are in the public domain; some procedural markups also are human readable. However, human readability does not ensure complete understanding of the markups — descriptive or procedural; some markups may make sense only to machines. Descriptive markups form the basis of markup languages. As Charles Goldfarb, one of original inventors of markup languages, said: "*Markups should describe a document's structure and other attributes and should completely divorce structure from appearance while facilitating indexing and generation of selective views.*"

Markup languages are not programming languages, but they basically allow for representation of text in an electronic form. Markup languages specify the following rules:

- A dictionary of markups allowed
- Meaning of markups
- When and where the markup is required
- Distinguishing a markup from the text

Markup languages provide a set of conventions that can be used for encoding texts. To reiterate, a markup language specifies symbols for markups, meaning of markups, distinction of markup from text and the type of markup required for a specific purpose. Markup languages ably deal with the problem of content management.

As stated earlier, SGML is one of the first standardized markup languages, and can be characterized as the mother of all markup languages. SGML provides markups that result in representation of an electronic text not dependent on specific devices or system and can be read over a wide variety of computers. SGML is a markup language and also a metalanguage. A metalanguage does not define a language but allows us to create a consistent markup language by providing the mechanics of a formal description of markup language (similar to providing grammar for the language). SGML is a very powerful and complex markup and metalanguage. Numerous software tools are available to create and validate SGML documents. SGML provides for almost an infinite array of markups, needs to be written only once and is platform independent. This leads to shorter lead times, reduction in cost and better control in document production.

SGML is governed by International Organization for Standardization (ISO) 8879, developed in 1986, and it is widely used in industry and commerce for large documentation projects. For example, SGML has been used to describe technical documentation of stealth bombers, patients' clinical records and musical notations. However, SGML is a pre-WWW language and is not specifically designed for the Internet. The use of SGML for specifying documents on the Internet is difficult, since no mainstream browser supports SGML. Additionally, though SGML provides structure, it does not provide style sheet standards, which deal with formatting and presentation of information, resulting in problems of presentation. SGML is widely used; however, it is not very useful in the Web environment.

Like SGML, XML is a markup language and metalanguage. However, XML is stripped of complexities, multifarious options and lesser-used parts of SGML. XML essentially is a subset of SGML. XML makes it easy to define document types, is easier to understand and program, can deal with multiple languages and is better suited for the Internet environment. XML is extensible, meaning capable of being extended or customized, and not fixed format and predefined (as HTML). Hence, XML can be used to design and define markups for an infinite variety of documents. XML allows transmission of data from server to browser, application to application, and machine to machine.

Exhibit 2. Differences in HTML and XML

HTML	XML
• Primarily used for web page layouts	• Can be used to store any kind of structured information
• Primarily defines format of a document through predefined set of markups or tags	• Allows creation and definition of markups o The authors can design their own document types o XML hypertext linking abilities are better than HTML o XML stylesheets provide far better facilities for a browser presentation and performance
• An *application* of SGML o Manufacturers' specifications may limit universal applicability	• A *subset* of SGML o Valid XML files are valid SGML files; can be used on the Web and in existing SGML environments
• Describes display format of the document	• Describes structure of the document
• Generally not human readable	• Can be made human readable

W3C (*www.w3.org/*), whose mission is to develop interoperable technologies (specifications, guidelines, software and tools) to lead the Web to its full potential as a forum for information, commerce, communication and collective understanding, develops the standards for XML. The standards designed or accepted by W3C are in the public domain. The design goals for XML 1.0 as listed on *www.w3.org/TR/REC-xml/* are:

- XML shall be straightforwardly usable over the Internet.
- XML shall support a wide variety of applications.
- XML shall be compatible with SGML.
- It shall be easy to write programs that process XML documents.
- The number of optional features in XML is to be kept to the absolute minimum, ideally zero.
- XML documents should be human-legible and reasonably clear.
- The XML design should be prepared quickly.
- The design of XML shall be formal and concise.
- XML documents shall be easy to create.
- Terseness in XML markup is of minimal importance.

HTML, the primary language used to describe and deliver documents in the Internet environment, is also an application of SGML. HTML uses concepts of hyperlinks, hypertexts and tags to browse files on the Internet; but it is neither as flexible nor as powerful as SGML. HTML, though simplistic, was at the right place at the right time. The use of HTML exploded as the Web expanded. However, HTML has many limitations. For example, HTML can only be used to define and deliver simple report-style documents — lists, tables, headings, and some hypertext and multimedia. This limitation is due to the fixed and predefined set of markups or tags used by HTML. These tags are used for primarily formatting documents, and support fixed and simple document structure. HTML provides static definitions of these documents and does not provide means to identify data, resulting in limited reuse and interchange of HTML documents. Searches on the Internet produce a large number of hits, since HTML does not identify contents of the documents. For example, it cannot differentiate between stocks (as in shares) and stocks (as in inventories). HTML's functionality has been variously extended by different vendors, and several incompatible versions exist. However, HTML has a large installed base and it will probably continue to exist in the Internet environment.

XML does not replace HTML; instead, it allows for definition of markup elements as one sees fit. In fact, XML has been applied to extend HTML, and the resulting language is called eXtended HTML (XHTML). This language permits document creation, content and delivery using features of both XML and HTML. Let us see the structure of XML that enables us to achieve these amazing features.

What is XML?

That is a billion-dollar question; and like most billion-dollar questions, it is difficult to answer. XML is a way of organizing and managing information, a constellation of supplementary technologies and a paradigm for information handling for the Internet age. Large volumes describe the guts of XML; however, we can only look at the fundamental concepts. First, creation of XML documents using XML markups will be discussed. Second, satellite technologies that expand the XML abilities — for example, dealing with numbers, voice, images and Web publishing — will be reviewed. Finally, XML tools and software that allow us to create XML documents and applications will be covered.

XML Document

XML document is a basic unit of information and consists of content and markups, and follows the rules of XML. The content can be text, numbers, images or equations. Exhibit 3 shows a simple example of an XML document. The upper part of Exhibit 3 shows a memo from a student to the faculty member; in the lower part, this memo has been converted into XML format.

The first line in the XML format (<?xml version="1.0" encoding="ISO-8859-1"?>) indicates the XML version and encoding used in the document. This line is required so

Exhibit 3. XML document

Memo

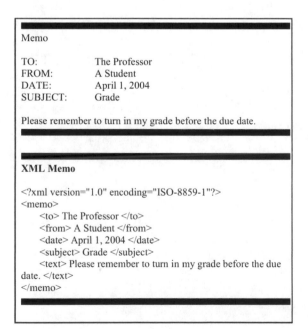

TO:	The Professor
FROM:	A Student
DATE:	April 1, 2004
SUBJECT:	Grade

Please remember to turn in my grade before the due date.

XML Memo

```
<?xml version="1.0" encoding="ISO-8859-1"?>
<memo>
    <to> The Professor </to>
    <from> A Student </from>
    <date> April 1, 2004 </date>
    <subject> Grade </subject>
    <text> Please remember to turn in my grade before the due
date. </text>
</memo>
```

that XML-aware applications can process the document. This memo conforms to XML specification 1.0 and uses the ISO-8859-1 (Latin-1/West European) character set. XML characters are based on an encoding system called Unicode that can handle up to 65,536 characters. These characters are used to represent various languages; for example, Latin, Greek, Hindi and Han ideographs (Chinese and Japanese language); additionally, various symbols sets have been defined. ISO is working on another standard called Universal Character System (UCS) that can handle up to 2 billion characters, ensuring that XML fulfills its promise of universal application. These standards enable XML to handle different languages and different symbols. Some of these XML standards and their uses are described in Exhibit 4.

XML documents must conform to XML syntax, meaning grammar of the language. Take a look at this syntax by studying Exhibit 3. The second line in the XML memo says <memo>, which means that this document is a memo. The term <memo> that comes first and tells us about the document is called *root element*. The root element includes everything between <memo> and </memo>. The next four elements (to, from, date and subject) are called *child elements*. The last line repeats </memo>, indicating the end of the root element. A person can easily infer that this XML document is a memo, which indicates that XML is human readable and self-descriptive to some degree.

Root and child elements give XML a tree-type structure. XML elements include everything from the beginning tag to the ending tag and things in between. An element can be mixed, simple or empty. A mixed element contains text and other elements. For example, root element <memo> is a mixed element since it contains other child elements. A simple element generally contains only text and an empty element contains nothing. The elements <to>, <from>, <subject> and <text> are simple elements and there is no empty element in our example. An element can also have an attribute, which provides additional information about the element. If, in our memo, we want to incorporate the date as an attribute of the root element memo, then we will define <memo> element as <memo date="April 1, 2004">.

Following are basic rules of XML syntax. Please remember there are numerous extensions to these rules.

- All XML documents should have a root element.
- All XML elements should have a beginning tag and an ending tag.
- XML tags are case sensitive.
- All XML elements are properly nested. That means both the beginning and ending tags for each child element exist within the body of parent element. (Exhibit 3 emphasizes this fact by indenting all child elements.)
- Elements should not overlap. For example, we cannot have:

  <to> The Professor <from>

  A Student </to> </from>
- Element names start only with letters and underscores and can only contain letters, numbers, hyphens, periods and underscores. For example, <from> or <_from> are valid but <from me> and <from-me> are not valid.

Exhibit 4. Character sets underlying XML

Specifications	Uses
Unicode ISO(International Organization for Standardization) Standards	Represents various natural languages in the world
IANA (Internet Assigned Numbers Authority) Character Sets	Represents different character sets
IETF (Internet Engineering Task Force) Standards and ISO Standards	Identify languages and countries
IETF (Internet Engineering Task Force) Standards	Identify the Internet resources

- Attributes values must be in quotation marks. Attribute in a XML document means a sub element defined within an element. For example, if the root element <memo> is expanded to add a date, then the root element will look like <memo date="April 1, 2004">. The value of sub element *date* should be in quotation marks, otherwise XML syntax is violated.

XML requires strict adherence to the syntax and brooks no deviations. An XML document that conforms to these rules is called *well formed*. The next question is where do we get those markup/tags, such as *to, from* and so forth? These are the tags that we created; remember, XML is a metalanguage. Then, following the grammar of XML, we generated a well-formed XML document. This can be called *free-form* XML. XML programs can understand it. However, this format is of little use, since in the free-form format meaning and structure of tags is not specified in any place. If a slightest mistake in typing tags is made, processing may come to a halt or be incorrect. It will be extremely difficult to debug errors, although many programs have simplified the process by automating debugging tasks. Additionally, errors in content cannot be detected by merely a well-formed XML document.

XML provides tools to model documents to overcome these problems. Document modeling involves specifying rules for a document. These rules define structure of the document and a list of its legal elements; they can provide definitions for the following items:

- Elements permitted in the document
- Attributes permitted in the document
- Parent element and child elements
- Order of child elements
- Number of child elements
- Contents of the element
- Data types for elements and attributes
- Default and fixed values for elements and attributes

Exhibit 5. DTDs

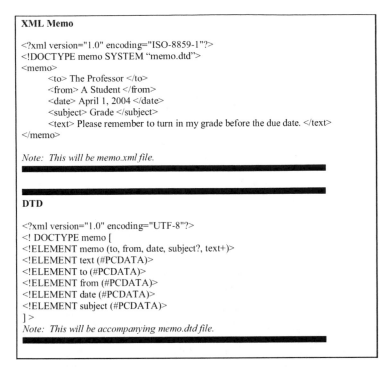

XML Memo

```
<?xml version="1.0" encoding="ISO-8859-1"?>
<!DOCTYPE memo SYSTEM "memo.dtd">
<memo>
        <to> The Professor </to>
        <from> A Student </from>
        <date> April 1, 2004 </date>
        <subject> Grade </subject>
        <text> Please remember to turn in my grade before the due date. </text>
</memo>
```

Note: This will be memo.xml file.

DTD

```
<?xml version="1.0" encoding="UTF-8"?>
<! DOCTYPE memo [
<!ELEMENT memo (to, from, date, subject?, text+)>
<!ELEMENT text (#PCDATA)>
<!ELEMENT to (#PCDATA)>
<!ELEMENT from (#PCDATA)>
<!ELEMENT date (#PCDATA)>
<!ELEMENT subject (#PCDATA)>
]>
```

Note: This will be accompanying memo.dtd file.

Any particular document (called *document instance*) can be compared with the document model to make sure the particular document is in conformity with the specified rules. This is called validating a document. A valid document is free from XML syntax errors, such as misspelled tags, improper order of tags or missing data; and follows all rules specified by the author. The two main tools provided by XML to validate documents are called Document Type Definition (DTD) and XML Schema.

A DTD is a formal description of a particular type of document. Using XML Declaration Syntax, DTDs describe what names are to be used for describing elements (elements consist of a start tag and an end tag), where they occur in the document and their interrelationships. DTDs can be located in the document with the tags and content or can reside in a separate file. XML documents with DTDs generally consist of two parts: the first part contains tags and content, and the second part formally describes syntax of the document. The XML document must contain tags and content; however, a very simple XML document may not need DTDs. For business uses, DTDs are, of course, crucial. A simple example of DTD will be used for illustrative purposes.

Exhibit 5 provides an example of DTD for a *memo* document. The third line in the DTD part introduces the elements in the memo. This document has three required header elements — to, from and date. The fourth header element, *subject*, is optional, which is specified by a question mark. The element *text* can have more than one occurrence (multiple paragraphs), which is identified by a + mark. The term *#PCDATA* refers to parsed

Exhibit 6. XML Schema

XML Memo

```
<?xml version="1.0" encoding="ISO-8859-1"?>
<memo xmlns="http://www.psu.edu/mo" xmlns:xsi="http://www.w3.org/2001/XMLSchema-
instance" xsi:schemaLocation="http://www.psu.edu/mo memo.xsd">
        <to> The Professor </to>
        <from> A Student </from>
        <subject> Grade </subject>
        <date> 2004-04-01 </date>
        <text> Please remember to turn in my grade before the due date. </text>
</memo>
```

Note: This will be memo.xml file.

XML Schema

```
<?xml version="1.0" encoding="UTF-8"?>
<xs:schema targetNamespace="http://www.psu.edu/mo" xmlns:mo="http://www.psu.edu/mo"
xmlns:xs="http://www.w3.org/2001/XMLSchema" elementFormDefault="qualified"
attributeFormDefault="unqualified">
  <xs:element name="memo">
    <xs:complexType>
      <xs:sequence>
        <xs:element name="to" type="xs:string"/>
        <xs:element name="from" type="xs:string"/>
        <xs:element name="subject" type="xs:string"/>
        <xs:element name="date" type="xs:date"/>
        <xs:element name="text" type="xs:string"/>
      </xs:sequence>
    </xs:complexType>
  </xs:element>
</xs:schema>
```

Note: This will be memo.xsd file.

character data; that is, text. Text should be a pure text and should not contain any unrecognized markup strings. The encoded memo will now be stored in a memo.xml file and the associated DTD will be stored in a memo.dtd file.

There are differences in this XML memo and the one in Exhibit 3. The DTD-based XML memo has a second line in the XML memo that indicates this document is based on a DTD, and the same DTD is given in the second part of Exhibit 5. The resulting memo output will be similar to the one in Exhibit 3. Both these formats can be used to display the document on-screen or print it on a standard form. However, the format in Exhibit 5 can be used to generate a new form based on each element. Any new memo (document instance) based on the given DTD can be validated by the DTD and debugging of errors will be easy.

The primary problem with DTDs is that the DTD syntax is not a valid XML syntax. Thus, support for XML and an additional support for DTD syntax is required when XML documents are processed. XML Schema is the other method of validation and is considered superior to DTD for various reasons. First, XML Schemas support data types such as numeric, alphanumeric or dates. This support enables us to describe permissible document content, to easily validate data and to convert data between different data types, to mention a few advantages. Second, XML Schemas use XML syntax, and the

Exhibit 7. Example of purchase order (Source: XML Spy, used with permission)

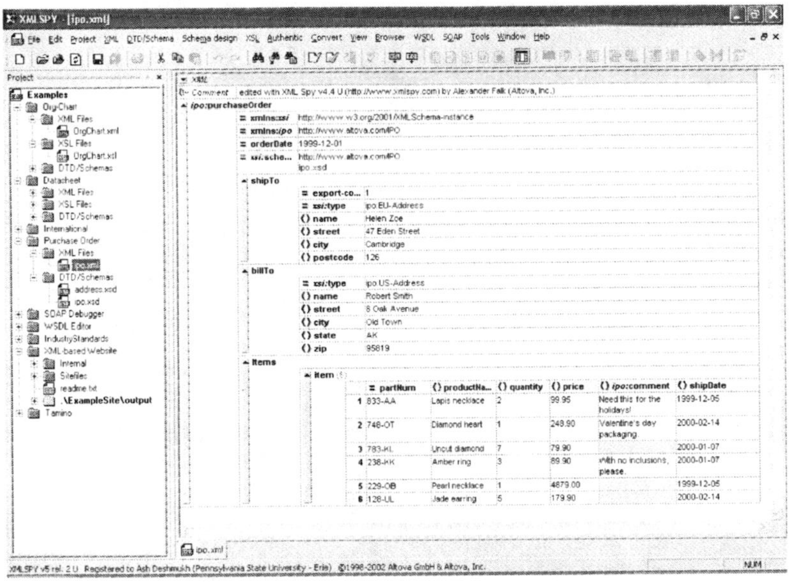

resulting documents look like XML files and can be processed using existing XML tools. Third, XML Schemas ensure correct data communication by clearly specifying expected format of data. Finally, XML Schemas based on XML are extensible, which allows for reuse of schemas or creation of your own data types.

Exhibit 6 shows the XML Schema for the memo. The XML memo document now contains a reference to XML Schema. The fourth line in the XML memo area xsi:schemaLocation="http://www.psu.edu/mo memo.xsd"> indicates the location of our schema. This location can be on a local drive; in the Web environment, a URL will probably provide this location. This schema is provided in the latter half of Exhibit 6. The later part of the third line in the XML Schema area xmlns:xs="http://www.w3.org/2001/XMLSchema indicates that elements and data types used in the schema conform to *www.w3.org/2001/XMLSchema/*. The fifth line identifies the element name as *memo*. The next line specifies the element *memo* as of complex type, because this element contains other elements such as to, from, date, subject and text. An element can be declared complex type due to several other conditions not discussed here.

Then, a correct sequence of the elements and the data type for each element is provided. The elements inside the sequence must occur in a given order. All the other elements — to, from, date, subject and text — are simple elements. A simple element in XML can contain only *text*. The XML Schema defines *text* broadly and includes data types such as Boolean, text strings and dates. In case of the elements to, from, subject and text, data type is specified as *string*, meaning these elements can contain only text strings. The element date is defined as *date* and not as a *string*, since this data field should only accept date format and no other data type. XML Schema travels with the original memo and can be used to validate the memo. This schema can also be used to generate similar memos. Any violations of rules of schema in the new memo can now be rapidly identified. These

Exhibit 8. XML purchase order and XML Schema (Source: XML Spy, used with permission)

XML Purchase Order

```
<?xml version="1.0"?>
<!-- edited with XML Spy v4.4 U (http://www.xmlspy.com) by
Alexander Falk (Altova, Inc.) -->
<ipo:purchaseOrder
xmlns:xsi="http://www.w3.org/2001/XMLSchema-instance"
xmlns:ipo="http://www.altova.com/IPO" orderDate="1999-12-
01" xsi:schemaLocation="http://www.altova.com/IPO
ipo.xsd">
    <shipTo export-code="1" xsi:type="ipo:EU-Address">
        <name>Helen Zoe</name>
        <street>47 Eden Street</street>
        <city>Cambridge</city>
        <postcode>126</postcode>
    </shipTo>
    <billTo xsi:type="ipo:US-Address">
        <name>Robert Smith</name>
        <street>8 Oak Avenue</street>
        <city>Old Town</city>
        <state>AK</state>
        <zip>95819</zip>
    </billTo>
    <Items>
        <item partNum="833-AA">
            <productName>Lapis necklace</productName>
            <quantity>2</quantity>
            <price>99.95</price>
            <ipo:comment>Need this for the
holidays!</ipo:comment>
            <shipDate>1999-12-05</shipDate>
        </item>
        <item partNum="748-OT">
            <productName>Diamond heart</productName>
            <quantity>1</quantity>
            <price>248.90</price>
            <ipo:comment>Valentine's day
packaging.</ipo:comment>
            <shipDate>2000-02-14</shipDate>
        </item>
        <item partNum="783-KL">
            <productName>Uncut diamond</productName>
            <quantity>7</quantity>
            <price>79.90</price>
            <shipDate>2000-01-07</shipDate>
        </item>
        <item partNum="238-KK">
            <productName>Amber ring</productName>
            <quantity>3</quantity>
            <price>89.90</price>
            <ipo:comment>With no inclusions,
please.</ipo:comment>
            <shipDate>2000-01-07</shipDate>
        </item>
        <item partNum="229-OB">
            <productName>Pearl necklace</productName>
            <quantity>1</quantity>
            <price>4879.00</price>
            <shipDate>1999-12-05</shipDate>
        </item>
        <item partNum="128-UL">
            <productName>Jade earring</productName>
            <quantity>5</quantity>
            <price>179.90</price>
            <shipDate>2000-02-14</shipDate>
        </item>
    </Items>
</ipo:purchaseOrder>
```

XML Schema

```
<?xml version="1.0" encoding="UTF-8"?>
<!-- edited with XML Spy v4.0 NT beta 1 build Jun 13 2001
(http://www.xmlspy.com) by Alexander Falk (Altova, Inc.) -->
<schema targetNamespace="http://www.altova.com/IPO"
xmlns:ipo="http://www.altova.com/IPO"
xmlns="http://www.w3.org/2001/XMLSchema"
elementFormDefault="unqualified"
attributeFormDefault="unqualified">
    <annotation>
        <documentation>
  International Purchase order schema for Example.com
  Copyright 2000 Example.com. All rights reserved.
 </documentation>
    </annotation>
    <!-- include address constructs -->
    <include schemaLocation="address.xsd"/>
    <element name="purchaseOrder"
type="ipo:PurchaseOrderType"/>
    <element name="comment" type="string"/>
    <complexType name="PurchaseOrderType">
        <sequence>
            <element name="shipTo" type="ipo:Address"/>
            <element name="billTo" type="ipo:Address"/>
            <element ref="ipo:comment" minOccurs="0"/>
            <element name="Items" type="ipo:Items"/>
        </sequence>
        <attribute name="orderDate" type="date"/>
    </complexType>
    <complexType name="Items">
        <sequence>
            <element name="item" minOccurs="0"
maxOccurs="unbounded">
                <complexType>
                    <sequence>
                        <element name="productName"
type="string"/>
                        <element name="quantity">
                            <simpleType>
                                <restriction
base="positiveInteger">
                                    <maxExclusive
value="100"/>
                                </restriction>
                            </simpleType>
                        </element>
                        <element name="price"
type="decimal"/>
                        <element ref="ipo:comment"
minOccurs="0"/>
                        <element name="shipDate"
type="date" minOccurs="0"/>
                    </sequence>
                    <attribute name="partNum"
type="ipo:Sku"/>
                </complexType>
            </element>
        </sequence>
    </complexType>
    <simpleType name="Sku">
        <restriction base="string">
            <pattern value="\d{3}-[A-Z]{2}"/>
        </restriction>
    </simpleType>
</schema>
```

Exhibit 9. Example of a complex document (Source: XML Spy, used with permission)

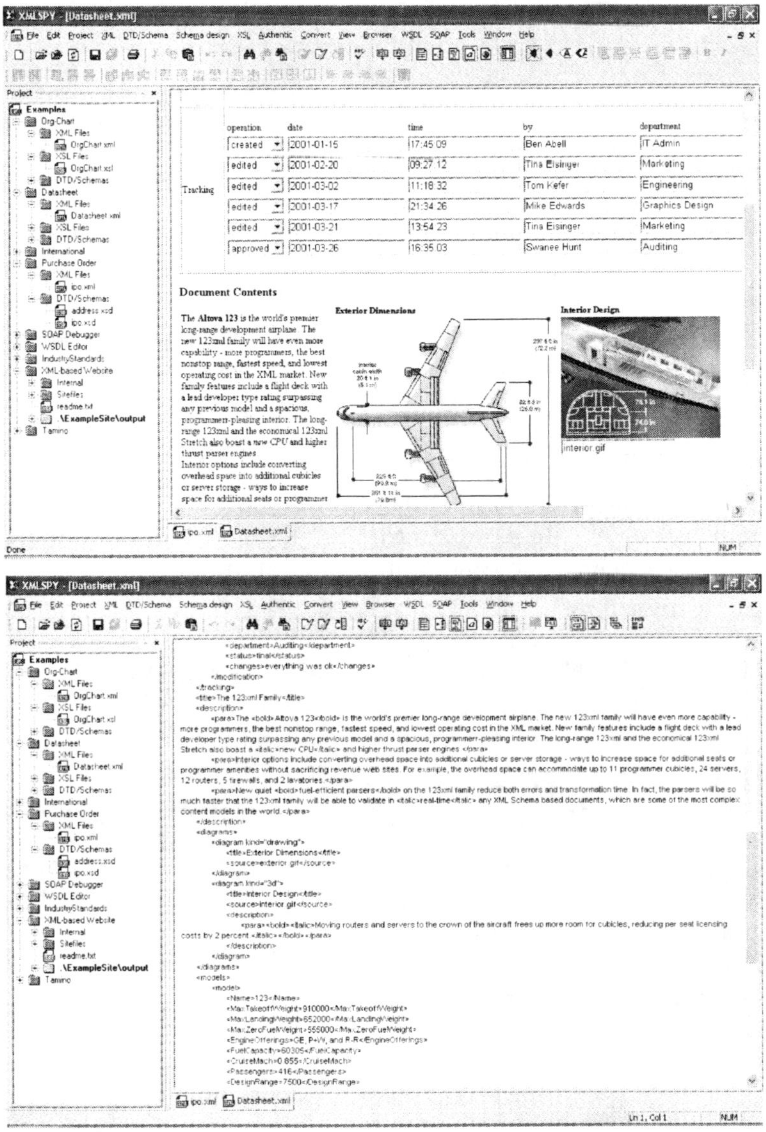

abilities are vital in large and repetitive documents, such as purchase orders or sales invoices.

XML allows for combination and reuse of other independently developed formats. Thus, different documents can be combined in one document; however, elements and names in those documents should be defined similarly. What happens when two documents contain the same name defined differently? For example, one document defines memory as *Random Access Memory (RAM)* and another document defines memory as *human memory*. If these two documents are merged then there will be a conflict on hand. XML provides a mechanism called *XML Namespaces* to deal with these situations. XML

Namespaces not only prevent name clashes but also tell the processing software how to treat the different groups of elements. For example, equations will be processed using certain XML rules and text will be processed using another set of XML rules. Namespaces in the XML document will be declared by using an attribute whose name is xmlns or has xmlns: as a prefix.

Exhibits 7, 8 and 9 are taken from XML Spy, which provides Integrated Development Environment (IDE) for XML. Exhibit 7 shows an international purchase order. The approximate actual format of the purchase order is displayed in the bottom right corner. This format is fairly common in the business world. The associated XML Purchase Order and XML Schema of this purchase order are shown in the Exhibit 8. This example shows how complex XML becomes once we start looking at real-world documents. The associated XML Schema uses all concepts such as XML Namespaces and complex types covered earlier. This XML Schema also uses many advanced concepts that are beyond the scope of this book. Exhibit 9 shows a document that contains datasheet, text and images. XML can easily handle these complicated documents. The partial XML tags for this document are shown in the next screenshot in Exhibit 9. This XML snapshot shows how the images are embedded in the document.

So far only bare basics of XML have been covered. XML is a versatile language and is not limited only to documents. XML provides a logical structure of the document and not the physical structure. The file can be physically at different locations and not necessarily at one location for XML documents to function properly. However, XML is not a programming language and, as such, XML is not executable. An XML file is processed using programs written in traditional programming languages.

XML Supplementary Technologies

XML consists of marking up of a text document. So how will XML fulfill its promise of leaping across national boundaries, linguistic differences and incompatible systems? XML is a modular language and there is an emergent set ·of modules increasing capabilities of XML. XML is armed with a host of supplementary technologies that enable these modules.[2] A broad categorization of these technologies is as follows:

- Validation and linking technologies
- Transformation technologies
- Processor technologies
- XML applications
- Security applications

XML provides a rich and flexible syntax to describe content. This very flexibility creates a problem of identifying valid XML documents. The validating technologies allow us to validate XML documents effortlessly, well, with little less effort! The primary validating technologies are DTDs and XML Schema, covered earlier. XML Schema is becoming

Exhibit 10. Examples of XML supplementary technologies

Validation and linking technologies	• XML DTD • XML Schema • XLink • X Base • XPath • XPointer • XFragment
Transformation technologies	• XSL • XSLT • Canonical XML • XQuery • XInclude
Processor technologies	• DOM • SAX
XML applications • *Non-text applications* • *Publishing on the Web* o *Web communication and services* • *Semantic Web and Resource Description Framework (RDF)*	 • MathML • SMIL • SMIL Animation • SVG • Voice XML/CCXML • XHTML • XFrames • XForms o CC/PP o SOAP/XMLP o WSDL/WSCL • RDF • RDF Schema
Security applications	• XML Signature • XKMS • P3P • Encrypted Data

increasingly popular and may become a dominant method. DTDs have a solid installed base, since DTDs are used in SGML, and are not likely to vanish in the short-term.

The popularity of the Web can be partially traced to its hyperlink capabilities. The user can jump from one page to another across Web sites and geographical boundaries. XML achieves this functionality using linking technologies. XML Linking Language (XLink) specifies the syntax for XML links, which creates and describes links between the Internet resources. This linking can be unidirectional or can connect several resources. The location of links can be separate from linked resources, and links can be associated with metadata (data that describes data). X Base supports XLink by providing connections with external resources such as images, style sheets and forms that can be processed, among other things. XPath, XPointer and XFragment are useful in addressing internal structure of XML documents. These syntaxes enable pointers pointing to parts of an XML file such as elements, character strings or other parts. XML Fragment Interchange Language can be used to send a part of the XML document, called a fragment, to a specified receiver.

Transformation technologies enable us to get a desired output from an XML document. eXtensible Stylesheet Language (XSL) can be used to design style sheets for XML documents to display on the Web. These style sheets use XML syntax and are processed with XML tools. XSL can transform XML documents to HTML documents and can also

Exhibit 11. Formatted memo in Word and associated style sheet for the Web

Memo

TO:	The Professor
FROM:	A Student
DATE:	April 1, 2004
SUBJECT:	Grade

Please remember to turn in my grade before the due date.

```
<?xml-stylesheet type="text/css"?>
<Word-Document
xmlns:HTML="http://www.w3.org/Profil
ML-transitional">
        <HTML:STYLE>
BodyTextIndent
{font-family:Times New Roman;
font-size:12pt;
text-align: left;
text-indent: 36.0pt}

DefaultParagraphFont
{font-family:Times New Roman;
font-size:12pt;}

NoList
{font-family:Times New Roman;
font-size:12pt;}

Normal
{font-family:Times New Roman;
font-size:12pt;
text-align: left;}

TableNormal
{font-family:Times New Roman;
font-size:10pt;}
p
{display: block;
 margin-bottom: 0.5 em;}
</HTML:STYLE>
      <BodyTextIndent>
          <p>&#1;</p>
          <p>Memo</p>
          <p/>
          <p>TO:          The Professor<
          <p>FROM:        A Student </p>
          <p>DATE:        April 1, 2004</
          <p>SUBJECT:     Grade</p>
          <p/>
          <p>Please remember to turn in r
            before the due date. </p>
          <p>&#1;</p>
      </BodyTextIndent>
</Word-Document>
```

transform a given XML format to another XML format. If an XML document uses a vocabulary not recognized by the system, then XSL Transformation (XSLT) can be used to create a desired vocabulary and then to process an incoming document. The other illustrative transformation technologies include canoncalization (Canonical XML), XML data query language (XQuery) and merging of documents (XInclude).

Processing technologies include software applications that interface with XML documents, read and process the XML file, and provide access to the content. These software modules are referred to as XML Processor or XML Application Programming Interface (API). One of the important API specifications is called Document Object Model (DOM). The W3C has approved DOM specifications for programmatically accessing structure and data contained in XML documents. DOM is a conceptual API for structuring, accessing and manipulating XML documents. DOM creates tree-based (root and children) representation of the XML document in memory and also defines a programmatic interface to traverse the XML tree and manipulate elements, attributes and values. In other words, DOM allows software programs to dynamically access and update the content, structure and style of documents. Microsoft and other software vendors have developed specific concrete examples of DOM that can be used with their software.

XML applications involve developing XML markups and syntax in a specific application area. XML can also be used as a metalanguage — then, which areas are using this metalanguage to develop XML-based markup languages and to what purpose? There are numerous XML initiatives in business and non-business areas. Conceptually, these applications can be divided into four categories:

- **Non-text applications:** XML, as already mentioned, can be used to handle non-text data. The non-text data includes, for example, numbers, images, multimedia, graphics and voice. Some illustrative applications include Mathematical Notation (MathML), which is a language used to handle mathematical functions; Synchronized Multimedia Integration Language (SMIL), which combines disparate multimedia objects in a coherent presentation; SMIL Animation, which provides an animation framework for XML; and Scalable Vector Graphics (SVG), which enables graphics in XML.
- **Publishing on the Web:** XHTML is an application of XML to HTML and can be used to publish Web pages. There are other applications; for example, XForms can be used to design Web forms.

Exhibit 11 shows the formatted memo used in the earlier section. This formatted memo was then run through XML Spy and the associated style sheet was generated. This style sheet is based on XHTML and will be needed to display the formatted memo exactly on the Web.

- **Web communication and services:** Languages in this area handle communications in the client-server environment, define protocols for exchange of information and describe Web services.
- **Semantic Web and RDF:** XML is also providing building blocks for *Semantic Web*. Semantic web refers to the extension of the current Web where information definition is standardized, enabling automated tools to process data. This standardization also leads to better linking of information and easier discovery, integration and reuse of data. Such a web will enable collaborative processing of data by humans and computers in a symbiotic fashion. The primary effort by W3C in this area is RDF. RDF is a framework for metadata, which enables machine-

Exhibit 12. Real-world application of XML

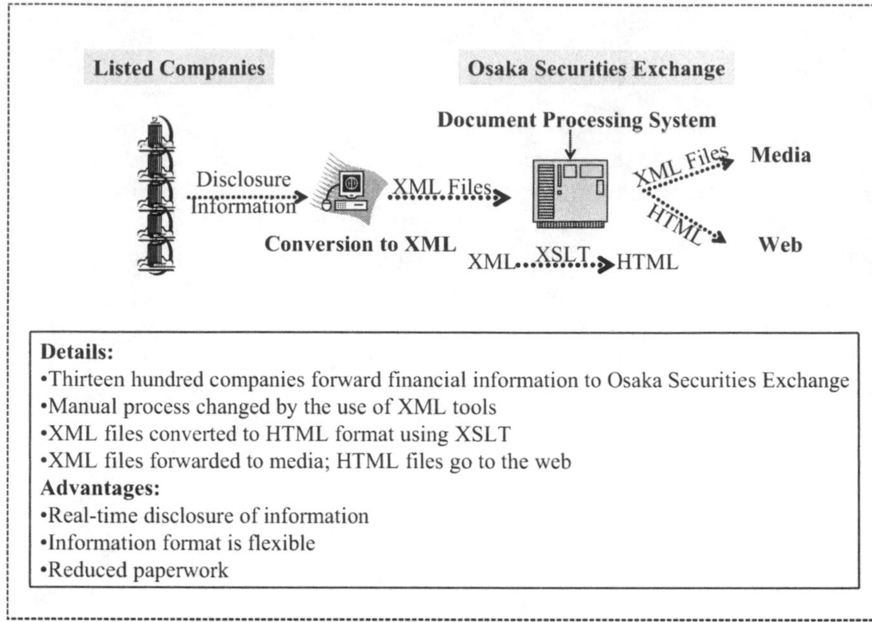
Listed Companies
Osaka Securities Exchange
Document Processing System
Disclosure Information
XML Files
XML Files
Media
HTML
Web
Conversion to XML
XML XSLT HTML
Details:
•Thirteen hundred companies forward financial information to Osaka Securities Exchange
•Manual process changed by the use of XML tools
•XML files converted to HTML format using XSLT
•XML files forwarded to media; HTML files go to the web
Advantages:
•Real-time disclosure of information
•Information format is flexible
•Reduced paperwork

understandable information. Such a framework shall promote interoperability of information among differing systems and enable automated processing. The applications will include better search engine capabilities; cataloging content and content relationship at various Web site, pages or even digital libraries; content rating; and description of intellectual property rights. RDF has many potential electronic commerce, security, entertainment and business applications. RDF heavily relies on XML technologies.

XML is increasingly being used in security applications. XML languages in this area include XML Signature for syntax and processing of digital signatures; XML Key Management Specification (XKMS) for use of public keys; Platform for Privacy Preferences (P3P) for privacy issues in the Web environment; and there are XML-based initiatives to encrypt data.

These comprehensive developments are mind-boggling. XML in a few years has progressed enormously and promises to usher in a new generation of Web and Web-based services. The usual caveat, of course, is that we are looking at emergence of a new technology or, rather, a set of technologies. Though the promise and potential is great, success in a great measure will depend on proper execution of different initiatives. The technology, even if perfectly developed, may not live up to its buildup. Given the momentum behind XML and the might of businesses and consortiums backing XML, let us err on the side of hope!

XML Tools and Software

XML has applications in numerous areas. So, what software tools are available to create these applications? First, tools to design, edit and validate XML documents are needed. Second, tools to display XML pages, manage XML databases and create XML-based content are required. Third, user-friendly software packages to read and process XML documents also are necessary. Different XML software tools exist to cater to these areas. XML tools can be broadly categorized as follows: XML and XSL editors; XML parsers; XML browsers; XML database, content management and desktop publishing tools; XML APIs; and specialized XML software. Microsoft Office 2003 has built-in XML Schema capability available to all users, which may spur wider use and acceptance of XML.

XML and XSL editors enable XML authoring. These tools can be used for XML editing and validation, schema editing and validation, XSL editing and transformation, and conversion of existing documents to XML documents, among other things. Tools for Windows and Macintosh platforms can be explored by accountants interested in XML. Given that all business information is being transformed into this digital dialect, accountants mastering this area will have unique advantages in business and accounting. Many tools offer GUI interface and are easy to use. XML parsers check that the XML document conforms to XML syntax, and validating parsers confirm that the document matches the DTD, which may be specified internally or externally. These can be standalone or integrated in a comprehensive tool.

If XML is used to create Web content, then XML-enabled browsers are required to view those Web pages. Currently, a number of XML browsers exist, and Internet Explorer (5.0 and above) and Netscape (6.0 and above) provide partial XML support. XML database and content management tools help in converting databases; structured and unstructured documents, such as spreadsheet files, traditional programming files and Web pages; and other data formats, such as images, sound or video files to XML documents. The content management tools also help in presentation of data and documents on the Web. XML desktop publishing tools are similar to XML and XSL editors described earlier. XML API deals with the interface of XML documents with applications, and specialized XML software has functionalities that do not fit in earlier categories. These functionalities are very technical in nature and generally useful for XML programmers.

In the early days of XML, there was a proliferation of tools in every area. XML-specific Web sites mention hundreds of software tools to tackle every aspect of XML. As is the trend in the software industry, these disparate tools and various functionalities are being offered in integrated packages. These packages — for example, XML Spy — offer IDE to support various XML technologies described earlier. XML IDE does not substitute for traditional programming suites such as C^{++} or JAVA, databases and Web development IDEs. XML IDE applies conceptual XML technology to a specific programming application running on a specific operating system and uses a particular networking environment. However, XML IDE tools are easy to use and available on the desktop in a familiar Windows environment, and they are an excellent way to learn and apply XML.

Advantages and Disadvantages of XML

The primary advantages of XML are:

- XML is a subset of SGML and is a very powerful and flexible language applicable to document- and transaction-centered processing.
- XML is device- and (programming-) language independent, provides interoperability to data and information.
- XML allows industry groups to develop their own markup languages, which should meet the needs of those groups more efficiently and effectively.
- XML writing, interpretation and implementation are relatively user-friendly.
- XML is suitable for Web purposes, thereby opening doors to various e-commerce applications.
- Can be made human readable
- XML is supported by W3C, and standards are in the public domain. In the financial area, such public acceptance can translate into seamless transfer of data among banks, financial institutions, stock exchanges, SEC and public accountants.

The primary disadvantages are:

- XML standards must be adopted by all parties involved in the interchange of information.
- XML standards, once developed, need to be managed and maintained continuously.
- XML can become fragmented like HTML and face incompatibility problems.
- XML follows strict formatting rules and has high startup costs.
- XML adds overhead to data transmission.
- There will be costs involved in conversion of data, training and use of XML.ROI depends heavily on universal adoption of XML.
- XML implementation can create radical changes in workflow and cause user-resistance-type problems.
- Inflated expectations may lead to disillusionment and backlash from industry groups.

XBRL

XBRL, formerly known as eXtensible Financial Reporting Modeling Language (XFRML), is causing excitement in the accounting community. The XBRL initiative started in 1998 under the auspices of the American Institute of Certified Public Accountants (AICPA). The potential of this project soon became clear, and XBRL.org was formed to coordinate efforts in this area. XBRL.org is now an independent organization called *XBRL International* and supports XBRL standards in the international arena. This organization is a non-profit consortium and has more than 170 members (a number that will only increase in the future) who represent leading businesses, major national accounting bodies, software vendors, non-profit organizations and governments. XBRL International has released XBRL specifications 2.0 and 2.1. These and other ancillary specifications are royalty-free, in the public domain and freely licensed to any user.

XBRL is an application of XML in the financial reporting arena. XBRL uses accepted financial reporting standards, and allows automatic exchange and reliable extraction of financial statements across all software and technologies. Financial reporting includes annual reports, SEC filings, reports from companies to investors, regulators, investors, and financial analysts, general ledger information and audit schedules. This definition is inclusive and not exhaustive. Financial reporting does not refer to market data such as security prices — FinXML and RIXML are the languages that deal with market data (see Appendix A). XBRL is reporting oriented, not transaction oriented. XBRL aims to streamline the financial supply chain — companies, the accounting profession, data aggregators, investment community, accounting software vendors and other users.

Exhibit 13. Timeline for XBRL

Year	Developments
1997	• Charlie Hoffman (CPA, Knight, Vale & Gregory, Washington, US) proposed using XML for financial reporting
1998	• AICPA conducted a pilot study to build a prototype–called XFRML (eXtensible Financial Reporting Modeling Language)
1999	• AICPA forms a steering committee–XBRL.org, about a dozen companies join the effort
2000	• XFRML became XBRL o First specification released o US CI (Commercial and Industrial Firms) taxonomy released o APRA (Australian Prudential Regulatory Authority)–the first company to implement XBRL 1.0
2001	• Specification 2.0 for XBRL released • Core requirements for general ledger released
2002	• Draft of taxonomy for IASC (International Accounting Standards Committee) released • Several international symposiums held • More than 170 organizations have joined the effort under the umbrella of *XBRL International*
2004	• XBRL Specification 2.1 approved

Exhibit 14. Definition of XBRL

- **XBRL IS**
    - XML based standard format for financial reporting
    - XBRL facilitates drill down of information
    - XBRL is extensible, users can increase its applicability
    - XBRL can be used transfer a single item of financial data or a financial database
    - XBRL standards are in the public domain
- **XBRL is NOT**
    - XBRL does not set new accounting standards
    - XBRL does not create a generic chart of accounts
    - XBRL does not translate GAAP (Generally Accepted Accounting Principles)
    - XBRL is not a privately owned standard
    - XBRL does not capture data at the transaction level

Structure of XBRL

XBRL is a markup language and, as such, we need to understand specified markups, definitions of markups and existing mechanisms to validate those markups. Supplementary technologies to create, process and transfer XBRL documents are also necessary to complete our understanding. This journey will be similar to XML in the earlier sections. First, XBRL markups, XBRL documents and XBRL Schemas that validate these documents are covered. Second, transformation and processing technologies that support XBRL are examined. Finally, XBRL tools and software that enable real-world implementation of the language are discussed.

XBRL Taxonomies

XBRL handles financial data, so markups or tags that describe financial statement items, such as inventory, receivables and net income, are needed. Do not forget that these financial statement elements are related; for example, current assets can be calculated from cash, accounts receivable and inventory, among other things. The problem is that there is neither a standard definition of individual items nor an internationally acceptable format for financial statements. There is additional industry and firm-specific terminology; banks will use different terms than, say, an automobile manufacturer. Within banks, there are different levels of voluntary disclosures that are bank-specific. Comprehensive definitions that will take care of differences in the GAAP, differences in industry and firm terminology, and also factors in relationships between financial statement elements are needed. A great deal is being asked of a markup language. Let us study concepts of XBRL specifications, taxonomies and instance documents to get a deeper understanding of how this reporting challenge is met.

XML specifications XML Schema, XLink, XML Namespace, Xpath and XSLT are used to develop XBRL specifications. XBRL specifications provide a set of normative rules that tell us how to develop valid XBRL instance documents and taxonomics. We need instance documents and taxonomies to markup financial reports. So what are these instance documents and taxonomies? Conceptually, an instance document is a collection of marked up financial facts, and a taxonomy document provides meanings, definitions and interrelationships among those facts. The XBRL specification defines XML elements and attributes used to create XBRL instance documents. The taxonomies are developed by concerned users; they may be national accounting bodies, specific industry groups or individual firms. XML meta model in the XBRL specification provides a language that can be used to define new elements and taxonomies of elements as desired by the users.

Now let us take a look at taxonomy. Taxonomy refers to a particular classification system. The taxonomy documents, in XML terms, can be called a dictionary of markups. Taxonomies define content of the document and, in essence, are XML Schemas. XBRL taxonomy is a dictionary or a classification system for financial facts. These financial facts come from standard accounting practices; for example, in the U.S., financial facts will be in accordance with the U.S. GAAP. The taxonomy provides definition of these financial facts. The taxonomy also provides relationship between those concepts and can even supply calculations to express those relationships.

No single taxonomy can cover the world's diverse need for financial reporting. Outside of the U.S., initial emphasis was on developing the taxonomy for the International Accounting Standards (IAS). Not all countries have adopted the IAS. Concurrent efforts focused on developing taxonomies for each country, referred to as jurisdictions. This is an ongoing effort, and different countries are at different levels in developing relevant taxonomics. Almost all major industrial countries have initial taxonomies for country-specific GAAP in place. The next level is to develop taxonomies for each industry within the country. The requirements and terminology for each industry is different, and we

Exhibit 15. XBRL taxonomies I

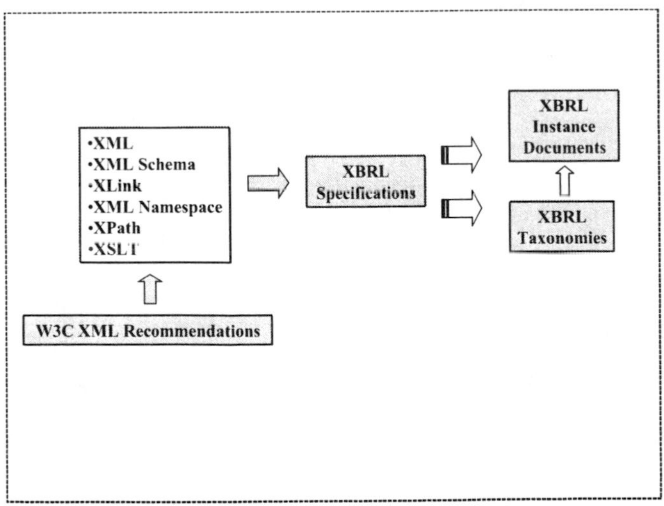

Exhibit 16. XBRL taxonomies II

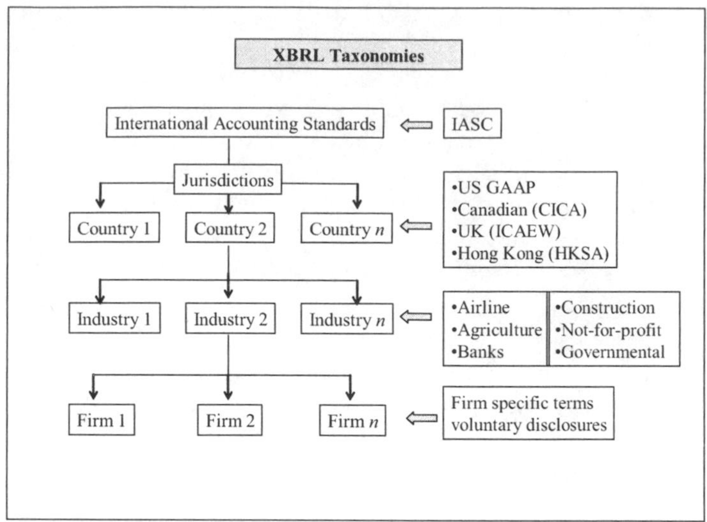

need taxonomy to cover each industry. The IAS, country-specific GAAP and industry-specific terminology taxonomies will be in the public domain. Finally, taxonomies to cover firm-specific terminology and voluntary disclosures by individual firms are also needed. A firm may also develop a taxonomy for internal reporting and/or consolidations, which may not be in the public domain. XBRL is extensible and allows development of new markups, which are compatible with the existing framework as long as the rules of XBRL are followed. The illustrative examples of following taxonomies in the U.S. indicate the extensive efforts and wide range of applications in this area:

- XBRL for financial statements
- XBRL for management reporting
- XBRL for general ledger
- XBRL for tax returns
- XBRL for EDGAR filings
- XBRL for assurance services (audit schedules)
- XBRL for authoritative literature
- XBRL for business reporting
- Industry specific taxonomies
- Taxonomies created by private parties for internal reporting purposes

Taxonomy creation is a complex task. People involved must have knowledge of relevant accounting principles and XBRL specifications. This is a multi-disciplinary effort.

Exhibit 17. U.S. GAAP CI taxonomy directory detail

ID	22
Preferred Namespace Prefix	us-gaap-ci
Official Name	**U.S. GAAP Commercial and Industrial (CI) Taxonomy**
Namespace Identifier	http://www.xbrl.org/taxonomy/us/fr/gaap/ci/2002-10-15
Description	This financial reporting taxonomy is intended to provide detail-level accounting terms that will allow commercial and industrial-type companies that conform to U.S. GAAP to tag financial statements in XBRL.
Taxonomy Date	2002-10-30
XBRL Version	XBRL V2
Current Location	http://www.xbrl.org/taxonomy/us/fr/gaap/ci/2002-10-15/us-gaap-ci-2002-10-15.xsd
Status	Public Working Draft
Home page or printout of Taxonomy	http://www.xbrl.org/taxonomy/us/fr/gaap/ci/2002-10-15/default.htm

Financial facts can be collected by reviewing financial statements, annual reports and relevant accounting standards, among other things. These facts need to be formatted according to XBRL specification to create an XBRL-compliant taxonomy. Once created, taxonomies undergo several levels of reviews to ensure accuracy and completeness. Initially, taxonomy drafts are circulated as *public working drafts*, which may change after the public review process.

XBRL International has a final say on taxonomies. A *recommended taxonomy* has the same official status as XBRL specification. An *approved taxonomy* refers to XBRL-compliant taxonomy that has been developed by XBRL International or has undergone a public review process. *Acknowledged taxonomy* is created by outsiders and listed by XBRL International on its Web site; XBRL International only assures that this is an XBRL-compliant taxonomy and in the public domain. *Final taxonomy* is assigned a version number and is permanently available on the XBRL International's Web site.

Let us take a detailed look at a specific taxonomy — the U.S. GAAP CI taxonomy. The directory details for U.S. GAAP CI are shown in Exhibit 17. This taxonomy is in a public working draft stage; it combines different taxonomies for delivering financial statements. These different taxonomies are: XBRL International's INT-GCD (Global Common Document) and INT-AR (Accountant's Report); XBRL U.S. taxonomies USFR-NAMDA (Notes and Management Discussion Analysis), USFR-GFC (General Concepts), USFR-PT (Primary Terms), USFR-SEC-CERT (SEC Officers Certification, mandated by Sarbanes-Oxley Act of 2002) and USFR-MR (Management Reports). These taxonomies together meet the financial reporting needs of companies that follow FASB standards, can be roughly grouped under the commercial and industrial category, and have commonalities in reporting elements in their financial statements.

A taxonomy consists of elements, attributes or datatype definitions. The taxonomy may also include a relationship between elements or relationship of elements in one taxonomy with elements of another taxonomy. Exhibit 18 shows partial entries for current assets in the U.S. GAAP CI taxonomy in tabular format. Each row corresponds to one element. The taxonomy contains the following details which are illustrated in Exhibit 18.

- **ID:** ID indicates the unique number of the element in the taxonomy.
- **Weight:** Weight indicates the relationship with parent elements. A weight of 1 indicates that all the child elements' values are multiplied by 1 and added or rolled up. This summation or rolling up gives us the value of parent element. For example, parent element *Current Assets* can be derived by adding child elements cash, AR, inventory and so forth. The account *Allowance for Doubtful Accounts* needs to be subtracted (indicated by –1) from *Accounts Receivable Trade* to get *Net Receivables*. The term *Assets* indicates a weight of *0*, meaning no further roll up is involved.
- **Balance:** Balance indicates whether the balance is debit or credit.
- **Type:** Type indicates the data type, such as monetary, text, shares or decimals.
- **NS (Namespace):** NS refers to the taxonomy to which the element belongs. Since the U.S. GAAP CI taxonomy combines various taxonomies, we see references to different taxonomies in this column.
- **Label/Description:** A name of the financial elements is provided with a description of that element. There can be multiple labels in different languages.
- **References:** This refers to the authoritative literature used to obtain a description of the financial element. The reference mentioned can include a reference name of the literature, reference number of the literature, reference chapters, and reference paragraphs and subparagraphs. The description for the term *Assets* comes from the Statement of Financial Concepts 6; if desired more details can be accommodated.

Then, in Exhibit 18, there are two views of the taxonomy; the first one is a tree view. This view starts with *Document and Entity Information* that deals with name of the company and the author(s) of the document. Then we see sequential elements of the financial statements. The second view shows dictionary form taxonomy elements, which provides definitions of elements. Here, definitions of cash-related elements are highlighted. Note that element numbers are different in the dictionary view.

This entire taxonomy contains 1,460 elements required to describe the core financial statements under U.S. GAAP CI. These elements can be used to create income statement, balance sheet, statement of cash flows, statement of stockholder's equity, notes and management discussion and analysis, auditor's report, management report and SEC officers certification.

Technically, an XBRL taxonomy document is a valid instance of an XML Schema document and generally consists of a package of six interrelated XML files. The contents of each row shown in Exhibit 18 are stored in this package of XML files. These files are: XML Schema File (.XSD file) and XML Linkbases (.XML files). The XML Linkbases consist of five files: references, presentation information, calculation relationship between elements, labels and definitional relationship between elements. The reference file provides references to the authoritative literature. These references can be detailed

Exhibit 18a. Partial description of elements in the U.S. GAAP CI taxonomy

ID	Weight	Balance	Type	NS	Label	Description	Reference
303	0	Debit	Monetary	usfr-gc	Assets (usfr-gc: Assets)	Probable future economic benefit obtained or controlled by an entity	Con 6
304	1	Debit	Monetary	usfr-pt	Current Assets (usfr-pt: TotalCurrentAssets)	Sum of all current assets - those assets that are reasonably expected to be realized in cash or sold or consumed within a year or within the normal operating cycle of the entity	
305	1	Debit	Monetary	usfr-pt	Cash, Cash Equivalents and Short Term Investments (usfr-pt: CashCashEquivalentsShortTermInvestments)	Cash and short term investments with an original maturity less than one year, including restricted cash	
306	1	Debit	Monetary	usfr-pt	Cash and Cash Equivalents (usfr-pt: CashCashEquivalents)	Cash and short term, highly liquid investments that are readily convertible to known amounts of cash and are so near their maturity that they present negligible risk of changes in value due to changes in interest rates - usually with an original maturity less than 90 days, This includes restricted cash, treasury bills, commercial paper and money market funds and other operating cash balances	SFAS 6; ARB 43 6
307	1	Debit	Monetary	usfr-pt	Cash (usfr-pt: Unrestricted Cash)	Unrestricted cash available for day-to-day operating needs	FAS 95 7
318	-1	Credit	Monetary	usfr-pt	Allowance for Doubtful Accounts (usfr-pt: AllowanceDoubtfulAccounts)	Estimate of uncollectible trade A/R that reduces the gross receivable to the amount expected to be collected	

and drill down to paragraphs and subparagraphs of relevant literature. The presentation file contains an order in which elements described in the taxonomy appear in the financial statements. The order presented is not applicable in every circumstance; however, it represents the most common way to present the information. The calculation file contains the information about weights. A weight of 1 indicates that this particular element will be added with other child elements to derive a parent element. A weight of –1 indicates that this element will be subtracted to derive the value of a parent element. The labels file provides a complete description of each element in the taxonomy. The description can be in different languages, such as Japanese or German. The definitional file creates the parent-child relationships required to generate the financial statements. These linkbases are connected to each other to facilitate data retrieval.

Exhibit 19 shows how the element *Cash* is stored in these different files. A beginning of the XML Schema and the description of the element *Cash* is shown in the XML format.

Exhibit 18b. U.S. GAAP CI – taxonomy elements: Tree view

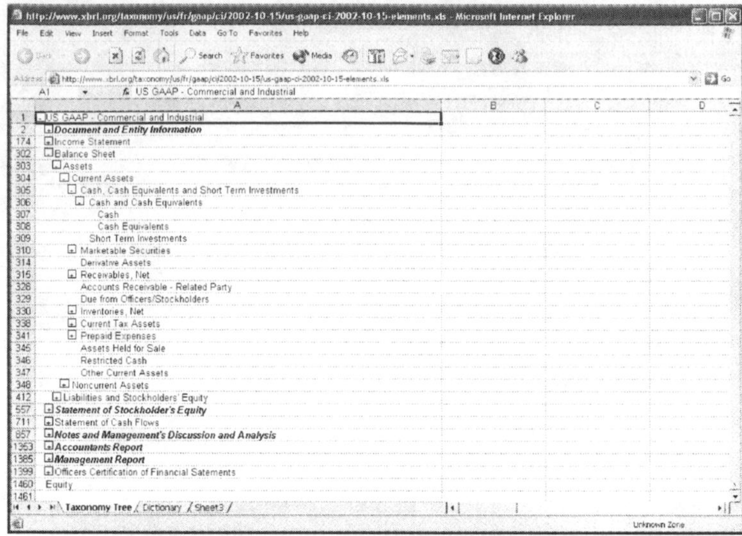

Exhibit 18c. U.S. GAAP CI – taxonomy elements: Dictionary view

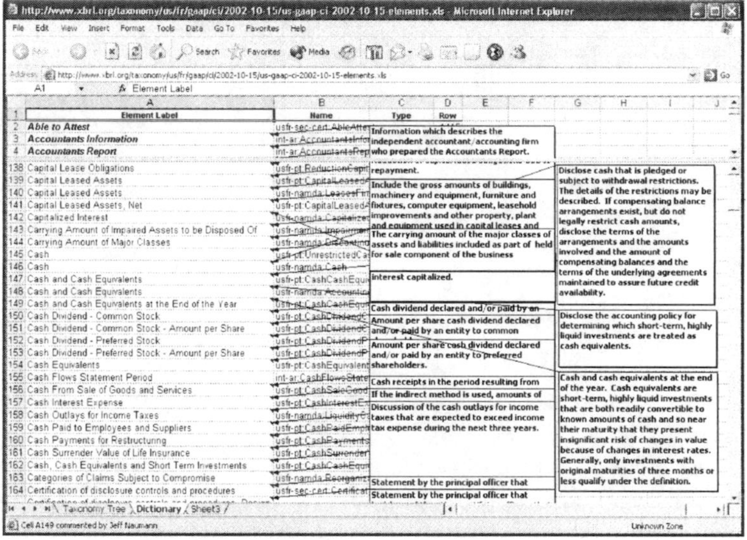

The .XML files are complicated and contain several entries for accuracy and completeness. Exhibit 20 shows the partial representation of *usfr-pt-2002-10-15.XSD* file for the element *Cash*.

Exhibit 19. Taxonomy files

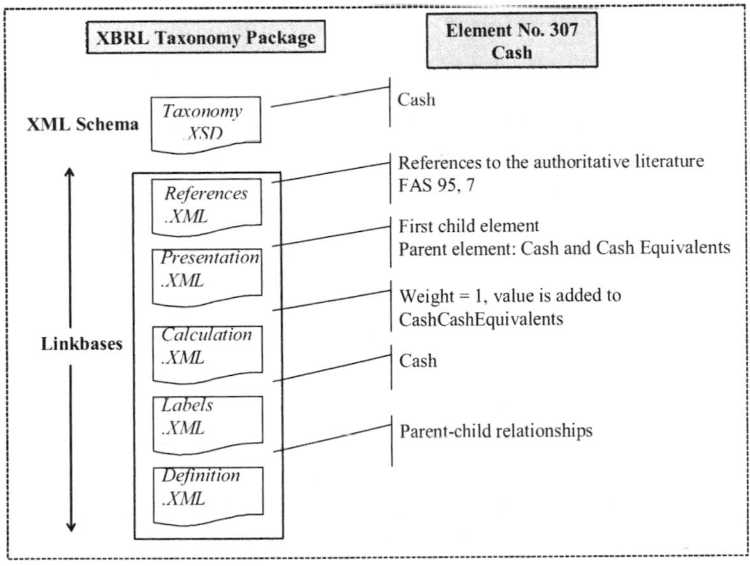

Exhibit 20. Partial representation of usfr-pt-2002-10-15.XSD file

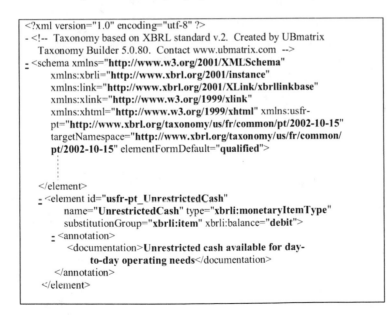

```
<?xml version="1.0" encoding="utf-8" ?>
- <!-- Taxonomy based on XBRL standard v.2. Created by UBmatrix
   Taxonomy Builder 5.0.80. Contact www.ubmatrix.com -->
- <schema xmlns="http://www.w3.org/2001/XMLSchema"
      xmlns:xbrli="http://www.xbrl.org/2001/instance"
      xmlns:link="http://www.xbrl.org/2001/XLink/xbrllinkbase"
      xmlns:xlink="http://www.w3.org/1999/xlink"
      xmlns:xhtml="http://www.w3.org/1999/xhtml" xmlns:usfr-
      pt="http://www.xbrl.org/taxonomy/us/fr/common/pt/2002-10-15"
      targetNamespace="http://www.xbrl.org/taxonomy/us/fr/common/
      pt/2002-10-15" elementFormDefault="qualified">
         :
         :
   </element>
   - <element id="usfr-pt_UnrestrictedCash"
        name="UnrestrictedCash" type="xbrli:monetaryItemType"
        substitutionGroup="xbrli:item" xbrli:balance="debit">
     - <annotation>
          <documentation>Unrestricted cash available for day-
               to-day operating needs</documentation>
       </annotation>
    </element>
```

XBRL Instance Documents

Once the taxonomies are in place, we can create XBRL instance documents. XBRL instance documents describe financial facts; it can be a single item such as *Current Assets*, or a complete *Annual Report*. In creating these instance documents, we need taxonomies, since taxonomies provide definitions and XBRL formats for these financial facts. The process is comprised of the following steps:

- Generate financial data using accounting software. XBRL-compliant software can create instance documents without intervention. If not, data can also be entered manually or exported to third-party XBRL software.
- Use the appropriate taxonomy. For example, if financial statements of commercial and industrial companies under U.S. GAAP are being prepared, then U.S. GAAP CI taxonomy (discussed earlier) will be required. No single taxonomy is adequate to cover the financial reporting need of corporations. The software for creating extensions to an XBRL taxonomy is required before XBRL is widely adopted and used.
- Map data generated by accounting software to the taxonomy. Most of today's software provides a method for manual *drag and drop* to map the data to taxonomies. This method is available in Word and Excel in Microsoft Office 2003.
- Create an instance document. To reiterate a few points:
  - The instance document is XML- and XBRL-compliant
  - The instance document contains company financial data
  - The instance document uses both industry-created taxonomies and company-specific extensions to the XBRL taxonomy
  - The instance document can now be transformed into a report format or can be processed by other software programs

XBRL does not create reports in a WYSIWYG format. XBRL instance documents must have a style sheet that formats an XBRL document properly. XBRL facilitates data transfer, not data formatting. The XBRL files have separate XML style sheets files (.XSL files). These files can format documents in the required format; for example, as a PDF file, HTML file or Word file. These style sheets can be developed using several software languages; however, XML tools are rapidly being developed to standardize and simplify the process.

Technically, XBRL instance documents follow syntax defined by XBRL. This syntax enables software applications that process instance documents to find, extract and analyze financial facts efficiently and effectively. This syntax is defined using XML Schema and this schema defines following elements: item, context, tuple (one row or one record) and group. An item represents a single financial fact or business measurement. Financial facts can be numbers or text, such as notes to financial statements. Context

Exhibit 21. XBRL instance documents I

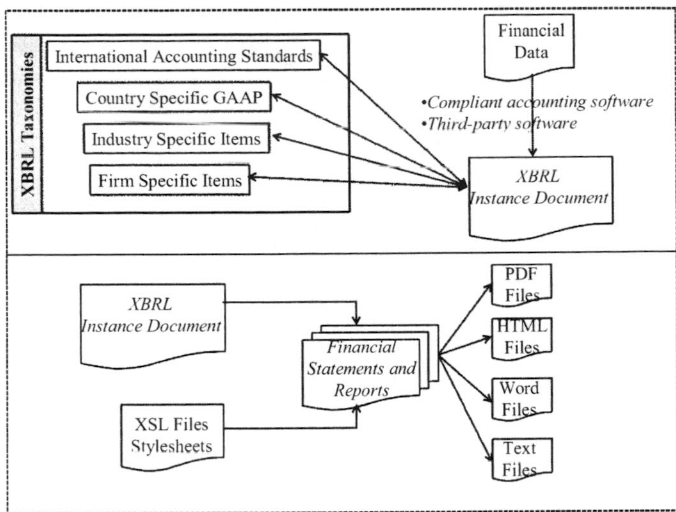

Exhibit 22. XBRL instance documents II

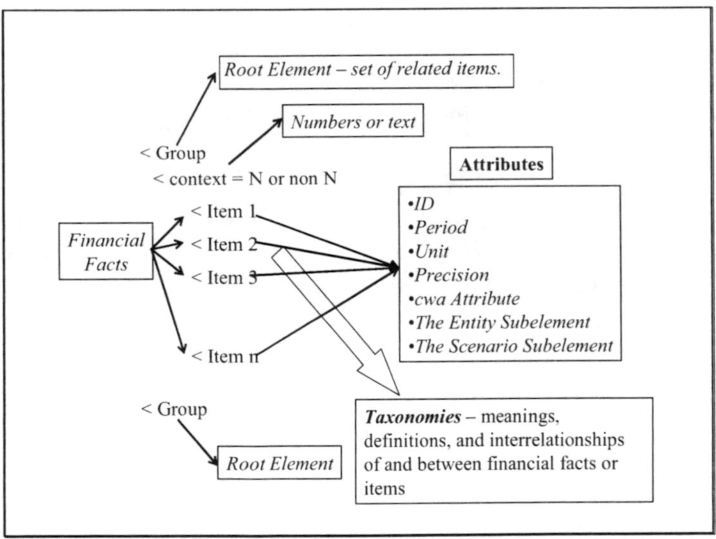

elements (numeric or non-numeric) hold the necessary information for providing proper context to the financial facts. Context elements have the following attributes:

- **ID:** Identifies the context — numeric or non-numeric
- **Period:** Provides chronological background to the item. For example, *instant* refers to a specific point in time and is useful for balance sheet and statement of cash

flows. Another description, *duration/endDate*, means a period of given length of time or ending as specified, which is useful for describing income statement.

- **Unit:** Specifies a relevant standard for measurement. For monetary measurements, we have standard currency designations; for example, in the U.S., dollars are used for measurement.
- **Precision:** Shows the arithmetic precision of the measurement. For example, precision="10" means numbers can be expressed up to 10 significant decimal digits.
- **cwa Attribute:** Refers to *closed world assumption*. If this condition is true, then the information in the document is complete and new values can be calculated based on data in the document. If not, then we should not attempt to calculate new values. This attribute is applicable only in the numeric context.
- **The entity subelement:** This subelement identifies the organization (name of the company, department, individual, etc.) to which the document pertains.
- **The scenario subelement:** This subelement enables handling of actual, reported, budgeted, restated and pro-forma formats. Additional valid markups for internal reporting purposes can be designed and used because of this subelement.

The tuple element allows management of interdependent business facts. For example, manager's name can be associated with manager's title, and a set of facts — manager's title/manager's name — can be used in multiple occurrences. The last element in this series is group element. This element *group* is a general grouping mechanism that helps in combining related items. It is the designated root element for XBRL instance documents.

Take a look at the XBRL instance document in Exhibit 23. This document shows Cash Flow Statement for Microsoft for 6/30/2002. Line numbers have been added to provide easy reference in the following explanations. The document is simple; however, not all lines are explained. Line 1 indicates that this is an XML document based on XML recommendation 1.0. The encoding employed is utf-8 (UCS Transformation Format 8) as defined by ISO standards. Line 2 is a comment indicating that this document is written at the University of Kansas in XBRL version 2.0. Line 3 starts with <group, which is a root element. In this XBRL instance document, we are combining statement of cash flow-related items.

The xmlns in line 3 implies that a namespace declaration is being made, followed by a colon that separates xmlns and the namespace prefix. This namespace declaration allows software applications to detect XBRL documents and/or to differentiate taxonomies in the same document. Then there is an equal sign, and the location for the namespace — in this case, Web address — is shown in double quotations. Line 3 associates the taxonomy for XBRL instance to the default namespace. Group element also occurs on the last line, 73, following XML conventions. The namespaces used in lines 4, 5 and 6 are ci, KU and ku. These namespaces are for taxonomies; we know the taxonomy U.S. GAAP CI; other taxonomies at Kansas University (KU and ku) are also being used. Lines 7 and 8 define the link namespace and the xsi namespace. Line 9 identifies the schema file (xbrl-instance.xsd) defining the taxonomy referred to in Line 8.

Exhibit 23. XBRL instance documents III

```
<?xml version="1.0" encoding="utf-8" ?>
- <!-- KU: XBRL v.2 -->
- <group xmlns="http://www.xbrl.org/2001/instance"
    xmlns:ci="http://www.xbrl.org/us/gaap/ci/2001/us-gaap-ci-2001"
    xmlns:KU="http://www.fraank.eycarat.ukans.edu/taxon"
    xmlns:ku="http://www.fraank.eycarat.ukans.edu/taxon"
    xmlns:link="http://www.xbrl.org/2001/XLink/xbrllinkbase"
    xmlns:xsi="http://www.w3.org/2001/XMLSchema-instance"
    xsi:schemalocation="http://www.xbrl.org/2001/instance xbrl-instance.xsd">
  - <numericContext id="NC1" precision="10" cwa="false">
  - <entity>
    <identifier scheme="www.sec.gov">Microsoft</identifier>
    </entity>
  - <unit>
    <measure>ISO4217:USD</measure>
    </unit>
  - <period>
    <instant>2002-06-30</instant>
    </period>
    </numericContext>
    <ci:netCashFlowsOperatingActivitiesIndirect.netIncome numericContext="NC1" label="Net
      income">7.829E9</ci:netCashFlowsOperatingActivitiesIndirect.netIncome>
    <ci:adjustmentsToReconcileCashFlows.depreciationAmortizationCashFlowsReconciliation numericContext="NC
      label="Depreciation amortization and other noncash
      items">1.084E9</ci:adjustmentsToReconcileCashFlows.depreciationAmortizationCashFlowsReconciliation>
    <KU:uknown numericContext="NC1" label="Net recognized (gains)/losses on
      investments">2.424E9</KU:uknown>
    <ci:adjustmentsToReconcileCashFlows.otherAdjustments numericContext="NC1" label="Stock option income ta
      benefits">1.596E9</ci:adjustmentsToReconcileCashFlows.otherAdjustments>
    <ci:adjustmentsToReconcileCashFlows.changesInDeferredIncomeTaxes numericContext="NC1" label="Deferred
      income taxes">-4.16E8</ci:adjustmentsToReconcileCashFlows.changesInDeferredIncomeTaxes>
    <ci:adjustmentsToReconcileCashFlows.otherAdjustments numericContext="NC1" label="Unearned
      revenue">1.1152E10</ci:adjustmentsToReconcileCashFlows.otherAdjustments>
    <KU:uknown numericContext="NC1" label="Recognition of unearned revenue">-8.929E9</KU:uknown>
    <ci:changeInWorkingCapitalIndirect.changeInReceivables numericContext="NC1" label="Accounts receivable">
      1.623E9</ci:changeInWorkingCapitalIndirect.changeInReceivables>
    <ci:changeInWorkingCapitalIndirect.changeInOtherCurrentAssets numericContext="NC1" label="Other current
      assets">-2.64E8</ci:changeInWorkingCapitalIndirect.changeInOtherCurrentAssets>
    <ci:changeInWorkingCapitalIndirect.otherChanges numericContext="NC1" label="Other long-term assets">-
      9000000.0</ci:changeInWorkingCapitalIndirect.otherChanges>
    <ci:changeInWorkingCapitalIndirect.changeInOtherCurrentLiabilities numericContext="NC1" label="Other curre
      liabilities">1.449E9</ci:changeInWorkingCapitalIndirect.changeInOtherCurrentLiabilities>
    <ci:changeInWorkingCapitalIndirect.otherChanges numericContext="NC1" label="Other long-term
      liabilities">2.16E8</ci:changeInWorkingCapitalIndirect.otherChanges>
    <ci:netCashFlowsOperatingActivities.netCashFlowsOperatingActivitiesIndirect numericContext="NC1" label="N
      cash from
      operations">1.4509E10</ci:netCashFlowsOperatingActivities.netCashFlowsOperatingActivitiesIndirect>
    <ci:proceedsFromIssuanceOfEquity.commonStock numericContext="NC1" label="Common stock
      issued">1.497E9</ci:proceedsFromIssuanceOfEquity.commonStock>
    <ci:paymentForRepurchasesOfEquity.commonStock numericContext="NC1" label="Common stock repurchased"
      6.069E9</ci:paymentForRepurchasesOfEquity.commonStock>
    <ci:netCashFlows.netCashFlowsFinancingActivities numericContext="NC1" label="Net cash used for financing"
      4.572E9</ci:netCashFlows.netCashFlowsFinancingActivities>
    <ci:paymentsForAssets.propertyPlantAndEquipment numericContext="NC1" label="Additions to property and
      equipment">-7.7E8</ci:paymentsForAssets.propertyPlantAndEquipment>
    <ci:paymentsForAssets.purchasesPaymentsForInvestments numericContext="NC1" label="Purchases of
      investments">-8.9386E10</ci:paymentsForAssets.purchasesPaymentsForInvestments>
    <ci:proceedsFromSalesMaturityOfAssets.investmentProceeds numericContext="NC1" label="Maturities of
      investments">8654000.0</ci:proceedsFromSalesMaturityOfAssets.investmentProceeds>
  <ci:proceedsFromSalesMaturityOfAssets.investmentProceeds numericContext="NC1" label="Sales of
```

Exhibit 23. (continued)

```
61    investments">7.0657E10</ci:proceedsFromSalesMaturityOfAssets.investmentProceeds>
62      <ci:netCashFlows.netCashFlowsInvestingActivities numericContext="NC1" label="Net cash used for investing">
63        1.0845E10</ci:netCashFlows.netCashFlowsInvestingActivities>
64      <ci:endOfPeriodCashAndCashEquivalents.netCashFlows numericContext="NC1" label="Net change in cash and
65        equivalents">-9.08E8</ci:endOfPeriodCashAndCashEquivalents.netCashFlows>
66      <ci:netCashFlows.effectOfExchangeRateOnCash numericContext="NC1" label="Effect of exchange rates on cash
67        and equivalents">2000000.0</ci:netCashFlows.effectOfExchangeRateOnCash>
68      <ci:endOfPeriodCashAndCashEquivalents.beginningOfPeriodCashAndCashEquivalents numericContext="NC1"
69        label="Cash and equivalents beginning of
70        year">3.922E9</ci:endOfPeriodCashAndCashEquivalents.beginningOfPeriodCashAndCashEquivalents>
71      <ci:cashFlows.endOfPeriodCashAndCashEquivalents numericContext="NC1" label="Cash and equivalents end o
72        year">3.016E9</ci:cashFlows.endOfPeriodCashAndCashEquivalents>
73    </group>
```

Line 10 refers to the attributes that apply to all items in the group. Numeric context refers to type of data required to provide context for a financial fact; in this case, the data type is numeric, since we are dealing with the cash flow statement. The maximum number of digits that will be used by any item in the group is 10, which is defined by precision. The term *cwa* refers to closed world assumption; this condition is false, which means that the processing application should not calculate new values based on the information given in this instance document. If the *cwa* assumption is false, then the XBRL document does

Exhibit 24. XBRL instance documents IV (Source: www.fraank.eycarat.ukans.ed/, used with permission)

Microsoft
Cash Flow Statement

Label	2002-06-30
Net income	7829.00
Depreciation amortization and other noncash items	1084.00
Net recognized (gains)/losses on investments	2424.00
Stock option income tax benefits	1596.00
Deferred income taxes	-416.00
Unearned revenue	11152.00
Recognition of unearned revenue	-8929.00
Accounts receivable	-1623.00
Other current assets	-264.00
Other long-term assets	-9000000.00*
Other current liabilities	1449.00
Other long-term liabilities	216.00
Net cash from operations	14509.00
Common stock issued	1497.00
Common stock repurchased	-6069.00
Net cash used for financing	-4572.00
Additions to property and equipment	-770.00
Purchases of investments	-89385.99
Maturities of investments	8654000.00*
Net cash used for investing	-10845.00
Net change in cash and equivalents	-908.00
Effect of exchange rates on cash and equivalents	2000000.00*
Cash and equivalents beginning of year	3922.00
Cash and equivalents end of year	3016.00

Note: * All values except this are in millions

not hold all the facts necessary to perform further computations. Lines 11, 12 and 13 identify the entity to which the information relates; in this case, Microsoft. Entities can also describe a subsidiary of a company, departments or cost/revenue centers. Lines 14, 15 and 16 describe the unit of measurement; U.S. dollars for our document. Lines 17, 18 and 19 identify the period; for the statement of cash flows, it is a date or an instant, 2002-06-30. XBRL can accommodate different date formats.

Lines 21 to 72 describe various items that constitute statement of cash flows. In line 21, ci refers to the taxonomy namespace defined in line 4, then the item or element name is given. The name in line 23 indicates that we are calculating net cash flows from operating activities using the indirect method, and the label for the first item is net income. The numeric context is defined earlier and labeled as NC1. The amount is mentioned between greater-than and less-than signs. The lines up to 72 describe various items in the statement of cash flows. Note that negative numbers, such as in lines 30 and 31, have a negative sign. This statement of cash flows is a good example of an instance document, though this document does not cover all the components of XBRL syntax.

The statement of cash flows is a simple document. As we add more details, the XBRL instance documents will become complex. This XBRL instance document can be used to create the statement of cash flows in a variety of formats, provided we create appropriate XSL files. For example, Exhibit 24 shows the approximate HTML output of this XBRL instance document. We can define different style sheets and create output as a PDF file, Word file or text file.

XBRL Tools and Software

XBRL is a markup language and in itself does not do anything. A host of supplementary tools are required to bring XBRL to life. XBRL tools can be broadly classified into the following categories:

- Taxonomy-related tools
- Document instance-related tools
- Programmatic tools
- XBRL Repositories

Taxonomy related tools enable viewing, editing and building of taxonomies. These tools are important, since extending taxonomies will be necessary for company-specific financial statements. The XBRL viewing tools allow viewing and printing of taxonomies. The editing tools allow us to add, delete or change the existing taxonomy. Finally, taxonomy-building tools can be used to build or create taxonomies, if necessary from scratch. The taxonomy creator can also help in preparing documentation for taxonomies.

Remember, instance documents are nothing but financial reports tagged by XBRL. The instance document-related tools allow creating, viewing, editing and validating instance documents. Many accounting software packages are planning to support mapping of the accounting system to XBRL taxonomy, thereby partially automating creation of XBRL instance documents. Some tools even map data warehouses to reporting taxonomies. Third-party software packages allow creation of instance documents from scratch or editing of imported instance documents. Few software packages even process instance documents to produce a generic output. Instance documents need to be validated to confirm that they match the schema specified by the XBRL specification. There are software tools (even Web-based) that take the file and check the validity of that file against the taxonomy file. XBRL International maintains an extensive list of tools on its Web site.

The instance documents need to be accessed by the software and processed. The programmatic access to structure and data in the XBRL document is facilitated by XBRL DOM. XBRL DOM is technically a software application (API component) embedded in the application software, such as Microsoft Excel or UB Matrix Studio. XBRL DOM makes working with XBRL instance documents user friendly, insulating the user by taking care of validating and linking tasks. XBRL DOM changes with changes in XBRL Schema specification and XBRL specification. Thus, users need not be conversant with the latest changes to validate and edit instance documents. There also are XBRL extractor tools that help to extract XBRL data from Web pages and other sources. Microsoft released an XBRL tool, *Microsoft Investor Analyst*, that works with Excel and imports XBRL-formatted documents in the spreadsheet for further analysis. Now this tool has been supplanted by Microsoft Office Tool for XBRL™ Prototype, available at *www.nasdaq.com/xbrl/*.

XBRL repositories refer to a consolidated collection of financial statements and reports in XBRL for various companies. Currently, *www.edgar-online.com/* has an extensive collection of SEC filings in XBRL format. Other Web-based solutions can convert non-XBRL documents into XBRL format. The University of Kansas Ernst & Young Research Center has an intelligent agent (a software program that automatically performs certain functions based on the occurrence of specified events) that can extract SEC filings and convert those into XBRL format, among other things. XBRL search engines (not yet developed) that search for XBRL on the Internet and intranets will be useful for financial users and the research community.

Audit and Control Issues in XBRL

Audit and control issues in XBRL are just beginning to be analyzed. Applications of XBRL span the entire spectrum of financial and managerial reporting. These applications will profoundly affect audit and control mechanisms. The purpose of this section is not to cover all these areas; however, it is to briefly identify areas that are immediately affected due to the introduction of XBRL. Conceptually, the simple questions are:

- How will XBRL financial statements be used? They carry all the same challenges that paper-based reports contain, but add the extra dimension of divisibility.
  - Will companies and auditors give assurance on XBRL instance documents as a whole?

  - What about a small piece of the whole, such as earnings per share calculation?
- How do you know if the appropriate taxonomy is being used?
- How do you know if the taxonomy is correct, especially if it is internally developed?
- How do you know XBRL instance documents are properly marked up?
- How do you ensure the integrity of tagged data?
- How do you ensure accuracy and integrity of style sheets to guarantee proper output?
- What are the appropriate auditing and sampling procedures to audit these control issues?

The XBRL tagged financial statements in the Web environment, or even in a non-Web environment, can be used either as a whole or in part. A financial statement can provide a hyperlink that can take a user to a different analysis, presentation or calculation. These may be integral to the financial statements or addenda. The audited parts of financial statements are not distinguishable from non-audited parts. The question is, how far does the auditing assurance go? What ways let the user know of the audited and non-audited information? What are the auditor's duties and what type of disclosures are needed in such a case? These are the global questions that demand answers before we even look at the mechanics of taxonomy creation and use.

Numerous taxonomies can be used to create XBRL instance documents. The next area of concern is appropriateness of the taxonomy being used, the version of taxonomy being used, match between requirements of a financial report and taxonomies, and the accuracy of mapping financial data with the taxonomies used. If the taxonomy is internally developed, it needs to be validated and vetted for accuracy and completeness. The controls over taxonomy choice, creation and editing need to be installed and monitored. Accounting software automates many of these functions; in this case, output needs to be evaluated on a sample basis. Additionally, controls over creation, viewing and editing instance documents are required.

The XBRL instance document contains markups, and these markups need to be accurate. If the document is not correctly marked up, then it may not be processed correctly. Automated controls over error correction, isolation of incorrect files and appropriate computer messages should be in place. These controls need to be validated and tested. Once the accuracy of instance documents is ensured, then questions of tracking changes in those documents arise. The standardized procedures for change and maintenance of these documents need to be in place, especially if documents are displayed on the Web in real time. The issues of authorization and authentication in the networked environment need to be analyzed carefully.

The actual auditing procedures are being discussed by the profession. However, these auditing procedures are not new. Many auditing techniques are already in place for similar applications; for example, EDI. Many standard auditing procedures in computer-based information systems are probably applicable in these areas. Accountants and auditors should be aware that with the promise of XBRL there is some peril of control issues.

Conclusion

XBRL is backed by major accounting bodies, professional accounting firms, software vendors and even governments, and is the only XML-based initiative in the financial reporting area. XBRL taxonomies are being developed in a wide range of areas, from financial statements to tax and assurance services and, no doubt, even more creative applications will come online. XBRL tools are rapidly being deployed, and the basic software infrastructure is in place. XBRL promises a seamless transfer of financial data across different information technologies and also to overcome lingual and national barriers. Recent empirical research indicates that using XBRL results in better acquisition and integration of information for individuals.

However, to fulfill these promises, substantial upfront investments are required. The richness and variations in financial reporting will probably result in complex taxonomies. Developing, validating and maintaining these taxonomies are major tasks. Since XBRL is based on XML specifications, as XML changes XBRL needs to be updated, which probably will be an ongoing task in the near future. Accounting software, analytical tools, skill sets for accountants and the nature of auditing and internal controls will certainly change.

Summary

XML is an attempt to standardize data and information transfer, which has been an Achilles heel for the Internet. XML is being applied in different areas – from music and religion to sciences and business. Businesses are moving strongly into a digital world, full of markups for all recordable business events. Financial data will not be an exception to this rule. As accounting deals with financial data, it is inevitable that XML will affect accounting. Markup languages such as XML use markups to identify the structure of documents. Markups can be procedural or descriptive. Procedural markups are software specific, used for formatting the document and not useful if that specific application is not being used. Descriptive markups contain information about logical structure of text and content in the document. These are used in markup languages.

Markup languages specify symbols for markups, meaning of markups, ways to distinguish markups from content of the document and purposes of different markups. SGML is one of the first markup languages and has wide applications. SGML is not suitable for the Internet, and is not supported by most browsers. XML is a subset of SGML, and is specifically developed for the Internet. The X in XML stands for extensible, meaning users can define their own markups and develop markup languages for specific purposes.

An XML document is a basic unit of information and must strictly follow the syntax rules of XML. XML syntax consists of different rules — for example, each document must have a root element. A well-formed XML document follows all rules of XML. To provide an explanation for markups, XML employs mechanisms of DTDs or XML Schema. DTDs provide explanation of tags and the syntax of the document. XML Schema is similar to

DTD; however, it supports different datatypes, is written in XML syntax and is extensible. XML Schema is replacing DTD as a method of document validation.

XML merely marks up the document, so how do we process these documents? XML is armed with a host of supplementary technologies. Validation and linking technologies enable us to validate XML documents and provide hyperlink capabilities. Transformation technologies allow display of XML documents in various output formats. Processor technologies permit software applications to process XML documents. XML applications are in areas of music, animation and Web publishing, to mention a few; and different XML-based languages are being developed in these areas. There are also various XML-based security initiatives.

The major initiative for the accounting community is XBRL. This XML-based language is designed to standardize financial and business reporting. XML specifications are used to develop XBRL. XBRL has two main components: XBRL taxonomy and XBRL instance documents. XBRL taxonomies are classification systems for financial facts. Taxonomies are being developed for IAS, nation-specific GAAPs, and industry- and firm-specific terminology in each country. Functional taxonomies, such as financial statements, general ledger, tax returns and assurance services, are also being developed.

XBRL instance documents describe financial facts; it can be one financial item or a complete set of financial statements. XBRL instance documents can handle numeric and non-numeric data; different units of measurement; multi-period financial statements; and actual, budgeted or pro forma reporting. Numerous software tools are being developed to create, edit, view and maintain taxonomies and instance documents. XBRL promises many benefits, but there are associated costs. Taxonomy creation and maintenance is a complex task, and is consuming resources of the accounting community. Audit and control issues raised by XBRL applications are just being addressed. XML is a dynamic language, and as XML specifications change, XBRL also will change. Accounting software, analytical tools, skill sets for accountants, and nature of auditing and internal controls will continue to evolve accordingly.

References

A gentle introduction to SGML. (2001). University of Illinois, Chicago. Retrieved January 11, 2003, from www.uic.edu/orgs/tei/sgml/

Arbortext. (2002a). *A guide to SGML and its role in information management* (white paper). Retrieved January 9, 2003, from www.arbortext.com/

Arbortext. (2002b). *Evaluating SGML vs. XML from a manager's perspective* (white paper). Retrieved January 9, 2003, from www.arbortext.com/

Bergholz, A. (2000, July-August). Extending your markup: An XML tutorial. *IEEE Internet Computing*, 74-79.

Bosak, J. (1996). *XML – Questions & answers.* International SGML/XML User's Group. Retrieved January 21, 2003, from www.isgmlug.org/n3-1/n3-1-18.htm

Bovee, M., Ettredge, M., Srivastava, R., & Vasarhelyi, M. (2002, Fall). Does the year 2000 XBRL taxonomy accommodate Current business financial reporting practice? *Journal of Information Systems,* 165-182.

Brown, J. (2001, May 18). Microsoft rolls dice on XML. *Computing Canada*, 11.

The Canadian Institute of Chartered Accountants, Information Technology Advisory Committee. (2002). *Audit and Control Implications of XBRL* (white paper). Retrieved January 17, 2003, from www.cica.ca/multimedia/Download_Library/Standards/Studies/English/CICA-XBRL-0502-e.pdf

Case study: Osaka Securities. (2002). Fujitsu. Retrieved January 10, 2003, from http://xml.fujitsu.com/en/case/disclosure_sys/index.html/

Deshmukh, A. (2003, March). XBRL. *Communications of AIS*, *13*(16), 1-40.

Hodge, F, Kennedy, J., & Maines, L. (2004). Does search facilitating technology improve the transparency of financial reporting? *The Accounting Review*, *79*(3), 687-703.

Hoffman, C., & Strand, C. (2001). *XBRL essential.* New York: AICPA.

Hyatt, J., Deitiker, G., & Gallagher, T. (1997). *How electronic publishing at Northern Telecom radically improved document quality and reduced information time-to-market.* AGAVE. Retrieved January 13, 2003, from www.agave.com/html/newsworthy/news_nortel.htm/

International Organization for Standardization, ISO 8879. (1986). *Information processing – Text and office systems – Standard Generalized Markup Language (SGML).*

Kim, L. (2002). *Document framework: Unifying XML content management and database systems for the Internet* (white paper). Beverly: Altova Inc.

Levitt, J. (1998, May). The making of a markup language. *Information Week*, 70-80.

Livermore, G. (2002, December). XML is a strategy not a technology. *Mortgage Banking*, 54-58.

Mohan, S. (1995, April 3). Markup language a mixed bag for publisher. *ComputerWorld*, 53.

Peis, E., & Fernandez-Molina, C. (1998, September). Enrichment of bibliographic records of online catalogs through OCR and SGML technology. *Information Technology and Libraries*, 161-172.

Penler, P., & Schnitzer, M. (2002). *Web enabled business reporting – for the banking industry*. Ernst & Young. Retrieved January 14, 2003, from www.ey.com/global/download.nsf/International/WEBR_Sept02_Whitepaper/$file/ Sep02_WEBR_Whitepaper.pdf

Randell, B., & Sknonnard, A. (1999). *A guide to XML and its technologies*. Microsoft. Retrieved January 13, 2003, from http://msdn.microsoft.com/library/default.asp?url=/library/en-us/dnxml/html/xmlguide.asp/

Ray, E. (2001). *Learning XML*. Sebastopol: O'Reilly Publications.

Resource description framework, FAQ. (2002). World Wide Web Consortium. Retrieved January 16, 2003, from www.w3c.org/rdf/faq/

Richard, J. (2002a). *The anatomy of an XBRL taxonomy* (working paper). XBRL. Murdoch: Murdoch University. Retrieved January 17, 2003, from www.xbrl.org.au/

Richard, J. (2002b). *The anatomy of XBRL instance documents* (working paper). XBRL. Murdoch: Murdoch University. Retrieved January 17, 2003, from www.xbrl.org.au/

Richard, J. (2002c). *An introduction to XML/XBRL* (working paper). XBRL. Murdoch: Murdoch University. Retrieved January 17, 2003, from www.xbrl.org.au/

Richard, J. (2002d). *Naming conventions Used in XBRL taxonomies* (working paper). XBRL. Murdoch: Murdoch University. Retrieved January 17, 2003, from www.xbrl.org.au/

Richard, J., & Tibbits, H. (2002). Understanding XBRL. *CPA Australia NSW Branch Workshop*. XBRL. Retrieved January 17, 2003, from www.xbrl.org.au/training/NSWWorkshop.pdf/

Salminen, A. (2002). *XML family of languages: Overview and classification of W3C specifications*. University of Jyvaskyla, Finland. Retrieved January 18, 2003, from www.cs.jyu.fi/~airi/xmlfamily.html/

Schmelzer, R. (2001). The "pros and cons" of XML. Waltham: Zapthink Research Report. Retrieved January 21, 2003, from www.zapthink.com/report.html?id=ZT-XMLPROCON

Shin, R. (2003). XBRL, financial reporting and auditing. *The CPA Journal, 13*(12), 61-65.

Shobowale, G. (1998, October/November). SGML, XML and other document-centered approaches to electronic medical records. *Bulletin of the American Society for Information Sciences*, 7-10.

The Unicode Standard. (2002). Unicode. Retrieved January 21, 2003, from www.unicode.org/

Walsh, N. (1998). *A technical introduction to XML*. N. Walsh. Retrieved January 21, 2003, from http://nwalsh.com/docs/articles/xml/

Willis, M., Tesniere, B., & Jones, A. (2003). *Corporate communications for the 21st century* (white paper). PriceWaterhouseCoopers. Retrieved January 21, 2003, from www.bnet.com/abstract.aspx?&scid=1515&docid=52817

XBRL (2.0 and 2.1) specification. (2001, 2004). XBRL. Retrieved January 21, 2003, and June 5, 2004, from www.xbrl.org/

XBRL FAQ. (2004). XBRL. Retrieved January 21, 2003, from www.xbrl.org.au/faq and www.xbrl.org/Faq.htm

XBRL U.S. Domain Working Group, U.S. Financial Reporting Taxonomy Framework. (2002). *U.S. GAAP Commercial and Industrial Extension Taxonomy*, Public Working Draft, Release Date: 2002-10-15. XBRL. Retrieved January 21, 2003, from www.xbrl.org/taxonomy/us/fr/gaap/ci/2002-10-15/us-gaap-ci-2002-10-15.xsd" \t "_blank

XML (1.0) specification. (2001). World Wide Web Consortium. Retrieved January 25, 2003, from www.w3c.org/

XML Namespaces FAQ. (2001). Ronald Bourret. Retrieved January 21, 2003, from www.rpbourret.com/xml/namespacesFAQ.htm

XML Spy, XML integrated development environment (white paper). (2002). XML Spy. Retrieved January 10, 2003, from www.altova.com/

Endnotes

1 A substantial part of this chapter is taken from Deshmukh, A. (2003). XBRL. *Communications of AIS*, *13*(16), March, 1-40.

2 A poster depicting comprehensive treatment of XML technologies used to be available on the Web site *www.zapthink.com/reports/poster.html/*

Appendix A: Applications of XML-Based Languages in Accounting

XML specification 1.0 establishes rules for creating good XML. XML applications develop good rules of XML in specific areas of interest. The Web site, *www.xml.org/*, details the name of the standard, organization(s) involved in developing the standard, category for the applications and XML examples. This site lists more than 60 areas where XML applications are under development. XML applications are in business and non-business areas. In the context of business, XML applications can be broadly categorized as vertical industry applications and horizontal or e-business applications. For example, the vertical industries listed are accounting, advertising, automotive, software and waste management; horizontal industry applications are in the areas of databases, e-commerce, supply chain management and financial reporting. There are a number of overlapping initiatives in the vertical industry and horizontal business applications. Non-business applications are in the fields of chemistry, economics, mathematics, music and religion.

Let us take a quick view of typical XML initiatives that are affecting or will affect the accounting function. We take an accounting cycle approach and identify XML-based languages that may affect individual accounting cycles. There is some overlap here, and it is identified as these developments are described. Some of the initiatives are competing in nature and some span more than one area. The initiatives that affect finance and security markets are shown under Finance. Developments listed here are illustrative and not exhaustive; new initiatives are coming online rapidly. These primary developments are shown in Exhibit A_1.

ebXML, BizCodes, BASDA e-Business XML cXML, XML Voucher and XML EDI will affect Web-based sales orders and related activities. Electronic Business using XML (ebXML) aims to develop a standard method to exchange business messages, conduct trading relationships and communicate business data in common language. BizCodes initiative is also an attempt to provide one standard format for global e-business interchanges. BASDA e-Business XML standard is developed so orders and invoices

Exhibit A_1. XML-based languages and accounting cycles

Accounting Cycle	Transaction Type	XML Application
Revenue Cycle	• Sales order • Credit approval • Shipping • Billing • Payment	ebXML BASDA e-Business XML BizCodes cXML ECML IOPT VISA XML Specification XML Voucher BIPS
Expenditure Cycle	• Review of inventory • Choosing a supplier • Purchase order • Receipt of goods • Receipt and payment of the bill	cXML eCX XML XML-EDI ECML IOPT VISA XML Specification XML Voucher BIPS XML UPS Tracking
Conversion Cycle	• Product design • Production planning and control • Manufacturing • Inventory control	PDML PDX
Financial Reporting	• Source journals • General ledger • Financial reporting	XBRL
Finance	• Derivatives, interest rate swaps • Capital markets • Transfer of financial data	fpML FinXML FIXML RIXML MDML IFX OFX

can be directly exchanged between different accounting applications. This standard will automate existing accounting functions by eliminating incompatibility between systems and resultant manual entries. XML EDI uses XML and EDI technologies together to provide a next generation of EDI. This standard aims to express existing EDI mechanisms in XML syntax, thereby creating a more flexible version of EDI. This version is expected to be cheaper and affordable to small businesses. XML EDI affects both sell-side and buy-side activities. EDI transactions will not be replaced; however, the XML technologies may broaden the use of EDI.

Coupons, loyalty points and gift certificates accompany the payment and delivery of goods in the real world. XML Voucher defines voucher (a logical entity that represents a right to claim goods or services) properties in XML syntax. This standard provides for a voucher-trading model, requirements for Voucher Trading System (VTS) for secure circulation of vouchers, and Generic Voucher Language (GVL) for a description of different types of vouchers. These vouchers need to be connected with related revenue accounts for automated entries. This development will also reduce manual entries, since coupons and gift certificates do create paper-based systems.

There is a profusion of standards in the electronic payments area. Electronic Commerce Modeling Language (ECML) standardizes electronic payments on the Web by providing a set of hierarchical payment-oriented data structures that supports electronic wallets. This standard provides functionality such as confidentiality, non-repudiability of transactions, automated payment scheme selection and smart-card support.

Electronic payment systems are varied and contain Secure Electronic Transactions (SET), Mondex, CyberCash and DigiCash, among other things. Internet Open Trading Protocol (IOTP) subsumes these protocols and aims to provide systems that resemble traditional paper-based methods of trading. The aim here is to provide definitions of trading events, such as negotiation of who will be parties to the trade, how the trade will be conducted, the presentment of an offer, method of payment, provision of a payment receipt, and delivery and receipt of goods in a way that two unfamiliar parties in e-commerce can complete the transaction successfully. Use of this protocol will make cash management easier and curb online fraud. The ideal here is global interoperability.

The Bank Internet Payment System (BIPS) secures financial transactions for a bank and its customers over the Internet. This standard uses existing technologies wherever possible and uses new protocols to bridge gaps. The idea is to maintain banks' role as a trusted agent in transactions in the virtual world. For customers, this protocol offers less costly transactions, more convenience and flexibility in payment options. These standards sometimes are overlapping, but mostly target different areas and can be expected to solve some of the thorniest problems in e-commerce.

The expenditure cycle and conversion cycle directly relate to Supply Chain Management. The illustrative initiatives in this area are cXML, eCX XML, VISA XML, PDML and PDX. Commerce XML (cXML) is designed to facilitate communication of business documents between procurement applications, e-commerce hubs and suppliers. cXML supports electronic product catalogs (similar to paper catalogs; the primary use is to convey product and service content to buyers), punchout catalogs (these interactive catalogs allow buyers to choose between different options and configure the product), procurement applications and order-receiving systems (accepting and processing of purchase orders). This format competes with mail, fax and EDI formats.

Electronic Catalog XML (eCX XML) has a slightly different emphasis. It is developed to promote electronic catalog interoperability. This standard primarily deals with catalog structure, dynamically described product information and catalog updates. A purchasing procedure substantially changes in this environment. Employees can order from their desktops and payments may be made electronically. Separation of duties and automation of internal controls through workflows need to be carefully evaluated. The integration with activity-based costing systems may also pose a challenge.

VISA XML specification is a standard for automation of B2B purchasing functions and monitoring of travel and entertainment expenses. This standard is not limited to Visa Card payment, but supports multiple payment types. Currently, this standard supports line-item invoice details for procurement, airline and travel itinerary data, lodging information and car rental information. Future releases of the specification are for specific industries.

Online product design, development and manufacturing are already supported by most of the ERP software packages. XML developments will make standardization easier. Product Data Markup Language (PDML) supports interchange of product information between commercial systems or government systems. Product data information often needs to be exchanged inter- or intra-company; and for government contractors, the information exchange is more intensive and continuous. To meet the needs of these groups, PDML is being developed. The other type of product information exchange takes place when company has a network of Original Equipment Manufacturers (OEMs), manufacturing service providers and parts suppliers. Product information exchange is lifeblood for such virtual networks. Product Definition Exchange (PDX) is a standard for the e-supply chain. This initiative is focused on exchange of product information between OEMs, manufacturing service providers and component suppliers.

In the finance arena, there are initiatives that deal with derivatives, capital markets and financial data transfer. Financial Products Markup Language (fpML) enables automation of flow of information across entire derivatives partner and client networks. The financial services industry has already developed standard contracts for derivatives. The prediction was that the current 5-day preparation time for a derivative contract would be cut down to 1 day by 2005. SwapsWire, a network of investment banks, has already implemented fpML for interest swaps. A SwapsWire spokesperson said that a typical financial institution handles 380 trades in a week, and an average staff person handles approximately 9 trades per week. The company expects to significantly increase the productivity of staffers by using automated contracts.

FinXML is a framework for defining vocabularies for the capital markets. This framework is expected to support a universal standard for data interchange within the capital markets. Currently, FinXML supports interest rates, foreign exchange and commodity derivatives, bonds, money markets, loans and deposits, and exchange-traded futures and options. Research Information Exchange Markup Language (RIXML) is an industry-standard dialect of XML that deals with management of research information, which includes equity research, fixed-income research, and events and calendars. This specification is targeted toward financial services firms such as brokerage houses, asset management companies, mutual fund managers and securities houses.

Interactive Financial exchange (IFX) specification is a framework for transfer of financial data, which is developed by major financial institutions. Currently, IFX provides support for bank statements download, credit card statement download, funds transfer, consumer payments, business payments, brokerage and mutual fund statement download, and bill presentment and payment. Open Financial Exchange (OFX) is similar to IFX and currently supports consumer and small-business banking; consumer and small-business bill payment; and bill presentment and payment, including stocks, bonds and mutual funds. OFX is developed by Microsoft, Intuit and CheckFree.

This description covers a few areas in XML-based languages in the context of accounting cycles. XML is in flux, and new developments and changes in existing applications are rapid and frequent. A visit to *www.xml.org/* will indicate that there is an explosion in XML standards and applications. XML effects on information transfer and management will be pervasive and affect every area of the business domain, and even arts, sciences, education and government. These developments will affect accounting and finance in due time. The exact implications for accounting are not very clear at this point, except for the well-known XBRL initiative. However, these developments will definitely affect transaction processing, internal controls, audit trails and accounting workflows. There will be meaningful changes in information management for security markets, banking and financial institutions. Information-intensive industries will certainly benefit from the coming standardization.

Chapter IV

Electronic Data Interchange

What is Electronic Data Interchange?

Before the dawn of the computer age, intra- and inter-business activities, especially purchasing and selling of products and services, were paper-intensive. Paper documents such as purchase orders, invoices, shipping notices, and bills of lading needed to be prepared in multiple copies. These copies had to be approved, signed, preserved in files for a certain duration, forwarded to trading partners and processed in a myriad of ways. Purchasing and selling activities rippled through the entire organization and tied in manufacturing, logistics, accounting, finance and human resources, among other areas. The documents then multiplied exponentially. Additionally, these documents were organization-specific, meaning there were no standard formats. The lack of standard format resulted in extra processing time; incoming purchase orders needed to be converted into the organization's sales order. In the 1960s, giant corporations had to deal with a mountain of paperwork and employ armies of clerks to process those documents. The associated costs and their effect on the bottom line alarmed managers. The idea of electronic surrogates for these documents and Electronic Data Processing (EDP) began to look attractive. In the late 1960s, the idea of an electronic exchange of standardized documents had taken a firm root in the transportation industry. The age of EDP has arrived and EDI was on the forefront of the wave and became more sophisticated over the next several decades.

EDI is easy to mistake for many electronic communication formats devised over the last decade. However, EDI has a distinct personality of its own. Formally, the definition of EDI (The Accredited Standards Committee Cases X12, *www.x12.org*) says:

> *"The movement of business data electronically between or within firms (including their agents or intermediaries) in a structured, computer-processable data format that permits data to be transferred without re-keying from a computer-supported business application in one location to computer-supported business application in another location."*

This definition highlights various unique features of EDI. Business data is transmitted electronically, does not need re-keying, can pass through networks and/or storage mediums, and does not need human intervention for flow, capture or processing. Data processing is generally done by business applications specifically designed to process the incoming data. The description so far matches with FTP, e-mail, fax or many other e-commerce applications. The key distinction between EDI and other forms of e-commerce is *structured format of data*. Paper documents, e-mail or fax do not have a specific, universally accepted data format. These forms of communication are handled using computers, manually or by a combination of both. In EDI, a need to minimize human intervention requires that data must be understood by the communicating computer systems. That means data must be pre-formatted and should be based on standards acceptable to the trading partners, and computers must be programmed to understand the incoming format of data.

Exhibit 1. EDI and other forms of communication

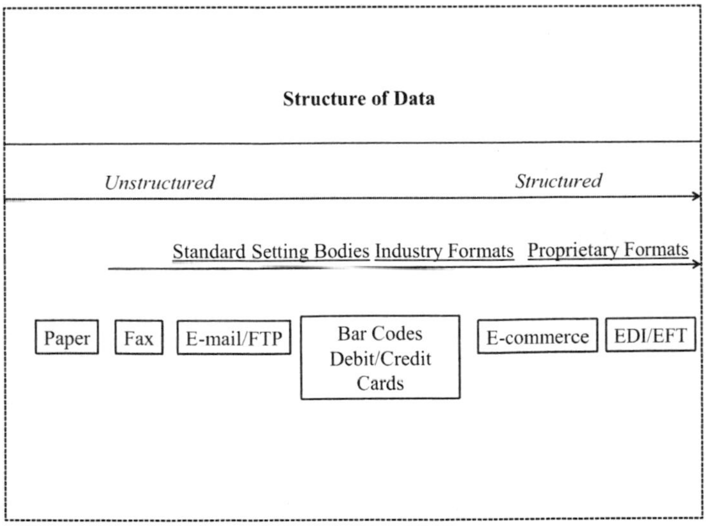

Structure of Data

Unstructured → *Structured*

Standard Setting Bodies Industry Formats Proprietary Formats →

Paper | Fax | E-mail/FTP | Bar Codes Debit/Credit Cards | E-commerce | EDI/EFT

EDI Standards and Standard-Setting Organizations

The idea of a standard document, as mentioned in Chapter 1, originated during the Berlin Airlift. Incoming cargo was accompanied by documents that were non-standard, in different languages and in different formats, which caused a logistics nightmare. The U.S. Army logistics officers designed a standard manifest to replace these non-standard documents. The standard manifest could be transmitted via telephone, telex or radio. The standard became a success; thousands of tons of cargo per day were tracked using these manifests. This very same idea resurfaced in the 1960s. Corporations, led by the transportation industry, began to employ standardized documents in electronic format.

Initially, standards were devised by individual corporations. These standards were in proprietary formats and were incompatible with other standards. Interestingly, some proprietary standards are still used, though corporations are steadily moving to generic standards. By the late 1960s, the transportation industry reached a critical mass of users. Different standards were hindering growth and acceptance of EDI. The TDCC was formed to create EDI standards for shipping, rail and trucking segments of the transportation industry. TDCC published its first set of standards in 1975. Then the Grocery and Food industry also launched its initiative in the EDI arena. To unify these disparate efforts for EDI standards, ANSI (*www.ansi.org*) started coordinating efforts for generic standards in the late 1970s. ANSI was founded in 1918 to administer and coordinate development of national standards in various areas. ANSI does not develop standards, but provides a forum where interested parties such as professional societies, trade associations, industry groups and government can come together and write and maintain standards.

Exhibit 2. Timeline for EDI standards and organizations

Time	Developments
Pre-1960	Standard manifests designed for cargo transportation during the Berlin Airlift.
1960-1970	• *Early 1960s*: DuPont and Chemical Lehman transmit cargo information in EDI-type formats. • *Mid 1960s*: Shipping manifests transmitted through telex that could be automatically converted into computer processable data. • *Late 1960s*:Transportation Data Coordinating Committee (TDCC) formed to establish EDI standards.
1970-'80	• *1975:* TDCC publishes the first set of EDI standards. • *1977:* Grocery and food industry launches a pilot project to assess the feasibility of EDI. • *1978:* ANSI develops generic EDI standards -- ANSI X.12
1980-'90	• *1982:* Automotive industry employs EDI; GM and Ford mandate EDI for suppliers. • *1985:* EDI for Administration, Commerce and Trade (EDIFACT) starts developing international EDI standards. • *Late 1980s/Early 1990s:* Federal government starts using EDI.
1990-2000	• XML-developed. XML/EDI standards begin to take shape. • EDIINT (EDI over the Internet) initiatives

Exhibit 3. ANSI X.12 transaction set for invoice (810)

					Segment Description	Required	Max. Use
ISA					Interchange control header	Mandatory	1
	GS				Functional group header	Mandatory	1
		ST			Transaction set header	Mandatory	1
			BIG		Beginning segment for invoice	Mandatory	1
			REF		Reference number	Optional	12
			N1		Name	Optional	1-50
				N3	Address information	Optional	2
				N4	Geographic location	Optional	1
			ITD		Terms of sale	Optional	>1
			IT1		Baseline item data (Invoice)	Optional	999,999
			NTE		Note/Special instruction	Optional	100
				DTM	Date/Time reference	Optional	10
			TDS		Total monetary value (Summary)	Mandatory	1
			SAC		Allowance charge	Optional	25
				TX1	Tax	Optional	10
			CTT		Transaction totals	Mandatory	1
		SE			Transaction set trailer	Mandatory	1
	GE				Functional group trailer	Mandatory	1
IEA					Interchange control trailer	Mandatory	1

The Accredited Standards Committee (ASC) X.12 has been entrusted by ANSI to develop EDI standards. These standards by the committee are codified in ANSI X.12. The Data Interchange Standards Association (DISA) serves as a secretariat for ASC X.12 and published an entire set of X.12 standards in one single volume. These standards have been in use in the U.S. Parallel to ANSI, other organization that is active in the EDI standards area is the United Nations rules for Electronic Data Interchange for Administration, Commerce and Transport (UN/EDIFACT,www.unece.org/). This initiative began in Great Britain, and initial efforts were in developing EDI standards for Europe. However, now EDIFACT develops internationally accepted standards. EDIFACT standards are influenced by ANSI X.12 standards, and there are many common structural characteristics; however, there are some differences in formats and structures of these standards. The unification of these standards is a work in progress.

Under the broad umbrella of ANSI X.12 and EDIFACT, there is a host of other standards. The different industry groups have industry-specific standards; for example, retail, insurance, transportation, automobile and banking have their own EDI standards. XML-based EDI has been gaining momentum in recent years, and there are separate standards for different industries under this group. There is also a movement to integrate EDI with the Internet, moving away from proprietary networks, covered by EDIINT standards. The other illustrative areas include standards for object-oriented EDI, product and data harmonization in EDI and messaging systems in EDI. The dynamic nature of this area can be understood by checking these Web sites: *www.disa.org/* and *www.ietf.org/*. These sites have comprehensive information about standards that affect the electronic exchange of information, along with a comprehensive list of standards for EDI. These standards will probably continue to change and evolve in the foreseeable future.

So what are these standards and how do they work? The basic components of the standards, both ANSI X.12 and EDIFACT, are similar. First, standards provide the syntax and encoding scheme that specify the structure of data. In EDI, the data structure makes data independent of machines, systems and storage media; and allows for common interpretation. The structure is also modular — meaning changes in part of the message

Exhibit 4. An invoice mapped to the EDI format

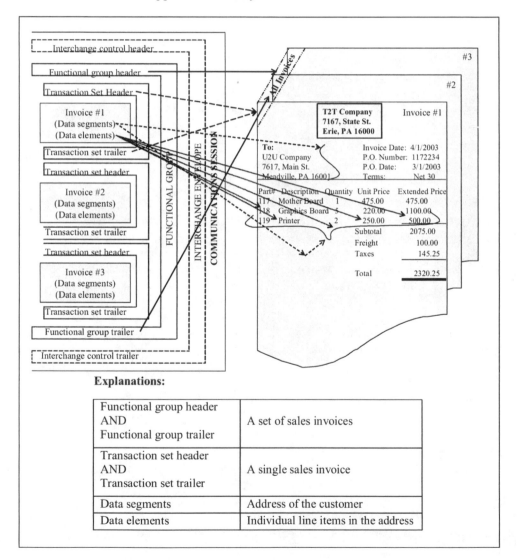

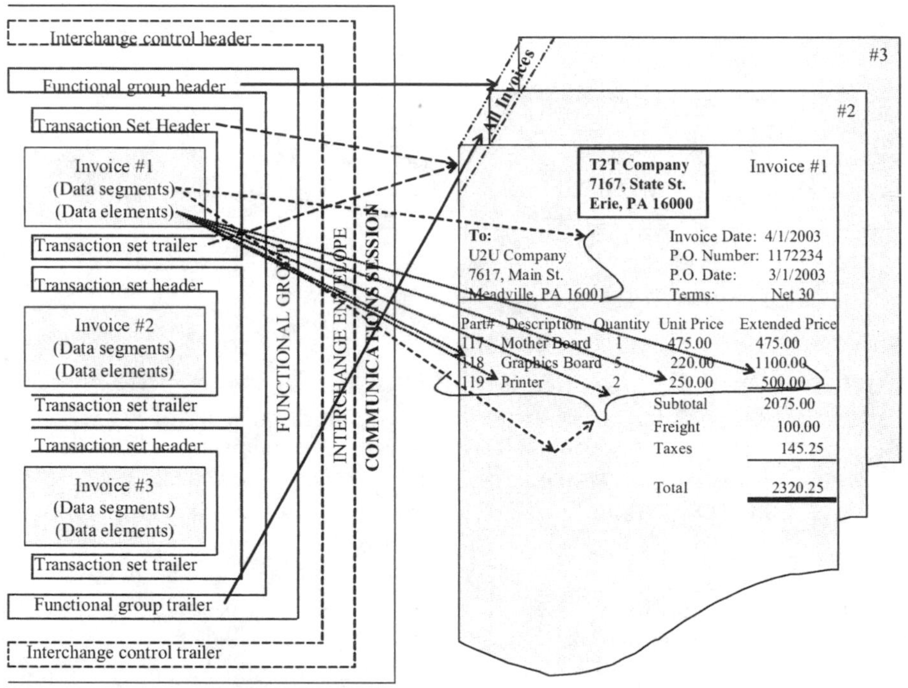

Explanations:

Functional group header AND Functional group trailer	A set of sales invoices
Transaction set header AND Transaction set trailer	A single sales invoice
Data segments	Address of the customer
Data elements	Individual line items in the address

do not need changes in other parts. Second, standards provide for data dictionary. This dictionary defines business terminology such as date, time, address and currency in special EDI terms. Third, standards provide a way to combine basic blocks of information (called data elements) such as date, time, account number and supplier's name and address, to create a complete document such as invoice (called a transaction set). We will look deeper at ANSI X.12 standards to get some understanding of the inner workings of EDI.

Traditional business activities — for example, sales transactions — are based on exchange of various documents, such as request for quote, sales order, shipping notice, bill of lading and invoice, to mention a few. EDI standards pattern EDI messages on a transaction basis. A complete representation of invoice (810) in ANSI X.12 format is shown in Exhibit 3. This format is taken from ANSI X.12 standards and it shows EDI segment name, segment description, whether the segment is mandatory or required, and maximum number of times the segment can be used. Invoice-specific items are as follows — ST to ITD segments describe the invoice header section, IT1 to DTM segments describe invoice details, and TDS to CTT segments describe invoice summary details.

The same transaction set is mapped to an invoice in Exhibit 4. The EDI message at the left-hand side indicates structure of the message. EDI message, in the U.S., means the entire data stream, including interchange header and trailer. There are five components: the interchange control structure, functional groups, transaction sets, data segments and data elements. The shaded region at the right-hand side shows a series of sales invoices. Each sales invoice, in EDI terminology, will be considered a *transaction set*; and a collection of invoices, that is, group of similar transaction sets, will be considered a *functional group*.

Exhibit 5. Invoice (810) converted to EDI message

	Invoice Header
ST*810*001	Header information, transaction set control number
BIG*20030401*INVOICE#1*20030301*1172 234***DR	Invoice number and date
CUR*SE*USD	Currency U.S. dollars
REF*PK*12345	Packing slip reference
N1*BY*T2T COMPANY*92*123456	Name of the supplier
N3*7167 STATE ST	Address of the supplier
N4*ERIE*PA*16000	Address of the supplier
PER*AR*JOHN SMITH*PA*4455667	T2T account representative number
N1*BT*U2U COMPANY*92*654321	Name of the customer
N3*7617 MAIN ST	Address of the customer
N4*MEADVILLE*PA*16001	Address of the customer
ITD*01*03****30	Terms of sale – Net 30
DTM*011*20030331	Shipping date
FOB*CC****MI*T2T COMPANY	FOB – shipping
	Invoice Detail
IT1*000117*QTY*1*MB*475.00*000118*Q	Part number, quantity shipped, and price information
TY*5*GB*220.00*000119*QTY*2*P*250.00	Part number, quantity shipped, and price information
	Invoice Summary
TDS*2320.25	Total amount of the invoice
TX1*ST*145.25*7.00	Applicable taxes
CTT*1	Total IT1 segments
SE*20*001	Transaction set control number

A transaction set consists of data segments; each data segment is comprised of data elements of variable lengths. Data elements are analogous to information in the line item, and data segments are analogous to the entire line item or the logical collection of line items. For example, line items in customer address such as street, city, state and country will be considered data elements. Data elements can be numeric, decimal, identifier, string, and date or time; have a minimum and maximum length; and an indication whether the element is required or optional. A collection of data elements will result in a data segment; when all line items in the customer address are combined, we get a data segment that identifies the customer. ANSI X.12 standards provide a data element dictionary that maps business terms such as date, address and so forth to the EDI message. Each data element in EDI will have a reference number cited in the data element dictionary. These standards also specify which data segments can be used in the message, sequence of the segments, optional or required nature of the segments, whether the segment can be repeated and, if yes, rules regarding repetition (loops) of the segments.

A comprehensive collection of data segments will be called a *transaction set*. In other words, the sales invoice (being a transaction set) will consist of data segments that will define company name and address, customer name and address, information about ordered parts, prices, freight and taxes. The structure of transaction sets is threefold: header and trailer area, detail or line item area, and summary area.

1. **Header and trailer area:** The transaction set header consists of a transaction identification number and transaction set control number. The transaction identification number is a three-digit number that uniquely identifies type of the transaction; for example, 810 means invoice. A wide range of business documents (approximately 250) for different industries have been standardized by ANSI X.12. A list of frequently used transaction identification numbers and the names of corresponding documents are listed in Exhibit 6.

   Transaction set control number is a unique sequence number assigned to each data segment, and the last number in that sequence identifies the total number of data segments. For example, if there are five data segments, then the first data segment will have a control number such as 0001 and the last data segment may have a control number 0005. The header area contains the transaction set control number associated with the first data segment. The transaction set trailer area indicates that the transaction has ended, total number of segments included, and the transaction set control number (generally the same number included in the header area).

2. **Detail area:** This area consists of data segments that provide information regarding quantity, price, catalog numbers, part numbers and product description, among other things. The sequence of segments may form a loop that may be repeated; for example, 810 IT1 (baseline item data) can be repeated 999,999 times. In case of an invoice, each loop will approximately correspond to each line item on the invoice.

3. **Summary area:** This area can contain summary information such as total price for the invoice and/or it may include control information such as number of lines in a sales order or hash totals.

Exhibit 6. EDI-capable documents in different functional areas

Accounting and finance	• 810 • 812 • 820 • 826	• Sales invoices • Debit/Credit memos • Payment order/Remittance advices • Tax reporting
Purchasing	• 850 • 855 • 865 • 869 • 870	• Purchase Orders (PO) • PO acknowledgments • PO changes/adjustments • Order status inquiries • Order status report
Inventory management	• 830 • 844 • 846	• Planning schedules • Product transfers and resale • Inventory advice
Marketing	• 832 • 840 • 843 • 845 • 852	• Prices/Sales catalogs • Request for quote • Return requests for quote • Price authorizations • Product activity data
Logistics	• 853 • 856 • 858 • 859	• Routing and carrier instruction • Advance shipment notices • Shipment status messages • Freight details and invoices
Manufacturing	• 830 • 866	• Planning schedule • Production sequence
General	• 997	• Functional acknowledgment

The set of *transaction sets* will be enveloped in a functional group. A functional group header will precede all transaction sets and a functional group trailer will succeed all transaction sets. As shown in Exhibit 4, functional group envelopes transaction sets of three invoices. The functional group header consists of a functional ID code that identifies the transaction set; for example, sales invoice or purchase order, application codes for the sender and receiver, and date and time, among other things. The functional group trailer identifies the number of included transaction sets and the data interchange control number, which is assigned by the sender. In the ANSI X.12 standard, a functional group receipt is acknowledged by a functional group acknowledgement (or functional acknowledgement), which indicates that the transaction sets have been received and can be processed. Remember, this communication takes place between computer systems. The Interchange Control header and trailer that surround the functional group do not contain EDI-specific information; however, they identify the sender and receiver, the date and time of transmission, and the version of X.12 being used in the transmission.

Exhibit 5 shows the conversion of the invoice shown in Exhibit 4 into an EDI message. Exhibit 5 uses elements of a transaction set as indicated in 810 transaction set and details of the invoice to create an EDI message. On the left-hand side are lines of the EDI message, and on the right-hand side are the meaning of those lines. The invoice header (ST to ITD), invoice details (IT to DTM) and invoice summary (TDS to CTT) are delineated to clearly indicate how the invoice gets transformed into an EDI message. The interchange control header and functional group header are not shown for the sake of simplicity.

Infrastructure for EDI Solutions

An effective implementation of EDI requires a firm infrastructural foundation. The infrastructure for EDI includes translation software, communication software, hardware for data transfer and security, and legal trading partner agreements. The process begins with accounting software preparing the required document, such as purchase order or advanced shipping notice in electronic format. This process also works for paper documents, which can be typed and entered in the EDI software. However, using paper documents negates benefits of the EDI system.

The translation software then translates the document or a batch of documents in EDI format (and vice versa); the EDI syntax and coding scheme must be followed precisely. The translation software (called *translator*) is a crucial piece in the EDI system. The primary task of translator is to convert outgoing messages from the seller's unique format to a standard EDI format and to convert incoming EDI messages to the buyer's unique format that can be further processed by the buyer's accounting software. The translation process consists of three steps. First, a file conversion program in the translation software formats data from the business application so data can be accepted by the EDI formatting software. Second, the EDI formatting software takes data output from the file conversion program and reformats it in the EDI standard format. Third, the communication software prepares the data for transmission. The translator also performs certain secondary tasks. The incoming message can be validated by the translators; if there are any errors, an error file can be generated. The translator also generates functional acknowledgments when it receives messages. Some useful features of the translator are enumerated below.

- The translator should support major EDI standards such as ANSI X.12 and EDIFACT. Additionally, it should support required industry specific standards, for example, automotive, groceries, or transportation industry
- The translator should support a data-mapping functionality for a wide range of incoming and outgoing messages, including multiple and nonstandard transaction sets.
- The translator should seamlessly integrate with the existing accounting system; for example, packaged software, ERP systems or legacy systems. Or, the vendor should be willing to provide a customized solution.
- The translator should automatically generate functional acknowledgements.
- The translator should require minimum manual intervention. Tasks such as scheduling, archiving of messages, table lookups and generation of turnaround documents should be done automatically.
- The translator should have an appropriate reporting facility to generate standard or custom reports.
- The translator should have connection facilities for trading partners' networks, the Internet and/or dial up telephone lines.

Exhibit 7. Infrastructure for EDI solutions

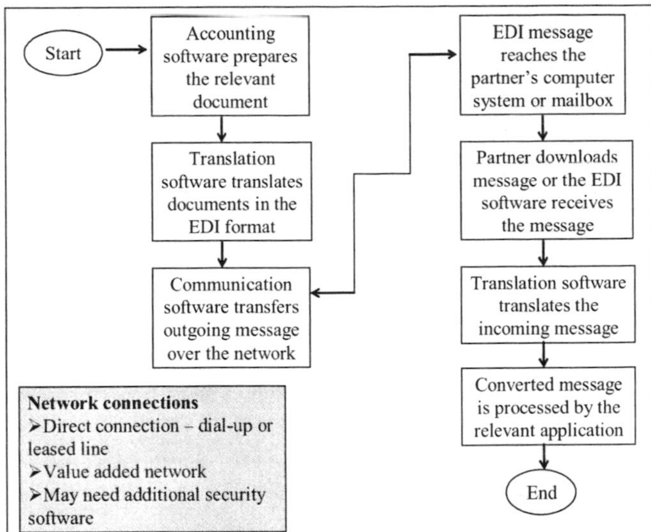

Dozens of companies provide translator software; however, due to industry consolidation, this number is constantly changing. Translation software is available as a standalone module as well as part of integrated EDI solutions offered by the same company. For example, Exact Macola software uses GENTRAN by Sterling Software as translator for its EDI module; however, Sterling Commerce also offers a variety of e-commerce suites and products that use the same translator software.

The translated document is transferred by the communications software over networks to the partner's computer system. Data transfer can be achieved by direct connections or by logging into the partner's computer system. The connection can be direct, such as regular phone lines or dedicated leased phone lines, broadband lines or Digital Subscriber Line (DSL). The choice depends on frequency of the EDI messages. If the messages are processed in a batch mode and only need a few hours for transmission, then regular phone lines may be a viable choice. However, as frequency of the messages goes up, number of EDI partners goes up, and/or usage of other online applications goes up, dedicated lines are more useful. The communication software should be capable of supporting multiple protocols to support these connections.

Indirect connections take place through third-party networks, referred to as Value Added Networks (VANs). A VAN is a private network provider. Basically, VANs move data, especially large and sensitive files, between companies. The term *value added* denotes that these networks add services that are not readily available on public networks. A list of additional services is quite lengthy, and includes handling of all connectivity-related issues, such as providing various communication options, protocol conversions and electronic mailboxing; security-related issues, such as privacy, authentication, data integrity and storage of data for audit trail purposes; consulting services; and other

Exhibit 8. Value added networks

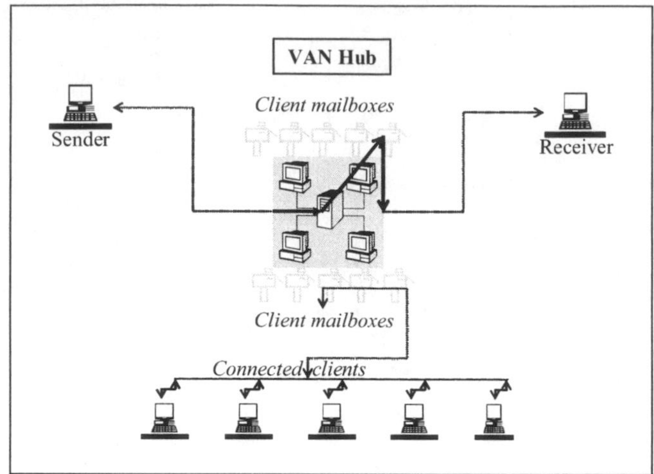

miscellaneous services, such as connecting to other VANs, EDI to e-mail conversion, EDI to fax conversion and electronic catalogs.

In EDI, generally, VAN is used as a post office. VANs provide electronic mailboxes for trading partners. The trading partners dial in or otherwise connect with the VAN and deliver messages. For example, the sender will dial in and connect with the VAN and deliver a purchase order. This order will be enclosed in an envelope and the address on the envelope will notify the order's destination to the network. The order will be placed in the mailbox of the appropriate supplier. The supplier will then log into the network and retrieve the purchase order, and the resulting functional acknowledgment will be placed in the sender's mailbox. Generally, every client of the VAN receives two mailboxes, first for incoming and second for outgoing EDI messages.

The basic service model described above is generally enhanced by VANs by offerings of additional services. For example, VANs can send advance notification that a message has arrived in a mail box; if there is no mail, then a *no mail* status can be displayed; downloading and uploading of messages can be automated using telecommunication sessions; and the same communication session can be used to deliver messages to different trading partners. The VAN will also wait after a message is delivered for acknowledgment of receipt of that message. It is important that the message is delivered once and only once. If the same message is delivered twice, it might be processed twice. Detailed transaction logs are maintained by the VAN to ensure an audit trail and accuracy of the EDI messages. Additional services include EDI translation, secure e-mail and management reporting, among other things.

VAN is a crucial link in the EDI chain. To protect interests of both sides, there is generally a legal agreement between the VAN operator and the customer. This agreement covers various areas; for example, description of the services, pricing structure, disaster recovery procedures, liability and damages due to disruption of services or errors on part of the VAN, security of messages, confidentiality and integrity of messages, provisions for independent third-party review of the VAN security, and procedures for termination or extension of the agreement.

The legal trading agreement, on the other hand, is between trading partners. The origins of these agreements can be traced to days when electronic EDI transactions did not have the same legal status as paper-based transactions. Interestingly, commercial law has not yet kept pace with EDI practice. The trading agreements fill the gap and provide a legal basis for EDI transactions. A trading agreement is also necessary to eliminate disputes that arise in an electronic environment. Since there is no comprehensive *EDI Law*, each trading agreement is unique. The contract can be a few lines to an elaborately drawn document that can only fit in a three-ring binder. The American Bar Association (*www.abanet.org/*) provides *Model Electronic Data Interchange Trading Partner Agreement and Commentary*, a booklet that can be obtained from the association.

The EDI trading agreement addresses the primary issue of establishing validity of transactions that do not have a paper trail. The agreement also deals with many technological issues unique to the EDI environment. Generally, these agreements cover following areas.

- Defining nature and scope of the EDI trading relationship. For example, discussions of electronic transactions, scope of the agreement, enforceability of the contracts, implicit contracts created by the EDI transactions and so forth.
- The EDI formats and documents used by the transacting parties
- EDI software specifications
- Third-party network specifications
- Security, integrity and confidentiality of EDI messages
- Responsibility for disrupted, garbled or corrupted messages and remedial action
- Cost issues
- Trading partner guidelines — for example, a checklist to assess partner readiness for EDI

This agreement is not an absolute necessity for EDI transactions. As EDI has gone mainstream and become an accepted business practice, importance of the agreement has somewhat declined. Many trading partners do not use a legal agreement of any form whatsoever. However, most major corporations will insist on a formal agreement.

Accounting Software and EDI

Accounting software primarily connects to the EDI chain via translator. The extent of integration between the translator and accounting software gives rise to various EDI configurations. The first level is where there is no integration between the translator and

Exhibit 9. Translator interface with accounting systems

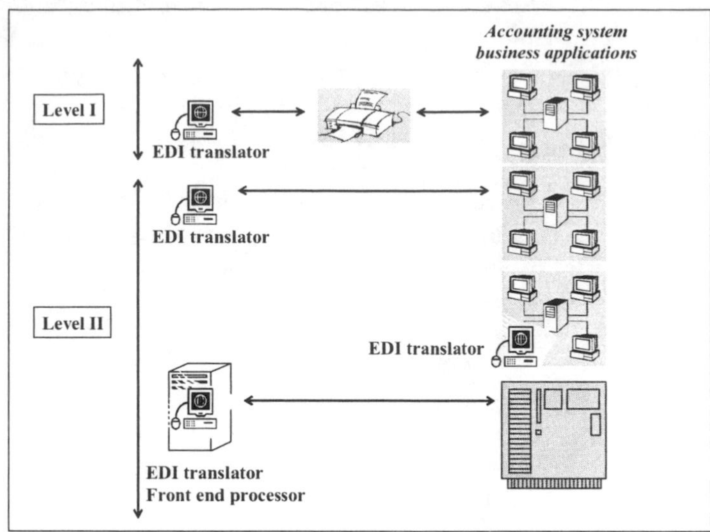

the accounting system. In the second level, the translator is integrated with the accounting system. The configurations in this level include translator being connected to the network via custom-developed software. The translator can also come integrated with the accounting software, pre-configured and ready for required EDI messages. In the mainframe environment, the translator can be mounted on the front-end processor that receives the incoming EDI messages and communicates with business applications.

Many smaller companies have simply purchased the translator software and used it as a stand-alone piece of software. The incoming EDI messages are translated by the translator, and the resulting documents, such as purchase order, are printed out. Then these documents are manually processed by the concerned departments. The outgoing messages are keyed into the translator from the outgoing documents generated by the accounting system. This type of arrangement is useful for companies that have few trading partners and a low frequency of EDI messages.

This solution is low cost, since it avoids the costs of integrating EDI software with the existing accounting system, does not affect workflows and still makes the company EDI capable. There are also considerable problems with this arrangement. First, the translator is merely used as a fax machine, where paper documents are passed back and forth. Second, manual data entry creates possibilities for additional errors in the accounting system. The outgoing messages create more problems, since all data needs to be reentered; rekeying of all information needs to be done in EDI format; and the outgoing messages frequently lack EDI-specific information, such as terms code qualifiers or ship-to qualifiers, which must be captured at the time of data entry. Some complex documents such as Advanced Shipping Notification (ASN) may need multiple entries. Data entry operators need considerable EDI expertise to accomplish these tasks. Finally, this

Exhibit 10. MACOLA EDI module

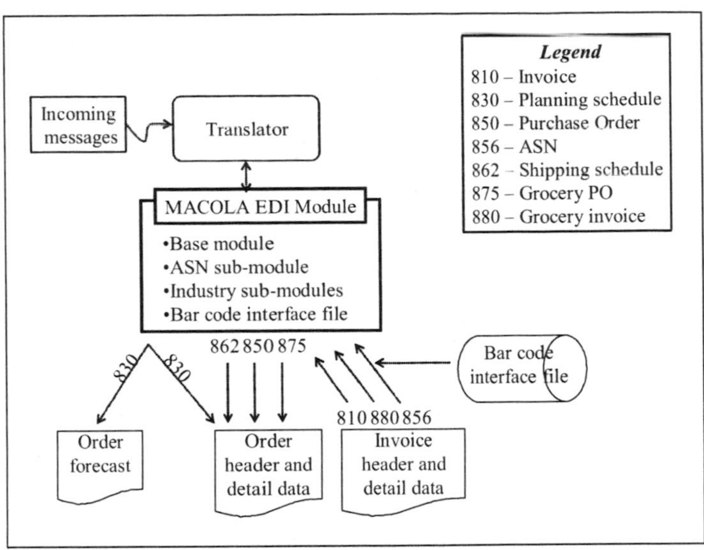

arrangement deprives the organization benefits of EDI, such as reducing errors and improving cycle time.

Integration of the translator with the accounting system can be achieved in two ways. First, a custom solution can be developed. This approach precisely tailors the solution to the needs of the organization. However, this approach can be expensive, and if the customized solution is not planned properly, it can lead to inflexible systems that do not scale with the organization. The majority of the mid- and higher-end accounting software packages offers integrated EDI capabilities. Either development is done in-house or is accomplished by integrating third-party products with the software. These products transfer responsibility for tracking and maintaining changes in EDI standards to the software companies, enable tracing of integration problems to one source for tech help, and can come with pre-mapped and pre-configured EDI capabilities. However, EDI capability, scalability, price, expertise and support for different industries and standards vary with different types of accounting software.

The EDI module in the Macola Progression Series is used to illustrate real-world implementation of EDI in accounting software. Macola primarily serves mid-size corporations, and the software is likely to be used by suppliers of major corporations like WalMart, GM or Ford. Macola Software had a historical manufacturing focus, and has extensive EDI capabilities. Macola had an integrated EDI solution, and its EDI module is comprised of a group of software and utilities packages. These various packages are described below.

- **The translator:** The translator used by Macola is called GENTRAN: Director of Windows, provided by Sterling Software. This software has the ability to connect with various VANs, directly connect with clients, generate functional acknowledgments and validate inbound and outbound EDI files. This translator converts incoming EDI files to an intermediate flat file format and passes those files to the base module, and takes outgoing intermediate flat files and converts them to EDI format.

- **The base module:** This module has three components — base integration logic, cross-reference file maintenance programs and standard systems tools common to different modules. The base integration logic helps create both inbound documents (such as orders) and consequent outbound documents (such as invoices). The incoming EDI orders are integrated with the Macola order entry module and the outgoing invoices are generated from Macola invoice data. The incoming orders are validated against the Macola data format and exceptions are written to the *exception file*. An audit report can be run against the exception file to determine which files need manual intervention. Additionally, EDI data is written to another file to keep a copy of data for further reference. Then, the validated data of inbound orders is ready to be processed by the software. The outbound invoices are created from Macola formatted invoices. These invoices can be printed. The base module then converts the e-version of Macola formatted invoices to an EDI format specified by a trading partner. The invoices are in the form of intermediate flat files, and are ready to be processed by the translator. The processing is generally done when the user chooses the appropriate menu option. The file conversion uses cross-reference files that contain *customer cross-reference files,* which hold customer-specific information, and *item cross-reference files*, which contain the entire ANSI EDI standard. These files convert data to and from the trading partner's identification codes and also help customize the EDI module.
- **The sub-modules:** If the company needs any EDI capabilities over and above the base module, then optional sub-modules can be purchased. These modules are generally industry-specific, for example, the ASN sub-module or the automotive sub-module.

  The ASN module is used to convey shipment details to the customer. The information includes carrier information, pallet and box bar code data, and description of the items and packages. The *Macola White Paper* on EDI says that ASN is one of the most complex EDI documents and can have up to five levels of detail. ASNs are required by the automotive industry and many retail trading partners. If a mistake is made in the ASN, if the ASN is missing or if the ASN is late, many automotive companies will refuse to pay for the shipment or will inflict heavy penalties on the supplier.

  The automotive sub-module deals with the planning schedule (830) and the shipping schedule (862). The planning schedule contains forecast information for the trading partner's requirements; Macola handles up to 13 weeks of forecasting information and integrates the planning schedule with the master scheduler module. The shipping schedule informs vendors of the release date for each shipment. Both of these are critical documents for automotive companies and their suppliers.

- **Bar code interface file:** The bar code interface file supplements the ASN sub-module. Bar code data collection systems generate bar code labels (termed as Uniform Code Council/UCC 128) at the point of packing. The bar code numbers are mandatory on most ASNs. If the company uses a third-party bar code data collection system, then the bar code interface file can be used to read the bar code labels, import data and populate the ASN.
- **The trading partner:** This is a collection of files that contain EDI file specification details for each trading partner. The translator uses these files to print, view, enter and translate the documents; these specifications also include conversion of Macola data to EDI format and vice versa. If a document is to be manually entered, then these files can help in printing and/or entering that document into the system.

The prior description is a simplistic description of the Macola EDI system. The real-world EDI/accounting systems are very complex and are getting more complex as more functionality is loaded in. The majority of mid-level and almost all higher-level accounting packages either offer an integrated EDI or third-party EDI solution to customers.

Financial EDI

EDI permitted organizations electronic transfer of purchase and sales documents. However, payments and processing of payments were still paper-based, negating some of the benefits of the EDI system. FEDI enables organizations to exchange payment and remittance information electronically, thereby allowing them to handle payables and receivables using the EDI system. The stringent EDI data formatting rules are applied to these electronic fund transfers and, hence, the name FEDI. The types of information that can be transferred include remittance advice, payment and check details, account analysis, lockbox receipts, letters of credit information and electronic acknowledgments. FEDI is sometimes viewed as *closing the EDI loop*. FEDI can be defined as (Ferguson, 2000):

> *"The electronic transfer of payments, payment-related information or other financial documents between a bank and its customers or between business partners, in a standardized, computer readable format."*

FEDI deals with transfer of funds and related remittance information. Hence, it involves intermediary financial institutions, at least one bank but generally two or more. Banks have been moving funds amongst themselves electronically for several decades by using electronic funds transfer (EFT) . The roots of FEDI can be traced to EFT, and to understand FEDI it is first necessary to understand EFT.

EFT is not merely electronic transfer of information; it is called by some transfer of value, meaning dollar amounts get transferred. Currently, there are four major ways of executing EFT. The three real-time methods are: FedWire developed by Federal Reserve, Clearing-

Exhibit 11. Remittance advice (820) converted to EDI message

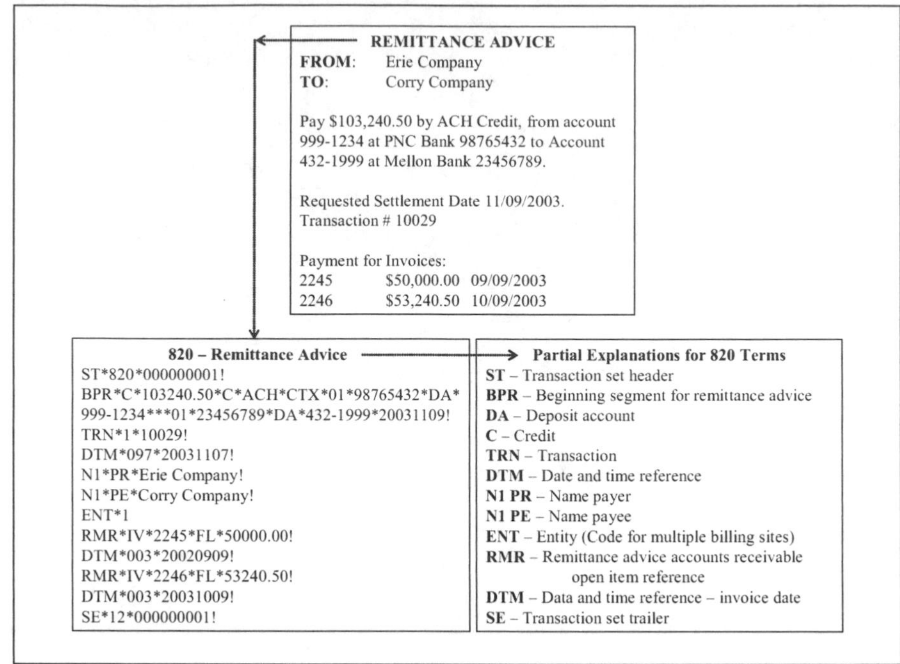

REMITTANCE ADVICE
FROM: Erie Company
TO: Corry Company

Pay $103,240.50 by ACH Credit, from account 999-1234 at PNC Bank 98765432 to Account 432-1999 at Mellon Bank 23456789.

Requested Settlement Date 11/09/2003.
Transaction # 10029

Payment for Invoices:

2245	$50,000.00	09/09/2003
2246	$53,240.50	10/09/2003

820 – Remittance Advice

```
ST*820*000000001!
BPR*C*103240.50*C*ACH*CTX*01*98765432*DA*
999-1234***01*23456789*DA*432-1999*20031109!
TRN*1*10029!
DTM*097*20031107!
N1*PR*Erie Company!
N1*PE*Corry Company!
ENT*1
RMR*IV*2245*FL*50000.00!
DTM*003*20020909!
RMR*IV*2246*FL*53240.50!
DTM*003*20031009!
SE*12*000000001!
```

Partial Explanations for 820 Terms
ST – Transaction set header
BPR – Beginning segment for remittance advice
DA – Deposit account
C – Credit
TRN – Transaction
DTM – Date and time reference
N1 PR – Name payer
N1 PE – Name payee
ENT – Entity (Code for multiple billing sites)
RMR – Remittance advice accounts receivable open item reference
DTM – Data and time reference – invoice date
SE – Transaction set trailer

house for Interbank Payment Systems (CHIPS) and Society for Worldwide Interbank Financial Telecommunications (SWIFT); on the other hand, Automated Clearinghouse Transfers (ACH), the fourth method, is a batch system. A brief description of these methods is provided.

- **FedWire:** This is an electronic network or communications system that connects the Federal Reserve and its branches; government agencies such as the Treasury and more than 9,000 depository institutions are connected to this network. FedWire is a real-time transfer of money through this network, using Federal Reserve account balances. The transfer mechanism starts when the sender's bank debits the sender's account and informs its local Reserve bank to send a transfer to another Reserve bank that serves the receiver's bank, if sender's and receiver's banks are in different Federal Reserve districts. The receiver's bank notifies the receiver of the transfer and the funds are immediately available. The two Reserve banks settle the transaction through what is called Interdistrict Settlement Fund. If the sender's and receiver's bank are in the same district, then only one Reserve bank processes the entire transaction. In the year 2000, the total volume of transactions over FedWire approached close to $400 trillion.

  The Federal Reserve network can also be used for communicating instructions to other banks; the payer can obtain a confirmation number to help track the payment through the system; and the payee can get a message that the account has been

Exhibit 12. Mechanisms of EFT

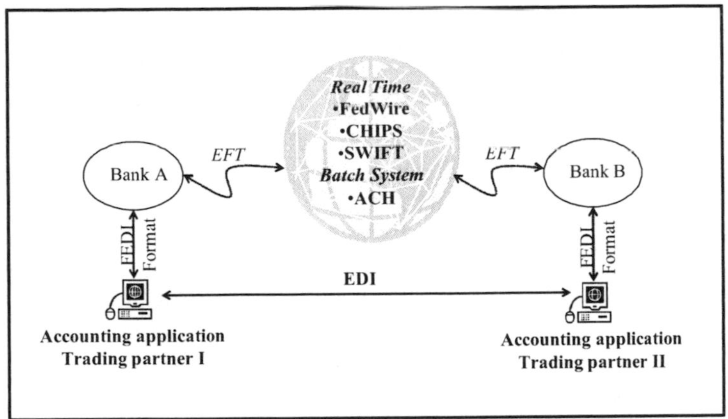

credited. The FedWires are very secure, work in real time, and the payment is guaranteed by the Federal Reserve and cannot be reversed. However, the real-time nature of transactions makes FedWire labor intensive and expensive for routine business use. The FedWire format also limits the amount of payment-related information that can be transferred and frequently requires human intervention for interpretation.

- **CHIPS:** This, similar to FedWire, is an electronic payments system that connects New York City and affiliated banks. CHIPS is privately owned and operated by the New York Clearing House Association. This association used to be a group of the largest New York City financial institutions, but now includes non-New York banks. Historically, CHIPS focused on foreign exchange transactions and handled approximately 95% of all U.S.-dollar payments between countries. CHIPS now also focuses on domestic business. CHIPS is both a customer and competitor of FedWire. Currently, the total-dollar volume of transactions in a year over CHIPS rivals FedWire.

  CHIPS operates as a netting system when moving funds. For example, if Bank A owes Bank B $500 million and vice versa, then there will be no actual movement of funds. The netting can be multilateral also; if Bank A owes Bank B $500 million and Bank C owes Bank A $500 million then Bank A's payment to Bank B will be queued until a corresponding receipt arrives from Bank C. The net effect on Bank A's cash balance will then be zero. Payments that have no match will be held until the end of the day and then settled; these payments are final immediately.

  The advantages and disadvantages of CHIPS are similar to FedWire. However, in 2001, CHIPS added FEDI functionality by expanding the data set that can be carried with payment information. The ancillary information such as invoice numbers, discount details, rebates and so forth can be sent via 9,000-character data set. This data set supports ANSI X.12, EDIFACT, XML and other user-defined formats.

CHIPS has also introduced a *Universal Payment Identification Code* that facilitates electronic payments between businesses.

- **SWIFT:** SWIFT is a non-profit organization organized by European bankers. More than 7,000 financial institutions in approximately 200 countries are affiliated with this network. SWIFT, similar to FedWire and CHIPS, provides a secure and efficient system for electronic transfer of funds. In the absence of central authority such as the Federal Reserve, payments are cleared by the corresponding banks. The access to SWIFT is through member banks only.

  SWIFT's format (*www.swift.com/*) is a proprietary format designed to handle payment instructions, letters of credit, confirmations, balance information and so forth. SWIFT messages are referred to by category numbers called Message Transfer (MT) numbers. A SWIFT message will consist of name and code of the originating and receiving bank, date and time, name and code of the person authorizing the transaction, name and account numbers involved in the transaction, a description of the monetary asset being moved and MT category of the transmission, and also will allow for some standardized pre-defined descriptive phrases. The new SWIFT MT 103 and MT 103+ formats have added extra space (9,000 characters) for payment-related information and support ANSI X.12 and EDIFACT standards.

- **ACH:** ACH is a secure, private electronic payment transfer systems that connects the majority of the banks (commercial, credit unions or savings and loans) in the U.S. The National Automated Clearing House Association (NACHA) is an organization of these commercial banks that sets standards and rules for ACH transfers. NACHA also handles research, pilot programs and marketing for ACH transfers.

Exhibit 13. ACH payment formats

Format	Use	Data Capacity
Corporate transactions		
CCD – Cash Concentration and Disbursement	Cash concentration and account funding and some types of corporate payments	94 characters
CCD+ – CCD with addenda	Used by the U.S. government in payment of invoices, taxes and trade payments	94 characters and an addenda of up to 80 characters (***Note***: Addenda records contain payment-related information)
CTP – Corporate Trade Payment	Corporate-to-corporate payments	94 characters and an addenda of up to 4,990 records (80 characters each)
CTX – Corporate Trade Exchange	Corporate-to-corporate payments	94 characters and an addenda of up to 9,999 records (80 characters each)
Consumer transactions		
PPD – Prearranged Payment or Deposit	Direct deposit of social security, payroll	94 characters
POS – Point of Sale	Point of sale (terminal) transactions	94 characters
MTE – Machine Transaction Entry	Automated Teller Network transactions	94 characters
CIE – Customer Initiated Entry	Bill payments from home (banking or telephone)	94 characters

This service first was initiated in California and was used for Social Security payments. Initially, government transactions constituted the bulk of fund transfers; however, the volume of corporate transactions is rising rapidly. ACH is primarily designed for high-volume transactions processed in a *batch* mode. The transacting company transmits the electronic payment information, which contains details of the payer and payee, account numbers and the receiver's financial institution, to Bank A. Bank A sorts the transactions and all on-us (transactions involving Bank A or its branches) are settled immediately and the company's account is debited for all (*not* only for on-us) payments. Bank A then (generally at the end of the day) merges transactions received from other companies and transmits the information to the local ACH. If the receiver's bank is served by a local ACH (intra-regional transactions), then transactions are forwarded to that bank for settlement. If not (inter-regional transactions), then the local ACH forwards those transactions to the ACH that serves the receiver's bank. Federal Reserve gets information about the transactions from the involved ACHs. Then the account at the sender's bank is debited and the receiver's bank is credited. The receiver's bank, after receipt of transactions, will credit the receiver's account.

ACH transaction files begin with the file header record that designates physical characteristics of the file and identifies the originator of the batches. The transaction batches follow the file header. The batch header identifies the originator of transactions and provides a brief description of debits or credits. The detail entries follow the batch header, and information in the batch header applies to all detail entries in that batch. The batch header, along with the detail entries, provides complete information, such as name, account number, amount, debit or credit and so forth, to relay the payment to the ultimate receiver.

ACH transfers handle a variety of transactions — corporate and consumer. ACH transfers are used to handle both consumer and corporate transactions. A brief discussion of corporate ACH formats is necessary to better understand EFT; consumer transactions, however, are beyond the scope of this book.

- *CCD and CCD+:* This format is primarily used for cash concentration (consolidation of funds) and also some types of corporate payments. The data capacity of this format is only 94 characters (and for CCD+ a small addenda that can contain remittance advice information); as such, it cannot carry ancillary payment information. These formats can be processed by almost all banks.
- *CTP:* This format provides more addenda space than CCD. But the extra space provided in this format is not governed by specified standards; as such, extra information does not have universal interpretation. In addition, many banks are incapable of processing this format.
- *CTX:* This format has additional space (more than CTP). However, this format overcomes limitations of CTP by standardizing the data format. CTX addenda are in essence ANSI X.12 document 820 (Payment order/Remittance advice). CTX format envelops the 820 EDI format in the ACH envelope, thereby making it FEDI capable. This format is slowly gaining acceptance, though not all banks can process it.

The fixed cost of ACH transactions is high, but the variable cost is low. Since ACH transactions have exceeded required critical mass, it is one of the cheapest methods of money transfer, and is appealing to businesses. The cost per ACH transaction continues to decline.

EFT is integral to successful execution of FEDI. The primary problem in using EFT formats for FEDI results from data capacity limitations of EFT formats. Businesses need not only information related to the mount of the invoice but also details concerning payments, such as invoice numbers, adjustments, and other related documents. The newly emerging EFT data formats that are supplementing or subsuming EDI standards do not have data capacity limitations. The changes in this area are fast and furious. CHIPS, SWIFTS and NACHA are entering into new e-service areas such as security, trust and controls in financial services. New software products can now generate ACH-compatible data right out of accounting software, and XML standards promise to make these transfers transparent and simple. The future is here, but not everywhere. The technical capabilities of the banks and companies vary widely. These different stages of technological development have given rise to various types of paper and EFT, paper and FEDI, and pure FEDI business processes. Some of the common types of FEDI are shown in Exhibit 14.

FEDI I depicts a scenario where transacting parties use the same bank, and all involved entities are FEDI capable. Business A transmits 820 (Payment Order and remittance advice) to the common bank, detailing amounts and ancillary payment information. The bank processes the information, debits and credits the trading partners, and forwards 820 to Business B. Business B receives payment and the details of payment, and processes it directly through its accounting software.

Exhibit 14. Different types of FEDI

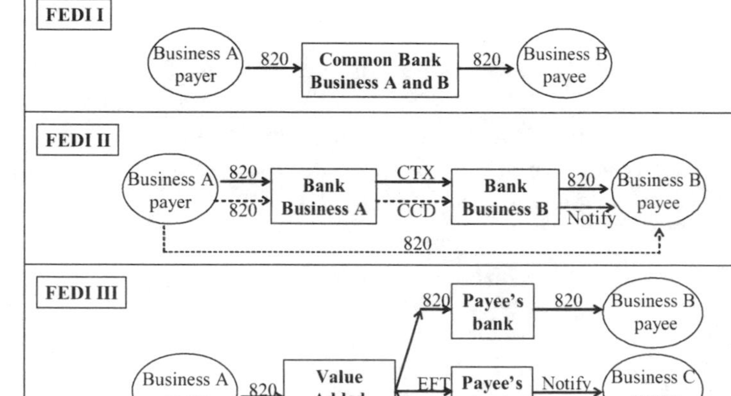

In FEDI II, Business A and Business B use different banks. The diagram describes two cases — one shown by solid arrows and one shown by dotted arrows. In the case shown by solid arrows, both banks are capable of processing the CTX format. Business A transmits 820 to its bank. The bank processes the transaction and envelopes 820 into CTX format as shown in Exhibit 15. The CTX is required since value (or funds) will be transferred from one bank to another bank. The CTX format carries transfer of funds information and addendum to the CTX envelope, which carries the remittance advice information. The funds will be transferred to Business B's account, and 820 carrying payment information and remittance advice details will be transmitted to Business B for further processing. In the dotted-arrows scenario, Business B's bank is not CTX capable. In this case, Business A will transmit 820 to its bank and also to Business B directly. Business A's bank will extract the payment information from the 820 and transfer the funds electronically to Business B's bank using the format required by that bank — for example, CCD. Business B's bank will transfer the funds to Business B's account and notify Business B that payment has been received. This information will be reconciled with remittance advice (820) details received from Business A.

ERADS is also used to transfer information concerning remittance details. ERADS uses an e-mail or fax system in conjunction with EFT. The funds are transferred through regular electronic channels using EFT formats; however, the ancillary information is faxed, e-mailed or FTPed to the payee. If the FEDI transaction volume is low, then this method provides a cost-effective alternative to the processing of 820s.

FEDI III shows a Value Added Bank (VAB). VAB is a financial service provider with FEDI capabilities and VAN capabilities. VAB is capable of accepting EDI-formatted documents such as 820. VAB can process 820 in various ways. The 820 can be transmitted as 820 to a FEDI-capable bank and directly to a FEDI-capable business. If the payee's bank

Exhibit 15. CTX envelope and 820

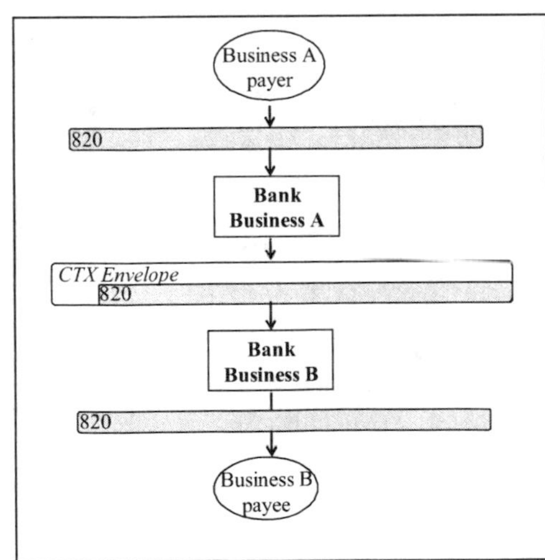

is not FEDI capable, then money can be transferred using one of the EFT formats. If the payee wants printed checks, then checks are printed and mailed to the payee. Additional options such as fax notifications, conversion of data to proprietary file formats and communications over the Internet are also available. As shown in Exhibit 14, Business A only needs to transmit 820 to VAB and further processing in the required format is carried out by VAB. This enables Business A not to worry about FEDI capabilities of the trading partners.

FEDI is also used in reengineering of work flows. Perhaps the most well-known example is Evaluated Receipts Settlement (ERS), also known as invoiceless process, self billing, pay-on-receipt or payment-from-receipt. ERS is used in manufacturing organizations and their suppliers; for example, automotive and electronics. ERS is based on a pre-negotiated price for goods and services. The price is conveyed using price lists or catalogs, or may form part of the written contract with an agreed-upon shelf life (30 or 60 days). A purchase order is generated by the purchaser that includes quantity, price, freight, tax and other relevant billing items, and then is submitted using EDI (other methods can be used). The supplier acknowledges receipt of the purchase order using ASN (856). The products are supplied using an itemized bill of lading (or packing slip) that contains references to the purchase order or contract. The bill of lading is validated by reconciling ASN with the purchase order.

If price can be gleaned from the purchase order, then the payment amount can be determined by reconciling the purchase order with the receiving report. In this case, the invoice becomes a redundant document and does not provide additional information. Once the quantity of goods is entered into the system, payment information can be generated using relevant data, such as prices, freight, taxes and so forth. JD Edwards' software factsheet claims that once you enter the receipt information the system will automatically create vouchers, edit and calculate taxes and discounts, and generate appropriate journal entries. The payment will be electronically transferred to the supplier's account. ERS eliminates non-value added activities and documents, and also reduces manual intervention.

EDI in the E-Era

EDI/XML

EDI, as a mature technology, enjoys a strong installed base and well-established standards. However, EDI is inflexible and static; if EDI standards do not meet a business need, there is no way to deviate from standards and still implement EDI. The standards only deal with data transfer; there is no mechanism to transfer processing rules and desired ancillary information. This, of course, gives rise to exacting procedures to map data from the company's database to the EDI standards and vice versa. Competing standards, ANSI X.12, EDIFACT and industry-specific standards, have caused fragmentation of the market. If a supplier following the ANSI X.12 standard decides to supply

Exhibit 16. Differences in EDI and XML

EDI	XML
1. Data is marked by using segments and elements.	1. Data is marked up by using tags.
2. Data elements can be numeric, decimal, identifier, string, and date or time; have a minimum and maximum length; and an indication whether the element is required or optional.	2. Data restricted to strings without format. However, standards are rapidly evolving in this area.
3. Segments names generally have three characters.	3. Tag names are not restricted in length.
4. Document structure is defined by message definition that is programmed in the software.	4. Document structure is described in the Schema that generally travels with the document.
5. Standards primarily defined ANSI X.12 and EDIFACT.	5. Multiple standard setters involved; standardization is just beginning.
6. Generally VANs used for data transfer and is not browser capable.	6. Can use the Internet and is browser capable.
7. Messages not human readable	7. Messages can be human readable.
8. EDI is optimized for data transfer.	8. XML is optimized for easy programming. Data transfer may require far more bandwidth than EDI.

goods to a company following EDIFACT standards, then that supplier may incur extra costs due to specialized translation software, training and/or developing interfaces. The Internet, compared to VANs, offers cheaper communication options that cannot be efficiently exploited by EDI in its current format. The complexity of EDI is reflected in the multi-year implementation cycles and its inability to penetrate small- and medium-size companies.

EDI needs to be updated for the Internet/e-commerce age. This updating ideally should preserve EDI's roots by providing backward compatibility and should give EDI wings by providing open standards, analytical capabilities and ease of use. Enter XML! The basic idea behind XML/EDI is to envelop EDI messages in the XML format. Exhibit 17 shows a rather simple example of *Address Segment* in the EDIFACT code and the related XML wrapper. XML can be used to develop DTDs or XML Schema for each EDI transaction. The EDI code now stands enveloped in the XML format, and XML carries additional information, such as style and formatting characteristics. The XML formatting information will allow the EDI information to be viewed by users in the exact required format, which may include an exact replica of a paper document or form such as order forms, catalogs or healthcare claims. This ability supports transfer of business documents and transaction-based information. On the other hand, the EDI-specific information can also be extracted from the XML format by use of programming languages such as JAVA; and can be accessed by machines for EDI processing.

The XML wrapper is just the beginning of XML/EDI. A standard infrastructure agreed upon by industry, government and standard-setting bodies needs to be developed. The evolution has begun, and the new conceptual framework proposes fusion of five different technologies to make EDI flexible and dynamic. These technologies are: XML, EDI, knowledge templates, software agents and global data repositories.

Exhibit 17. EDI message in XML format

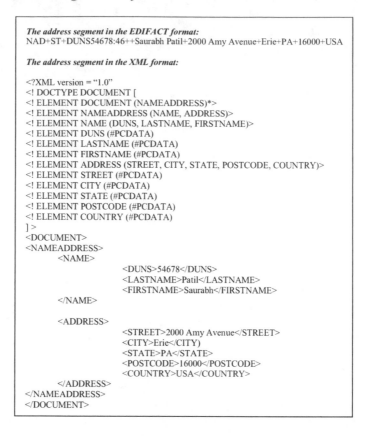

The address segment in the EDIFACT format:
NAD+ST+DUNS54678:46++Saurabh Patil+2000 Amy Avenue+Erie+PA+16000+USA

The address segment in the XML format:

```
<?XML version = "1.0"
<! DOCTYPE DOCUMENT [
<! ELEMENT DOCUMENT (NAMEADDRESS)*>
<! ELEMENT NAMEADDRESS (NAME, ADDRESS)>
<! ELEMENT NAME (DUNS, LASTNAME, FIRSTNAME)>
<! ELEMENT DUNS (#PCDATA)
<! ELEMENT LASTNAME (#PCDATA)
<! ELEMENT FIRSTNAME (#PCDATA)
<! ELEMENT ADDRESS (STREET, CITY, STATE, POSTCODE, COUNTRY)>
<! ELEMENT STREET (#PCDATA)
<! ELEMENT CITY (#PCDATA)
<! ELEMENT STATE (#PCDATA)
<! ELEMENT POSTCODE (#PCDATA)
<! ELEMENT COUNTRY (#PCDATA)
]>
<DOCUMENT>
<NAMEADDRESS>
        <NAME>
                    <DUNS>54678</DUNS>
                    <LASTNAME>Patil</LASTNAME>
                    <FIRSTNAME>Saurabh</FIRSTNAME>
        </NAME>

        <ADDRESS>
                    <STREET>2000 Amy Avenue</STREET>
                    <CITY>Erie</CITY)
                    <STATE>PA</STATE>
                    <POSTCODE>16000</POSTCODE>
                    <COUNTRY>USA</COUNTRY>
        </ADDRESS>
</NAMEADDRESS>
</DOCUMENT>
```

The foundation for this framework is provided by XML. The XML envelope empowers an EDI message. XML provides the syntax that transports data and related information across networks. EDI message identifiers can be supplemented or supplanted by XML. EDI formatting is preserved and transported in the XML envelope, providing complete backward compatibility. The existing investment and installed base remain protected. EDI data transfer, even in the XML envelope, is static, meaning only data is transferred, with no information about what to do with it. To make data dynamic and interactive, the receiver should be able to understand business concepts represented in the data stream and apply business-specific rules to that data for appropriate processing. This process is multifaceted and multi-layered. The incoming data must be analyzed to evaluate the role and syntax of each piece of the interchanged data, understand sequencing of the data stream, determine steps in the processing of data, call on the appropriate programs, move processed data from one stage to another and account for interactions of these different processes.

Knowledge templates and software agents can be used to deal with this complexity. Knowledge templates include rules for presentation and processing of data. These templates resemble a spreadsheet format in layout and are supplemented by DTDs. These

Exhibit 18. Convergence of XML and EDI

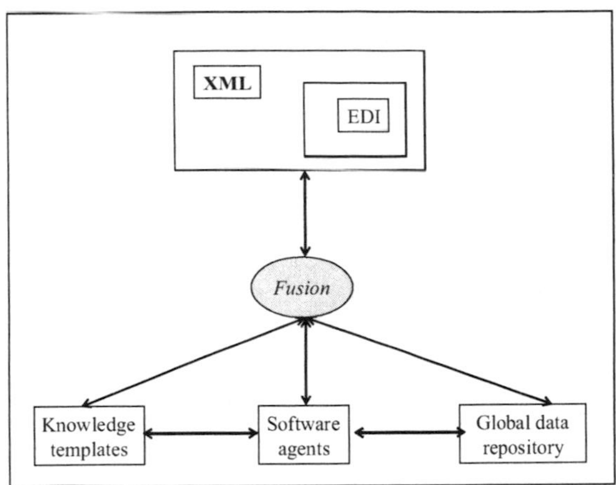

templates and DTDs enable understanding of different organizations' data, presentation of data in a format desired by the end user and identification of required processing of data. Software agents interpret templates to make out work requirements, can automatically create knowledge templates for new jobs and/or look up existing templates, and allow user requirements to be expressed in natural language terms. JAVA and ActiveX can be used to create software agents, and XML can be used to transport agents to the desired location. The global data repositories provide universally accepted definitions and descriptions of common business objects, DTDs, EDIFACT or ANSI X.12 dictionaries, and business rules and requirements for trading partners, industry, and federal and state governments. The purpose of a global data repository is to provide a semantic foundation for interacting businesses by allowing knowledge templates and software agents to automatically look up meanings and definitions of business documents, processes and rules.

The XML/EDI is a work in progress and can evolve in different and unpredictable directions. Primary research questions deal with how to faithfully represent EDI data in the XML format, how to build industrial strength intelligence in XML documents and how to develop universally acceptable definitions of various business documents and processes to be included in the global data repository. The XML/EDI Group is already proposing ideas and discussion papers on various standards involved. Developing XML/EDI will be a collaborative effort involving businesses, EDI and Internet standard-setting bodies, government and academic communities, and may continue for decades.

The successful XML/EDI combination should provide many benefits. These advantages include increased connectivity with different networks and less reliance on VANs, easy access to EDI messages via browser and the Internet, expanded character set and multilingual capabilities, elimination of translation software, and reduction in need for trading partner agreements. The primary disadvantage of XML is increased requirement for bandwidth. As seen previously, translation of one line of an address segment takes many lines in XML. Generally, bandwidth is not considered a constraining factor; however, if businesses start widely using XML/EDI, then consumption of bandwidth due to large XML files may cause unforeseen problems.

EDIINT

Traditionally, EDI messages trekked over VANs. This method provided needed security and control features — however, at premium prices. Initially, efforts were made to replace VANs with ISPs; this solution did not work very well, because of unresolved security problems. However, *EDIINT*, spearheaded by the IETF (*www.ietf.org/*), has spawned numerous initiatives to facilitate transfer of EDI messages over the Internet. EDIINT takes the EDI messages and transports them over the Internet and at the same time endeavors to provide VAN-level security and functionality. The primary objective of EDIINT is to increase the use of EDI by enabling small- and medium-size businesses to participate in EDI. This increase is to be achieved by use of the Internet in communicating EDI messages, simplifying implementation processes and making them cost-effective, and providing tools that make transfer of data transparent to the user.

EDIINT does not change the basic structure of EDI messages. EDIINT is a set of protocols that allows exchange of structured data such as EDI messages over the Internet. The protocols define how a legacy EDI message is wrapped into a Multipurpose Internet Mail Extensions (MIME) envelope, encrypted and transmitted over the Internet. The MIME envelope allows for transport of the EDI messages, proprietary file formats or Web forms formatted in HTML or XML. The encryption is done using Pretty Good Privacy (PGP) protocol or Secure/MIME (S/MIME) protocols, and the transmission protocol is TCP/IP. A connection method can be dial-up, point-to-point, VAN or the Internet.

The initial generation of data is identical in traditional EDI and EDIINT. Data is produced by business applications in the form of proprietary flat file formats and then get converted into ANSI X.12 or EDIFACT format by the translator software. The resulting EDI data

Exhibit 19. Differences in traditional EDI and EDIINT

	Traditional EDI	**EDIINT**
Formatting of the message	ANSI X.12 or EDIFACT	ANSI X.12 or EDIFACT Proprietary flat files, Web forms (HTML or XML)
Enveloping layer	X.12.5 Protocol for ANSI X.12 and ISO9735 for EDIFACT	MIME envelope on top of the EDI envelope, FTP, HTTP
Transport layer	VAN protocol, generally X.25 packet switching networks	TCP/IP
Physical layer	Direct connections Dial-up lines VANs	Direct connections, dial-up lines, VANs, the Internet

is generally enveloped by X.12.5 protocol in ANSI X.12 standard and ISO 9735 in EDIFACT standard. This envelope identifies sender, receiver, data content standard and version by assigning control numbers. These functions are performed on EDI Gateway. Gateway functions generally involve mapping, enveloping, de-enveloping, logging of transmission activity and communicating of the messages. If the EDI Gateway resides on another machine, a communications program takes data from machine to machine.

The EDI message then moves to the EDIINT server. This server takes the EDI file and formats it using S/MIME format as an S/MIME file. The sender's and receiver's addresses are converted from EDI to e-mail addresses, the message is encrypted and encoded, and then digitally signed. The EDI message is sent from the sender's EDIINT server to the Internet e-mail server as a secure e-mail attachment. The receiver's EDIINT server then decrypts the incoming messages and authenticates data by confirming data integrity. The S/MIME attachment gets decoded, the e-mail addresses get converted to EDI addresses, and the EDI message travels to the receiver's EDI Gateway. The EDI message then can be processed by business applications after passing through the translator. The transmission is logged at the EDI Gateway and also at the EDIINT server at both ends. If the receipt acknowledgement is received, it is processed; if it is not received, appropriate error messages are generated and corrective action is taken.

There are numerous other variations of the EDIINT scheme. For example, a rather simple method is to use Web forms formatted using HTML or XML; this method is sometimes referred to as Web-EDI or lite EDI. This variation is useful where trading partners are small and have no desire to invest in EDI. Here, the trading partner accesses the Web server of the EDI-enabled partner. The Web server contains several business documents, such as purchase orders as *forms*. These forms look like their printed counterparts. The Web

Exhibit 20. Traditional EDI message over the Internet

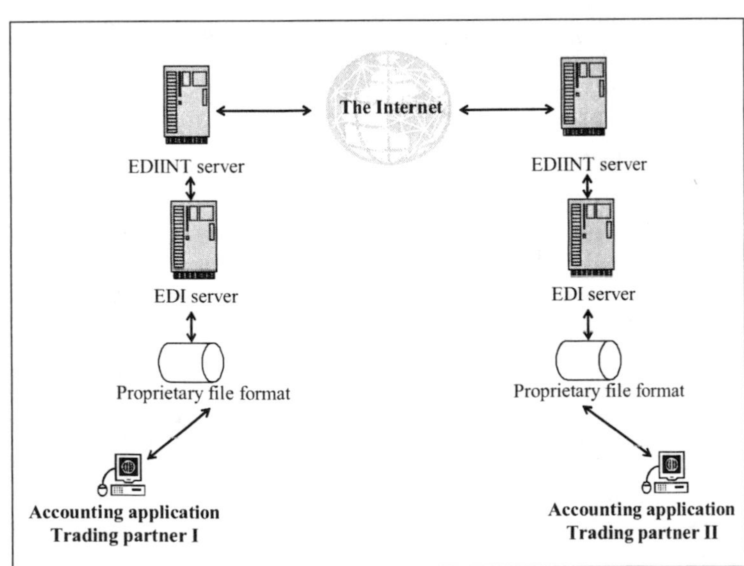

Exhibit 21. Web forms and EDI

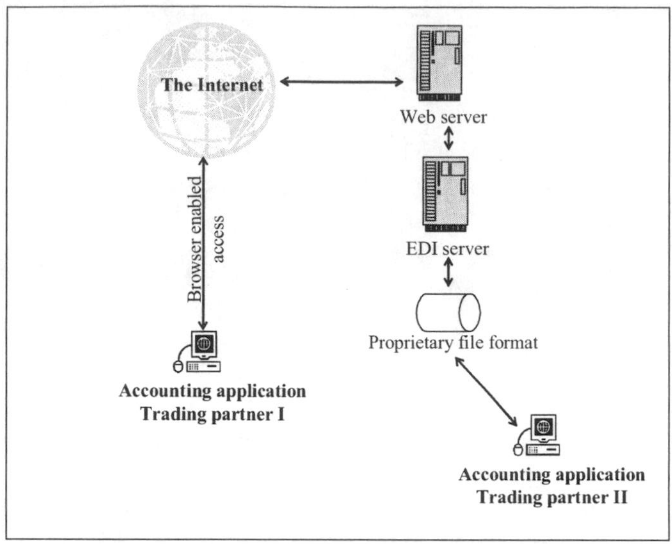

server can be accessed via standard browser over telephone lines. The trading partner logs onto the Web server and fills in relevant forms. Once a form is submitted, the server side programs (generally written in JAVA or Active X) package the form in the EDI-type message. This message then moves on to the EDI translator and is translated into a proprietary format and processed by the accounting system.

Several reasons exist for why incoming forms are packaged as EDI messages and are not directly integrated with the back-office system. First, if EDI is installed and operational, then the organization already has a robust and well-tested interface. This interface has been tested for necessary functionality and integrated with the accounting system; plus, the necessary investment has already been made. Second, the existing EDI applications have the required security and controls. Finally, it avoids the extra cost associated with new interfaces, new programs and new security features.

This EDI method involves investment in EDI only on the part of the dominant trading partner. The small trading partners can participate in the business simply by using browser and phone lines. However, the main disadvantage is that the small trading partners do not have back-office integration with the EDI system. The full benefits of EDI, of course, are not available in such circumstances. Human intervention on the small trading partner's site can delay the entire process. And, if incoming orders are printed and processed, then we are again looking at a fax-to-EDI-to-fax type scenario with all its inherent disadvantages.

IBM (*www.ibm.com*) offers services to small businesses to become EDI capable through what is called *Web Data Transfer* and *Forms Exchange.* This service was spun off in 2004; however, this application is very interesting and worthy of study. Web Data Transfer allows for exchange of EDI and non-EDI files between trading partners through a Web

Exhibit 22. IBM solution for Web forms/orders

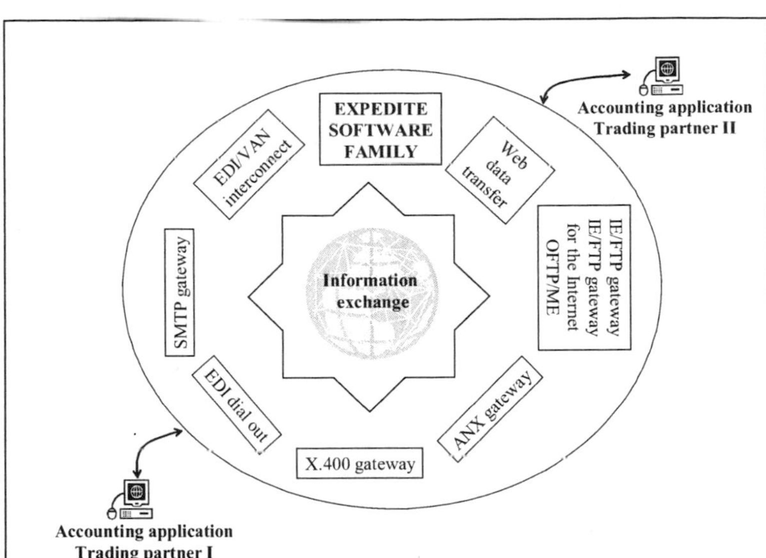

browser and Internet connection. File formats such as EDI, binary, text or XML can be exchanged, and proprietary file formats, such as Excel, can be automatically converted into EDI format. Forms Exchange provides for exchange of electronic forms, including EDI- and XML-formatted forms such as orders and invoices, using a browser and Internet connection. Forms can include data entry forms such as purchase order, invoices and ship notices; presentation forms such as (again) purchase orders, invoices, and ship notices that need to be viewed and printed; and turnaround forms, such as ship notices generated in response to a purchase order. The trading partner can send and receive Web-based electronic forms, upload and download forms from accounting software (the service even supports QuickBooks and Peachtree) and respond to the trading partners.

The infrastructure for these services is provided and hosted by IBM and is called *information exchange*. This infrastructure and related MQSeries software provide for in-network translation of Web-based forms into EDI, XML or another format as desired by the trading partners. Like VANs, IBM also provides mailboxes (in and out) to the trading partners. *Information exchange* is not only an EDI solution, but it also provides an array of e-business solutions and, according to IBM claims, provides a reliable infrastructure for those solutions. The essential components of this information exchange are described below:

- **Expedite family of products:** This family of software products is primarily installed on the client side; that is, trading partners will have this software installed on their machines. The software supports a variety of operating software and hardware platforms, facilitates interface with accounting software, and manages notifications and communications of electronic messages.

- **EDI VAN interconnect:** If the trading partners use other VANs, then this software manages connections with IBM and other service providers.
- **SMTP gateway:** The Simple Mail Transfer Protocol (SMTP) gateway allows use of the Internet in transferring EDI and non-EDI files.
- **EDI dial Out:** This feature enables EDI-formatted data to be transferred to trading partners who do not use the Information Exchange services of IBM.
- **X.400 gateway:** This enables users of X.400 (a standard messaging protocol that allows data to travel over different networks) to exchange data with non-users of X.400 and vice versa.
- **ANX gateway:** The Advanced Network exchange (ANX) is a private network preferred by the automotive industry. The ANX gateway allows ANX-enabled and ANX non-enabled users to exchange data, with or without being an ANX subscriber.
- **IE/FTP gateway and IE/FTP gateway for the Internet:** These gateways allow information exchange subscribers to send and receive files over VANs and the Internet. If the data transfer is over the Internet, then audit trail information, backups and listings of the mailbox contents are provided. Standard Internet security protocols and encryption of files are used for authentication, data confidentiality and data integrity.
- **OFTP/IE:** This provides an interface between the *Organization for Data Exchange through Transmission* (ODETTE; used by European Motor Manufacturers) file transfer protocol and Information exchange services. This interface enables to and fro transmission of ODETTE data and Information Exchange data.
- **Web data transfer:** This is an entry-level Web solution that was described earlier.

IBM staked out e-business as a core service area just before e-business became a buzzword. But IBM is not the only solution provider in this area. The majority of ERP vendors have a full e-business functionality built into their products. Even medium- and small-accounting software manufacturers have built-in EDI support. However, IBM's solution is comprehensive and makes an excellent illustration for changes sweeping the EDI landscape.

Internal Controls in EDI

Evaluation of internal controls in the EDI environment encompasses technical, legal and audit considerations (Control techniques mentioned in this section are covered in detail in Chapter 10). The basic areas that should be covered include effects of automation, trading partner agreements, the EDI software and its interface with the accounting system, and the communication system. In security terms, we can classify these considerations as validity of transactions, mutual authentication of identity, end-to-end data integrity and confidentiality, non-repudiation of origins, auditability of transactions and backups for the system. The areas are not mutually exclusive, and EDI controls often times apply to more than one area.

- **Validity of transactions:** The primary question in EDI is the legal status of transactions, since the transactions occur without a manual authenticating signature. This question arose since commercial law was vague on various points such as electronic offer and acceptance, propriety of paperless transactions, competency and sufficiency of electronic evidence, and electronic audit trails and record retention, among other things. The UCC requires that the contract be signed and in writing if it involves sale of goods for more than $500. The signature authenticates the document, verifies origin of the document and makes enforcement of the contract possible. EDI transactions are not in writing nor do they contain any signature. Trading partner agreements attempted to rectify the situation by addressing some of these concerns in a bilateral framework. These agreements outline a mutually acceptable method of authentication such as digital signatures, passwords that allow access to each others' systems or any other method. For example, one way to bypass the problem is to send a blanket purchase order to trading partners at the beginning of the year; manually signed by a proper authority. The EDI purchase orders for the entire year then can be considered releases against the blanket purchase order and, as such, legally valid. The review of legal literature indicates that trading partner agreements are enforceable and will be upheld by courts.
- **Mutual authentication of identity:** Authentication is the process of verifying identity of the transacting party. It involves determining whether someone or something is, in fact, who or what it is declared to be. Authentication of identity has two facets: identity of the machines and identity of the humans operating the machine. The methods of authenticating machines depend on the manner of connection. If the partners connect using dedicated, secured lines, then the issue of authentication does not arise, since the connected machines do not change. In case of dial-up modems, VAN connection authentication can be carried out by means of static or dynamic passwords or personal identification numbers (PINs), passwords or PINs and security tokens, automatic callbacks and biometric techniques. The use of digital certificates is also increasingly common. A digital certificate establishes credentials of the transacting partner, is issued by a third party called the certificate authority, and uses encryption and digital signatures to establish identity.

  Establishing identity of a human at the machine end is primarily a matter of intra-organizational controls. It requires review of access controls and separation of duties within the organization. The human user is identified by something the user knows, carries or something about the user. These criteria include passwords, ID cards or biometric measures such as fingerprints. The internal controls in these areas should be reviewed. At a minimum, EDI access should be restricted and the system should employ log-on authentication. Another layer of control is generation of a functional acknowledgment. This serves as a receipt of the message and if the original message is not generated by the trading partner, then he/she will be alerted to the fact that an unauthorized transaction has taken place.

- *Data integrity and confidentiality:* Data integrity refers to the transfer of data without any modification, intentional or unintentional, in the transit. Data confidentiality refers to inability of unauthorized parties to access data. The standard controls that address these two concerns are listed below.
- *Encryption:* This process transfers text messages into a cipher or coded text that cannot be read by unauthorized users. A password or a key is needed to decrypt the file. There are many encryption algorithms of varying strength. The strength of encryption used in EDI depends on security concerns of the involved organizations.
- *Security algorithms:* Various algorithms exist to protect network communications, such as echo check, parity check or message sequence numbering, or request response techniques. A checksum value may be employed to seal the message that indicates that contents of the message have not been altered.
- *Communication protocols:* If the Internet is used for transmission, then standard Internet protocols such as Secure Sockets Layer (SSL) or S/MIME can be used to protect data integrity and confidentiality.

EDI translator packages reject messages that do not comply with EDI standards. The rejected messages, whether incoming or outgoing, should be collected in a separate file and analyzed carefully. The translation software also allows for on-screen error detection and correction facilities. These should be used with care, and additional errors due to manual intervention should be avoided. The trading partners' agreements generally cover these security procedures and should be reviewed.

Other potential problems exist in this area. For example, messages can be delayed in transit, can be misrouted or can be inadvertently sent twice or more. If the message is delayed or misrouted, the entire supply chain can get disrupted. Technical solutions can be useful to some extent. Most of the trading partners' agreements have procedures to deal with such a situation. However, VAN security has been quite effective and these problems have not figured in EDI. The trading partners' agreements also cover audits of VANs by mutually acceptable auditors.

However, precautions need to be taken against human error. If the same message is sent twice, it might be processed twice, causing loss to both parties. If the message contains errors, it might be processed with those errors. These errors are especially plausible in stand-alone translator systems. The operators should have appropriate training and education. The EDI system should also be physically isolated and/or should have log-on access controls.

- **Non-repudiation of origins:** Non-repudiation refers to proof that an electronic document was sent by the sender and received by the receiver. The three aspects of non-repudiation are: non-repudiation of origin, of receipt and of submission. Non-repudiation covers the problem of post facto denial of the electronic transaction by the transacting parties. First, it proves that the transaction took place;

second, it establishes identity of the transacting parties. The various controls that address non-repudiation can be summarized as follows.

- Digital signatures that accompany the electronic document for authentication purposes can also be useful for non-repudiation purposes; since digital signatures prove that the transaction was authorized and generated from a specific source.
- The EDI software generates automatic functional acknowledgment when the EDI message is received. VANs also provide automatic acknowledgments for messages sent and received. These acknowledgments, along with the generation of functional acknowledgments by the EDI software, serve to provide proof that the document was received.
- The use of digital certificates also serves to verify origin and receipt of the electronic document. The certificate authority keeps a time stamped and signed record of transmissions, along with the identities of the sender and receiver.
- Protocols like SSL authenticate connecting computers via public key handshake at the beginning of a secure session. If the transaction takes place over the Internet, then communication protocols such as SSL can provide assurance regarding origin and receipt of the electronic transaction.
- In case of VAN, the administrator keeps a log of documents delivered to and from each mailbox. This audit log also serves as a non-repudiation source.

- **Auditability of transactions:** Auditability of transactions refers to existence of an audit trail and ability to verify past transactions. The issues concerning validation, control and recording of transactions are dealt with earlier. The issue of an audit trail is considered below in *Backups*. However, the following questions need to be asked concerning auditability of transactions.
  - Has each EDI message received and sent been preserved?
  - What is the medium of storage? What are access controls over such storage medium? Is there a clear separation of duties for generation, maintenance and update of this storage medium?
  - Have the EDI messages been formatted, altered or changed in any way before storage? If yes, can original messages be recreated?
  - What are the controls for rejected or corrupted incoming and outgoing messages? Are error files preserved? Who has the authority to rectify errors and resubmit transmissions?
  - Have error detection and correction facilities in the translator program been verified (by the user, third-party or vendor)?
  - Do stored records contain authentication stamps and/or digital signatures?
  - Have records of how messages were sent, received and transferred through networks been preserved?
  - How long will EDI records be kept?
  - In case of the VAN, are audit reports by a third party available?

- **Backups:** Once the organization starts using EDI, especially integrated EDI, then business workflows are severely disrupted if the EDI software or communication network fails. The following questions are useful whether the company has a direct connection or transacts business via VAN.
    - What is the frequency and length of time of service outages?
    - What is the status of the back-up system?
    - How long does it take to activate back-up systems?
    - In case of failure, is the incoming data archived? How it is stored? How can the archived data be accessed?
    - What is the division of responsibilities for data lost in transmission?
    - What is the disaster recovery or business continuity plan? Is a copy available?
    - What kind of back-up systems does the VAN have for its phone lines and power supply?
    - In case of VAN, are audit reports by the third party available?

There is no such thing as absolute security, and even security policies are subject to cost benefit analysis. EDI, when properly programmed, runs by itself. The majority of controls is automated and shall work as programmed. VANs have been handling data for financial institutions and governments for a long time and, as such, have developed a high level of security. Generally, problems with VAN security have been few and far between. The primary problems exist in the areas of disruption of networks, manual intervention in the system and legal problems arising out of trading partners' agreements. The review of business continuity plans, organizational security policies and trading partners' agreements should cover these critical areas.

Benefits and Costs of EDI

EDI replaces paper via electronic transactions, thereby changing the nature of the workflows. The implementation of EDI takes multiple years, and significant benefits start flowing only after several years. EDI, like any complex technological solution, imposes costs and delivers benefits to the adopter; these are difficult to quantify due to intricacies of EDI projects. A summary of these benefits and costs is provided below.

Benefits

- **Customer service:** Many companies have adopted EDI after an important customer, such as WalMart or GM, has asked them to be EDI capable. If the business has significant dealings with these giant corporations, they get to keep the customer and stand to gain added business through increased efficiencies.

EDI allows a company to fulfill orders faster and accurately. However, research also indicates that cost justification of such improvements is very difficult, causing many companies to ignore a formal cost-benefit analysis. EDI is often justified on the basis of commitments to customers and differentiation of services and products.

- **Data accuracy:** Research indicates that EDI improves accuracy of data by reducing manual and other types of errors. For example, a distributor in the grocery industry reduced the invoice error rate from 20% to 1% and reduced the staff from 50 to less than five. Other examples include reductions in returned shipments, reductions in purchase order errors and optimization of transportation costs in the high-tech and pharmaceutical industries.
- **Decrease in cycle time:** Time between orders-to-cash may also decrease due to EDI. The paper-based system adds days before an invoice is ready, error rates that cause delay in payment increase, and paper checks take time to reach their destination. EDI automates the entire process; thus, as product delivery occurs, the invoice is sent to the customer. If FEDI is also used, then payments can also be received faster. However, delivery of payments is based on agreements with trading partners, and speedy delivery of the payments is not guaranteed. For example, GM used to pay electronically 3 days after the due date on the payment. These 3 days represented delay in the mail. Sears also had similar policies. However, faster billing at least eliminates delays on the part of the supplier.
- **Decrease in costs:** EDI accelerates reordering, and due to quick partner response, decreases uncertainty in reordering. This has significant effect on the safety stock hold by the corporation. Inventory levels can be lowered without adding risk. For example, Pacific Bell used EDI and an inventory management system to reduce parts handling warehouses from 19 to two, maintaining the same level of service and realizing substantial savings.

  EDI also decreases the need for personnel due to automation of processes, realizing labor savings. Additionally, EDI eliminates or at least reduces paper handling, storage, retrieval and mailing costs.
- **Improvements in existing workflows:** EDI can improve productivity of the existing workforce. For example, a large metal fabricator employed buyers for its purchase function, and productivity of those buyers soared after EDI, since each buyer was able to handle more accounts and spend more time on the buying process. Sales and purchases information is now available in digital format, and can be used for managerial analyses. For example, in the late 1990s, K Mart was able to analyze sales information according to the region, metropolitan area, population density and other desired dimensions. This application is a precursor to full-blown CRM applications discussed in the revenue cycle.

  EDI might also be useful in auditing applications. Matching of invoice and payment can be done electronically, and the entire population can be covered. Universal computerization of accounting systems and automated auditing software, of course, makes this possible in the majority of cases.

Costs

- **Upfront costs:** The upfront costs of EDI can be summarized as follows.
  - *Hardware costs*: These costs depend on the existing infrastructure. EDI hardware includes personal computers, modems or dedicated lines for connecting with trading partners. Most businesses have this infrastructure and do not need to buy additional hardware.
  - *Software costs:* Software costs involve costs of translation and communications software. It can be off-the-shelf software used standalone or integrated with the existing system; or a new EDI-integrated system can replace a legacy system. The costs can vary from a few hundred dollars to tens of thousands of dollars, depending on the complexity of EDI implementation. However, EDI is a mature technology; powerful products and knowledge pools currently exist and can make the transition smoother.

    If EDI translator packages are purchased separately, then the existing systems need to be modified. The interfaces need to be rewritten, data need to be mapped from the existing accounting database format to the translator format, or data may need to be collected that is not collected in the existing system. If new data needs to be collected, the generation, processing and storage costs of this data need to be factored in. The software design, programming and testing are unique to each company.
  - *Changes in existing workflows:* As mentioned earlier, EDI can improve productivity of the existing workforce. To realize this potential, existing workflows and job descriptions need to be analyzed and redesigned to take advantage of EDI characteristics such as instantaneous availability of information, slicing and dicing of electronic information using reporting tools, and also possibilities of errors in the EDI system. These changes cost money due to disruption of the existing system, uncertainty caused by introduction of a new technology, and training and education.
  - *Training costs:* If EDI expertise does not exist in the company or new systems are being introduced, then a significant amount needs to be spent in training and education of personnel. Research indicates that these costs include systems design or re-design, training seminars, standards adoption, purchasing and distribution of purchasing manuals and user guides, establishing internal procedures and controls, and involvement in industry associations.
  - *Trading partner costs:* If a company is rolling out EDI and expects its trading partners to do the same, then it needs to sell the program to other partners. EDI is a high fixed-cost venture, and is not profitable until adopted by a critical mass of partners. Marketing and promotional costs can take various forms; for example, having a presence in trade shows, advertising of EDI capabilities, consulting for trading partners and, in some cases, buying hardware and software for partners. Negotiating formal or informal trading agreements can consume valuable managerial time. Small trading partners may also need continuing assistance for maintaining and expanding EDI.

- **Recurring costs**
  - *Administration costs:* Once the EDI system is in place, it does not need a great deal of attention. However, monitoring oEDI messages, error corrections and exception handling, program updates and maintenance, EDI standard and format changes and so forth are some continuing activities that cost money.
  - *Communication costs:* Communication costs depend on the method of data transfer. In case of leased lines, monthly fixed charges need to be paid. VAN charges depend on variables and can be confusing. These charges are based on certain monthly minimum and per-character charges; for example, $XX per month (2-year minimum) and $X per megabyte of data received and sent. Additionally, there can be a one-time connect charge. Trading partners may use different VANs, and there can be additional charges as messages are routed over different networks.
  - *Duplication of procedures:* If all trading partners are not EDI capable, the organization needs to maintain dual procedures to accommodate data flows. The need to maintain EDI- and paper-based transactions systems imposes recurring additional costs.

Estimating EDI benefits and costs is extremely difficult. There is no agreed magic formula, and different companies use different techniques to make estimates. The benefits are hard to quantify, and costs can vary from several thousand to millions of dollars. In many cases, the decision is made on the basis of faith. EDI Research Inc. conducted a survey in 1990, asking respondents to rank EDI benefits. The ranking obtained was:

1 Improved accuracy of data
2 Improved customer service
3 Reduced clerical errors
4 Faster access to information
5 Decreased delivery time
6 Decreased administrative time
7 Improved cash management and payment practices
8 Lower inventory costs

The survey also noted that the payback period for EDI projects was estimated to be 2.5 years; however, EDI projects were *not* mainly justified on a cost basis, and estimated cost savings realized by EDI implementers were primarily guesstimates.

Looking Ahead

In 1998, the estimated EDI global revenue — that includes hardware, software, services and communication charges — was estimated to be $12 billion. Globally, approximately 350,000 organizations were involved in EDI; in the U.S., approximately 6% of the 10 million U.S. companies are EDI capable. Thomson EC Resources EDI forecast indicated that EDI will continue to grow at the rate of 18% from 1997 to 2002. By 2000, EDI was expected to surpass paper as a most important mode of information exchange for large- and medium-sized businesses. And some estimates put EDI transactions at $1 trillion by 2003. The accuracy of these forecasts can only be ascertained down the road. The installed base, robust operations and heavy investments continue to keep EDI a viable business operation.

The e-revolution has refined EDI by throwing up open standards, using the Internet in communications and providing alternate means of EDI for small businesses. Trends that outline the future of EDI are slowly emerging. Experts seem to agree that influence of XML, Web-based EDI and low-cost EDI solutions will be most important in the coming days. The use of XML has the most promise of changing inflexible and static EDI structures and making them flexible and dynamic. This concept is immensely appealing, but successful execution remains an issue. The XML-based infrastructures are in infancy and may take years before they acquire industrial strength. The majority of businesses are taking baby steps as they test the new and unproven technology and are in no hurry to tear down the existing EDI structures.

Until 1998, approximately 95% of EDI traffic was on VANs. The percentage was expected to drop to below 50% in 5 years, as the Internet was being increasingly used for transferring EDI messages. Advances in the security and stability of the Internet have accelerated the pace. Businesses are attracted to this area since it promises immediate cost reductions. The use of VANs will not disappear, since VANs have been aggressively pricing their services and many businesses still do not trust the open infrastructure of the Internet.

Penetration of EDI in small- and medium-size businesses remains a concern. The browser-based or form-based solutions, as the one offered by IBM, are fast becoming cheaper alternatives to traditional EDI. These alternatives offer EDI benefits to all trading partners. Bigger partners can get all suppliers on board while smaller partners can have benefits of EDI; and it may also encourage many smaller businesses to trade with larger enterprises.

Summary

This chapter provides a comprehensive introduction to EDI. Accounting and finance departments are intimately involved with the implementation of EDI and FEDI, and aspiring accountants need to understand the fundamentals of this technology. The origins of EDI date back to the idea of standard manifest floated during the Berlin Airlift.

Today, EDI has strict standards of data formatting and data transmission that differentiate EDI from fax and e-mail. EDI standards are maintained by two main organizations — ANSI X.12, primarily used in the U.S.; and EDIFACT, primarily used in Europe (it has also gained international acceptance).

The infrastructure for EDI includes translation software that translates incoming EDI messages into proprietary data format and vice versa, communication software that transmits data over VANs or the Internet, associated security measures and trading agreements that define rules of the game. The majority of the medium and almost all large accounting software vendors offer EDI functionality, either integrated or available via third party.

EDI can also be used to transmit payments and other payment-related information, and this version is called FEDI. Banks have been using EFT by employing FedWire, CHIPS, SWIFT and ACH to transfer funds between themselves for the last several decades. FEDI formats, such as 820, are increasingly supported by the proprietary bank formats. FEDI closes the EDI loop by automating the entire process. FEDI penetration is slow because of technological problems giving rise to various types of paper and EFT, paper and FEDI, and pure FEDI processes. FEDI has been used extensively in reengineering of purchasing and accounts payable functions by large corporations.

EDI is being increasingly transformed by applications of XML and the Internet, which promise to add previously unthinkable functionality to EDI and a vastly reduced cost of transmissions. However, both these approaches are experimental and need a lot of work before being widely accepted. These two trends according to most experts will most influence the EDI future. EDI in any format provides robust security features for validity of transactions, mutual authentication of identity, data integrity and confidentiality, non-repudiation of origins, auditability of transactions and backups.

Benefits of EDI include improved customer service, increased data accuracy, decreased cycle time, decreased transaction costs and improvements in existing workflows. There are, of course, upfront costs such as hardware, software, changes in existing workflows, training costs and trading partner costs; and recurring costs, such as administration and maintenance costs. The estimates of upfront costs vary from tens of thousands to millions of dollars, depending on the intensity of the EDI project.

EDI continues to evolve and change. EDI is becoming cheaper and more capable with every iteration. There are formidable problems in developing new frameworks and paradigms; however, the work continues. The basic promise of EDI is to lower costs and cycle time. These objectives remain relevant in every business age. The installed base and heavy investments promise that EDI will be with us for a long time.

References

Albright, B. (2003, March). EDI for the masses. *Frontline Solutions*, *3*, 12-13.

Batson, B. (1997). *EDI and the Internet*. Texas Instruments. Retrieved February 7, 2003, from www.ti.com/sc/docs/scedi/new/batson.htm

Bednarz, A. (2002, February 18). EDI service providers expand range. *Network World*, 27-28.

Bragg, S. (1997). *Advanced accounting systems*. Altamonte Springs: The Institute of Internal Auditors.

Copeland, K., & Hwang, J. (2001). *Electronic data interchange: Concepts and effects*. Internet Society. Retrieved February 7, 2003, from www.isoc.org/inet97/proceedings/C5/C5_1.HTM

Electronics Industry Data Exchange Association. (n.d.). *EIDX business models for electronic business*. Retrieved February 9, 2003, from www.eidx.org/

Evaluated receipts settlements and tax compliance: A report of the steering committee task force on EDI audit and legal issues for tax administration. (2001). Federation of Tax Administrators. Retrieved February 10, 2003, from www.taxadmin.org/fta/ftapub.html

Ferguson, D. (2000a). Financial EDI: A required business practice before the turn of the century. *EDI Forum: The Journal of Electronic Data Interchange*. Reprinted in *Fundamentals of Electronic Commerce Handout, Proceedings of Financial Electronic Commerce Conference*, April, Chicago.

Ferguson, D. (2000b). The real facts of EDI in 1997. Thomson EC Resources. Reprinted in *Fundamentals of Electronic Commerce Handout, Proceedings of Financial Electronic Commerce Conference*, April, Chicago.

Forms exchange and Web data transfer user's guide. (2001). IBM. Retrieved February 10, 2003, from www.ibm.com/services/interchange/

Freibrun, E. (2001). *Electronic data interchange and the law*. Eric S. Freibrun, Ltd. Retrieved February 10, 2003, from www.freibrunlaw.com/articles/artic13.htm/

Grannan, P. (1997, November). Electronic commerce today: Financial EDI solutions for tomorrow. *Management Accounting*, 38-41.

Grant, C., & Ferguson, D. (2000). EDI is not a "dead man walking!" *The Journal of Electronic Commerce*. Reprinted in *Fundamentals of Electronic Commerce Handout, Proceedings of Financial Electronic Commerce Conference*, April, Chicago.

Guidelines for using XML for electronic data interchange. (2002). GeoCities. Retrieved February 10, 2003, from www.geocities.com/WallStreet/Floor/5815/guide.htm/

Hill, N., & Ferguson, D. (1989, March). Electronic data interchange: A definition and perspective. *EDI Forum: The Journal of Electronic Data Interchange*, 5-12.

Hill, N., & Ferguson, D. (2000a). Electronic data interchange and electronic funds transfer: The basics. *EDI Forum: The Journal of Electronic Data Interchange*. Reprinted in *Fundamentals of Electronic Commerce Handout, Proceedings of Financial Electronic Commerce Conference*, April, Chicago.

Hill, N., & Ferguson, D. (2000b). Introduction to EFT and financial EDI. *EDI Forum: The Journal of Electronic Data Interchange*. Reprinted in *Fundamentals of Electronic Commerce Handout, Proceedings of Financial Electronic Commerce Conference*, April, Chicago.

Hill, N., & Ferguson, D. (2000c). The EDI revolution and bank strategy. *EDI Forum: The Journal of Electronic Data Interchange*. Reprinted in *Fundamentals of Electronic Commerce Handout, Proceedings of Financial Electronic Commerce Conference*, April, Chicago.

Hruska. (1995). The Internet: A strategic backbone for EDI? *EDI Forum*, *8*(4), 83-85.

Introducing IBM interchange services for e-business. (2001). IBM. Retrieved February 10, 2003, from www.ibm.com/services/interchange/

Krizner, K. (2001). Web interface extends value of EDI investment for automotive supplier. *Frontline Solutions*, *2*, 16-21.

Macola Software. (2001). *Macola's Electronic Data Interchange white paper* [Progression Series 7.5]. Exact America. Retrieved December 9, 2002, from http://exactamerica.com/macola/

Mak, H., & Johnston, R. (2000). Tools for implementing EDI over the Internet. *The Journal of Electronic Commerce*. Reprinted in *Fundamentals of Electronic Commerce Conference, Proceedings of Financial Electronic Commerce Conference*.

Marchal, B. (2001). *Electronic data interchange on the Internet*. NetScape. Retrieved February 10, 2003, from http://developer.netscape.com/viewsource/marchal_edata.htm/

Mason, D. (1990). The state of U.S. EDI: 1990. *EDI Forum: The Journal of Electronic Data Interchange*, *1*, 17-25.

Millman, H. (1998). A brief history of EDI. *InfoWorld*, *20*(14), 83.

Montana, J. (n.d.). *Legal issues in EDI*. Retrieved February 12, 2003, from http://xnet.rrc.mb.ca/recmgmt/articles/article20.htm/

Peat, B., & Webber, D. (1997). *Introducing XML/EDI – The eBusiness frameworks*. Retrieved February 12, 2003, from www.geocities.com/WallStreet/Floor/5815/start.htm/

Pushkin, A., & Morris, B. (1997, November). Understanding financial EDI. *Management Accounting*, 42-46.

Roche, T. (2001). *How to avoid legal disputes arising out of Electronic Data Interchange – The EDI trading partner agreement*. KK&R Law Firm. Retrieved February 13, 2003, from www.kkrlaw.com/articles/edi/htm/

Sawabini, S. (2001, January/February). EDI and the Internet. *The Journal of Business Strategy*, 41-43.

Scala, & McGrath. (1993). Advantages and disadvantages of electronic data interchange. *Information and Management*, *25*, 85-91.

Stultz, A., & Sigler, K. (2001). *Demystifying EDI*. Plano, TX: Wordware Publishing, Inc.

The future of EDI in business-to-business electronic commerce (white paper). (2001). ZDNet. Retrieved February 13, 2003, from http://whitepapers.zdnet.co.uk/0,39025945,60029473p-39000529q,00.htm

Trombly, M. (2001, April 9). Automated clearing house. *ComputerWorld*, 44.

Utility industry group implementation guideline for EDI. (2002). The Utility Industry Group. Retrieved February 13, 2003, from www.uig.org/guide/chapter3.htm/

Varon, E. (2001). The once and future EDI. *CIO*. Retrieved February 13, 2003, from www.cio.com/archive/ec_future_edi.html

Vollmer, K. (2001). The Internet will determine the future of EDI. *Internet Week*. Retrieved February 13, 2003, from www.internetweek.com/columns01/beat/720001.htm/

Chapter V

The Revenue Cycle

Revenue Cycle Activities

The revenue cycle deals with the delivery of products or services to customers and consequent collection of cash from customers. The standard transaction flow in the revenue cycle can be characterized as follows: sales order comes in from the customer; credit department approves credit; warehouse assesses the inventory and releases goods; shipping department ships the goods; the customer is billed based on the sales order and shipping documents; and eventually cash is collected from the customer. Traditionally, the sales department received sales orders by paper, fax, EDI and, sometimes, even verbally. The incoming sales order is in fact a purchase order from the customer, often times in the customer company document format. The purchase order then gets converted to the standard sales order and processed. If an order arrives through EDI, then purchase and sales order formats are pre-approved and based on partner agreements. The majority of companies will input the sales order in their accounting system. It will be routed to the credit department for credit approval. The credit will be approved based on prior history of the customer or, if the customer is new, by obtaining relevant credit information. The approved sales order will be forwarded to the warehouse. Here, inventory availability will be checked, goods will be released and stock release documents will be generated. The shipping department will ship goods when those arrive on the shipping docks. The documents involved are a shipping notice and bill of lading.

Exhibit 1. The revenue cycle

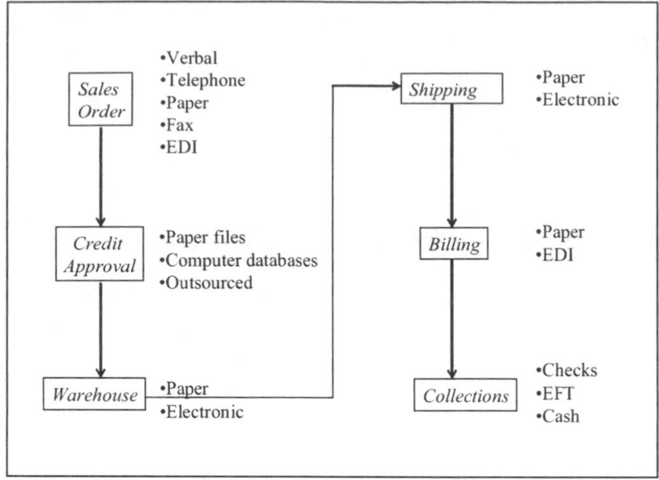

The billing department receives copies of the sales order, the approved sales order, stock release and shipping notice. The billing department will then reconcile these documents and bill the customer. The entry will be made in the accounts receivable journal and, subsequently, summary totals transferred to the general ledger.

The collection process begins with check and remittance advice, which contains payment-related information, coming to the mail room. These two are separated and the check and remittance list (a list of all received checks) goes to the cash receipts department. The check is deposited and the remittance list and remittance advice are forwarded to the accounts receivable department. An entry is made in the accounts receivable ledger and the summary totals are forwarded to the general ledger. Internal control measures include comparing bank deposits with the summary totals of the accounts receivable ledger and bank reconciliations.

General activities in the revenue cycle are easy to describe; however, there is no standard processing set up for these activities. The types of documents involved, processing methods, billing methods, internal controls and collection methods vary depending on the technology, industry and market focus of the involved businesses. The sophistication of the accounting software package or ERP system, extent of the integration among homegrown legacy systems and accounting software, and extent of the coordination among departments are also some deciding factors. The practices range from manual documents to highly automated, Web-enabled methods. Of course, no one solution is right for all companies.

The Internet and ERP have injected many changes in the revenue cycle. Sales orders can arrive on the Web through EDI, B2B or B2C storefronts, online exchanges, CRM or Sales Force Automation (SFA) software. In the cases of sales orders that need credit decisions in a few minutes, Web-based credit services offer automation of the entire credit approval process. Picking items in the warehouse is controlled by sophisticated WMSs, some of

Exhibit 2. E-changes in the revenue cycle

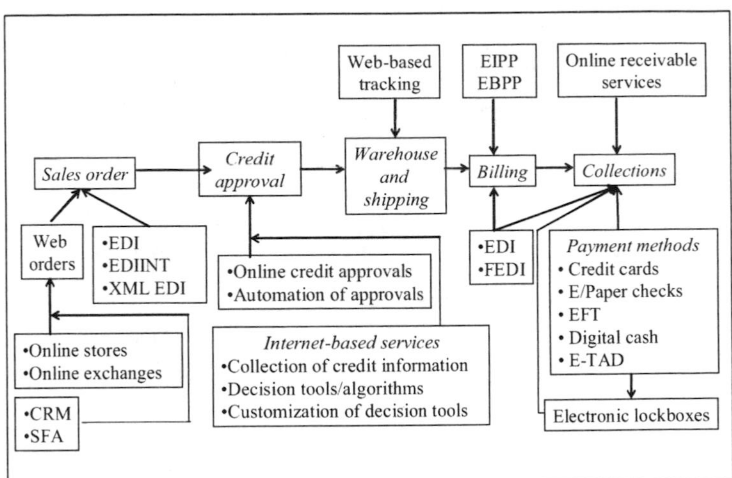

which are Web-enabled. Shipments can be tracked or monitored using the Internet. The billing function can be handled as Electronic Invoice Presentment and Payment (EIPP) and/or by FEDI. Payments can be made using negotiable electronic instruments or digital cash in addition to traditional methods. Online receivable services can automate the entire receivables process. An electronic lockbox[1] enables automatic downloading of cash collections to accounting software. And, depending on the integration with the accounting system, further processing, such as posting to accounts receivable and general ledger, can be automatically performed. These changes are explored in this chapter.

The chapter is organized as follows: First, automation of sales orders is discussed in the context of CRM. This discussion also covers intersecting areas between CRM and accounting. Second, the online credit approval process is described. The credit approval process can be partially automated, fully automated or Web enabled, and all of these variations are covered. Third, warehousing and shipping, with special emphasis on Web-based monitoring of shipments, is discussed. Fourth, EIPP and EBPP processes, models for EIPP and EBPP, and advantages and disadvantages of these methods, are reviewed. Fifth, online management of receivables and electronic payment methods in B2C and B2B transactions are comprehensively analyzed. Finally, a summary rounds off the chapter.

Sales Orders

Sales orders can arrive via Web, EDI and the EDI variants, online exchanges, or CRM or SFA software. Conceptually, there is little difference in online orders and offline orders. The proper processing of online orders requires substantial integration of the front-end

Exhibit 3. Customer life cycle management and periodic accounting (Source: www.jimnovo.com/)

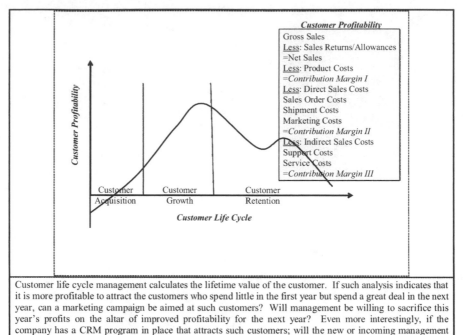

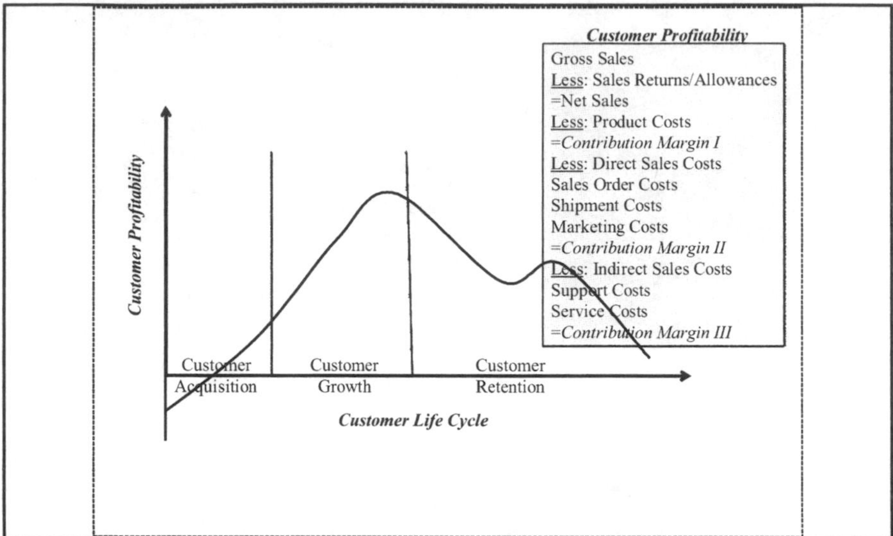

Customer life cycle management calculates the lifetime value of the customer. If such analysis indicates that it is more profitable to attract the customers who spend little in the first year but spend a great deal in the next year, can a marketing campaign be aimed at such customers? Will management be willing to sacrifice this year's profits on the altar of improved profitability for the next year? Even more interestingly, if the company has a CRM program in place that attracts such customers; will the new or incoming management keep it going?

Some believe that periodic financial accounting is one of the causes of CRM failure. The periodic financial accounting has been accused of short-term orientation. On the other hand, many successful managers have argued importance of meeting this quarter's numbers. The truth probably is in the middle somewhere. However, analyses of the customer profitability need to consider these ramifications.

systems with the back-end accounting systems. Organizations need to precisely coordinate credit approvals, inventory availability and shipping methods, among other things. A number of online companies faced severe problems in processing incoming sales orders; especially in the good old days of the dot-com era.

A basic understanding of CRM in the revenue cycle will be helpful for accountants. CRM intersects with accounting, especially accounts receivable analysis, and offers non-traditional ways of analysis. The term CRM, though extensively used, lacks a standard definition. The basic idea is to understand behavior of customers and assess the profitability of customers. CRM is not a new concept. Tools such as paper-based records, telephone interviews, focus groups and marketing surveys have been used for CRM purposes. The advent of the Internet, data warehouses and data mining technologies offer more sophisticated ways to manage the customer relationship process. The objectives of CRM include improving customer service, increasing efficiency and effectiveness of call centers and marketing channels, cross selling of products, discovering new customers and improving profitability of existing customers.

CRM endeavors to focus disparate pieces of information such as customer behavior, customer demographic and financial data, sales and marketing, channel effectiveness, and service and support functions to establish a better relationship with the customer. CRM includes managing prospective and existing customers, coordinating various marketing channels to effectively market products, and integrating customer support functions with the back-end office systems. These functions are managed using CRM software; the software suite being only a means to an end. CRM can be classified into three categories.

- **Operational CRM:** This component of CRM deals with integration of all customer touch points or interactions; for example, different sales channels such as Web, phone, fax and face to face; service centers; call centers; and human contact. The integration strives to increase efficiency and profitability of customer interactions.
- **Analytical CRM:** The customer data created by operational CRM is captured in a data warehouse or repository. This data is mined by data mining algorithms. The analytical capabilities of CRM can help identify profitable customers, products and regions; conduct life cycle analysis on customers; recognize productive salespersons; and provide sophisticated sales forecasting abilities. Additional areas of analysis include observing past customer behavior, predicting customer behavior in the near future and identifying cost-effective marketing strategies. Many of these analytical methods go way beyond the aging analysis of accounts receivable.
- **Collaborative CRM:** This area deals with creating seamless interactions with customers through different channels such as e-mail, brochures, catalogs, newsletters, chat rooms, call centers, help desks and newsletters.

These three components are not entirely independent. There has been a swirl of jargon in this area — customer asset management, customer relationship planning and customer life-cycle management, to mention a few. Most of these terms refine the basic meaning of CRM, not very important to the theme of this book. SFA, a forerunner of CRM, has essentially become a subset of CRM. SFA includes equipping members of the sales force with machines to connect with corporate databases and enable them to check status and pricing of products, view customer contracts and conduct high-level reporting and analysis. SFA can result in direct interface with the accounting system for observing inventory levels and placing sales orders.

SAP CRM Tools

CRM is a complex topic and intersects with marketing, sales, service, finance and logistics departments; additionally, it has a strong strategic component, requiring involvement of top management. The components of CRM software are examined to understand CRM functionalities. CRM packages consist of a constellation of modules and are connected with the base ERP or back-end accounting system. All of the leading ERP vendors offer CRM tools, and numerous software vendors sell CRM tools for organizations of all sizes,

Exhibit 4. The functional view of SAP CRM

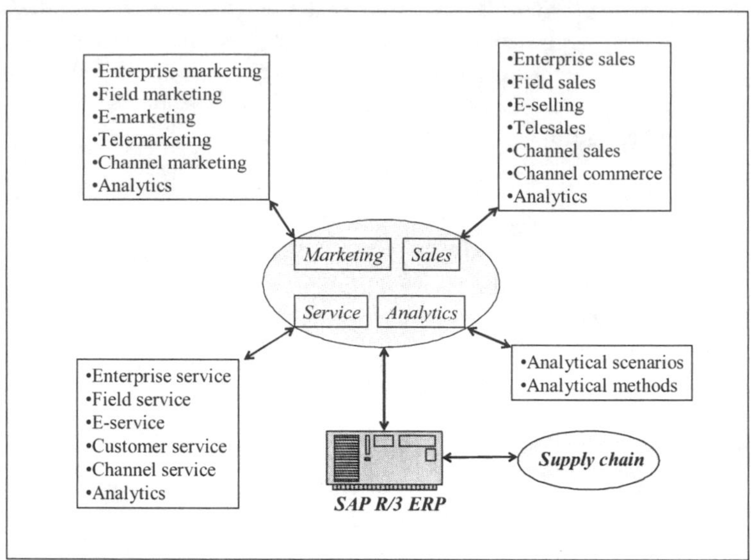

Siebel Corporation being the market leader in this segment. SAP and Oracle tools are primarily used in this book, though different software suites are used when appropriate. SAP provides all its e-business solutions on a platform called mySAP.com. The list of e-business solutions is lengthy and continues to expand as SAP brings forth more functionality under this umbrella. The suite of CRM tools falls under this platform and gives a good idea regarding existing state of the art in this area. Following is a bare-bones description of a very complex software suite.

SAP CRM tools manage four different customer-centric functions: marketing, sales, service and customer analytics. This is a functional view of SAP CRM capabilities. This review highlights reach of the CRM tools in customer-related functions, covers a lot of marketing ground and contains a number of marketing buzzwords and jargon. The description here, though, focuses on a high-level review of CRM functionalities.

The marketing function in the SAP CRM is supposed to support the entire marketing cycle, from planning to analytics. The capabilities of the marketing function are illustrated below.

- **Enterprise marketing:** Marketing efforts across the enterprise can be managed using Enterprise Marketing. Specific marketing activities supported are marketing planning, marketing budgeting, product management, customer segmentation, trade promotion management, campaign management, lead management and personalization of marketing efforts.

- **Field marketing:** These capabilities are similar to enterprise marketing, though these are aimed at marketing initiatives at the regional or field level.
- **E-marketing:** Marketing campaigns over the Internet are enabled here. Capabilities include catalog management, content management, personalization, one-to-one marketing and customer segmentation.
- **Telemarketing:** Telemarketing capabilities using call lists and interactive scripts are enabled in this function.
- **Channel marketing:** Marketing efforts can be coordinated with channel partners by providing relevant information, consistent branding, appropriate incentives and measurement tools.

Sales functionalities are geared toward sales teams. The idea is to establish a consistent sales process that supports sales activities. Functionalities are described below.

- **Enterprise sales:** Features include integrated sales planning and forecasting, account and contact management, opportunity and pipeline management, sales methodology analyzer, task and activity management, incentives and commissions management, sales order management, quotations and contracts, logistics management and analytics.
- **Field sales:** These capabilities are similar to enterprise sales, though these are aimed at marketing initiatives at the regional or field level.
- **E-selling:** Using the Internet to establish Web fronts and support Web-based sales activities is supported here.
- **Telesales:** Features here include lead management, pipeline and opportunity management, call scripting and prompts, call lists, Web chat, e-mail response, voice call back, sales order management, and quotations and contracts.
- **Channel sales:** Capabilities are similar to enterprise sales, but these are available to channel partners.
- **Channel commerce:** Features include virtual showroom, distributed catalog and content management, distributed order and inventory management, hosted order management and hosted partner sites, which enable collaborative sales activities with the partners.

Service is an important component of CRM. Service activities span a spectrum from planning to actual delivery of services, and need comprehensive software tools for management. The illustrative functionalities of service function are given below.

- **Enterprise service:** Service efforts across the enterprise can be managed using enterprise service. Specific service activities supported are service planning and forecasting, customer service and support, resource planning and optimization, knowledge management, installed base management, service order management and professional services.

- **Field services:** Capabilities are similar to enterprise service, and are aimed at service initiatives at the regional or field level.
- **E-service:** These capabilities can be used by customers to track orders, access Frequently Asked Questions (FAQs) and knowledge bases, and self-service. Features include parts catalog, knowledge management, request management, live customer assistance, account self-service, installed base management, complaints and returns management, and billing and payment.
- **Customer service:** Features include help desk, customer service and support, and complaint management. These can be used to manage customer contracts and complaint resolutions from a central place.
- **Channel service:** Capabilities are similar to enterprise service, but these are available to channel partners.

Analytics in the SAP CRM consist of analytical scenarios and analytical methods. The analytics do not only include performance measures but also optimization and planning tools. Analytical scenarios provide customer analytics, product analytics, marketing analytics, sales analytics, service analytics and interaction-channel analytics. These different measures come as pre-packaged solutions, and customized measures, if required, can be developed. Analytical methods, on the other hand, are a collection of tools and methodologies that can be used for performance measurement, trend prediction and

Exhibit 5. CRM analytics

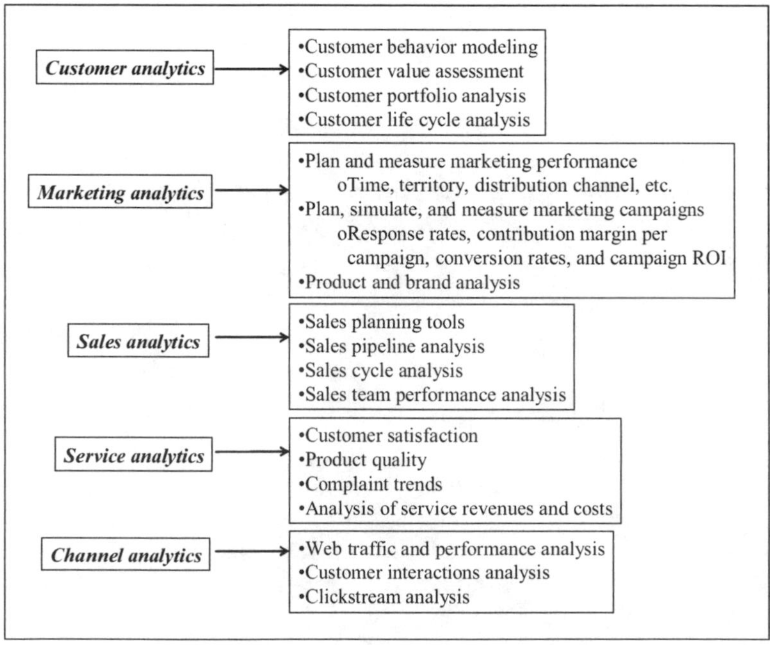

Exhibit 6. SAP CRM software suite

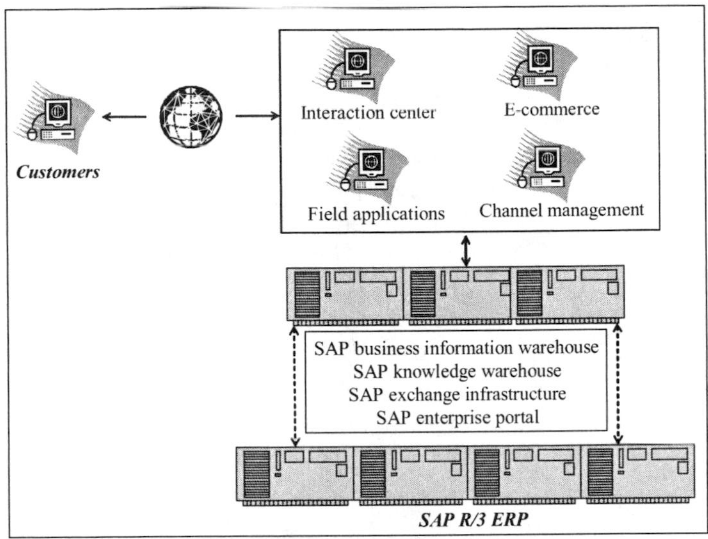

optimization of customer relationships. The analytics component is common to all functions and can be used in marketing, sales and service functions.

SAP CRM software modules operate on top of an ERP system in a symbiotic fashion. The leading vendors claim that their CRM tools will run on top of any ERP system. However, the practical difficulties of integrating systems from different vendors can be formidable, and should be kept in mind while evaluating these claims. CRM modules offered by SAP include the following components: business information warehouse, knowledge warehouse, exchange infrastructure, enterprise portal, field applications, e-commerce, interaction center and channel management.

First, let us look at the modules that enable CRM; these include business information warehouse, knowledge warehouse, exchange infrastructure and enterprise portal. These tools are used to support a variety of business processes and are not specific to CRM; reference to these software modules will be made in the next several chapters. These software modules are described here in the context of the CRM process. SAP Business Information Warehouse collects business data from the underlying ERP system. If the business uses modules from multiple ERP systems, then the business information warehouse module can be programmed to interface with those systems and collect required data. This module is optimized for the SAP ERP system, though not limited to it, and is a combination of database and database management tools. For example, in the context of CRM, this warehouse contains sales- and payments-related transaction data, sales- and service-call activity, key customer contacts and details of product sales. This data is available to sales, service and call-center personnel. Moreover, data can be questioned using query languages, downloaded to spreadsheets or used to generate reports with in-built reporting tools. Business information can be mined to derive key performance indicators, capture comments made by teams working collaboratively, and develop special alerts; for example, a drop of more than 5% in sales to an important customer would result in an alert to a specified sales manager.

The purpose of the knowledge warehouse is to store, organize, process and disseminate knowledge. This warehouse can contain business rules, best practices, business process information, and even decision support systems. Data can be in text or multimedia format. This module can also be used to create a training and documentation database. This enterprise-wide database can be used to cut down on the learning curve and training costs. Another building block of CRM tools is SAP exchange infrastructure. This exchange infrastructure supports different standards such as XML, Web Services Description Language (WSDL) and Simple Object Access Protocol (SOAP), along with different communication protocols. The objective is to enable collaborative business processes by cutting across various systems and protocols used within the organization. In the absence of such support, the costs of integrating different systems may become prohibitive.

The final base component is SAP enterprise portal, which provides a consistent navigation environment for corporate users. The ERP system can be run on mainframes, minis or microcomputers, and on a variety of operating systems. Thus, a typical organization — even if hosting an SAP ERP system — is likely to have numerous user interfaces. The enterprise portal integrates applications, data and metadata, and Internet information. This integrated information can then be used to provide reports as specified by users or can be shared across the organization. This module is used in what SAP calls financial insight, procurement insight and sale insight, which are essentially pre-

Exhibit 7. SAP CRM software functionalities

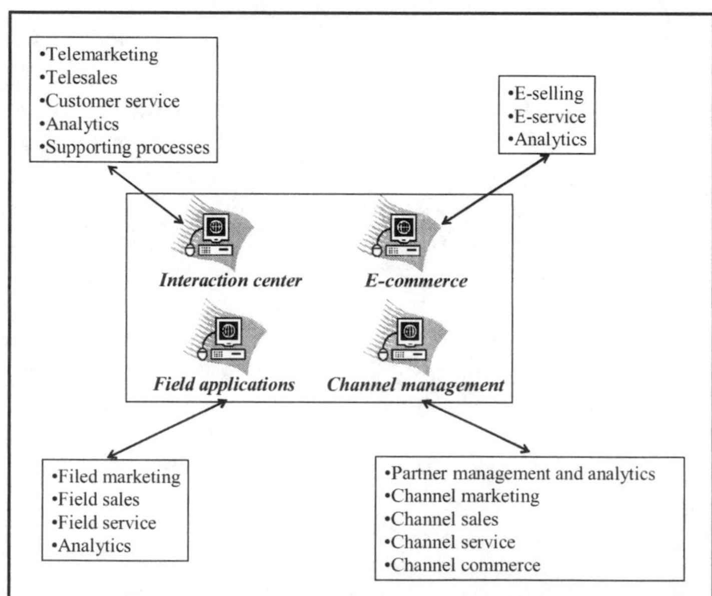

packaged business intelligence tools. Enterprise portals and business intelligence tools are discussed in depth in the general ledger cycle.

The integrated software modules that enable CRM functionalities are interactive center, e-commerce, field applications and channel management. The interaction center module handles contacts with customers; for example, telemarketing, telesales, customer service and interaction analytics. The E-commerce module enables e-marketing, e-selling and Web analytics. The field applications module supports field activities such as field marketing, field sales and field service. The channel management module handles all channel partner-related functions such as channel marketing, channel sales, channel service and channel commerce. These functionalities have already been discussed.

To reiterate, the preceding information is a bare outline of an extremely complex software suite. The demands on CRM tools are enormous, and these demands vary in different businesses and industries. As such, it is not surprising that software supporting these business processes is also large and complicated. In addition, the functionalities, jargon and supporting technologies are exponentially expanding as CRM matures. There can be practical problems in implementing such a package. The successes and failures of CRM initiatives are being researched; though the conclusions are still in their infancy.

CRM and Sales Orders

This section takes a detailed look at the e-selling functionality, which provides information regarding how SAP CRM tools deal with incoming sales orders on the Web. The e-selling functionality can be used to create Web-based storefronts. The Web sites required to transact business in the B2B, Business-to-Market (B2M) and B2C environment are different. The B2B environment involves long-term contractual and pricing arrangements, multiple buyers from a single customer and elaborate shipping requirements. The B2M environment is often characterized by connections with online exchanges and dealing with customers from around the world. Pricing information, inventory availability and product configuration capabilities often are expected by B2M customers. In the B2C environment, the Web site needs to be easy to navigate; electronic catalogs with multimedia content are often required; and shopping carts and credit card payment facilities are an absolute must. The e-selling functionality in the SAP CRM can be used to create these different types of Web storefronts.

These Web sites that serve different clientele need many supporting features to be effective. The first and foremost requirement is catalog or content management. The electronic purchasing process depends on the availability of products in the electronic format, referred to as electronic catalogs. The electronic catalogs provide information via text, graphics, pictures, audio and video, among other things. If product descriptions and selling terms and conditions are not electronic, then the buying process cannot be automated. The more detailed and searchable the product database, the easier is the job of the customers. Managing these electronic catalogs is called *content or catalog management*, in e-commerce jargon. Content management is a complex and costly process. The e-selling authoring tools can be used to create product catalogs. The electronic catalogs can be developed in different formats, such as XML, spreadsheet and

Exhibit 8. SAP CRM e-selling

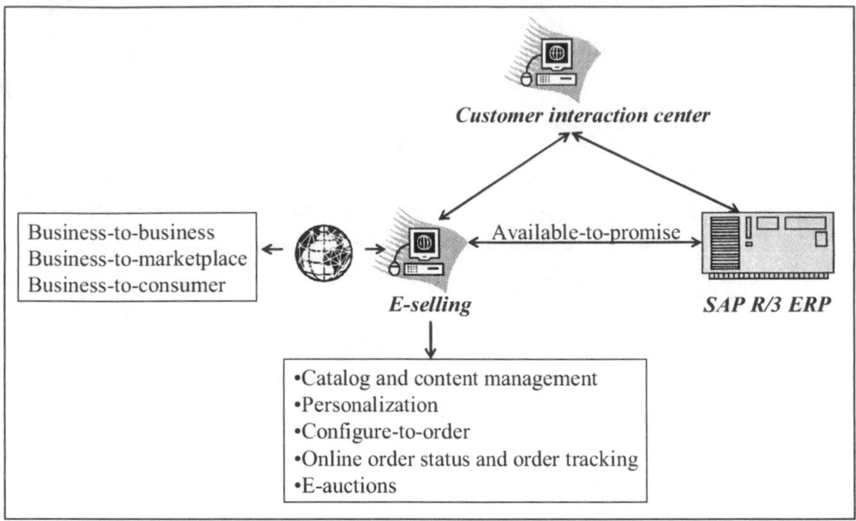

Comma Separated Value (CSV); and automatically uploaded to the Web site. The content can be changed, updated or modified. Additionally, these catalogs can also be imported from online exchanges and third-party content providers. The electronic catalogs are of no use unless they can be efficiently searched. The CRM tools also provide a search facility for users. The search tools are similar to the ones you may have encountered on the Internet — for example, Google.

The SAP CRM tools can offer self-service functionality for customers. Customers may be able to conduct a variety of activities, such as entering orders, tracking orders, issuing special instructions and viewing their accounts. A new customer can establish an account online and conduct business. Sometimes the software allows the customer to set up a customized screen available every time that customer logs in. These features relieve company departments from routine queries and paperwork while empowering customers to seek information in a timely fashion.

The customer can also see a personalized page based on his or her profile, preferences and purchasing history. The customer will see product recommendations, related product categories, and cross-selling and up-selling suggestions that facilitate one-to-one marketing. The CRM tools can also be used to create online product configurators. Customers can design products or customize products. Calculators can provide feedback on the prices for designed or customized products; knowledge bases can be used to provide relevant suggestions; and incompatible configurations are flagged and rejected. Such product configurators need to be connected to the back-end systems to ensure accuracy and product availability. The shopping carts, secure connections, and ability to handle credit card and procurement card payments can also be added to the Web site.

As the customer orders a product — self-designed, customized or off the shelf — availability and delivery dates need to be calculated. Factors such as current inventory, production capacity, shipping routes, shipping costs and time are considered in making available-to-promise check. The integration may extend all the way up to the supply chain, discussed in the Conversion Cycle. The SAP CRM and SAP SCM tools can be used to provide such integration. Once the order is in place and prices and delivery dates are confirmed, the customer should be capable of tracking orders, viewing invoices and querying appropriate personnel in case of problems. The SAP CRM tools, apart from these features, also provide hyperlinks to carriers' tracking systems.

The e-selling tools can be used to conduct online auctions to get rid of surplus goods and excess inventory. Bids can be solicited, the auction process can be monitored in real time and bids can be evaluated using multiple criteria with in-built algorithms. The Web storefront can also be connected with the customer interaction center. The customer can talk with service agents via phone, chat facilities or voice-over-IP options. Customers can also track service requests, connect and explore company knowledge bases, establish online user forums and access online technical support. Routing of customer requests and inquiries is based on automated workflows. These customer interactions and customer activities data are stored in a data warehouse. This data can be used to generate reports concerning customer behavior, retention reports, conversion reports, site metrics and sales analytics.

Accounting processes can become part of the CRM process. The customers can establish their own accounts, change contact information and periodically view those accounts. Credit approvals can be automated or performed online. The invoices can be automatically generated and electronically presented to the customers. In the B2B environment, invoices can be altogether dispensed with to support the ERS process. Payments can be made via credit cards or procurement cards and can be executed in the Web store. These developments are discussed in the next sections; however, at this stage please realize that some accounting processes can be handled by CRM software.

Credit Approvals

Traditionally, the credit approval process is reactive; that is, a sales order arrives and the credit department evaluates credit worthiness of the customer. The credit process can be classified in three phases:

- Assessing quantum of and collecting information about the customer
- Evaluating the information
- Deciding credit worthiness of the customer

Credit approval decisions encompass trade credit, consumer credit or equipment financing. The time and expense involved in credit decisions depends on whether the customer

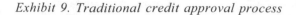

Exhibit 9. Traditional credit approval process

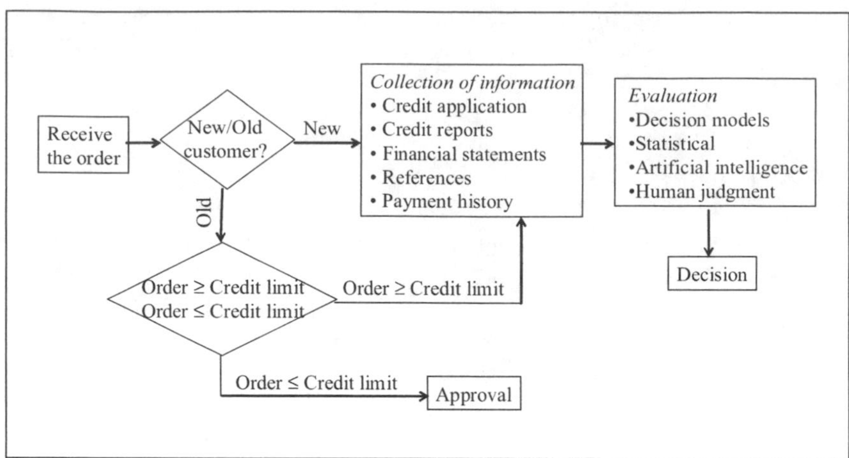

is new or established, availability of current information, whether an order is above or below the credit limit, algorithms applied to evaluate the credit worthiness of the customer, and other factors deemed important by the credit manager. This approach has worked fairly well in established traditional commerce.

However, in the new e-environment, this approach can be costly, delay credit approval and cause inconsistency in decision-making, and result in lost sales or uncollectibles. Now, incoming orders are automated, 24/7 and customers are geographically scattered. This environment forces corporations to respond to routine and non-routine credit approvals in real time. The traditional credit approval process may become a bottleneck in the revenue-generation process, since alternate suppliers are only a click away.

Historically, corporations have attempted a variety of techniques to accelerate the credit approval process; for example, reengineering, automation and artificial intelligence techniques. Internet resources provide other options to manage the credit approval process. Internet-based resources and services can be used to collect information on the customer, can provide standard and customized decision mechanisms, or can be used to automate the entire credit approval process.

The Internet has numerous resources to collect general information regarding new or prospective customers. The illustrative list of resources is provided in Exhibit 10 (A-I). The resources listed provide the following types of information:

- Financials, standard filings such as 10-K, 10-Q and S-8
- Address of the company, incorporation information, product lines and top management information
- Current and historical stock quotes and movements

Exhibit 10. Web-based sources for credit approvals

(A)	***Web resources – customer information***	*I. General customer information* ➢ Bloomberg.com ➢ Dowjones.com ➢ Edgar-online.com ➢ PRNewswire.com ➢ Reuters.com *II. Specialized services* ➢ Choicepoint – Choicepoint.net ➢ Experian.com ➢ Lexis – Netlds.com
(B)	***Web resources – decision tools***	➢ Dun and Bradstreet – dnb.com ➢ Experian.com ➢ FairIsaac.com
(C)	***Web resources – comprehensive credit approval management***	➢ Dun and Bradstreet – dnb.com ➢ eCredit.com ➢ Experian.com ➢ eFinance.com

Note: The above lists merely give some examples, but are not meant to be an exhaustive list of either resources or services. Additionally, nature of the services provided changes rapidly; please check the web sites for current information.

- News and current events such as mergers, acquisitions, new products and new personnel
- Industry and sector news

These services provide a good starting point in the credit approval process. Costs vary based on the brand name of the service, depth of the information desired and extent of the required information. However, information concerning small businesses or international businesses can be hard to obtain.

Specific information regarding the customer can also be obtained using the resources listed in Exhibit 10 (A-II). These Web-based companies collect information from various sources and compile a comprehensive information portfolio. Available information is as follows:

- Name, address and contact information
- History of the business
- Financials, financial summary, key financial indicators and graphics
- Credit lines
- Credit score based on proprietary models
- Telephone, fax and Web address
- Names and information of the top managers
- Lines of business, product lines and Standard Industry Codes (SIC)
- Public filings concerning tax liens, judgments and liens, and UCC filings

- Competitors
- Country risk analysis

The information provided is quite comprehensive and, according to vendors, updated constantly. These services are cost effective even for ad-hoc queries and accessible by a browser; search and retrieval of this information is available in real time. For example, prices can vary from $X per query to thousands of dollars for an annual contract. Information on small businesses, privately held businesses and international businesses is also available. The disadvantages of these services are difficulty in verifying accuracy and integrity of the information, continuing need for cost-benefit analysis and stability of the service.

Internet-based services also provide tools to aggregate the information to derive credit rankings. Illustrative sites that provide these tools are shown in Exhibit 10 (B). The risk assessment tools use proprietary algorithms but also allow customization based on criteria specified by the customer. For example, a vendor can tailor the program to a specific company's needs, design rules and criteria based on that company's input, offer standardized decision engines, interpret results and push the results to the credit manager's desktop. The decision engines employ a variety of algorithms; for example, advanced statistical methods, expert systems and artificial intelligence techniques. The users need not understand technical intricacies of the program, but should have a general understanding of the strengths and weaknesses of various algorithms. The outputs of the system can include a credit risk score, comparison of risk level of the business with other businesses, background information regarding the business and other items specified by the user. These services can be tailored to small businesses, international businesses or large businesses.

Exhibit 11. Web-enabled credit approval process

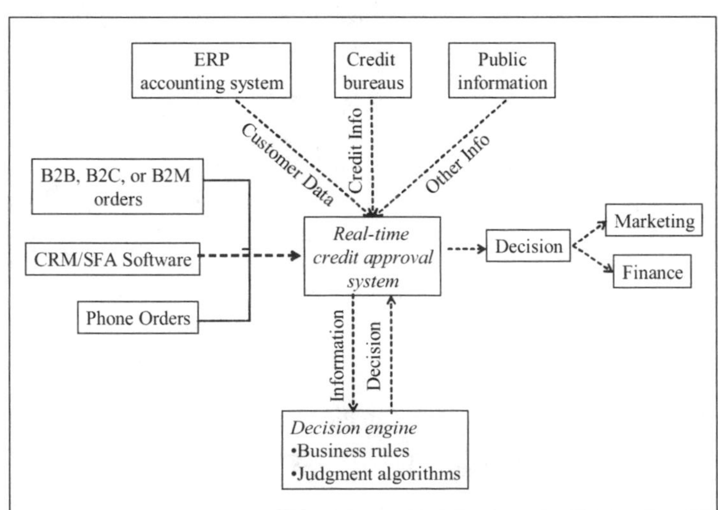

The primary advantages of these decision tools are: minimized manual intervention, reduced cycle time for decisions, consistency in credit policy enforcement and reduced operating costs. However, the tool needs to be chosen carefully, and there are upfront and recurring costs, such as software and hardware investment, programming and validating the tool, continuing maintenance or monthly payments to Web-based services.

The traditional, off-line credit grantors will benefit from the resources listed so far. However, in the case of Web orders, the credit decision must be delivered in minutes or seconds. This calls for automation of the entire credit approval process. The credit approval decision can be completed in a matter of minutes. Web-based services that provide such support are listed in Exhibit 10 (C). The process flow can be described as follows:

- Business installs the automated credit decisioning system. The system needs to be integrated with a legacy accounting or ERP system, connected with approved credit bureaus, able to access designated public information sources and be embedded with the required decision expertise.
- Customer information is forwarded to the credit system once the sales order arrives. The credit system pools data from the accounting system, credit bureaus and public information sources.
- The collected information is filtered through the decision engine to arrive at a credit score and the consequent decision. The decision engine is provided by the vendor and is generally customized by the business.
- If the decision is *yes*, then the system can generate the necessary documentation or can forward the decision to the approved personnel or machine.
- Exceptions are handled on basis of the rules programmed in the system.

The costs and successes of such services are based on a variety of factors; for example, transaction volume; difficulty in integrating a credit system with accounting systems; types and number of credit bureaus used; and intangible costs, such as process redesign or reengineering, and resistance from the credit personnel, among other things.

A number of factors should be considered before using the Internet. An illustrative list follows:

- The speed with which credit needs to be approved.
- The frequency of routine vs. non-routine (such as exceptions, high-dollar value items or risky customers) credit approval decisions. The higher the frequency of non-routine decisions, the lesser the use of the credit approval system.
- Accuracy and integrity of the information available on the vendor's Web site.
- The decision tool should be evaluated for accuracy, customization capabilities, expertise and training required for using the tool, updating routines and data import/export capabilities.

Exhibit 12. Tools of the trade: eCredit.com

The leading provider of Internet-based credit solutions is eCredit.com. The company has been around almost a decade and has survived the dot-com carnage. Different types of products offered by eCredit.com are as follows:

Decision desktop: This is a collection of analytical tools that helps in assessing individual customer risk and the overall risk exposure of a company.

- *Portfolio analysis* -- allows benchmarking a customer's financial profile with other peers as defined by SIC codes. Other options include comparison using geographic location and business size; the analysis can be supplemented with expert comments and graphs.
- *Financial analysis* -- calculates pre-defined financial ratios and cash flow projections, compares financial statements and allows *what if* analysis.
- *Business hierarchies* -- build relationships between related businesses, such as parent and subsidiary, to provide a 360-degree view of the risk exposure.
- *Scoring* -- develops a scoring system and customizes score cards.

Equipment financing expert: This helps lessors in granting credit. This product includes a *process automation engine* that allows a business to implement its proprietary knowledge and business rules in a credit-granting decision. Data can be input manually, via FTP, using the Internet or through remote workstations. The documentation is automatic. This product can interface with the ERP systems to access customer data collected by the business and use it in the analysis.

nFusion Suite: This Web-based credit approval system integrates and automates the entire credit approval process. The suite includes decision automation technologies as described in the *decision desktop*, a centralized database repository that collects data from internal accounting systems and external content providers such as credit bureaus, and a decision engine that has business rules and procedures and is capable of producing scorecards.

The *instantdecision* module is a base for nFusion Suite. This module automates origination of a credit request at the point of sale either through Web screens or third-party systems, automatically gathers data from credit-granting institutions, analyzes data using programmed decision rules and, finally, communicates the decision. If the credit-granting decision cannot be reached by the system, then an in-depth financial analysis can be performed. The Suite also includes workflow management tools.

RapidCollect™ automates the collection process. The primary objectives of this tool are to reduce bad debts, improve cash flow and lower days sales outstanding. This tool automates many routine administrative tasks, provides analytical and performance measurement tools, and can be used to implement a uniform collections methodology throughout the organization.

- Ability of the automated service to integrate with existing legacy or ERP systems.
- Relative costs involved in in-house vs. outsourced credit approval decision. For example, costs saved — such as redeployment of credit personnel, no investment in software and hardware, no recurring maintenance expense; against costs incurred — such as lost expertise, treatment of exceptional cases, monthly payments, cost of dedicated connections and stability of the service provider.

The Internet has opened new ways to approach credit approvals. The Internet-based resources can speed up the credit approval process and support various degrees of automation. Various levels of services are offered by such Internet-based companies. Acquiring information about the customers from proprietary and public databases, feeding customer information into decision tools available on the Web or customizing the entire credit approval process; whatever the requirement, the Internet can be profitably leveraged to improve the credit approval process.

Exhibit 13. Case studies for eCredit.com: Gateway and Cisco

Gateway Corporation

Gateway Corporation builds and sells computers to consumers and businesses. The computers can be built to the customer's or business' specification. Gateway's business is based on high volumes and low margins. In 1997, Gateway financed $377 million; about 20% of Gateway's customers used installment-type financing, and 60%-70% used credit cards. Gateway benefits if the customers move from credit cards to financing, because Gateway saves the upfront fee (average 1.85%) on the credit cards and earns about 4.5% on the financing side. These percentages make a great difference in a low-margin business. Gateway installed an online credit system from eCredit.com to streamline its credit approval and financing processes in 1997. Gateway used the system to check online credit and offer individuals and small businesses financing by partnering with multiple finance partners. Mark Scoular, director of business development in Gateway's financial services division, indicated that a loan application can be processed in 15 seconds, and completing the paperwork is much faster. He added that reviewing loan applications is a fully automated process and two people oversaw loan applications worth more than $4 billion, out of which $2 billion were financed. The percentage of customers availing of the financing option had gone up considerably. Gateway was also able to generate new revenue streams such as loan origination, develop customer profile information for CRM, and use its financing arm for some of the financing deals.

Gateway's financing program later faced some difficulties. It goes to show that any automated or Web-based method can only be as intelligent as the programmers who program it.

Cisco

Cisco is a giant company that sells Internet networking products. Cisco also used eCredit.com's software. The experience for Cisco was positive. However, Cisco faced the following problems:

- Interfacing of eCredit.com's software with the ERP system (Oracle) was time consuming. Development time, estimated by Cisco, was approximately 60 days.
- Cisco had an automated credit application process. However, only 25% of applications came back electronically; the rest were mailed or faxed. These non-electronic applications had to be manually keyed, delaying the credit decision.
- Cisco leases a lot of its equipment. Leasing business rules are different, and Cisco had to develop a separate interface for its leasing activities. Cisco used an outside firm to develop an e-lease product.

Warehousing and Shipping

Once the sales order is approved, the tasks of picking goods in the warehouse, making a picking list and shipping the product take place sequentially. These tasks involve warehousing and shipping, which are tightly integrated. Warehousing refers to storing of the product, and shipping is primarily a logistics function; the shipment can be to the customer or from the supplier. In this section, warehouse aspects pertaining only to delivery of products to the customer — that is, *outbound logistics* — are discussed.

The warehouse management and picking processes are often managed by WMSs. WMSs were created to control the movement and storage of materials within a warehouse. WMSs then evolved to encompass light manufacturing, transportation management, order fulfillment and even accounting processes. Many suppliers of WMS exist, and these systems span a spectrum, from material tracking systems all the way to ERP-type systems.

The order fulfillment process in the e-commerce age became e-fulfillment process. Initially for many e-tailers and now for many e-enabled established businesses, order fulfillment remains a challenge. In the e-environment, especially for retailers, order volume is higher, orders are parcel-sized and orders may need many vehicles for transportation, since customers are geographically scattered and trucks are sometimes only partially filled.WMSs can address many of these problems.

The core functions of the WMS system in outbound logistics are as follows:

- WMS supports various methods of directing incoming goods to proper locations and replenishing goods as required.
- WMS also performs ancillary functions, such as packing goods, verifying goods, holding goods, staging and loading goods.
- WMS supports various methods of picking goods from the shelves. The logic of picking goods depends on combinations of item, order, quantity and/or location, and is generally supplied by the user.
- WMS enables designing an optimum path for movement of materials, efficiently utilizing storage space in the warehouse and assuring a proper storage configuration.
- WMS can handle dangerous and hazardous materials by designating those to special areas.
- WMS saves on shipping costs by calculating the proper container size for packing items.
- WMS can automatically create and forward ASN to the customer.

The advanced functionalities of WMS may include order allocation and router, freight and parcel management, foreign trade zones management and retail compliance. WMS functionalities are growing; however, if the organization has an existing ERP system, the WMS needs to be integrated with ERP, CRM, material handling equipment and supply chain planning. Web-enabled WMS also allows for tracking an order from inception to end on the desktop using a browser.

The primary use of WMS and the Internet is their ability to track a shipment in transit. The majority of businesses believe that carrier selection and shipment tracking using the Internet are big factors in staying competitive. Numerous online companies specialize in shipment tracking. The process works as follows: The shipments are turned over to the carrier – road, rail or by air. The vehicles transmit the movement status to the concerned carrier. The carrier periodically updates status of the shipment and transfers information to the Web site of the shipment tracking company. The online company collects

Exhibit 14. Internet-based shipment tracking

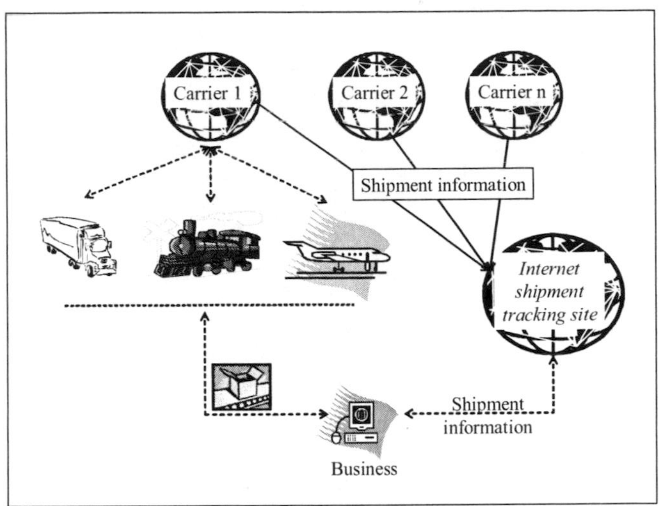

information from various carriers and provides timely reports to the business. Shipments can be tracked by bill of lading number, purchase order number, Return Material Authorization (RMA) number or shipper reference number. Instead of using an online company, a business can also obtain information directly from a carrier. The infrastructural issues are more complex, though the basic process remains the same. Internet-based shipment tracking and related software is useful to accountants in the following areas:

- Handling sales and purchases cut-offs more precisely
- Auditing freight bills for overcharges, duplicate charges and unrecognized shipments
- Tracking of performance measures for shippers, such as load tender accept and reject percentages, on-time pickup and delivery, and ratio of multiple claims
- Analyzing volume by carrier, lane, equipment type or customer, and to perform *what-if* analyses
- Reducing operating costs and administrative overheads

Visibility of shipments is a first step in the shipping area. A number of pre- and post-shipment activities can be affected by the Web-readiness of the carrier. First, an accurate estimate of shipment charges based on contractual arrangements can be obtained from the carrier database. Exact quotations are useful in case of frequent shipments and helpful in managing cash flows. Second, a bill of lading can be created electronically, transmitted to the carrier and printed at the source. Shipping labels can also be created at this time. Third, the carrier can be informed directly about the pickup information. A log of pickup requests is useful in monitoring carrier performance. Fourth, as already mentioned, shipment tracking ability is required. Shipment tracking ability should be supplemented with the ability to reroute shipments in transit. Fifth, regular notification of shipment status — either through e-mail or other electronic means — at predefined intervals is necessary. Businesses can monitor shipments delivered on time, delayed shipments and lost shipments, and should be able to take corrective action. Finally, the ability to electronically retrieve documents, such as bill of lading, delivery receipt and packing lists; and Web access to standard forms and documents, such as certificate of origin and customs information and report creation tools are extremely helpful.

Billing

Billing methods differ in the B2B and B2C environment. The standard method of billing in a B2B transaction involves reconciliation of sales order, credit approval, shipping notice and stock release, among other things; and then the bill/invoice is prepared. The process can be paper based, electronic or a mix. Incoming payments need to be matched with the invoice, order number and shipping notice. Finally, the accounts receivable subsidiary and general ledgers should be updated to reflect correct status of the customer. The payments can be via cash, checks, credit cards and EFT, to mention a few. Businesses may need multiple billing accounts per customer, which may have separate review processes.

The B2B billing process is complex, error-prone and expensive; billing disputes are fairly common. An EDI-based process referred to as ERS (also known as invoiceless process, self billing, pay-on-receipt or payment-from-receipt) has been used to reengineer the billing/payment process. However, EDI does not have a critical mass, and ERS is not universally used[2]. In the B2C environment, billing methods differ depending on the industry. For example, if items are purchased in a store, the bill will be handed over immediately; however, in case of telecom residential services or utilities, the paper bill will be forwarded directly to the customer's home. The paper-based bill is generally paid by consumers by a check; however, payment methods may also involve credit cards or EFT.

The estimates of total number of bills in the U.S. economy vary between 27 and 30 billion (approximately 12-15 billion B2B bills and 15-18 billion B2C bills). Businesses and consumers annually write approximately 68-70 billion checks, which is the highest check usage among industrialized nations. In B2C billing, consumers spend an average of 2 hours per month writing checks and spend $100 per year in associated costs, such as postage, late fees and returned checks. Bill presentment and payment costs businesses and consumers $80 billion per year; and internal processing costs for businesses are around $45 billion per year. Can these costs be reduced by using the Internet? Gartner Group estimates that using Web-based billing and payments, B2B companies can save $7.25 and B2C companies $0.55 per bill. Apart from cost reduction, Web-based billing can have strategic applications in the customer service area and CRM.

EIPP and EBPP Processes

EIPP for B2B and EBPP for B2C transactions are the Web-based innovations to streamline paper-based billing and payments processes. The core idea behind EIPP and EBPP is to provide customers a facility to receive, pay, review, analyze and query bills primarily over the Internet. There are many similarities in the way EIPP and EBPP operate; however, EBPP is simpler, since the B2C environment is relatively less complex than the B2B environment.

First, let us take a look at the modus operandi of EIPP and EBPP. The Web-based billing and payments process includes billers (sellers — the party who bills), customers (buyers), financial institutions and intermediate service providers. The generic steps involved in EIPP and EBPP can be summarized as follows.

- **Enrollment:** The customer has to navigate to the biller's Web site and enroll in the program. The front end of the Web site should have capabilities for the customers to enroll online. The critical self-service abilities in this area include account creation, account management and payment options. The biller, after positively identifying the customer, issues account number, user ID and password. If the customer has already created these data fields, they are confirmed and made operational. Data provided by the customers can later be used in CRM.

  The design of bills and invoices is a challenge due to the multimedia nature of the Web. Additionally, in the B2B environment, sometimes an invoice can be hundreds of pages long. In print format, the choices are rather drab; basically, black and white. The Internet offers a rich array of colors, graphics and animation to make bills more informative and entertaining. This stage provides opportunities for marketing messages, up- or cross-selling, and personalized messages to the customer. A whole new field of *digital documents* deals with problems in this area.

- **Data extraction and formatting:** The next step is data extraction and appropriate formatting of data in the digital format. The process for biller in EIPP and EBPP is

Exhibit 15. Differences in B (bill) and I (invoice)

Bill	Invoice
• Serving consumers -- relatively straightforward	• Serving businesses -- relatively complex
• Bill reflects charges and payment activity for the consumer	• Invoice provides details of services provided or items purchased
• Bill tells customer amount due and where to send payment	• Invoices may contain information used to allocate costs
• Contains few line items -- generally read and approved by the same person	• Invoices are matched, reviewed and approved; then paid by the cash/treasury department
• Bills paid as billed; lower rate of disputes	• Invoices not paid as invoiced; higher rate of disputes (up to 15%)

Exhibit 16. EIPP/EBPP process

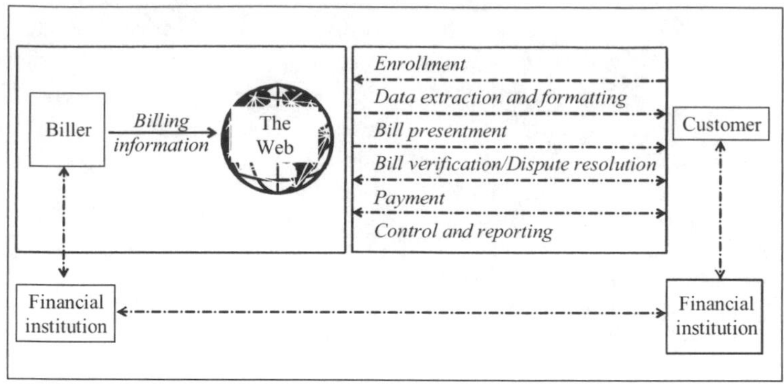

same. The data needs to be extracted from the back-end accounting systems, and data formats can range from software specific to ASCII files. This data needs to be readied for digital delivery through the appropriate format; for example, HTML or XML formatting. The customer may desire a digital document and printed invoice; the digital bill also needs to be formatted in a printer-friendly format. Data may need to be summarized in case of complicated bills and invoices.

- **Bill presentment:** In this stage, a digital bill is presented to the customer. Delivery methods may include e-mail, fax and palm device; posting on the biller's Web site; or forwarding the bill to a third-party Web site. A combination of methods can also be used; for example, posting the bill on the Web site and notifying the customer of the posting by e-mail. Digital bills can also be delivered on mobile phones and televisions. Hotel industry all over the world has used the delivery of check-out bills via close-circuit television for many years.

  The electronically delivered bills and invoices occasionally do not reach the destination due to e-mail or transmission failures. A failure detection and recovery mechanism is needed to identify such instances and take corrective action.

- **Bill verification and dispute resolution:** The customer then interacts with the bill by reviewing details, posing questions, verifying accuracy and doing analytics, if these capabilities exist. The review process in the B2C setting is relatively simple, since generally only the customer reviews and approves the bills.

  B2B transactions have an elaborate approval process, where the invoice is routed to various departments before getting approved. In the B2B, and to a lesser extent in the B2C environment, dispute resolution procedures also need to be formalized in the workflow. Approximately 5% to 15% of B2B transactions are disputed. Disputes can arise due to billing errors, partial or wrong shipments, promotional or early payment discounts, or other myriad reasons.

- **Payment:** The customer should be allowed a variety of remittance options, such as using the customer's own server, online banks, Web portals, ACH or credit card networks and, finally, a simple printed check. The customer should be able to control for full or partial payments, payment dates or consolidation of bills for payments.

In the case of a B2B transaction, the remittance information is captured by the EIPP system and forwarded to the biller. This information is necessary for accounts receivable reconciliation and can be automatically uploaded to the back-end accounting system.

- **Control and reporting features:** The strategic benefits of EIPP/EBPP are available when customer viewing habits, payment behavior and visit logs are accumulated. These databases are then mined using data mining algorithms to extract information that can be used in marketing and customer service. The control and reporting features should provide abilities to monitor, summarize, report and save such vital data.

Conceptually, the idea of electronic billing and payments seems efficient and effective. However, there are number of challenges in the area. First, who should host the Web site to post the bills, the seller or the buyer? In the EBPP environment, the question is, will the consumer travel to different Web sites to collect bills? To answer this question, different models proposed and/or used in this area need to be examined. Then there are issues of front-end design of the Web sites, design of the electronic bills, data conversion from legacy systems, internal controls for electronic delivery and acceptable remittance options.

Models for EIPP and EBPP

There are three primary models for EIPP and EBPP — direct model, consolidator model and Internet post-office model. These models differ in terms of implementation, workflows, costs, benefits, controls and customer relationship capabilities.

In the direct model, the biller establishes the Web site for displaying bills and acts as a service provider. Customers browse to the Web site to obtain bill information. The biller controls design of the Web site, design of the bill, collection of the customer data, marketing messages, and enrollment and dispute resolution. Customers are required to visit the biller's Web site periodically, collect billing information and arrange for payment.

In the B2B environment, direct biller can be either a seller or a buyer. If the seller establishes a Web site, then the buyers are expected to review their bills on the seller's Web site. This process is similar to the standard biller model described earlier. The seller-direct model is a traditional model applicable for existing trade relationships where payment terms and credit limits are pre-specified. Seller direct remains a popular choice for sellers who issue a high volume of invoices or have high-value invoices. This model is used in manufacturing, telecommunications, utilities, health care and financial services.

Exhibit 17. Direct biller model

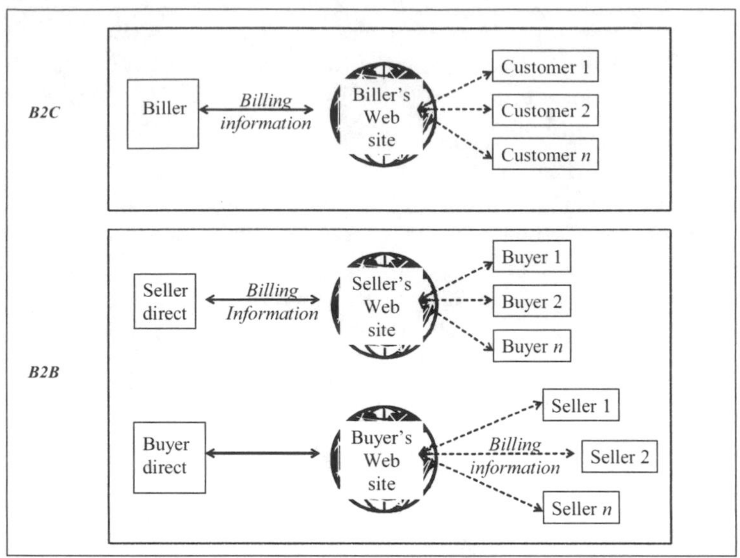

On the other hand, if the buyer establishes the Web site, then the sellers have to post their bills on the buyer's site. The buyer will review the bills periodically and arrange for payments. The question is, why should sellers agree to post their bills on the buyer's site? The choice between seller- and buyer-direct models depends on who is dominant in the relationship. Large buyers such as Wal-Mart, who are interested in purchase-order-driven invoicing and payment processes, generally can implement buyer-direct models. The existing trading relationships and high volume or value of invoices are prerequisites for this model, as in the seller-direct model.

Customers enjoy several advantages in the biller-direct model. First, this process is similar to paper-based billing. The customer navigates to the Web site, reviews the bill and pays the bill. Second, dispute resolution is faster, since the customer is interacting directly with the biller. The biller can provide analytical facilities such as reviewing past bills, comparing bills, calculating average bill and looking at seasonal variations in the bill, such as in a utility bill. Third, if the customer wishes to add a new service or discontinue an existing service, it can be done quickly. The majority of credit card companies employ the biller-direct model. Finally, the seller must incur start-up and operational costs for the Web sites and recurring maintenance and security costs.

Problems with the direct model are as follows: First, customers have to visit different Web sites to gather billing information. This in itself is not a problem; however, customers may encounter different interfaces, different payment mechanisms and different Web site designs, causing acceptance problems. Second, the biller-direct model lacks the ability to present consolidated bills. For example, if the customer gets one consolidated bill for various services and pays that one bill, then the customer saves considerable time in the process. Such one-stop billing is difficult in the direct model, since each biller essentially posts only his/her bills on the Web. Third, there are management problems for the customer, such as tracking e-mail notifications, keeping bookmarks and visiting Web sites. Finally, the seller has to convince a critical mass of customers to join the online billing process. If the seller does not dominate the market, marketing a biller-direct model can be tedious and expensive. The seller also has to bear the costs of Web site construction and back-end systems integration.

The second EIPP/EBPP model is the consolidator model. The term *consolidator* refers to the organization, generally Web based, which consolidates bills from various billers and provides a single user interface to the user. Customers can view all their bills and pay for them at one place. A consolidator is essentially an intermediary who collects and aggregates bills and invoices from multiple sellers and posts those on the Web for the benefit of multiple buyers. Additional value-added services, such as factoring, escrow, insurance, credit ratings and payment processing may also be made available by the consolidator.

The consolidator model can be further divided into two models – the thick consolidator and the thin consolidator. The thick consolidator collects billing data that is in summary and detailed formats. The customer can view bills online, access previous bills, investigate line item details, run analytics and do pretty much anything possible under the biller-direct model. The thick consolidator manages the entire customer relationship. The thick consolidator generally provides technical infrastructure and standards for formatting and publishing of digital bills. In the B2B setting, this model can bring together a large number of smaller sellers and buyers. The success of this model depends on the thick consolidator's ability to attract and retain a critical mass of sellers and buyers.

Exhibit 18. Thick consolidator model

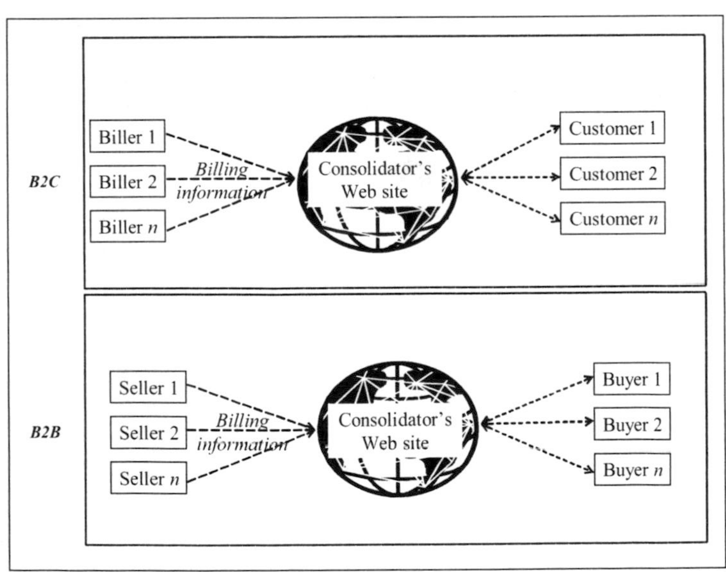

Major banks and Internet portals with established brand names can probably play a role of thick consolidator.

CheckFree Corporation (*www.checkfree.com/*) is one of the leading consolidators in the EBPP area. CheckFree consolidates bills from hundreds of billers and presents them to its customers. Currently, CheckFree has approximately 5 million U.S. consumers and processes 4 billion payments each year. CheckFree does not charge upfront fees to the users; it is a free service. CheckFree offers various options for payment, such as debit cards, credit cards, paper checks and EFT, among other things. CheckFree guarantees privacy and security, and also accepts responsibility for late payments and unauthorized payment on customer accounts. Many corporations offer consolidator and EIPP/EBPP services; for example, BillingZone, American Express, Discover and Intuit.

The primary advantage for customers is having a single point of contact with multiple billers. The interface is standardized, bills look similar and there is only one Web site to visit. In the B2B situation, sellers and buyers can leverage technology resources of the consolidator, such as handling multiple data formats, analytical tools, security infrastructure and dealing with multiple transmission protocols. The initial set-up and recurring operating expenses of the Web site can now be avoided.

There are several disadvantages of this model. First, the level of bill/invoice details is not as deep as in the biller-direct model. Because the billers follow technology standards set by the consolidator, formatting and presentation capabilities are limited. Second, the level of interactivity decreases considerably in the thick-consolidator model compared to the biller-direct model. For example, requesting a new service, changing the existing service or performing in-depth analytics is either more difficult or non-existent. Sellers

Exhibit 19. Thin consolidator model

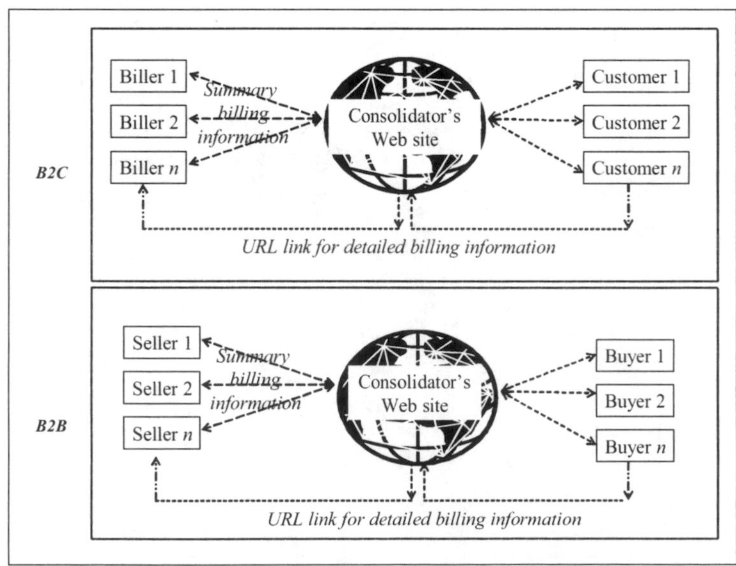

are not able to exploit marketing and service opportunities of the new medium. Finally, a thick consolidator generally cannot consolidate all bills for the customers. Customers may be forced to visit multiple consolidator sites, though not as many as under the biller-direct model, negating some of the benefits of the model.

To offset some of the disadvantages of the thick-consolidator model, the thin-consolidator model was invented. The thin-consolidator model follows an industry-wide technology standard rather than a proprietary standard of the thick consolidator. Thus, billers can follow the same technology standards as they post bills and invoices on the Web sites of various consolidators. The bills posted on the thin consolidator's site only consist of a summary. The customers can review and pay the bills on the thin consolidator's site. If they need additional details, such as line items or analytical tools, a Web link on the consolidator's Web site takes them to the biller's Web site. This model recaptures some of the advantages of the biller-direct model. Interactive customer service, advanced analytics and cross-marketing activities can be implemented. The development of industry-wide standards remains a barrier in the adoption of this model.

The third model is called the Internet post office model. This is primarily useful in the EBPP area. Different billing organizations and financial institutions are connected with an Internet post office. The Internet post office is a hub that can be managed by a Web portal, brokerage firm, bank or any other intermediary organization. The billing organizations will send bills to the Internet post office, and those will be delivered to the customer. Data on the customer's bank accounts is maintained by trusted organizations such as Certificate Authorities. When the customer makes a payment decision, automated procedures gather information about the customer's bank accounts and initiate payment. The success of such a model depends on the data standards for EBPP, security and privacy protections, national biller directories and intelligent agents (a software program

Exhibit 20. The Internet post-office model

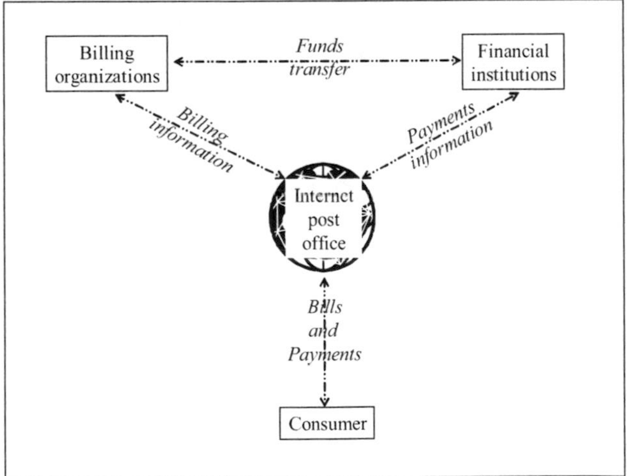

that automatically performs certain functions based on occurrence of specified events) that can gather information from disparate sources. National post offices are best equipped to offer the Internet post office service. In Canada, Australia and New Zealand, national post offices are already offering these services; for example, Canada Post Corporation, the Bank of Montreal and TELUS Corporation offer a service called *epost* (*www.epost.ca/*) that is essentially the Internet post office.

Infrastructure for EIPP and EBPP

The infrastructure requirements for EIPP and EBPP are similar, but not identical. The following discussion primarily focuses on the EIPP/EBPP software that manages end-to-end electronic billing and payment processing, and not on operating systems and hardware. Needless to say, functionalities differ across various software packages. The first problem for EIPP/EBPP software is extraction of data from accounting systems in the desired format. Accounting systems can vary from old legacy systems to the latest ERP systems. The legacy systems use different file formats for printing bills and invoices. These print formats are captured by the EIPP and EBPP software to create digital bills and invoices. The ERP software is generally capable of producing output in Web-viewable format and can be directly used by the EIPP/EBPP software.

Various operating systems run legacy and ERP systems, such as Sun Solaris, Windows and UNIX, among others. The EIPP/EBPP software for data extraction should be able to interface with these operating systems. Software functionality should include the ability to handle a large volume of transactions, large bills (capabilities range up to hundreds

Exhibit 21. Infrastructure for EIPP/EBPP

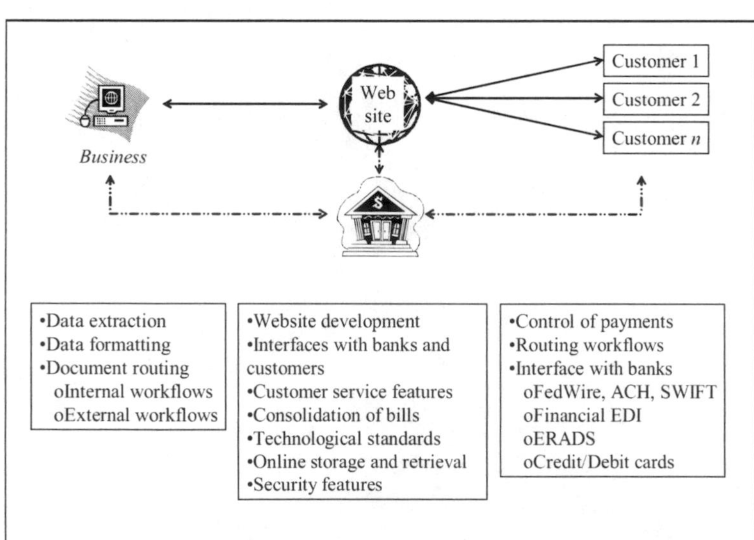

of thousands of pages) and large volumes of bills, graphical utilities to define data extraction rules for various bill types, creation of summary statements and the capability to match extracted data to the desired output format. The data extraction rules can also create header and trailer records for mathematical functions, such as calculation of payments totals, batch totals and batch count.

Output formats for an invoice or bill can be HTML, XML, image files or PDF, which are Internet-viewable formats; printed invoices and statements remain as a backup format. The EIPP/EBPP software provides standard templates for invoice creation, tax forms and logical controls, such as conditional IF statements, date and amount formatting, and audit controls. The software also has a document router that will route documents to the billers' or consolidators' Web sites. Capabilities sometimes include the ability to format summary data according to consolidators' specifications. These digital documents are archived online and indexed for easy retrieval. The standard biller-side control and reporting features include ability to access online documents, logging customer visits and payment behavior, data mining abilities and report generation capabilities.

The output can also be presented on e-mail, fax, palm device, cell phones and pagers, and can be remotely printed. The EIPP/EBPP software needs to be integrated with the Web application software. The messaging software to facilitate communication between concerned parties is also required. The EIPP/EBPP software also monitors delivery of the invoice to the customer. If the software detects failure in delivery, then alternate routes, such as printing and posting of the invoices, are invoked.

The EIPP software resides on the billers' and payers' systems. On the payer side, the EIPP software provides the ability to route the invoice to appropriate approvers. Ideally, the software should also be able to integrate with the back-end accounting system. This enables functionalities such as management of different supplier accounts, routing of invoices through approval workflows as defined by accounting software, tracking invoices online, assigning general ledger account numbers and running analytical routines. The EBPP software does not generally reside on the user side, since the Web sites are accessed using a browser.

On the payment side, the EIPP software provides creation of NACHA-compliant transactions, FEDI-type transactions and check printing ability for payroll and payables. The check printing software can be integrated or add-on to the EIPP software. The software has wizards (automated help tools) that enable creation of transaction numbers, bank account details, vendor payment information and addenda requirements. The payer can control amount to pay, payment format and settlement date. Payments are automatically released on a pre-specified settlement date. Reporting utilities can generate reports such as summary payable, details of payables and payment dates for various suppliers, among other things. In the EBPP software, the payer-side payment utilities primarily reside on the billers' or consolidators' Web sites and not on the payer's system.

The EIPP/EBPP software needs to provide an interface with the banks or financial institutions. Payment types such as FedWire, SWIFT, ACH, financial EDI, EFT, credit/debit cards and printed checks should be supported by the software. The EIPP software often provides wizards to create transactions with required payment options. Some vendors support ERADS, where payment moves through the financial institutions and remittance details are forwarded by e-mail or fax. If the seller uses electronic lockboxes, then the EIPP software should interface with these lockboxes to update accounts receivable files.

The hosting of Web-based bill presentment is done either in-house in case of direct billers or on the consolidator's Web site if a third-party is used for bill consolidation. Consolidators need to collect bills from various billing organizations. Conversion of bills into a required format is generally standardized. The consolidator has to develop technology standards in collaboration with the billing organizations and provide software tools to accomplish data extraction and conversion. Consolidators also need to collaborate with banks and financial institutions for collections from customers.

Security is an important requirement for acceptance of EIPP and EBPP. Standard security features on EIPP and EBPP software include firewall, intrusion detection software, high-quality encryption and message transmission security.[3] On the user side, software can be administered by the system administrator. The system administrator authorizes users and assigns log-in privileges. Log-in activities of users are recorded, and this information is available to the administrator. This log can provide auditability of the invoicing and payments process. The organizations can institute additional controls at the desktop level. The EBPP software also provides authentication and authorization controls for users. Many EBPP service providers make explicit guarantees for privacy, security and unauthorized payments.

Organizations wishing to offer EIPP/EBPP have several choices. First, the service can be developed, delivered, operated and managed in-house. This provides for a customized system tailored to the needs of the organization; however, it calls for considerable expertise and deep pockets. Second, packaged software can be purchased and integrated with the back-end accounting systems. Off-the-shelf packages have strong capabilities and can handle transactions for large organizations. Third, the entire EIPP/EBBP operation can be outsourced. There are vendors who can provide infrastructure and programs to manage operations of companies of all sizes. The key items that need to be addressed are as follows:

- Interface of existing cash or bank management systems with the EIPP/EBPP software
- Technological and security standards and their implementation in the existing environment
- Changes in the business workflows and internal controls
- Changes in accounts receivable and accounts payable processing
- Measurement of costs and benefits, and calculation of ROI
- Marketing of the system to customers and/or suppliers

Advantages and Disadvantages of EIPP and EBPP

The advantages of EIPP and EBPP accrue to all parties involved in the process. These include businesses that implement EIPP and EBPP, customers that join online billing and trading partners. Advantages are both tangible and intangible. EBPP and EIPP are supposed to provide strategic benefits and cost reductions. These can be summarized as follows:

- **Businesses:**
  - *Customer service:* Improvements in customer service is a motivating factor for many businesses to implement electronic invoicing. Customers can create their own accounts, track purchases and control payments. Analytical tools can be provided that will help customers compare and contrast invoices and bills. Changing of existing services, discontinuation of existing services and addition of new services is facilitated. Any other additional information can be provided via Web links.

    Digital documents can be downloaded by customers and uploaded to back-end accounting systems, reducing error rates. High-value customers can be given limited access to back-end accounting systems, say for order tracking. Invoices and bills can be presented in different languages and different formats for international customers. Such facilities can enhance customer loyalty and retention rates.
  - *Marketing opportunities:* Online customer databases can be used to deliver targeted marketing messages. There are opportunities for up-selling and cross-selling to customers. Online salespersons can assist customers with products and finalize orders immediately. EIPP also makes it easy to measure the effectiveness of marketing campaigns to existing customers.
  - *Cost reductions:* Direct cost savings include reduction in making, printing and mailing of bills. If the customer pays electronically, there are associated savings in the reduction of cash float, paper handling of incoming checks and manual entries in the accounting system. Businesses reduce their day's sales outstanding and improve cash management.

    Indirect savings result from self-service abilities provided by EIPP and EBPP. A large number of customer service inquiries are related to billing. A clearly designed electronic invoicing facility can provide answers to many routine questions, thereby reducing expensive customer support.
- **Customers:**
  - *Convenience:* In the B2C setting, activities such as obtaining billing information, analyzing bills, asking questions and controlling payments are easier for customers, as compared to paper-based bills. Customers can also download these bills directly into their personal money managers and avoid duplicate manual entries. The posting of payments can be confirmed relatively quickly, and accounts can be verified on an ad-hoc basis anytime. This will reduce wait for bank statements and canceled checks.

    For B2B partners, elimination of paper bills results in operational efficiencies. Electronic bills can also be easily integrated in the electronic workflows offered by different ERP packages. Disputes can be resolved online, approvals are faster, discounts are rarely missed and cash flow projections are relatively more precise.

- *Cost savings:* These result from elimination of paper-based processes. Expensive activities such as opening of incoming mail, manual reconciliations and paper-based checks can be reduced if not eliminated.

EIPP/EBPP is a new technology and faces inherent problems of introduction and adoption of a new technology. Crucial for success is adoption of the technology by a critical mass of users. In the absence of such users, the technology is not profitable and does not succeed in the marketplace. Problems with EIPP/EBPP can be summarized as follows.

- **Business:**
  - *Upfront and recurring costs:* The biller or the consolidator has to incur upfront costs to build the Web site and its integration with the back-end accounting system. There are also costs of developing technology standards for digital bills and invoices. These standards are required to handle multiple data input/output formats, deal with various transmission protocols and interface with customers' accounting software through a browser front end. Trading partners may need training and education in using EIPP, and those costs are sometimes borne by the biller.

    Recurring costs include maintaining the Web site, upgrading the Web site, maintaining and modifying technology standards, and administrative costs.
  - *Marketing costs:* The developer of EIPP/EBPP has to market the electronic invoicing services. Unless the critical mass of users accepts the concept, these services cannot become profitable. The biller has to design incentives, devise marketing campaigns, and educate partners to enroll and use EIPP/EBPP services.
  - *Risk management:* If the banks or financial institutions use a consolidator to present bills, they concede direct operational control. Risk management procedures routinely used by financial institutions, some mandated by federal regulations, must be followed by the EBPP providers. Federal regulators have expressed concerns in these areas.
- **Customers:**
  - *Information collection:* Customers have to navigate to the various Web sites to get billing information. Multiple sites mean managing multiple enrollments, multiple access routines and multiple data formats. In the B2B setting, the buyer needs to integrate an accounts payable system with multiple seller sites and has to comply with seller payment options.
  - *Learning curve:* There are initial costs in learning EBPP for customers. In case of EIPP, specialized training and education programs may be necessary to train accounting personnel.

- *Enrollment problems:* Customers should be able to subscribe and unsubscribe from the service. Conditions such as enrollment for at least 1 year, fees for subscribing or unsubscribing, and online problems can add costs to the service. Given the current state of online services, such scenarios are not only possible but likely.
- *Resistance to adoption:* First, consumers are reluctant to change their banking habits. Many people do not see much advantage in joining online billing. Second, consumers have repeatedly expressed concerns regarding privacy and security on the Web. Unless these concerns are addressed appropriately, EBPP may not achieve critical mass. Third, many billers are not capable of delivering electronic bills. That limits the number of bills available on the Web and discourages consumers, since paper-based bills continue to pour in. Some billers are waiting for a critical mass of users before offering EIPP/EBPP, creating a classic catch-22. Finally, from billers' perspective, there is a lack of industry-wide standards for data exchange.

EIPP/EBPP was touted as a *killer application* of the 21st century. However, the acceptance rates for EIPP/EBPP have not been very encouraging. The value proposition that looked so strong on paper did not work in the real world. As the technology matures, adoption rates are beginning to move upwards, but not as wildly forecasted as in earlier years. A treasury automation survey of Fortune 1000 companies indicated that approximately 40% to 50% businesses are interested in EIPP and EBPP, and approximately 10% have already adopted EIPP/EBPP. This survey also revealed that the three most important reasons for adopting EIPP/EBPP were cost reduction, service improvement and elimination of billing errors. A report from Gartner Group suggests that only 9% (B2C setting) and 2.3% (B2B setting) adoption rates are required for a positive ROI. Giga Information Group, on the other hand, estimates that EIPP/EBBP services can become profitable when adoption rates are 12% to 15%. EIPP/EBPP does not have a large installed base; however, awareness among businesses and consequent adoption rates continue to inch upward.

Receivables and Collections

Online Management of Receivables

Receivables management involves collection of receivables, post-collection activities and financial analytics. The collection of receivables includes contacting the customer via telephone calls or e-mails, customized dunning letters, resolution of disputes, face-to-face contact and any other activities to speed up collections. Post-collection activities include matching incoming payments with invoices to get correct accounts receivable; follow-up with customers via calls, letters or e-mails; and generating financial reports, such as an accounts receivable aging schedule. Financial analytics involves performing ratio analysis, cash flow analysis and determining working capital status.

Exhibit 22. Online receivables management

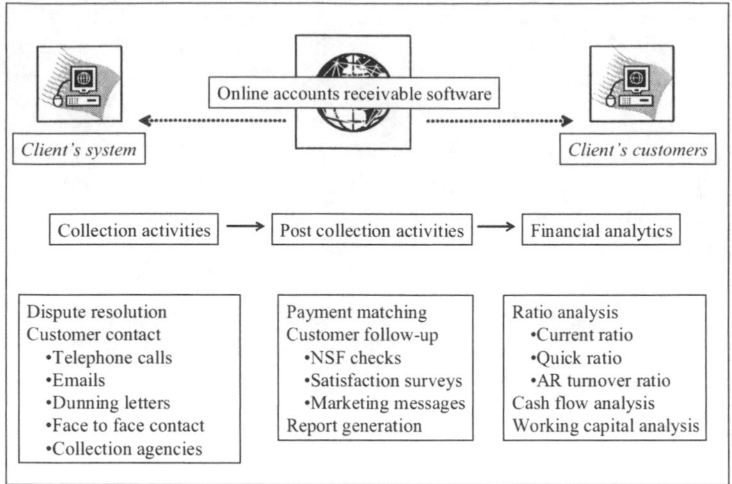

The Internet has not generated new processes to displace existing receivables management. The primary effects of the Internet in this area are to move paper-based or manual processes online and reengineer existing processes. Numerous online organizations offer online receivables management. These services generally develop a comprehensive software suite to handle various accounts receivable management functions. These online organizations also partner with accounting software vendors, enabling integration of their services with their client's systems. These services are often industry- and software-specific.

Online services start with credit evaluation of the client's customers, covered earlier. Services provided in the collection services area are generally transparent to the client's customer. The letters and paper-based bills that go to the client's customer are on the client's logo, checks are drawn on the name of the client and aforwarded to the client's lockbox or physical location. Clerical work is handled by the online organization. Detailed account information is available on the Internet and includes balances, payments, status of delinquent accounts and transaction histories, among other things. Many of these organizations also offer EIPP/EBPP, factoring, processing of returned checks and ancillary marketing services. Marketing services might include delivery of marketing messages, frequent shopper-type programs, data mining, customer profiling and automatic e-mails.

The topic of *factoring of receivables*, sometimes referred to as accounts receivable financing, needs further examination. Online financing companies have changed the dynamics of factoring. A significant number of small- and mid-size businesses need to factor accounting receivables. The factoring of receivables means sale of receivables to a financing company. The financing company buys the receivables at discount and/or charges factoring fees. A certain percentage of receivables, for example, 80% of the invoice price, is immediately handed over to the business. If the receivables are collected in a timely fashion, the remaining 20% (less discounts or factoring fees) will also be paid. Depending on the terms of the agreement, the risks of collection may or may not be passed to the financing company.

The online factoring process has reduced paperwork considerably. The majority of online factoring companies have forms and ancillary documentation on the Web site that can be filled and submitted online by businesses wishing to factor receivables. However, other processes are in a varied state of automation. A few companies have automated the entire process. For example, 21st Century Capital has the following process: The entire application and documentation process required for enrollment is online. The application and ancillary documentation can be filled and submitted online. Identity of the business or person wishing to avail the facilities is verified through *Equifax eIDVerifier™*, which serves as an online notary public substitute. The *I Agree* button serves as a surrogate for a signature and authenticates the factoring agreement.

The process of printing invoices and mailing them to the financing company has also been eliminated. 21st Century's Web site provides online tools for creating and storing digital invoices. Supporting documents, such as purchase order, shipping documents and bills of lading, need to be faxed. The faxed documents are converted into digital documents and stored with the invoices. These can be viewed, downloaded or printed by authorized parties. Payment data is also posted on the Web site, which is useful in managing cash flows.

These services are primarily marketed to small- and mid-size corporations. Some online companies also cater to non-profit organizations and universities. The large corporations generally have a necessary accounts receivable management infrastructure in place. Large corporations may use these services on a selective basis in a specific area. Online receivable management companies are in flux, and are rapidly consolidating or disappearing. A proper choice of partner is absolutely necessary in this area.

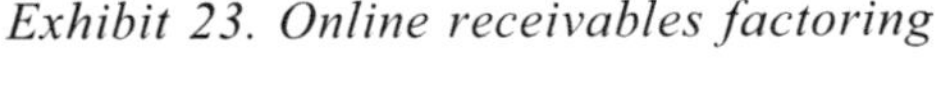

Exhibit 23. Online receivables factoring

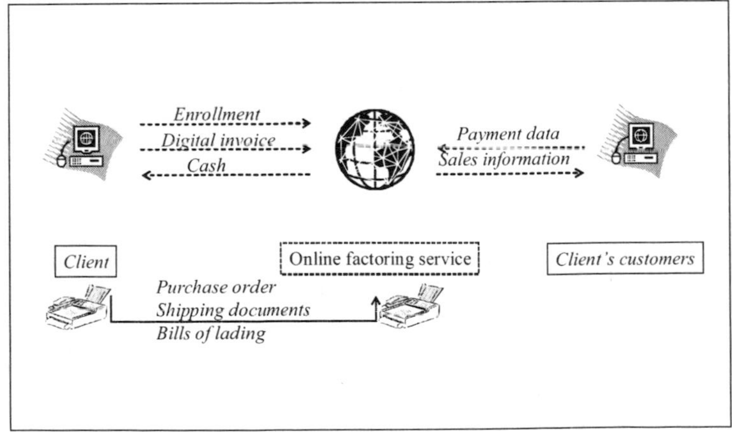

Electronic Payment Methods

Standard payment methods and Web-era payment methods can be broadly classified into three categories. First, the customer receives goods or services and informs the financial institution, which then makes the payment to the business. Second, the customer provides payment information to the business either by phone, fax, e-mail or Web site, and this information is validated by the bank and payment is transmitted to the business. Finally, the customers make direct payments to a business without any intermediate financial institution. The first two methods have existed for decades as standard payment methods in B2B and B2C transactions. The standard ways of making payment have been check, credit cards and EFT.

The third method of bypassing financial institutions and making payments directly surfaced in the Internet age. Customers have paid in cash for hundreds or thousands of years, so the idea of digital cash was floated. The dot-com era spawned a variety of digital cash payment methods suitable for e-commerce. The majority of these digital cash inventions, especially in the B2C area, have not been successful. Needless to say, digital cash does not bypass financial institutions completely, since the customer has to purchase digital cash some place. Several payment methods also have altered the basic credit card payment model, with varying degrees of acceptance in the marketplace. On the other hand, a few online payment methods in the B2B area have been viable. In this section, the focus is on different electronic payment methods used in e-commerce.

Initially, in the B2C area, there was an explosion in online payment methods. The number of online companies offering these services has been declining, but remains quite strong.

Exhibit 24. Transaction clearing — Yahoo! categories (Source: www.yahoo.com)

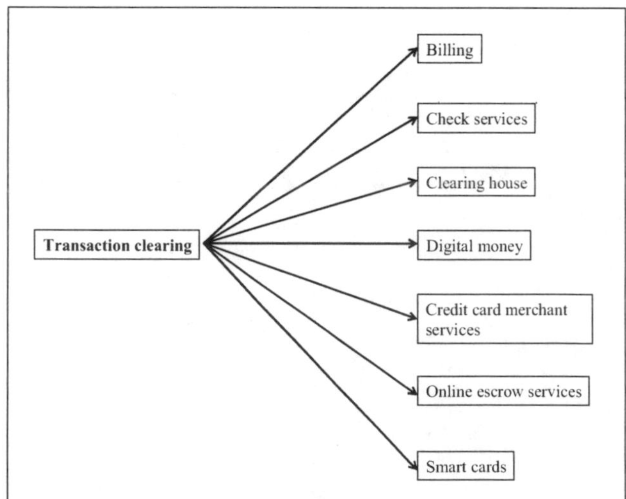

Exhibit 25. Types of online payments

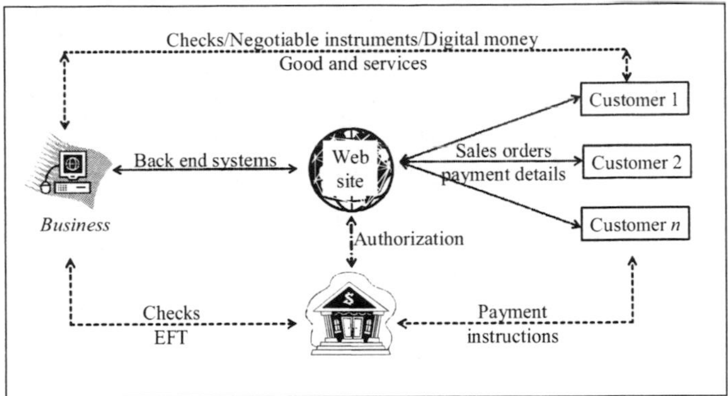

First, payment methods in this area are examined. These methods can be conceptually classified in five categories: credit cards and checks, stored value cards, replenishment accounts, phone-based billing and micropayments. Some of the methods are now crossing over to the B2B area, and the distinctions are not exact. Second, electronic wallets that support these payment methods are discussed. Third, developments in the B2B area are discussed. A number of commonalities in the B2B and B2C areas exist; however, payment methods more prevalent in the B2B world are stressed in the ensuing discussion. Finally, electronic lockboxes are discussed. Remember, most of these technologies are not new, but generally at least a decade old. These are being refined for wider applications in the online world.

B2C Payment Methods

Credit Cards and Online Checks

Currently in the B2C area, a credit card is the most prevalent method of payment. In the U.S., there exists an excellent infrastructure to support credit card payments, and for consumers there is legal liability protection. Credit card essentially consists of name, number, expiration date and magnetic stripes. The number system in credit cards is based on ANSI Standard X4.13 (1983), and the numbers convey certain information; for example, if the first number is 3 then it is a travel/entertainment card, if the number is 4 then it is a visa card and so forth. The magnetic stripes encode the information provided in front of the card.

The credit card payment mechanism is simple. When the card is passed through the card reader, the stored information is transmitted to the credit card company. This information is verified, the amount charged is assessed to be within the credit limit on the card, and then payment is approved. In the Internet environment, instead of a magnetic strip, the concerned person provides information by filling in onscreen questions. Approximately 85% to 90% of online payments are done by credit cards. However, credit cards pose many problems in e-commerce, especially from a security perspective:

- Credit cards are designed for face-to-face commerce. Identifiers such as name, social security number and signature are irrelevant in e-commerce. There have been efforts by some credit card companies to introduce PINs in online transactions for additional security, though enrollment is voluntary.
- Credit card data, basically name and card number, can be easily stolen. Card numbers do not change and are stored on merchant servers, and can become easy targets for hackers.
- Credit cards are easy to duplicate.
- Credit card fraud costs run into tens of billions of dollars. There are no concerted efforts by credit card companies to create common fraud fighting utilities. However, there are increased signs of activity in this area, due to the rising frequency of online scams such as identity theft and phishing.

Checks remain another popular method of payment on the Internet. The checks can be mailed in after purchase. However, check payments can also be effected online in real time, and there are numerous online check verification services. The check verification and approval mechanism is very similar to the credit cards. The customer makes a purchase and decides to pay by check. The payment option is selected. Then the customer is directed to the online check verification service. The customer is asked to fill in a blank check on the screen, sometimes called a virtual register, which includes the usual information and also bank account and routing numbers. The online service

Exhibit 26. Online checks[4]

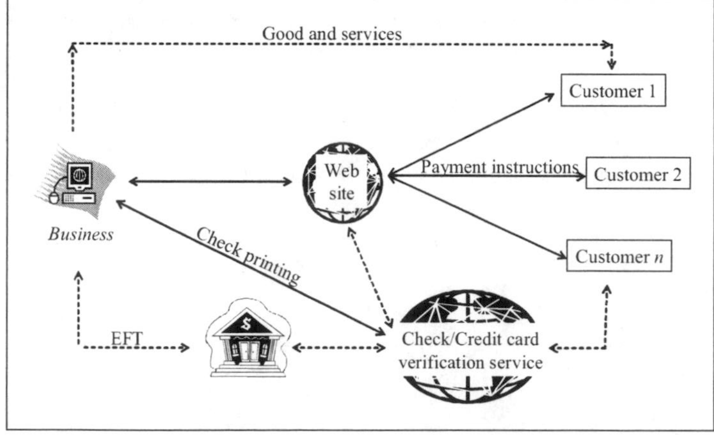

Exhibit 27. A conceptual representation of virtual check (Source: www.echeck2000.com/echeck_gateway.asp "\t" _blank")

First Name Last Name Check Number

Address

City State Zip Code

Phone

Amount

Pay to the Order of

Bank Routing Number Bank Account Number

Additional Information

E-mail Address Birth Date

Driver's License Number Merchant Reference Number

contacts the bank, confirms the account and approves the check. The process is transparent and the customer is not aware of the underlying steps.

The transfer of funds can be facilitated in different ways. The online service can transmit the check to the merchant, which is then printed and then deposited in the bank. The other method is to directly deposit the funds in the merchant's account through EFT. These services are also used for phone orders, fax orders or face-to-face business. For example, when a customer writes a check, it will be swiped through a reader. The information will be transmitted to the online service, which then follows the process described earlier. The online service approves or rejects the check in a matter of a few seconds or minutes. Additional services such as a log of transactions, NSF checks information, online availability and delivery of customized reports, and downloading of payment data to the merchant's desktop may also be available. Detailed information regarding electronic checks – standards, protocols, specifications and technology is available on *www.echeck.org/*.

The estimates for all types of check frauds range from millions to billions of dollars. Security precautions invariably include protecting blank checks, separation of duties, making checks tamperproof by using water marks, holograms and multi-colored printing, among other things. However, these precautions are not useful in the online environment. The problems and potential for fraud in online checks is similar to fraud in credit card payments. There are software products that assess risk in credit card and online check payments; for example, see *www.vscrub.com/*.

Stored Value Cards

Stored value cards, as the name says, store value in the card; for example, prepaid phone cards. The phone card can be used until the allocated minutes are exhausted. Generally, value in the stored value cards is cash. Stored value cards are useful in commerce, electronic or otherwise, when customers prefer to pay in cash. The value in the stored value cards is input by the customer by paying upfront cash or making arrangements with the bank or financial institution. Stored value cards can be dumb cards, meaning storing little information apart from the cash balances, or can be smart, meaning storing a great deal of information. The terms stored value cards, smart cards, and memory cards are used interchangeably in the business; however, stored value cards are not synonymous with smart cards. A smart card certainly stores value — money or information — but a stored value card is not always smart.

Banks have offered prepaid debit and credit cards to customers for a long time. Customers having problems in acquiring credit cards can opt for prepaid cards, which generally charge a hefty fee. These prepaid cards are similar to stored value cards. The primary difference in debit cards and stored value cards is that debit cards leave funds in the customer's account until the transaction is completed. The use of stored value cards has gone far beyond merely paying for goods; businesses have found a variety of uses for these cards. An illustrative list of applications of stored value cards follows.

- **Cash cards:** This term primarily refers to cards that hold cash, or prepaid cards. Businesses that issue cash allowances and refunds for returns to customers and employees can issue cash cards in lieu of cash or check. Few retail businesses mandate that these cards can only be spent in the store; thereby limiting impact on cash flow. These cards can also be issued to employees who only need occasional access to cash and can be used on an imprest basis. Many students use cash cards on campus that obviates the need to carry cash.
- **Payroll cards:** These cards store cash equaling the net wages or salary of an employee. These cards can be redeemed at Point of Sale (POS) terminals or an ATM. Such cards save costs of printing, cutting and mailing checks. These cards are especially useful in the case of employees who refuse to accept EFT, do not want to cash checks or for any other reason only accept cash.
- **Family cards:** These cards are targeted at kids and teens. Parents fund the card and can monitor usage of the card either via online services or through regular statements. These cards can be used just like credit cards in online and offline businesses.
- **Gift cards:** These are similar to cash cards. Gift cards can be generally used at specified locations, such as a particular store or mall. These cards can be purchased over the Internet or at local facilities. If a specific store issues such a gift card, it is also referred to as a *merchant card.*
- **Incentive cards:** As the name says, these cards are given to employees for performance. These cards are issued instead of gifts, checks or prizes. Incentive

cards are generally cheaper than checks or gift checks and the cash is immediately available for consumption.

- **Mall cards:** These are prepaid cards that can be used at a particular shopping mall. These can be customized and bear a logo of the mall, or can be general mall cards.
- **Benefits cards:** Checks are generally issued for health care reimbursement costs or by government agencies for claims and benefits. The benefit card can be used to deliver value instead of checks.
- **Virtual cards:** This card is virtual, lacking a physical plastic counterpart. The card is represented by numbers and can be used as a credit card in the online environment. This can also be a debit account. In any case, this card provides anonymity in the online environment.

The advantages of stored valued cards can be summarized as follows. First, the cards can be used instead of cash, checks, traveler's checks or cashier's checks; additionally, these can be used at an ATM. Second, the cards operate similarly to credit cards and there is little or no learning curve. Third, these cards can be disposed of or can be reloaded repeatedly. Fourth, from the seller's perspective, only online equipment is needed to verify the validity of the card, and no expensive third-party approval is required. The management of electronic transfer of stored value is easier than management of cash and coins.

There are also disadvantages. First, funds need to be paid up front, forfeiting interest. Second is the fee structure associated with the stored value cards — some financial institutions are known for expensive stored value cards, and some cards lose value if not used in a specified time period. Third, if the card is lost, the process of reclaiming cash on the card can be tedious. Finally, the purchase protection and limited liability offered by credit cards is not always available on stored value cards.

Smart Cards

A smart card is a credit card-type, plastic card that contains an embedded general-purpose microprocessor, typically an 8-bit microcontroller, though higher-bit configurations are evolving. Sizes and shapes of the smart cards are also beginning to differ from the standard credit card. The microprocessor replaces the magnetic stripe on credit cards. This microprocessor makes the card smart by enabling thousands of times of more storage information. A smart card can contain different types of information; for example, social security numbers, bank account numbers, credit card numbers, private encryption schemes, health information and insurance details, among other things. Due to the superior storage capabilities, the smart card has been applied in different areas apart from funds transfer.

The smart card was invented in the 1960s; technology development occurred in different countries. Smart cards took off in the 1980s, when the semiconductor technology became capable of supporting advanced functionality in smart cards. The term smart card was invented in France and continues to be used today. ISO has issued numerous standards for smart cards. The standards for physical and mechanical characteristics are more

Exhibit 28. Smart card

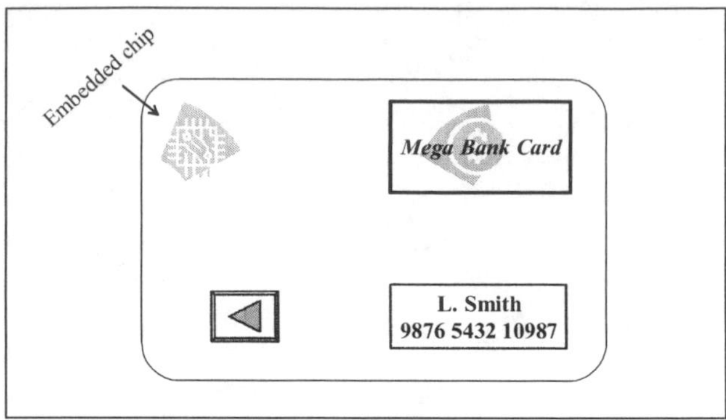

consistently observed than software standards. There are many competing standards formulated by companies, industrial consortiums and user groups.

The smart card consists of a single integrated chip that houses a central processing unit, Read Only Memory (ROM), RAM and programmable memory. Additionally, a smart card contains card software and input/output ports. The ROM portion of the smart card consists of the programs written during the manufacturing phase of the chip. RAM is used by the smart card when the card is interacting with a PC or with an application that requires a timely response. The programmable memory can be used to change the information contained on the smart card. The card itself contains personal identification information of the user, applications and data files, and a directory structure to identify data files. The Erasable and Programmable Read Only Memory (EPROM) is used to change the information; however, changes can be made only finite times, approximately 100,000 times. The size of each memory depends on the design of the smart card.

Exhibit 29. The evolution of the smart card

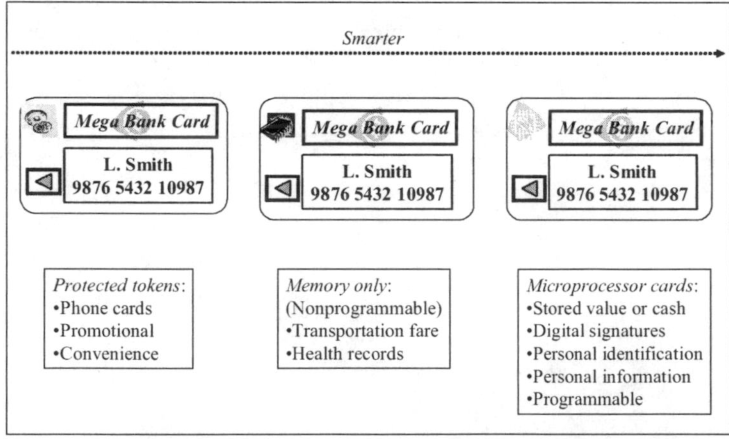

The card software consists of an operating system, utility and application software. The primary functions of the card software are to manage the internal information, communicate with the outside readers and implement security features, and can be used to customize an off-the-shelf smart card. Security features deal with protecting the accessing and processing of applications and data on the smart cards. The principles of cryptography and complex algorithms are used to hide the information from external observers. As the use of smart cards grows, the attempts to crack security are becoming sophisticated. The security features, in turn, are evolving. Input/output ports are used to connect with card readers and/or PCs.

Smart cards are generally read by an external reader. A smart card reader authenticates the merchant and the holder, then proceeds to make the transaction. There are two types of smart cards: contact and contactless. Contact cards are physically in contact with the reader, such as inserting in a slot or floppy drive of the computer. Contactless cards operate using radio frequencies and need not touch the reader. The range is pretty short; however, these types of cards are useful in security applications; for example, entering a secured area.

Smart cards are evolving continuously. The UltraCard Inc. (*www.ultracard.com/*) has introduced a smart card that uses a thin magnetic strip that can come out of the card. This card comes in contact and contactless forms. This magnetic strip can store up to 20 MB of information, and storage capacity is increasing. Due to the high level of storage, this card can store fingerprints, iris scans, photographs, voiceprints or similar biometric identification measures. The higher storage enables multiple security applications, allowing for private keys, certificate and public/private key infrastructure, among other things.[5] These measures, the company claims, will provide almost unbreakable levels of security. The card can only be accessed by organizations authorized by the user.

The smart card has found applications in many areas. For example, payments over the Internet, computer security and access, wireless communications, banking, identifica-

Exhibit 30. Architecture of a smart card

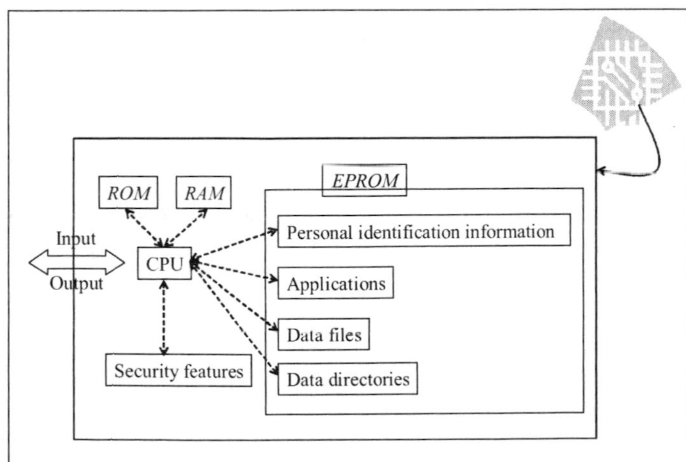

tion purposes and security; have all seen extensive use of smart cards. Smart cards are issued by a variety of organizations. Smart Card Alliance is a non-profit organization that works for acceptance of smart card technology. A visit to *www.smartcardalliance.org/* will show an extensive list of companies active in this area. Since we are interested in the use of smart cards in e-commerce, let us take a look at a smart card payment process.

Initially, the holder of the card needs to contact the bank and download the cash into the card. The holder can transfer the cash on the phone to a compatible card. In case of online transactions, the card is first inserted into the reader. Special hardware sometimes needs to be purchased by the user. The reader authenticates the holder and the merchant as valid parties to the transaction. Before transmitting the payment, the holder's reader receives the digital signature from the merchant. The card, after verification, sends its own digital signature, which is acknowledged by the merchant. Then cash is deducted from the holder's card and transferred to the merchant's account. The digital signature from the merchant's card is again confirmed by the customer's card, and the transaction is complete only after valid confirmation. The process is similar to a credit card; however, card readers on both sides validate the user, and issues of non-repudiation become irrelevant.

Smart cards have many advantages. First, smart cards have more functionality than dumb cards and can be programmed and/or perform local processing. These abilities enable a wide range of applications. Second, smart cards are more durable and secure, and store more information than existing credit cards. Security protocols of the card are not dependent on the communications channel and, as such, transactions can be conducted over unprotected public networks. Finally, smart cards can be used in different communication media, such as phones, personal digital assistants and PCs.

Despite these advantages, smart cards have not taken off in the U.S. The use of smart cards in Asia, Europe and Latin America is much higher than in the U.S. The expense of purchasing new hardware, familiarity with credit cards, liability protection and the lack of critical mass in adoption are some reasons cited in low usage of smart cards in e-commerce. Other significant concerns exist also, such as privacy, centralization of personal information at one place and greater governmental and/or corporate control. The momentum for smart cards, however, is building, and the forecasts for usage of smart cards show a steeply rising trend.

Replenishment Accounts

In this payment method, a third-party online vendor manages payment and payment information for the seller and buyer. PayPal (*www.paypal.com/*) and InternetCash (*www.internetcash.com/*) are the leading vendors that provide this type of service or variations thereof. With PayPal, the customer has to first navigate to the Web site of the online vendor and register. The customer provides information concerning bank account or credit card information. InternetCash, on the other hand, offers secure stored value cards for use on the Internet. Once the account is established, the customer can use services offered by the online service. Sellers also need to follow a similar process and register at the site. However, the seller has to put client-side tools on its Web site, provided by the online vendor.

Exhibit 31. Replenishment account payment process

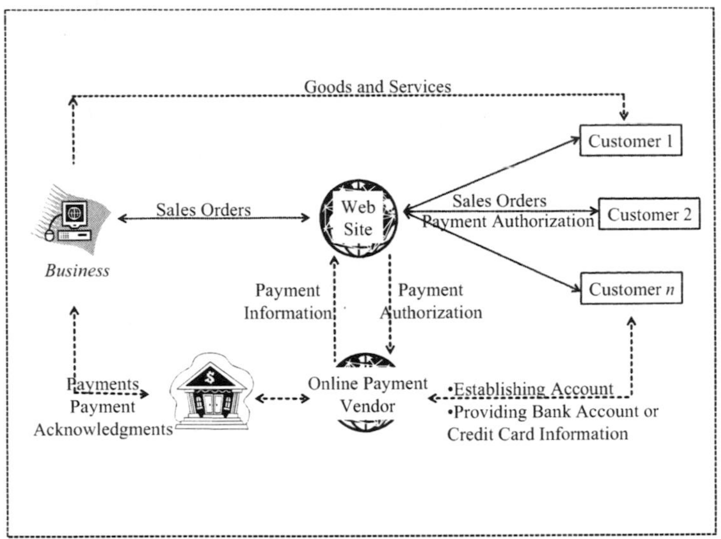

If the customer decides to purchase from a participating Web site, the customer clicks on the appropriate payment button. This button takes the customer to the Web site of the online vendor. Payment instructions are now delivered at this Web site. The online vendor, after due authorization and authentication, transmits payment to the seller. The payment is either charged to the credit card or debited from the customer's bank account.

After receipt of payment, goods or services will be delivered to the customer. The advantage of this method is instead of transmitting a credit card number or bank account information to each seller, the information needs to be stored only at one place. InternetCash uses digital signatures based on card numbers and customer PINs to authenticate the transaction. These online services also provide for a mediation process in case of dispute between seller and buyer. These services can also be used for recurring payment, such as subscriptions. PayPal even allows C2C payments; the only condition is the payers and the payee should have a valid e-mail address.

Phone-Based Billing

This payment method is generally used for buying digital goods and services, music, articles or games, and viewing pay-per-view sites on the Internet. In this method, purchases are charged to the customer's phone account. Currently, eCharge (*www.echarge.com/*) is one online company that offers phone-based billing. The customer has to navigate to the eCharge Web site and download a client-side piece of software. The seller also has to install a special icon on the payment page and install server-side software provided by the vendor. This software communicates with the eCharge server for completion of the transaction.

The customer downloads the product before payment. The downloaded digital product is encrypted and unusable. When the customer approves payment, the customer's modem is disconnected and dialed into a 900 number. The phone bill is charged at this dialing in. At the same time, the customer also receives a decryption string for the digital product. Then the modem is reconnected with the ISP's order confirmation and completion page. These transactions are transparent to the user.

This payment method does not need any personal information of the user. The necessary information is derived from the 900 number call. The customer receives the phone bill, pays the bill and the seller gets the payment. eCharge charges fees to the seller and the buyer, depending on the size of the transaction. Generally, there is also a ceiling on the amount of purchase for the customer. The phone-based system is easy to operate for both the seller and customer. This service is primarily aimed at approximately 30% of the U.S. population, who do not have credit cards but have telephone access. The drawback for the seller is that there is a considerable time lag in delivering service and receiving payment.

Micropayments

These services cater to transactions that are less than $1. However, the term *micropayment* is defined differently by different people. A standard definition describes micropayments as a low-value economic activity. Again, the term *low value* can be interpreted differently. The issue of micropayments arises especially regarding digital goods and products. A payment of a small amount using checks and credit cards is not economical. The payment mechanism then becomes a bottleneck in e-commerce.

Numerous innovations, such as Millicent protocol[6], arose to meet this challenge. The majority of these companies is now either out of business or provides different services in addition to micropayments. The whole area of micropayments never became as important as predicted by its proponents. Currently, micropayments do not prominently figure in e-commerce payment mechanisms. Many organizations serve the micropayments market; for example, eCharge, MicroCreditCard and Peppercoin. However, these companies handle micropayments in the framework of electronic payment methods described earlier.

Electronic Wallets

The electronic wallet, an e-counterpart of physical wallets, is not exactly a payment mechanism. These wallets facilitate management of online payments, especially credit and debit cards. An e-wallet contains customer-specific information, such as name, billing and shipping address, credit card numbers, bank account numbers and any other additional information as input by the user of the wallet. The primary purpose of the electronic wallet is to make online shopping convenient and secure by protecting and automating routine shopping functions.

Most Web sites have a standard way of authenticating users, especially with user IDs and passwords. As the number of Web sites used for online shopping increases, usernames and passwords become difficult to manage. Usernames and passwords are

Exhibit 32. Passport authentication mechanism

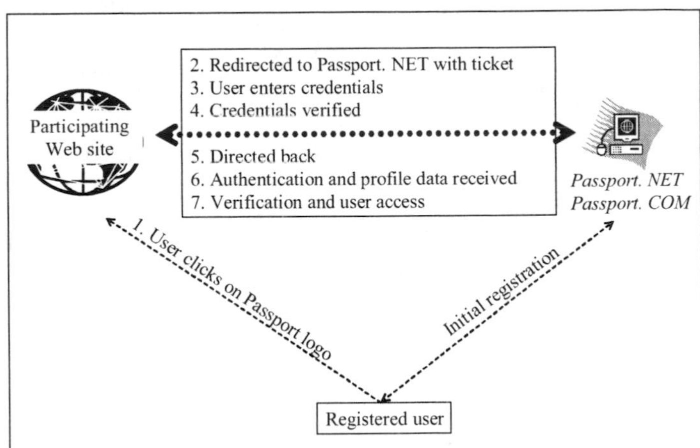

often generated on the spur of the moment and hard to remember. If the same username and password is used at every site, that can become a security risk. These Web sites also have different forms to fill in and different information is asked for. A few online merchants have simplified the process; for example, Amazon.com's single-click system. Electronic wallets simplify the online shopping process by storing necessary information securely and making it accessible.

There are two types of electronic wallets — client side and server side. Client-side electronic wallets need to be downloaded and installed on the consumer's machine. Such installation ensures security of the information, since the information is stored on the individual machine. Unless that machine is compromised, information remains safe. The problem with client-side electronic wallets is *portability*. If the consumer is using any other machine, the wallet becomes unavailable. This is a serious problem, since most consumers use at least two machines, and probably more. A number of dot-com companies initially offered client-side wallets, and most are out of business now.

The server-side electronic wallet resides on the server. The question is, whose server? The electronic wallet is provided by a provider such as Microsoft. Consumers access the provider's Web site and fill in the application to activate the service. The electronic wallets reside on the provider's servers and are accessible from any machine, including mobile phones, PDAs and digital TVs. The disadvantage of this method is that if the provider's server is compromised, a huge database of confidential information becomes available for misuse. The other problem is that this database can be misused by the provider. Questions regarding provider integrity, privacy policies and past behavior need to be raised and answered.

Take a look at Microsoft's .net Passport service — a server-side implementation. Passport includes the following services: single sign-in service, express purchase and kids passport service. Passport single sign-in service allows users to store commonly used information in the Passport profile. This information can be transmitted to the participating site if desired by the user. This takes care of user names, passwords and filling in of different forms. Passport express purchase service allows users to create an electronic wallet that can store billing/shipping information, credit card numbers and telephone numbers, among other things. Kids passport service allows parental control over information sharing with Web sites and monitoring of profile information.

Passport stores the following types of information — credentials, profile data and wallet information. Credentials are security-related information, such as passwords, PINs, security keys, and/or secret questions and answers. Profile data includes e-mail address, first and last name, birth date, gender and postal address, among other things. E-mail address is common to the credential field and profile data. A large portion of profile data is optional and not shared with other sites unless authorized by the user. Wallet information consists of name, billing and shipping address, credit card or bank account numbers, and telephone numbers.

Initially, a user has to register with the Passport service. This can be done at *www.passport.com/* or at participating sites. User data now resides on Microsoft servers. Once registered, the Passport service primarily performs the authentication function. The user is identified by verifying credentials at the participating sites. The process works as follows: The user browses to the navigating site and clicks on the Passport logo. This site then attaches what is called a *ticket*, a small amount of data revealing time of sign in and some other information, and redirects the user to Passport.com. The information tickets are transferred as appendages to URLs or cookies, rather than server-to-server communication. The information flowing between Web sites uses SSL7 for further protection.

On the Passport Web site, the user enters his or her credentials. These are verified and a cookie is attached to the user's browser. The user is redirected to the original Web site with encrypted packets of information. These packets contain an authentication ticket and any optional profile information as authorized by the user. The original Web site can now authenticate the user as a valid user by using software called Passport manager, which is installed on the Web site's server. The user is then allowed to access secure content and/or perform other functions. This process is transparent and the user is generally not aware of the redirecting of information between the Web sites. The Passport service encompasses more activities than described above; for example, there are additional security provisions if the user is browsing on public networks.

Initial hype predicted that electronic wallets will become a focal point in e-commerce. These wallets have found little acceptance. The basic question is, do consumers really need this type of service? The question has been partially answered in the marketplace. Next, for these wallets to be accepted, problems of standardization and interoperability need to be settled. Different types of electronic wallets are accepted by different online businesses. Consumers need to have multiple electronic wallets, which creates a problem of managing electronic wallets. Different security protocols were used by different wallets; many online businesses were not interested in becoming compatible with these formats. So electronic wallets could only be used at certain places. The situation is changing, but the problem of setting market-wide standards still exists, and plagues Microsoft.

B2B Payment Methods

The majority of payment mechanisms in the B2C world are used to some extent in the B2B world. The dominant forms of payments in the B2B world are ACH, FedWire, FEDI or similar systems. Banking or financial institutions are central to these transactions. A host of organizations exist to manage, facilitate or support these types of transactions. Many of these payment variations have been discussed earlier. However, there are few organizations that have successfully displaced a bank as a central institution. Actrade Financial Technologies was one such online company, and offered a successful product called Electronic Trade Acceptance Draft (*E-TAD*). The company is in bankruptcy courts, but the payment process is still worthy of study.

E-TAD originated from Trade Acceptance Drafts (TAD). Actrade used TADs in the international commerce before the advent of the dot-com era. In the year 2000, an e-version of the TADs was commercialized. E-TAD was similar to an electronic check, not issued by any bank, but issued by Actrade. E-TAD was described as a negotiable electronic payment obligation issued by a buyer to the supplier. This instrument was payable at a future date and could be endorsed. The clearance mechanism was through banking networks; however, E-TAD was encoded by Actrade technology. Buyers could issue one or more E-TADs, and the terms could be up to 6 months.

The process worked as follows: Buyers and suppliers had to enroll in the program at the Actrade Web site. Initial documents needed to be signed and forwarded to Actrade. The buyer's credit limit was assessed and approved. Only the buyers from the U.S. and Canada could participate in the program; suppliers could be anywhere in the world. Actrade was planning to expand the service to other countries. When the buyer purchased goods or services from the supplier, individual Web site, B2B exchanges or any other method, the buyer had to indicate the payment option as E-TAD. Payment request was then forwarded to the Actrade server for processing.

Exhibit 33. Conceptual representation of trade acceptance draft

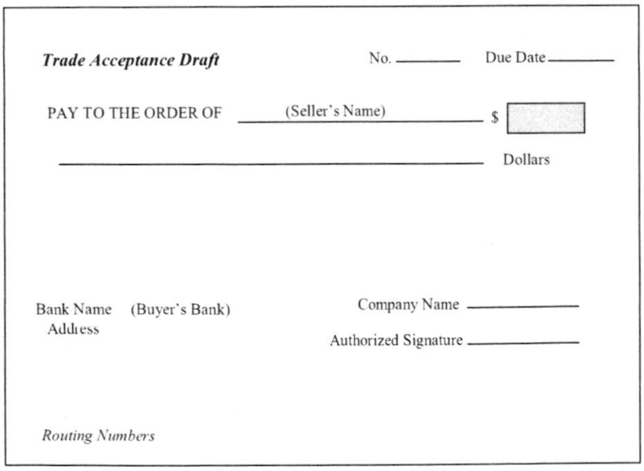

Trade Acceptance Draft No. ______ Due Date ______

PAY TO THE ORDER OF (Seller's Name) ______ $

______ Dollars

Bank Name (Buyer's Bank)
Address

Company Name ______
Authorized Signature ______

Routing Numbers

Exhibit 34. E-TAD

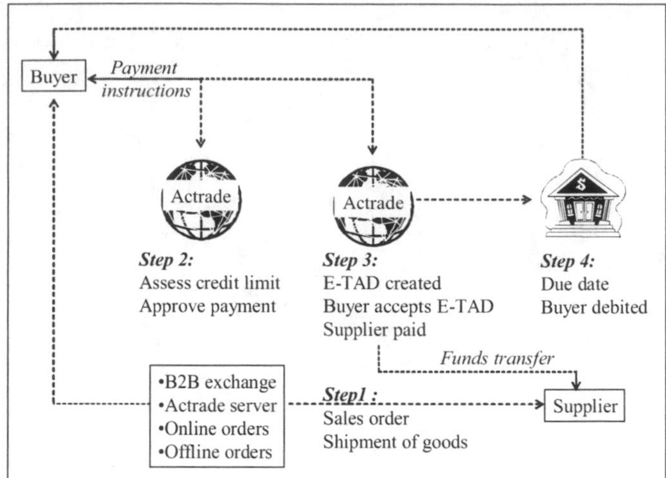

If purchases were made offline, then buyers had to log in to the Actrade server. The buyer submitted the necessary information, and after evaluating the buyer's credit status, the Actrade server would process the transaction. There were no enrollment fees for buyers or suppliers. If a payment was approved, the supplier was electronically notified and an E-TAD image was created. E-TAD was presented to the buyer for endorsement. At this endorsement, the buyer was deemed to have paid fully for the ordered goods or services.

Actrade then purchased the face value of E-TAD from the supplier — less, of course, discounts. The discount need not be paid by the supplier, depending on the terms; a discount could also be paid by the buyer or split between the buyer and the seller. The supplier received the payment in a couple of days. Actrade held the E-TAD up to the designated future date and then debited the buyer's bank account. The buyer got flexible payment terms and the supplier received immediate cash. Actrade took over the credit risk..

E-TAD was an online method for accelerating collections of accounts receivable. In that respect, it was similar to factoring or a bank line of credit. There were differences. E-TADs financed only one transaction, and were purchased by Actrade without recourse. E-TAD, being an unsecured method of financing, was similar to a bank line of credit, though there were no fees.

B2B electronic payment methods are varied and in flux. There are almost infinite variations of the payment methods described so far. Major payment methods and the leading vendors supporting these methods have been examined in this section. There are many players, software vendors, financial institutions, trades exchanges and ancillary hardware vendors — it is impossible to cover them comprehensively. Due to the nature of the online business, new players enter and old ones exit all the time.

Electronic Lockboxes

A lockbox is basically a collection and processing service provided by a bank or financial institution. Customers are given a specific address, generally a post box, for payment delivery. The address generally has a unique zip code for faster mail delivery. The checks at this post box are sorted, totaled, recorded and deposited. The details of these checks are then forwarded to the accounts receivable or credit department of the concerned organization. There are generally two types of lockboxes — retail and wholesale. Retail lockboxes use Optical Character Recognition (OCR) technology and are suitable for low-dollar and high-volume payments. Wholesale lockboxes manually process invoices, and payments are suitable for high-dollar and low-volume payments.

The paper-based lockbox invariably induces a time lag in payment information and creates problems for credit departments and working capital management. Enter electronic lockboxes! Electronic lockboxes can handle payments through ACH, FedWire, EDI payments or paper checks. Additionally, these lockboxes can be retail or wholesale. Paper checks are converted into digital images generally via OCR technology. Incoming payments are electronically processed and deposited. The accounting information is captured in the process and can be transmitted online to the concerned organization. The information can be provided on a disk or hard copy as desired.

The advantage of receiving information online is that it can be directly downloaded into accounting software. Accounting software then can automatically match payments, and unmatched payments can be reconciled manually. This system obviously results in operational efficiency by saving costs and time. The problems in this system are at the software design and interface stages. Many banks and accounting software vendors have teamed up to provide compatible solutions.

A similar technology can be used for electronic bank statements. At the end of the month, the bank transmits the bank statement electronically to the company. On the other hand, an electronic bank statement can be posted at a secure Web site and can be downloaded by the company. The bank statement is directly downloaded to accounting software and automatically reconciled. Anyone who has done bank reconciliation by hand will appreciate the automation. In the real world, the implementation can be difficult, since many bank accounts are used and multiple bank statements need to be downloaded; many banks may not even offer this service. The majority of leading accounting software packages can handle automatic download and reconciliation.

A Word on Digital Cash

Digital cash, also known as e-currency, Web money or electronic cash, has been around for at least a decade. The use of digital cash did not catch up as expected, and many pioneering organizations have gone under. Digital cash is still being used, however; for example, in smart cards, stored value cards, online casinos and by some pay-per-view Web sites. Some payment mechanisms described earlier use digital cash. The use of digital cash, still, does not have a critical mass. After the initial shock, the traditional methods of payment have become dominant in e-commerce.

A basic understanding of digital cash is still needed. To that end, characteristics of digital cash, problems associated with digital cash and prospects for digital cash are now examined. Digital cash, as the name implies, exists in the electronic realm. The first question is, how we can simply designate a string of 1s and 0s as cash? Digital cash is issued by a trusted entity, like a bank. The infrastructure of public/private keys and digital signatures enables the issue of digital cash. Banks can sign on blocks of digital data as representing cash using a private key, and customers and merchants can verify the digital cash using the bank's public key. A customer can use private keys to make withdrawals and deposits, and the bank can verify those using the customer's public keys.

Digital cash can be identifiable or anonymous. Identifiable digital cash contains information regarding the identity of the owner, and such money can be traced as it moves through the economy. Anonymous digital cash, however, does not contain information concerning the owner and does not leave a transaction trail. Anonymous digital cash is created using what is called blind digital signatures. This digital cash is similar to paper cash floating in the system.

These two types can be stored online and offline. Online digital cash denotes digital cash held by a trusted entity, such as a bank. If a customer wishes to use the digital cash, then he or she will contact the bank and the bank will transmit funds to the desired place. In offline storage, the digital cash will be stored by the user on some form of magnetic media. Offline anonymous digital cash poses complex security problems.

The foremost problem is preventing double spending. Digital cash is simply a string of digits; what is to stop users from merely copying it over and over and multiplying the cash at will? If smart cards are used, then the in-built hardware and software controls prevent duplication of digital money. In online transactions, where smart cards are not used, a bank gets contacted each time digital cash is spent. The bank advices the merchant whether the cash is still valid; if it is not, the merchant refuses to consummate the transaction. Offline anonymous digital cash, sans smart cards, can be traced if the in-built protocols reveal the transaction trail and identity of the user. To protect the privacy of the cash holder, such revelation takes place only if the digital cash is double spent. However, the implementation of such a protocol is difficult, and security of anonymous offline digital cash is not foolproof.

Theoretically, there are numerous advantages of digital cash. Digital cash can protect privacy of the users; provide protection from fraud; and have properties such as portability and divisibility, making it ideal for micropayments. Digital cash can be convenient in making payments, reduce paper expenses and is easier to carry around. Problems essentially revolve around making digital cash tamper-proof, having universal standards for acceptance, recovering digital cash after the magnetic media crashes or is stolen and not allowing criminals and terrorists to use it for undesirable activities. There are other complex issues of money supply, competition with national monetary systems and legality.

Digital cash initially created a great deal of debate and excitement. Online identifiable digital cash is still being used, especially in conjunction with smart cards. The use of offline anonymous digital cash is hampered due to various factors, not to mention the political climate prevailing after 9/11. Digital cash has created a niche for itself and will continue to exist. As with many innovations, digital cash may catch on in due time and course.

Summary

The e-developments that affect the revenue cycle have been reviewed in this chapter. The revenue cycles starts with the sales order. In the Web environment, sales orders can arrive via online storefronts, online exchanges, EDI or CRM/SFA software. The instantaneous arrival of orders puts a premium on integration of front-end activities with back-end accounting systems. CRM deals with comprehensive management of customer touch points, behavior, data and marketing efforts. CRM software connects with the back-end accounting systems and may come with tools that enable self-service abilities for customers. CRM data mining tools also analyze customer profitability in different ways than traditional accounting methods.

Credit approval is the next step in the revenue cycle. The Internet provides different types of tools to manage credit approvals. First, many Web sites provide information about public, private and/or international corporations for a fee. The types of information provided and reliability of the information, though, needs to be evaluated. Second, numerous Web sites provide decision tools that can be used to determine credit worthiness of the customer. These tools are pre-programmed but can be customized, if desired. The decision tools can be Web based or downloaded to the user's desktop. Finally, there are Web services that automate the entire process of credit approvals and deliver a decision within minutes. These services use ERP databases, credit bureau reports, public information and proprietary decision tools for decision making.

Warehousing and shipping has also changed due to the Internet. Warehousing is managed by WMS, which controls the storage and movement of materials in the warehouse. These can be Web enabled and can automatically start filling incoming orders. Additionally, WMS can be used to monitor shipments using the Internet. Some online organizations specialize in providing information regarding shipments in transit by obtaining information from different carriers. Shipment visibility is only the starting point in the shipping area. A number of pre- and post-shipping activities, such as getting shipping charges, creating and transmitting a bill of lading, rerouting of shipments in transit and electronic access to shipping documents, can be simplified using the Internet.

Billing has evolved due to EIPP and EBPP. These mechanisms provide customers a facility to receive, pay, review, analyze and query bills over the Web. There are three primary models for EIPP and EBPP – direct biller model, consolidator model and the Internet Post Office Model. The models differ based on ownership of the Web site, modes of collecting information and payment methods. All of these are being employed in the real world. A number of companies provide infrastructure for EIPP/EBPP and include software vendors, hardware manufacturers, intermediaries and financial institutions.

EIPP/EBPP is being sold for strategic reasons such as customer service rather than for cost reduction. Electronic billing has not captured the market as initially forecasted, though adoption rates are increasing.

Online receivables management services now automate the entire process, which includes presenting sale documents, collecting receivables, post-collection activities and financial analytics. Specialized online factoring services can buy receivables and advance cash on the Internet. Electronic payment methods in B2C transactions now include online checks, smart cards, replenishment accounts, phone-based billing and micropayments. Electronic wallets that support these various methods of payment are available. In the B2B area, specialized services such as E-TAD could be used. Finally, digital cash technology has been briefly reviewed. Digital cash is used in many online activities, though it never lived up to its original promise. As with many innovations, digital cash may catch on in due time and course.

References

An overview of mySAP CRM (white paper). (2002). SAP. Retrieved February 25, 2003, from www.sap.com/

Analytical CRM (white paper). (2002). SAP. Retrieved February 25, 2003, from www.sap.com/

Analyzing Web site traffic (white paper). (2002). Net Tracker. Retrieved February 26, 2003, from www.sane.com/

Andreeff, A., Binmoeller, L., Boboch, E., Cerda, O., Chakravorti, S., Ciesieleski, T., & Green, E. (2001). Electronic bill presentment and payment – Is it just a click away? *Economic Perspective, IV*, 2-16.

Bartra, P. (2004, April). Will e-invoicing put a stop to the paper? *Director*, 38.

Bernstel, J. (2000, February). Presentment vs. personalization. *Bank Marketing*, 30-31.

Berson, A., Smith, S., & Thearling, K. (2001). *Building data mining applications for CRM.* New York: McGraw Hill.

Blakey, E., & Saliba, C. (2000). Smart cards stack the e-commerce deck. *ECommerce Times.* Retrieved February 27, 2003, from www.ecommercetimes.com/

Council for Electronic Billing and Payment. (2002a). *Business-to-business EIPP: Presentment models and payment options, part one: Presentment models* (white paper). Retrieved February 27, 2003, from www.crfonline.org/orc/pdf/ref17a.pdf

Council for Electronic Billing and Payment. (2002b). *Business-to-business EIPP: Presentment models and payment options, part two: Payment options* (white paper). Retrieved February 27, 2003, from www.crfonline.org/orc/pdf/ref17a.pdf

Cagliostro, C. (2003). *Primer on smart cards.* Smart Card Alliance. Retrieved February 28, 2003, from www.smartcardalliance.org/

Davidson, B. (2001, February). A good Web site aims to reduce shipping costs. *Dot.com Distribution*, 23-28.

Dilger, K. (1999, February). From ship to shore. *Manufacturing Systems*, 83-90.

Enos, L., & Blakey, E. (2001). *Alternative payment methods get no Respect online.* LinuxInsider. Retrieved February 28, 2003, from www.linuxinsider.com/story/7736.html

Enterprise intelligence with mySAP CRM, SAP solutions brief. (2002). SAP. Retrieved March 3, 2003, from www.sap.com/

E-selling with mySAP CRM, SAP solutions brief. (2002). SAP. Retrieved March 3, 2003, from www.sap.com/

EWallets: Past failure, future success? (2002). Datamonitor. Retrieved March 3, 2003, from www.datamonitor.com/

Farhoomand, A., & McCauley, M. (2001, October). Tradecard: Building a global trading electronic payment system. *Communications of the AIS*, *7*, 1-35.

Feare, T. (2002, May). Hot spots in e-fulfillment. *Modern Materials Handling*, 5-19.

Gamble, H. (2001, January). Lockbox technology. *Business Credit*, 103, 24-30.

Gateway credit story. (2001). The Industry Standard. Retrieved March 3, 2003, from www.thestandard.com/article/display/0,1151,152128,00.html/

Gutzman, A. (2001a). *An overview of B2B payment systems – part I.* ECommerce – Guide. Retrieved March 3, 2003, from www.ecommerce-guide.com/

Gutzman, A. (2001b). *An overview of B2B payment systems – part II.* ECommerce – Guide. Retrieved March 3, 2003 from www.ecommerce-guide.com/

Hayes, T. (2001, July/August). Will EBPP transform relationships? *Credit Union Executive Journal*, 6-12.

Hochgraf, L. (2003, August). Tools for top speed. *Credit Union Management*, 26, 38-40.

Hurt, S. (2003, April). Why automate payables and receivables? *Strategic Finance*, 33-35.

IBM Corporation. (2002) *Electronic bill presentment and payment: A strategic advantage* (white paper). IBM. Retrieved February 28, 2003, from www.ibm.com/

Judge, T. (2002, March). Tracking cargo with software, on the Web. *Railway Age*, 36-37.

Juptner, O. (2002). *Ebilling could save companies Millions.* E-Gateway. Retrieved March 5, 2003, from www.e-gateway.net/infoarea/news/news.cfm?nid=2442/

Kytojoki, J., & Karpijoky, V. (2000). *Micropayments – requirements and solutions.* Telecommunications Software and Multimedia Lab. Retrieved from www.tml.hut.fi/

Lacker, J. (1996). Stored value cards: Costly private substitutes for government currency. *Economic Quarterly*, *82*(3), 1-25.

Long, B. (2000, Winter). The evolution of today's payment system: E-commerce opportunities beyond electronic check presentment. *AFP Exchange*, 18-22.

Luo, W., Cook, D., Joseph, J., & Ganapathy., B. (2000). An exploratory framework for understanding electronic bill presentment and payment model selection. *Human Systems Management*, *19*, 255-264.

Malhotra R. (1999, July/August). Fuzzy systems and neuro-computing in credit approval. *Journal of Lending and Credit Risk Management*, 24-27.

McAndrews, J. (1999, July). E-money and payment system risks. *Contemporary Economic Policy*, 17, 348-357.

META Group. (2001). *Integration: Critical issues for implementation of CRM solutions* (white paper). Retrieved March 8, 2003, from www.metagroup.com"\t"new"

Microsoft. (2003). *Microsoft.NET Passport, review guide*. Microsoft. Retrieved March 5, 2003, from www.microsoft.com/

mySAP CRM Interaction Center. (2003). *SAP solution brief.* SAP. Retrieved February 26, 2003, from www.sap.com/

mySAP CRM Marketing. (2003). *SAP solution brief.* SAP. Retrieved February 26, 2003, from www.sap.com

mySAP CRM Sales. (2003). *SAP solution brief.* SAP. Retrieved February 26, 2003, from www.sap.com

mySAP CRM Service. (2003). *SAP solution brief.* SAP. Retrieved February 26, 2003, from www.sap.com

Parson, M. (2000). The accidental rise of smart cards. *Red Herring*. Retrieved March 6, 2003, from www.redherring.com/mag/isue109/1300.html/

Patel, J., & Fenner, J. (2000). Electronic billing software steps up. EBS. Retrieved March 6, 2003, from www.ebs.com.mx/ebscd/EBPP_Resources/billingworld.html/

PitneyBowes docSense, electronic bill presentment and payment. (2002). Pitney Bowes. Retrieved March 6, 2003, from www.docsense.com/

Rees, M. (2001, May/June). Electronic bill presentment and payment – A major new organizational resource. *The British Journal of Administrative Management*, 14-15.

Schmidt, D. (2000). *Internet B2B payment systems: The challenges faced*. Smart Pros. Retrieved March 6, 2003, from http://accounting.pro2net.com/x15206.xml/

Shacklett, M. (2000, March). Electronic bill presentment and payment is around the corner. *Credit Union Magazine*, 12-15.

Shirky, C. (2000). *The case against micropayments*. O'Reilly. Retrieved March 7, 2003, from www.openp2p.com/lpt/a/515/

Simpson, B. (2003, December). What's next for electronic payments? *Credit Card Management*, *16*(10), 38-46.

Sowinski, L. (2000, June). Customer relationship management software. *World Trade*, *13*, 70-71.

Spiotto, A. (2001). Electronic bill presentment and payment: A primer. *The Business Lawyer*, *57*, 447-473.

Stoner, J. (2001, September/October). A recipe for EBP success: Mid-Atlantic corporate FCU shares the ingredients of its electronic bill payment program. *Credit Union Executive Journal*, 12-16.

Strischek, D. (1996, January). Reengineering the credit approval process. *Journal of Commercial Lending*, 19-34.

The acceleration of treasury technology, PayStream advisors, corporate benchmark report. (2002, Summer). Billing.Org. Retrieved March 7, 2003, from www.ebilling.org/White_Papers/Acceleration_of_Treasury_Technology_-_PayStream.pdf

William, K. (2000, November). What's ahead for electronic billing and payment. *Strategic Finance*, 21.

Williams, P. (2001, Spring). E-billing: Right strategy, wrong time? *Public Utilities Fortnightly*, 20-24.

Wright, D. (2002, February). Comparative evaluations of electronic payment systems. *INFOR*, 71-85.

Endnotes

1 Lockbox is basically a cash collection and processing service provided by a bank or financial institution.

2 Please see Chapter 4 for discussion of these methods.

3 Please see Chapter 10 for a detailed discussion of these security techniques.

4 The information in this section is collected from the following Web sites: *www.cross-check.com/*, *www.lmlpayment.com/*, and *www.telecheck.com/*

5 Please see Chapter 10 for a detailed discussion of these security techniques.

6 Millicent protocol is a security protocol that supports purchases costing less than one cent.

7 Please see Chapter 10 for a detailed discussion of this security technique.

Chapter VI

The Expenditure Cycle

Expenditure Cycle Activities

The expenditure cycle consists of the ordering of goods and services from suppliers and consequent payments to the suppliers. The generic transaction flow in the expenditure cycle can be described as follows: inventory control reviews inventory records to determine order requirements. A purchase requisition(s) is created and forwarded to the purchase department. The requisition contains details of items and quantities required. The purchase department selects suppliers by using the approved list of suppliers or any other standard operating procedure established by the organization. The supplier is selected and a purchase order is created and forwarded to that supplier. Another copy of the purchase order goes to the inventory control department to notify it that goods are on order. The supplier ships goods to the warehouse, and a receiving report is created. The receiving report is forwarded to inventory control and accounts payable. Inventory control updates inventory records based on the receiving report.

The accounts payable department receives an invoice from the supplier and creates a voucher package by reconciling the necessary documents, such as purchase requisition, purchase order, receiving report and invoice. The voucher package is then approved with

Exhibit 1. The expenditure cycle

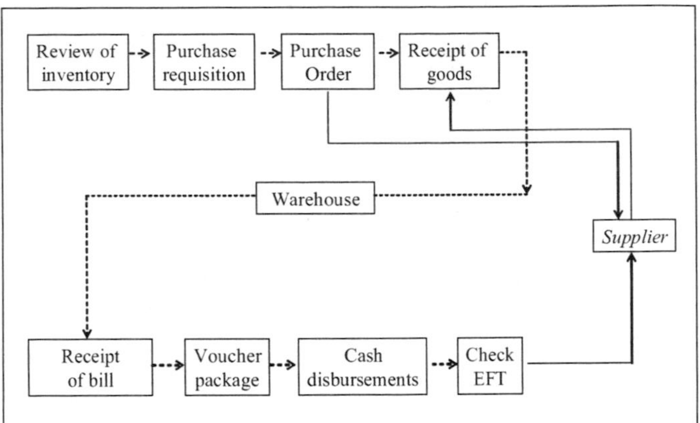

Exhibit 2. E-change in the expenditure cycle

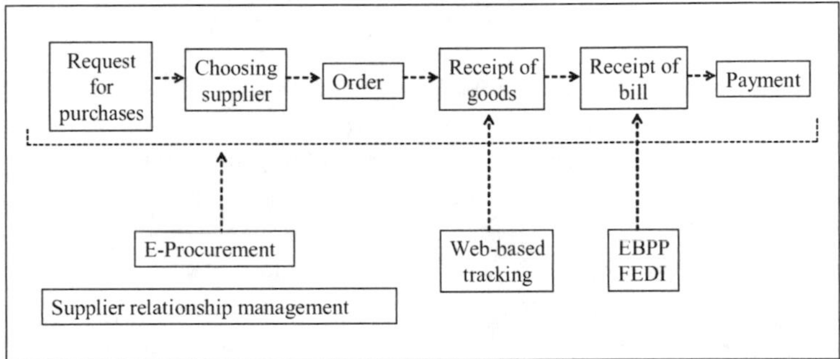

corrections, if any. The accounts payable subsidiary ledger is updated and summary totals are forwarded to the general ledger. The voucher package is forwarded to the cash disbursement department. A check is prepared and mailed to the supplier.

The generic steps in the expenditure cycle are similar across organizations; however, implementation of these methods spans a full spectrum, from manual methods to Web-enabled automated methods, to innumerable combinations in between. There is no one standard solution that fits all companies. The expenditure cycle has changed considerably due to the Internet and ERP. The review of inventory is automated and can be done over the Internet. Suppliers can tap into company databases and supply needed items based on inventory levels. The purchasing activities of today's corporations span the globe; suppliers can be based in different countries, and purchase staff may be empowered to conduct purchasing activity without specific approvals. The entire purchasing process can also take place over the Web in the absence of face-to-face contact. Supplier relationship management and e-procurement enable such activities by automating and Web enabling the majority of purchase functions. These tools can interact with the accounts payable module for payment processing. Other areas in the expenditure cycle that have been affected by the Internet, but not as glamorized, are management of expenses, such as travel and entertainment, and payroll systems. Fixed-assets management has also been Web enabled. Effects in the fixed assets area, however, are not as profound as those in purchasing and expenses.

This chapter is organized as follows: First, changes in order, receipt and payment activities in the expenditure cycle due to supplier relationship management and e-procurement are investigated. A detailed coverage of procurement cards is also provided. Second, online management of expenses, such as travel expenses and online travel centers, is covered. Online payroll management is comprehensively discussed. Third, changes in accounting for fixed assets are briefly reviewed. Finally, a summary rounds off the chapter.

Ordering, Receiving and Paying for Goods

The purchasing function of an organization involves a complex set of activities and interfaces with various internal functions, such as production, accounting and treasury, among other departments. Purchasing activities also include external entities, such as suppliers and shippers. Let us take a look at these various activities and changes wrought by the Internet. The first issue is: What are we purchasing? Depending on the business of the organization, purchases can include raw materials, supplies, services or capital goods. In this section, all these categories are discussed, though the detailed interactions of purchasing and production are discussed in the next chapter.

Purchasing activities, in the context of the expenditure cycle, consist of generating requisitions, selecting suppliers, creating purchase orders, receiving goods and paying suppliers. Illustrative additional activities generally *not* included in accounting texts are as follows: A strategy needs to be designed for selecting suppliers. Corporate objectives such as improving relationships with suppliers, minimizing costs of purchases, improving on-time deliveries or enforcing contract compliance dictate choice of suppliers. Suppliers can be in any corner of the globe. The next task often times involves tedious contract negotiations with the supplier and contract management. This task may involve interactions of geographically diverse teams and a complex set of documents.

Once a supplier is chosen and contracts negotiated, the routine activities of placing orders, receiving goods and paying for goods begins. The supplier can introduce new products and services that need to be evaluated on a regular basis. Suppliers also need to be assessed on numerous dimensions to ensure achievement of corporate objectives. This is an outline of activities involved in purchasing of direct or indirect materials or services. In the age of the Internet and ERP, these activities are integrated and generally inseparable. A set of software modules can manage the entire purchasing process.

Initial efforts in this area resulted in what is called e-procurement. E-procurement refers to the use of the Internet in purchasing direct or indirect materials; for example, Maintenance, Repairs and Operating (MRO) purchases, office expenses and travel expenses. E-procurement started with the use of the Internet for purchasing indirect materials, but soon expanded to include different activities, such as streamlining the purchasing process, consolidating product information from various suppliers and linking with online exchanges and marketplaces. Internet-based procurement was soon followed by SRM.

SRM started as a part of e-procurement, grew up to include sourcing and then became a comprehensive area for managing suppliers. Sourcing is considered more strategic – the right product, from the right supplier, for the right price. Procurement is considered to be more tactical — the objective is to eliminate paperwork and reduce costs. Hence, SRM is considered to be more comprehensive than e-procurement. Now, SRM includes e-procurement in addition to a host of different activities. Another term that may be encountered in the SRM field is *spend management*. This term refers to the management of spending or expenses on direct and indirect materials, services and commodities, which echoes the definition of e-procurement. Another term similar to SRM is Supplier Life cycle Management (SLM) and denotes similar functionalities, though theoretical definitions may differ.

SRM is defined as a set of suppliers facing practices enabled by a collaborative software suite. SRM primarily deals with sourcing of suppliers and procurement. There is much terminological confusion in this area; for example, how to differentiate between SRM and SCM? There are many similarities and overlapping activities. Different software packages may use different acronyms to describe similar functionalities. Generally, but not always, SRM will be considered a subset of SCM. SCM will be discussed as part of the conversion cycle in the next chapter. The definitions of these terms vary and explanations provided here are based on the generally accepted meanings of the definition. In any case, remember to focus on functions and not on labels.

Exhibit 3. Supplier relationship management

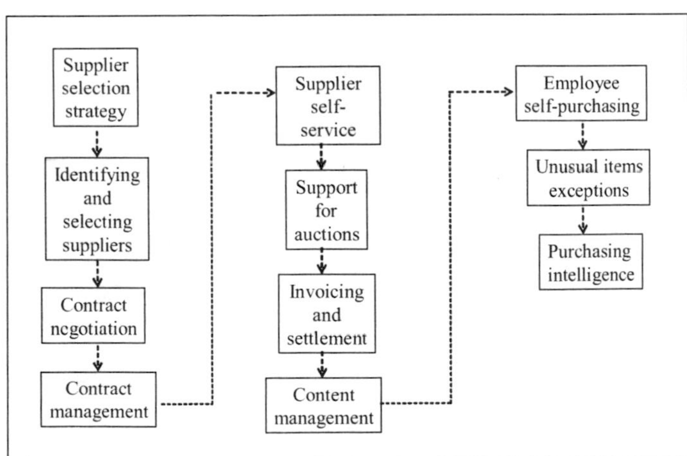

The rise of SRM was fueled by a range of factors. The shrinking of product life cycle and consequent need to redesign products or introduce new products, the trend toward global outsourcing, the movement toward viewing suppliers as partners and not adversaries, and the desire to squeeze costs from procurement were some main reasons. Traditional ERP-based purchase systems could not answer such questions as — Who are our top 10 suppliers?, Who are the worst suppliers? Why?, Who supplies the maximum quantity of item X? and Is supplier Y profitable? So, software vendors developed SRM software suites. SRM also supports knowledge creation and preservation; knowledge may not be lost due to employee turnover. The capabilities of this software suite have become more sophisticated with each iteration.

SRM enables a set of internal and external purchasing activities. These activities start at the strategy level and extend to purchasing intelligence. SRM is generally a suite of software modules and operates on top of an ERP system. All major accounting and business software vendors offer SRM functionality, but to a varying degree. The leading SRM modules in the market, at least on paper, present very comprehensive SRM functionalities. Let us take a sequential look at these different functionalities and understand their connections with the accounting system.

Supplier Selection Strategy

Supplier selection strategy is, by and large, driven by corporate objectives. SRM supports supplier selection strategy by providing quantitative data, projections and analyses, and by facilitating online collaboration by providing appropriate tools. Quantitative data includes patterns in spending and supplier performance, projections of future performance based on available data and changes in existing products and business, among other things. Analytical facilities in SRM enable detailed analysis of

Exhibit 4. Supplier selection strategy

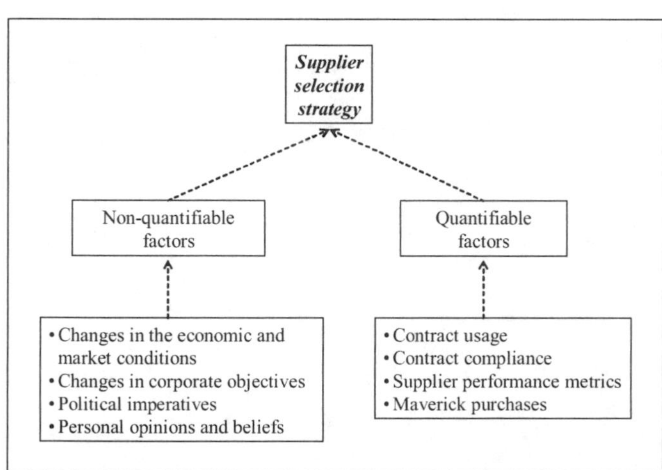

supplier contracts. Illustrative examples in the contract analysis include calculating the use of the supplier by organization, evaluating gaps in contract coverage and supplier performance, identifying purchases that do not conform to contracts and investigating purchases made from non-approved suppliers.

Data requirements may change, depending on the nature of materials provided by the supplier. For example, if supplies consist of commodities, then businesses deploy what is called *commodity business strategy* or *commodity strategy*. Such strategy generally demands in-depth cost analysis of purchases across business units, product lines, supplier locations or cost centers. On the other hand, if the supplier provides a unique product, then the supplier selection strategy may focus on locating another source and product design rather than on cost considerations. SRM modules generally combine data from the ERP system, or a data warehouse is created to support SRM operations. The tools provided by SRM include pre-built workbooks, pre-defined reports, customizable reporting capabilities and the ability to download and upload data from external analytical tools such as Excel and Access.

Non-quantitative factors in supplier selection strategy include changes in economic and market conditions, changes in corporate objectives, political imperatives and a number of other factors. SRM modules provide collaborative tools, such as virtual chat rooms and work rooms, discussion boards, project management tools, task managers and team management tools. These virtual tools are useful for strategy teams generally geographically dispersed and who need to get information from sources close to suppliers or markets. The strategies generally pursued are diversifying supplier base, decreasing inventory and reducing total purchase costs, increasing capacity by adding additional suppliers, focusing on few suppliers by narrowing supplier base or decreasing variability in supplies by rationalizing delivery schedules.

Identifying and Selecting Suppliers

The next step is identifying suppliers that complement the chosen supplier strategy. First, suppliers need to be discovered; second, they need to be qualified. The discovery phase is a complex process conducted by purchasing, engineering and production

Exhibit 5. Supplier contract negotiations

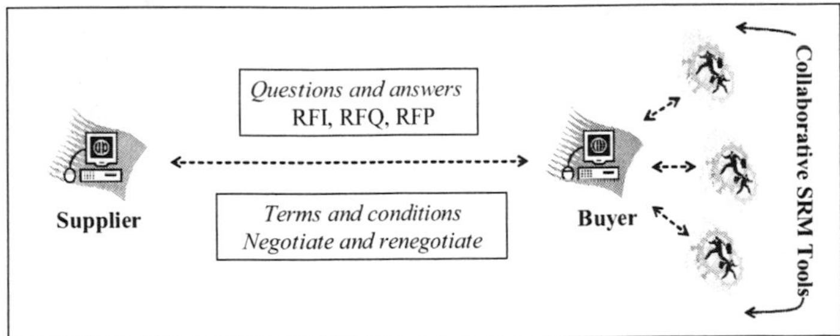

professionals. Information sources must be tapped by using phone, fax, paper catalogs and industry contacts. The discovery phase of identifying suppliers is facilitated by SRM tools. For example, online trading directories that can be searched based on various parameters can be made available on the employee desktop due to SRM tools. Direct links can be provided with external agencies such as eCredit.com and credit bureaus to assess credit and business risks of suppliers. The SRM tools provide a structured way to design and deliver Request for Information (RFI) to multiple suppliers, and collecting and analyzing responses. Suppliers can post replies on the buying organization's Web sites, and supplier replies can be evaluated and analyzed.

The supplier identification phase is followed by supplier selection. Suppliers are asked to provide Requests for Proposals (RFP) and Requests for Quotations (RFQ). Here again, availability of standard documents and Web capability smoothes the transaction flow. If suppliers are submitting bids, these bids can be managed online. The bids are standardized and can be analyzed on any required dimensions such as price, quality and delivery schedule. If supplemental information is required, it can be obtained online. SRM tools may also support multiple languages, multiple currencies and be able to deal with different time zones. Once the supplier is qualified and added to the approved list, that supplier is available to all departments and locations.

Contract Negotiations and Contract Management

Contract negotiations and contract management is also facilitated by SRM tools. These contracts are created by specifying terms and conditions, and are reviewed by lawyers, suppliers and management before final acceptance. The negotiation cycle is long and complicated. SRM tools help by providing online access to standard templates for contracts, and they centralize all ancillary documents in one place. Standard templates can be filled and customized online, and detailed and rich descriptions of requirements is possible. Suppliers can be given access to negotiations if their participation is preferred. Individuals in the organization can share their expertise and specific requirements at a central place. This knowledge base is useful in presenting a unified face to suppliers.

Once a contract is awarded, the SRM tools can automatically generate a customized contract and consequent purchase orders. Contracts, once awarded, are monitored for compliance with existing terms and conditions. The signed contracts can be shared widely within the organization for review and as models. If the contract is long term, the system can be programmed to generate sourcing rules that will guide new requisitions to desired suppliers. SRM tools provide usage statistics, purchase order histories and alerts if the supplier violates pricing, quality, delivery or service standards. The automated contract execution and increased visibility provides for a sound contract management.

Supplier Self-Service

SRM tools provide numerous supplier self-service abilities. These abilities are generally provided through a supplier portal or supplier-facing SRM module. These tools allow suppliers limited access to the buyer's systems. If suppliers are new or selected for the first time, they need to register with the buyer. Approved suppliers in the company database can register directly, and automatically generated user IDs and passwords are sent to them. Non-approved suppliers can also register, though there will be a review process. The registration process is easy, and most organizations offer multiple ways of registration.

Once the supplier is registered, the supplier can carry a variety of activities:

- Update addresses and contact data
- Create Web pages on the supplier portal to detail key information about themselves and to advertise their services
- Obtain information about their accounts. This information can be delivered through different reports, such as purchase order history, purchase order confirmations, invoice and payments information, details regarding contracts and other customized reports
- Upload information about their products
- Program software (limited); for example, a supplier can program for an automatic e-mail after a purchase order is received

Support for Auctions

Another tool that has been used to reduce procurements costs is auctions. The basic idea behind an auction is when an organization is selling a product, it will invite buyers to compete with each other, and sell the product to the buyer who offers the highest price. Traditionally, auctions have been used in many areas, particularly art and antiques, where the real price of the product may not be easily determinable. An auction offers a way to determine the market price while allowing sellers to obtain maximum price and permitting each buyer to bid according to his/her estimate of the market value of that item. There are different types of auctions, such as ascending prices where prices move upward, descending prices where prices move downward, sealed bid and many other variations.

Since we are not interested in auctions per se but only to the extent it is used in SRM tools, let us view auctions from the sourcing and procurement perspective. Auctions are used by corporations in purchasing direct and indirect goods, commodities and even complex customized products. A form of auction that has become popular is called *reverse auction*. In this auction, the buyer (note that the buyer is using the auction, not the seller) posts a requirement for a particular product for a particular price. Suppliers can view the price and bid their own price. All suppliers can view bids made by other suppliers and try to outdo each other. The supplier who bids the lowest price generally wins the order. These types of auctions have been in use for a long time, but became vastly more useful after advent of the Internet.

A reverse auction in the Internet environment works as follows: Suppliers allowed to participate in the auction are generally thoroughly screened. Since the low bid wins, the winner must be able to provide quality product comparable to higher bidders. The online auction is conducted on a secure Web site; suppliers may have to register in advance and, if necessary, are given training in online auctions. The rules and regulations stipulated by the auctioneer are final. Supplier IDs are masked and all suppliers are assigned alpha numeric codes. Bids will be forwarded from remote locations and suppliers can watch the bids in real time. The prices on the bids, but not the supplier names, are now common knowledge. The supplier who bids lowest generally wins the order.

SRM tools enable auctions via supplier portals or supplier-facing software. Supplier portals enable establishing private exchanges, which are set by the organization, linking suppliers and partners in a secure environment. Suppliers are already pre-screened; the supplier database is generally available online and information regarding auctions can be conveyed to suppliers using e-mails or other online methods. Suppliers can receive auctions and bidding information, log on to auction sites on the private exchange, view an auction in progress, and review call and bid information. In case of unique products, online supplier directories can be tapped for enlarging the supplier database.

The SRM software also provides decision tools for evaluating bids. If the price is not the sole criterion, evaluating bids in real time is extremely difficult. If factors such as quality, quantity, location and supplier reputation are factored in, decision makers face information overload. The decision tools in SRM can help rank incoming bids using ranks, weights and pre-defined user formulas. A multivariate evaluation of incoming bids is thus possible. SRM generally supports different types of auctions, not only reverse auctions, and different types of quotations. These capabilities support strategic and ad-hoc sourcing/procurement activities.

Electronic Invoicing and Settlement

The purchasing/invoicing and payment/settlement mechanism is the most important process for our purposes. This process is carried out using back-end ERP systems and SRM tools, such as supplier self-service and employee self-service. A purchase order is created by the purchasing system, based on either an automated review of inventory levels or on the employee purchase requisition. Suppliers can also monitor inventory levels and generate purchase orders if inventory reaches pre-specified reorder levels. This order process is called Vendor Managed Inventory (VMI) and is covered in the next chapter.

This electronic Purchase Order (e-PO) is passed on to the supplier portal and gets converted into an electronic Sales Order (e-SO) for the supplier. The supplier receives an e-mail or logs into the system and processes the e-SO. A response to the PO is created; if the response is in complete agreement with the initial PO, then the PO/SO is accepted

Exhibit 6. Invoicing and settlement

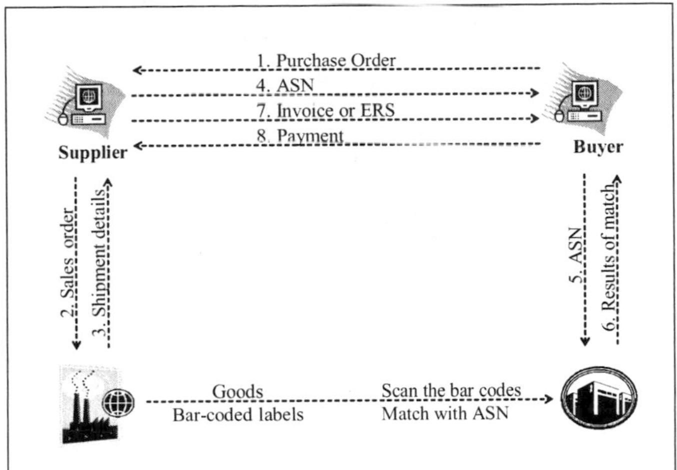

by the transacting parties. If there is a disagreement, online negotiations take place until a compromise is reached. If the POs are complex and changes are required as the work progresses, these changes can be monitored online. Revisions to the initial PO are archived and can be accessed for comparison purposes.

The user can also specify the status of purchases as taxable or tax exempt. This status is then carried forward to the PO; as explained later, sales and local taxes can complicate the purchasing mechanism. Account codes for accounts that need to be charged can be generated using workflow rules. The charges can be split across multiple accounting codes, multiple departments and/or multiple costs centers. If suppliers are based out of the country, prices can be designated in foreign and local currency simultaneously.

The purchasing process is somewhat different in case of long-term contracts. In this case, the supplier has agreed to certain pricing and quality terms for a given duration of time. The workflow in the ERP system is used to specify the sourcing rules. These workflow rules will be triggered if items covered under the long-term contract are required. These items will be matched with the approved supplier list, and an appropriate supplier will be chosen. Then the ERP system will generate required documents, such as a PO, and those will processed as described earlier.

The ASNs, described in the EDI chapter, are created by the supplier and transmitted electronically. ASN is essentially an electronic packing list and has elaborate formatting requirements. ASNs carry information down to the container level or to the PO-detail level, depending on the buyer's requirements. ASNs improve visibility of incoming goods; improve warehouse operations, such as receiving and putaway; and allow efficient use of receiving docks, due to the advance knowledge of shapes and sizes of incoming shipments. ASNs are required in EDI but can be used in SRM, and help automate the receiving process.

Exhibit 7. UPC – A bar code

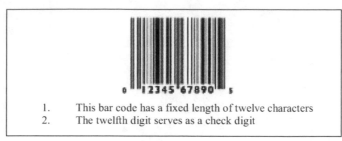

1. This bar code has a fixed length of twelve characters
2. The twelfth digit serves as a check digit

The supplier receives the e-PO and enters it into his/her system. The accounting system, after processing the PO, makes it available to the warehouse or WMS module. Orders are reviewed in the warehouse; items are picked off the shelves and packed. The packed items are reconciled against the PO to confirm shipment. Any differences in the original PO and packed items are noted. Data regarding item description, price and quantity is collected during the packing phase. This data is used to create an ASN. The EDI modules of the ERP software can automate this process.

The ASN is created and then used to print out bar-coded labels. Bar codes are rectangular patterns of lines that vary in width and spaces. Each pattern is assigned a specific character (0 to 9). Laser light reflects from those patterns and information in the lines or patterns is automatically recognized by bar-code readers. There are various types of bar codes; the common one used is UCC 128. The bar-coded labels used with ASN should have a specific format(s), be capable of being scanned and be legible. Labels that do not follow required guidelines need to be manually processed, and the supplier faces stiff penalties for non-compliance with bar-code rules.

The bar-coded labels contain information regarding packed goods and that matches with the ASN. The ASN is transmitted to the buyer, and the buyer's purchasing and receiving departments are alerted to the incoming goods. The ASN is increasingly being formatted as ASN XML; the XML ability is supported by the majority of SRM vendors. Shipments in transit can be monitored using the ASN and bar-coded labels. When the receiving department receives the container carrying goods, the bar-code label is scanned and information is matched with the ASN on file. The goods may be physically inspected, and can be transferred to the appropriate place in the warehouse. Once the bar-code information is scanned by the receiving department, the purchasing department is aware of the receipt and can monitor the shipment, whether it is in the receiving department or transferred to the warehouse.

The SRM tools provide electronic abilities for payment and settlement. The supplier submits an invoice electronically, which can either be created using a supplier portal or the supplier's accounting system. The invoice is matched with the ASN and PO, and then approved. In case of discrepancies, the invoice is routed to an appropriate manager for correction, and corrections can be confirmed with the supplier. Once the invoice is approved, it can be automatically paid according to the contractual terms and conditions. Payment can be made through EFT or by a paper check directly at the due date, and the due date can be automatically calculated to take advantage of available cash discounts.

Exhibit 8. Pay this supplier and you will pay dearly!

> The OFAC (Office of Foreign Assets Control) of the US Department of Treasury administers and enforces economic and trade sanctions as dictated by the US foreign policy and national security requirements. These sanctions are against designated foreign countries, terrorists, international narcotics traffickers, and those engaged in activities related to the proliferation of weapons of mass destruction. The USA Patriot Act passed after 9/11 fortifies the tools required to prevent, detect, and prosecute international money laundering and people responsible for financing terrorism. The organizations must monitor their payment and disbursement activities to make sure that undesirable entities are not being paid. Bottomline Technologies *(www.bottomline.com)* have devised a module called WebSeries Universal Payment Engine that scans the payment activities and checks these payments against a file containing a list of undesirables. Information concerning the undesirable entities is provided by the OFAC and continuously updated. The penalties for violation of these laws and regulations are stiff and expensive.

Payment information is transferred to the accounts payable and general ledger, and the back-end ERP system, after a review, posts those amounts to proper accounts. Suppliers can view their invoices and payments against those invoices on the supplier portal. This facilitates reconciliation of invoices by the supplier's accounts receivable department.

The SRM tools can also support the ERS process described in the EDI chapter. Incoming ASNs, often referred to as Advanced Shipment and Billing Notice (ASBNs), are identified and matched with the PO or contract terms, and a corresponding invoice is created by the back-end ERP systems or SRM tools. The invoice may also be eliminated. The amount due to the supplier can be calculated using the PO and ASN/ASBN, and be credited to the supplier. ASBNs frequently contain tax information for taxable shipments and can be automatically used in the invoice. The invoice is electronically transmitted to the supplier or posted on the supplier portal for review. This process is similar to the EIPP process described in the revenue cycle. This process differs from manual matching of PO, receiving report and purchase invoice, and then creating a voucher package. If the documents do not match, an exception report is forwarded to the authority specified in the workflow.

Content Management

The electronic purchasing process depends on availability of supplier products in the electronic format, referred to as electronic catalogs. Electronic catalogs can provide information via text, graphics, pictures, audio and video, among other things. If product descriptions and selling terms and conditions are not electronic, the buying process cannot be automated. The more detailed and searchable the product database, the easier is the job of purchasers. Managing these electronic catalogs is called *content management*, or *catalog management*. Content management is a complex and costly process. There are different ways to handle content management. First, suppliers can develop catalogs internally in the approved format and then upload the information. The consolidation of these catalogs is then done by SRM tools. Second, specialized content management services can manage consolidation of supplier catalogs. These services are useful for electronic marketplaces or exchanges where large numbers of buyers and sellers meet. Since most buyers and sellers are small and in need of a standard catalog format, the catalog management companies with standard protocols and software tools can be invaluable. Finally, the organization can get information from suppliers and author the catalogs and manage them or can even buy content from third-party providers. The SRM tools and large organizations generally follow the first method, since it is cost effective.

SRM tools provide self-authoring tools to suppliers. The electronic catalogs in different formats, such as XML, spreadsheet and CSV, can be automatically uploaded to the supplier portal or at a designated place in the buyer's system. Suppliers can control content and can change, update or modify the content to keep up with product changes. Additionally, these catalogs can also be imported from online exchanges and third-party content providers. The imported catalogs can be evaluated for quality and merged into a single file. The product information can be structured and organized using standard schemas such as United Nations/Standard Products Services and Code (UN/SPSC) or can be formatted in XML variants. Such standard schemas are useful in eliminating redundant and duplicate information, developing easy search mechanisms and assigning unique identifiers.

SRM tools also provide a search facility for users of the system. Electronic catalogs are of no use unless they can be efficiently searched. The search tools are similar to ones encountered on the Internet; for example, Google. These tools may be embellished for given business purposes. Oracle's iProcurment system offers facilities to search results by price and relevance. The relevance of an item is calculated based on occurrences of the search term in the given database. Additional search parameters include sorting by description, supplier and category. If you have used Amzon.com search engines, you already have a good idea as to how the process works.

Employee Self-Purchasing

As mentioned earlier, SRM rose from e-procurement, first as a tool set within the e-procurement area; then it consumed the e-procurement category. E-procurement began to facilitate the purchases of indirect materials, such as MRO items, office furniture, office supplies and machine parts; and services, such as janitorial, gardening and travel expenses. Costs associated with paperwork and approval procedures make these purchases very pricey. Generally, paper-based purchasing processes were not standardized, the number of suppliers could run in the thousands and approvals were time consuming, resulting in high transaction costs. SRM tools continue to provide the e-procurement functionality, which is also referred to as *employee self-purchasing*. The employee self-purchase process begins with identification of required items and then searching for those items in electronic catalogs.

The catalogs developed by the suppliers can be hosted on the supplier portal and browsed from the desktop by users. The content can also be managed by a third-party organization, hosted by online exchanges or hosted by the supplier at its own Web site. Hosting options are primarily determined by the relative power of the purchasing and selling organizations. An automotive giant company like GM can ask its suppliers to post their content on the GM-specified Web space, but a small company may have to use online exchanges or navigate to the supplier's Web site. The purchasing process is essentially identical no matter where the catalog is hosted; however, there are differences in the infrastructure that supports these purchases.

SRM tools also support internally developed electronic catalogs. Goods and materials purchased by the company are typically stored in different warehouses. Employees generally have no idea what is in stock and what is not. To offset this problem, internal store catalogs detailing availability of goods at various locations are developed. In case of selection of an item from internal catalogs, the SRM tools will produce an internal requisition. The internal requisition may be converted into internal sales orders and processed by the revenue cycle process; in cases where warehouses are treated as profit centers or internal service providers, they compete against external providers. If the required item is available both internally and externally, the user can choose the supplier if he/she is authorized to do so. Items selected from internal catalogs are delivered from the warehouse to the desired place, and the appropriate business unit or cost center is charged with the cost.

This search-and-buy process is similar to the one experienced in buying books or music CDs on the Internet. Required items are searched and selected; then a shopping cart is filled with those items. SRM tools offer a few refinements, such as saving a template of a shopping cart for recurring orders, searching based on product descriptions or product numbers, and filling the carts and putting them on hold until the designated time, which

Exhibit 9. Conceptual representation of workflows for approval of shopping carts

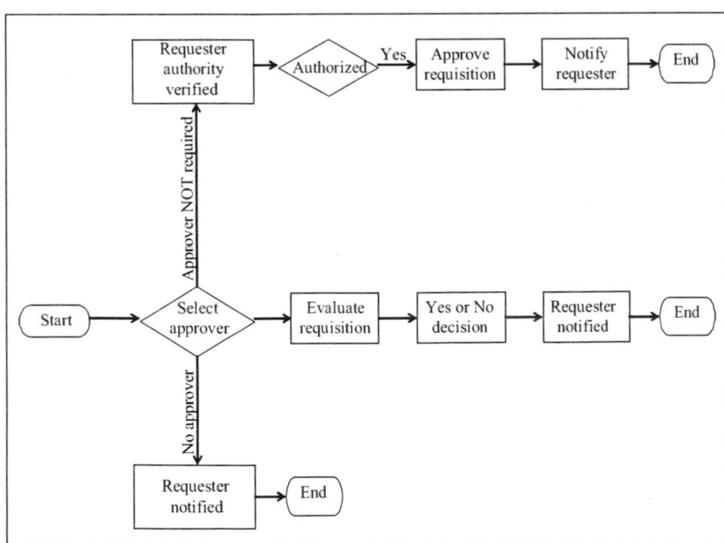

makes the corporate procurement process easier. Employees can add extra information to items selected; for example, if visiting cards are required, the required information such as name, address and title can be uploaded. Some SRM tools can be configured to create a purchase requisition based on the shopping cart.

The SRM tools read the product information in the shopping cart/purchase requisition and decide whether approval is needed based on pre-programmed decision rules; for example, the purchase amount exceeds a specified limit. If the answer is yes, the shopping cart/purchase requisition is routed to the designated manager. Users can attach text, URLs or files to the shopping cart if they wish to provide more information to the manager. The manager can then approve or deny the request. In case of approval, the shopping cart/purchase requisition is processed by the system; if not approved, the employee gets notification that products cannot be purchased or certain changes in products are required before approval. Approval workflow, such as the level of authority required for approval and specified purchase limits, can be modified by authorized personnel. For example, a manager going on vacation can assign approval rights to the other manager, thereby avoiding potential bottlenecks.

The workflow shows a status of the shopping cart/purchase requisition at all times; for example, approved, rejected, awaiting approval or approved with changes. The pending shopping carts/purchase requisitions can be cancelled by the originator if desired. When the shopping cart is approved, a PO is created by SRM tools or the back-end ERP system, depending on the configuration. The PO is electronically transmitted to the supplier; the transmission may be a message from accounting system to accounting system, e-mail or any other form specified by the buying organization. The PO can also be transmitted in different languages based on the preferences of the supplier.

Goods or services are then delivered by the supplier. The receiving report (also called *confirmation*) can be created by the employee who originally requested the purchase. Different routines are available in creating receiving reports. First, if the shipments or services are partial, a receiving report can be created but put on hold. Second, suppliers providing goods and services can automatically ask the system to produce receiving reports after delivery. Third, if the organization needs tighter internal controls, creation of receiving reports can be controlled by a central authority. For example, only the administrative assistant can confirm delivery of services for the entire department. This central authority receives goods or services and creates receiving reports. The invoices are submitted by the supplier and automatically reconciled with the PO and receiving report. On the other hand, the supplier delivery message (similar to ASN) can be used to create an invoice, as in the ERS process described earlier.

In the case of Web sites hosted by suppliers or online exchanges, the SRM tools provide what is called *punchout* capabilities. If the catalogs are hosted on the internal system, then searching for products is easy since it is a matter of searching over the private network of the company. When catalogs are outside the company's network, it is difficult to use tools embedded in the company's SRM or ERP. The SRM tools provide a capability that automatically links their network; that is, it punches out to the supplier's site and the supplier's site can be searched using the SRM tools. When products are configured, selected and loaded onto the shopping cart, the cart automatically links with the internal system of the buyer. The shopping cart or resulting purchase requisition is routed according to internal workflows. The problems with punchout are that each supplier's Web site is differently organized, meaning that there is a learning curve before a user can efficiently search the site. Also, internal search tools may not work uniformly across different Web sites.

The issue of integrating cost accounting systems with SRM tools has not been discussed much in the literature. ERP systems and SRM tools from the same vendor generally ease integration of cost accounting system with SRM. However, there were cases where existing activity-based cost accounting and project cost accounting systems were difficult to map to SRM tools. Accountants need to pay close attention to this area.

The SRM tools also provide for internal controls in purchases from electronic catalogs. First, the internal catalogs can be arranged in different views and the employees of different departments or different business units can access only certain items. Second, if rare or expensive parts are needed, these parts can only be accessed by qualified personnel having special clearance. Third, shopping carts created by employees can have pre-set spending limits, and time periods can be specified during which employees are allowed to make purchases. The expiry of purchasing rights after a certain time is useful in case of employees who have resigned or reassigned. Fourth, as soon as the shopping cart is created, the SRM tools check the inventory status to confirm that these items are truly required. Fifth, if the goods or services are not budgeted, the SRM tools can flag all such purchases and route those for special approvals. A message is also sent to the user so the user knows that he or she is running over budget and can take corrective measures. Finally, suppliers can confirm availability of the required items in real time; and in case of stockouts, alternative suppliers can be immediately tapped, making for an effective procurement process.

Procurement Cards

Procurement cards, also known as P-Cards or purchase cards, are credit cards issued to non-purchasing staff for purchase of low-dollar items and services; for example, indirect materials, supplies, services and small-value non-capital items. Bayer Corporation recently targeted temporary help, overnight shipments, meetings and event planning, uniforms and personal computers as additional areas for the use of procurement cards. Increasingly, procurement cards are also being used to pay for Internet purchases. A research report indicated that in 2001 approximately 60,000 procurement cards were in use in the U.S., and the total volume of transactions was around $45 billion; and, about 25% of Fortune 100 companies had adopted the procurement card program. These cards have also become a hit in governmental, non-profit and university settings.

Research studies have shown that in many organizations, 80% of purchases account for 20% dollar payment volume. The paperwork created for completing the requisition, order, approval, receipt, invoice and payment cycle for such purchases can easily overwhelm any system and result in considerable costs. Even if an ERP system is used, considerable overheads are involved in processing transactions for purchases of small items. Procurement cards decentralize purchasing authority by enabling employees to make purchases without a paper trail and reduce transaction processing costs considerably. However, credit card companies charge fees for issuing cards, and the fee structure varies according to the agreements with the card companies. This cost needs to be factored in a cost-benefit analysis of procurement cards.

Administration of procurement cards is generally handled by the department that implements the cards, or it can be centrally administered by a department, such as purchasing or finance. Introduction of procurement cards does not mean those cards will be used. Many organizations have adopted incentives/penalties for using/not using the cards. Procurement cards change purchasing activities and cause changes in the recording of transactions. The primary effect is in mapping purchases to proper accounts and processing receipt of goods.

Generally, the account structure in the general ledger in most organizations can support recording procurement card transactions. The major problem is in the number of transactions; recording of these transactions can be time consuming. This problem is often referred to as *reconciling with the financial system*. This problem is handled in a number of ways. First, few companies simply charge these transactions to what is called *procurement card purchases*; or, a few standard headings, such as office supplies, shipping supplies and operating expenses, may be developed and used to debit the transactions. Second, a dedicated person may collect and sort reports and assign proper accounts numbers. However, this method slows the system and adds costs.

Finally, procurement card reports coming from the credit card companies may be directly mapped to the general ledger and recorded. This method automates the process but adds upfront costs of programming. For example, Ericsson, a Swedish phone company that has implemented procurement cards, receives two files at the end of a month from American Express. The first file is an invoice to be paid to American Express and the second file

Exhibit 10. Procurement card purchase process

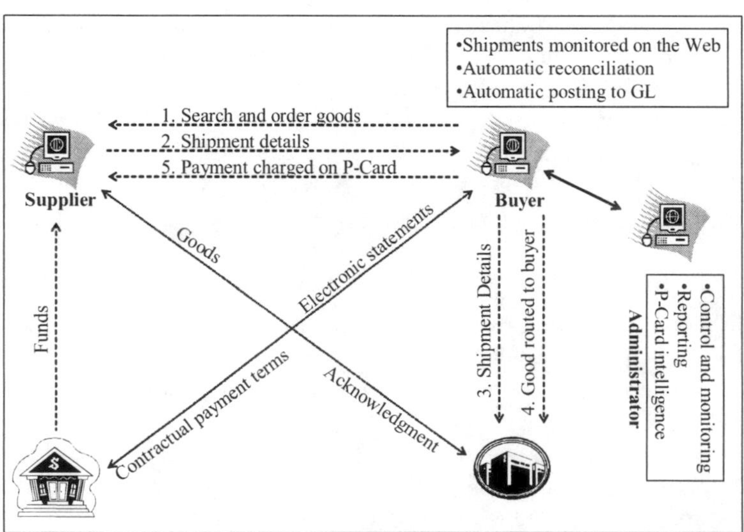

provides a breakdown of spending by card, department and/or cost center. The second file is directly input to the ERP system and accounting entry is completed.

There are also Web-based solutions (for example, P-Card Web Solution, *www.p-card.com/*) that allow a user to receive expense statements over the Web, which can be viewed via browser. This solution can come pre-mapped to the corporate database which, of course, involves upfront programming. Cardholders can then split the transactions based on item descriptions, categories and quantities, and assign the transactions to accounting codes specified in the general ledger; any invalid codes are flagged at the source. The user can then send a report to the general ledger and it can be posted directly or after a review.

Users can also record their orders on the online order form and can formalize entries after receipt of goods or services. The online order log or electronic record of purchases can be automatically reconciled with electronic statements received from the card issuer. After reconciliation, a transaction report is generated that can be routed to the manager, who may review and approve it. The accounting codes are assigned by the user and can be posted to the general ledger or the cost accounting system, depending on existing linkages.

This solution comes with what is called an *administrator* module. This function can be used to manage the procurement card life cycle. The administrator can monitor card activity and generate reports, such as sales tax, freight, 1099 and usage statistics. Card users can be added or deleted, or their rights can be modified from this central place. Text and multi-media entries regarding users, usage or suppliers can be added to the database for reference purposes. For small businesses, a list of suppliers who accept procurement cards can be provided. This list can be searched by SIC, Merchant Category Code (MCC), name and location, among other things.

Receiving of goods on procurement cards also needs to be handled separately. The objective is to reduce costs of small purchases, so the incoming small-purchase goods should not be subject to the formal receiving process. Receipt of goods or services is generally confirmed by one authorized employee; then the payment process can be initiated. If goods are coming to the receiving dock, there may be a special receiving area where only procurement card purchases are received. Another approach is to provide suppliers with special, bright labels that identify incoming procurement card purchases. These goods and supplies are directly forwarded to employees who ordered them and are not entered into the system. To achieve these objectives, the procurement card system needs to be connected with the receiving function. Information such as packing slip, tracking numbers, shipper and carrier names, and contact information of the person ordering goods needs to be available in real time to the receiving function.

Procurement cards can cause sales- and local-tax-related problems. Briefly: *Does information collected from the procurement card statements provide sufficient documentation to determine whether the correct sales and local tax was collected on the transaction at the point of sale?* Companies have developed special procedures to handle sales and state tax issues. Remember, businesses pay penalties if the appropriate sales tax is not paid, whether they are buying *or* selling.

The first approach is to make approved vendors contractually obligated to collect and remit appropriate taxes. Another approach is to educate employees concerning taxable and non-taxable sales. If sales are taxable, the vendor should be asked to provide a detailed breakout of sales tax, either on the invoice or on the shipping notice. Finally, many organizations have acquired sales tax exemption from every state where procurement cards may be used. The organization provides an exemption number to all employees or embosses it on the procurement card. The organization then accrues and remits the sales tax to various states based on the transactions. This method is cumbersome and can add considerable overheads.

There are a number of other approaches to handle this issue. Some organizations will simply remit the appropriate sales tax without any regard to the sales tax collected by the vendor, since the dollar items are small. Others might rely on vendors and take chances with the tax audit, since the dollar items are small. There also are other issues, such as purchases from minority- and women-owned businesses and separate reporting requirements, which are not discussed here.

Controlling procurement cards is certainly a challenge. The main problem is assuring that the procurement cards are only used as per the established corporate policy. Additional controls also need to be in place to prevent unauthorized use and theft of procurement cards. A number of internal controls can be designed to achieve these objectives. However, research has shown that procurement card programs are not beneficial if internal controls are strict and if cost allocations are taken very seriously. Remember, these cards are used to facilitate purchase of low-value items and generate low-cost transactions. If controls are very strict, employees may be discouraged from using procurement cards. An illustrative list of internal controls is provided.

- A card can only be issued by the authorized manager. There is written justification as to whom and why the card is being issued. There are standard operating procedures for stolen or misplaced cards.
- These cards are issued only to trusted employees after proper documentation and managerial approvals. In many cases, organizations even conduct background checks before issuing cards. However, issuing procurement cards is not only a financial issue. There is a delicate balance between trust and empowerment of employees who receive cards and low morale in employees who do not receive cards.
- The person who holds the card is responsible for all charges on the card. Ultimate liability rests with the company; however, the person is answerable to superiors for use of the card.
- Each card has a dollar maximum, and this maximum can be applied to daily, weekly or monthly transactions. Even limits on how many times a card can be used in a day or week can be set. These limits are set based on cost of the paperwork vs. dollars at risk in purchasing transactions. Most organizations set limits around $5,000 or less.
- Purchases can be restricted to approved suppliers. Such restrictions reduce *maverick buying*, which refers to purchases made from suppliers who do not have an existing contract or are not approved. If purchases are not restricted to approved

suppliers, there can be different types of restrictions; for example, suppliers (as identified by SIC code) selling alcohol or chemicals may not be paid using the card.

- There can be special procedures for purchases made over telephone, by fax or in person. Employees often times are asked to maintain a log of purchase information, such as items ordered, date ordered, order price and sales tax, if any. This adds to the paperwork, and there are wide variations regarding this control; many organizations do not ask for logs at all.
- Goods or services, when received, should be confirmed by the person who ordered them. A few organizations may require additional confirmation from an independent person, though many organizations will not ask for it.
- If the card is used in contravention of organizational policies and procedures, there is a standard investigation process. Disciplinary and legal policies are generally developed and, ideally, should be enforced.
- A standardized reconciliation process is carried out at the end of the month, where purchases made are matched against payment.
- There can be periodic audit of selected procurement cards or card transactions.

Now that procurement cards have been discussed, a question on your mind may be — why are we looking at these cards while reviewing SRM tools? SRM tools deal with a gamut of supplier relations and, as such, must support procurement cards. Procurement cards issued to employees are handled much the same way as described earlier. A single invoice is received from the credit card company that is paid, and cash is credited. The detailed breakdown of accounts is provided in another file and that file is directly fed to the ERP system. If the breakdown is separately maintained and entered into the system, then summary totals of this breakdown and a single invoice from the credit card company are automatically reconciled. If there are any discrepancies, a report is routed to the manager specified in the workflow.

Procurement cards can even be used in strategic sourcing. In this case, the procurement card is issued to the supplier, *not to the employees*. Controls over these cards are similar to those described for employee procurement cards. The SRM tools, during the requisition phase, identify suppliers that have been assigned procurement cards. The procurement card information is provided on the resulting purchase order. In case of employee self-service, shopping carts are automatically flagged for procurement card payment based on pre-defined profiles of the supplier and employee. The supplier can charge payments on the procurement card instead of providing an invoice. If more than one purchase order is generated, the SRM software can consolidate these charges and direct those to the supplier.

At the end of the month or a specified period, the credit card company sends an electronic statement of purchases charged on the procurement card(s). Now purchase orders and purchases charged need to be reconciled, and that can be a time-consuming chore. The SRM tools automate the process by generating what is called PO history feed. This history feed and electronic statements from the credit card company are matched and reconciled automatically. If the reconciliation does not have any exception, an invoice payable to the credit card company is created and forwarded to the accounts payable application of the ERP system. Remember, the primary difference between employee and supplier procurement cards from an accounting viewpoint is generation of the PO.

Unusual Items and Exceptions

SRM tools can also help handle items that are unique, find alternative suppliers when the supply chain is disrupted due to unforeseen reasons or if there are sudden changes in demand for goods and services. The SRM tools provide a space — SAP refers to this space as a sourcing cockpit — for consolidating information, such as data on substitute materials, an organization-wide list of approved vendors, alternative suppliers, and new and unique products. This information is compiled by the organization as part of the environmental scanning or as a routine precaution in conducting business. This space also provides links that connect to external databases on suppliers and products. These can be compiled as part of an industry-wide effort or by third-party vendors or trading partners.

This entire universe of information is now available to employees who have to cope with changes in products, processes or suppliers. There are tools to consolidate purchase requisitions from different units to avail of discounts, create open POs and circulate those to chosen suppliers, receive quotations from suppliers and compare them, and search for the best alternatives. The workflow of the ERP system can be automated so that if a supplier or product cannot be found, purchase requisitions are automatically routed to this space.

Purchasing Intelligence

Purchasing intelligence involves analysis of data collected by SRM tools, which is supplemented by external economic databases, competitor benchmarking and professional insights. Purchase intelligence can be used to evaluate corporate sourcing strategies, the potential for better sources, cost efficiencies and detailed analyses and reports. Illustrative examples of purchase intelligence are supplier scorecards, performance analysis and reports, and supplier ratings and categorization. There are numerous other reports that can be generated using SRM tools.

The strategic analysis of sourcing involves evaluating effects of sourcing decisions on key performance indicators for departments, businesses units or organizations. Key performance indicators are defined by top management and sometimes referred to as a procurement scorecard. These key indicators differ across strategies and businesses. A search for better opportunities includes standardizing and consolidating suppliers, monitoring supplier performance across multiple dimensions and optimizing supplier portfolios. Additionally, the organization itself must be monitored to ensure compliance with corporate objectives and policies. Such monitoring demands detailed analytical reports. Let us see what reports are available in a SRM suite.

SRM tools collect detailed operational information, such as volume of purchases, quality of products, price of products, delivery performance and compliance with contractual terms. The details can be made as fine as required by line item, product groups or supplier. This data can be used to benchmark and improve supplier performance on desired indicators and reduce the total cost of ownership. Operational data can be used to produce the following actionable reports:

Expenses and supplier analysis

- Spending per supplier, commodity, cost center, and average requisition
- Supplier on-time performance
- Supplier delivery lead times performance
- Supplier product reject ratios
- Supplier credit ratings
- Supplier ISO certification status
- Number of suppliers per commodity

Quality Analysis

- Warranty claims per product
- Total material rejections per supplier, per commodity
- Failure rates per supplier, per commodity

Financial Analysis

- Timeliness of payments
- Accounts payable turnover ratio
- Accounts payable to sales ratio
- Accounts payable per department, per business unit, per commodity
- Top suppliers by volume.

Suppliers who provide *service* as opposed to tangible goods may be measured for service responsiveness, quality assurance, measured quality and costs. Suppliers can be notified about their performance using supplier portals. Many organizations issue formal ratings to suppliers, informing them of their performance across pre-specified indicators. A FedEx supplier evaluation program provides the following guidelines for an effective program: First, measure value-added results and make sure that measurement costs do not exceed benefits. Second, do not be constrained by available data. For example, if the ERP system provides financial data but not performance data, do not automatically rely on financial data. Finally, develop easy-to-understand measures and keep them few in number. FedEx used four to six measures.

Management can also design other reports. For example, Oracle provides pre-defined reports on contract leakage performance. This report tracks maverick buying; that is, purchases made from suppliers who do not have an existing contract or are not approved.

This report will identify when maverick buying is exceeding the desired percentage and needs to be controlled. The SRM tools provide drill-down capabilities that allow investigating transaction-level data and specific contractual terms to search for reasons of maverick buying. Another pre-defined report tracks purchase-to-sales ratio. This report shows whether the costs of purchases relative to sales are within the desired limits. Additionally, one can factor in the financial stability of the supplier to identify sourcing risks. External data, such as supplier total revenues and its sales to the organization, can be compared to figure out dependency of the supplier on the buyer's organization.

A number of additional tools search databases developed using SRM software. The database can be queried using specialized languages, downloaded to spreadsheets or structured across multiple dimensions and analyzed accordingly. Reports can compare suppliers as a cross-section, across a period of time or against standards and benchmarks, among other things. Remember, supplier data can come from different departments, different business units or international subsidiaries and associates. These reports are only limited by the imagination of the analyzer.

SAP SRM Tools

SRM packages consist of a constellation of modules and are connected with the base ERP or back-end accounting system. SRM tools are offered by all the leading ERP vendors, and numerous software vendors sell SRM tools for medium-sized organizations. The required functionalities for each organization are different and, to repeat — there is no one standard solution. This section looks at SRM tools developed by SAP. SAP provides all its e-business solutions on a platform called mySAP.com. The list of e-business solutions is lengthy and continues to expand as SAP brings more functionality under this umbrella. The suite of SRM tools falls under this platform, and it will give us a good idea regarding existing state of the art in this area. What follows is a rather simple description of a very complex software suite.

SRM tools operate on top of an ERP system in a symbiotic fashion. All the leading vendors claim that their SRM tools will run on top of any ERP system. However, the practical difficulties of integrating systems from different vendors can be formidable and should be kept in mind while evaluating these claims. SRM tools offered by SAP include the following components: business information warehouse, knowledge warehouse, exchange infrastructure, enterprise portal, enterprise buyer, bidding engine, supplier self-service and catalog management tools by Requisite.

First, let us look at the modules that enable SRM; these include business information warehouse, knowledge warehouse, exchange infrastructure and enterprise portal. SAP business information warehouse and knowledge warehouse is not specific to SRM, but are described here in the context of an SRM process. SAP business information warehouse collects business data from the underlying ERP system. This module is optimized for the SAP ERP system, though not limited to it, and is a combination of database and database management tools. For example, in the context of SRM, this warehouse contains purchase- and payments-related transaction data, purchases and service-call activity, key supplier contacts and details of product purchases. This data

Exhibit 11. SAP SRM tools

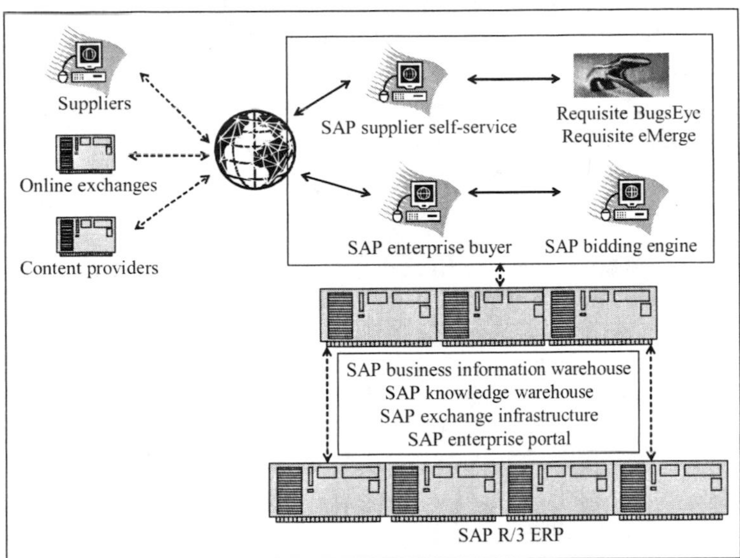

is available to purchase, production and maintenance center personnel. Moreover, data can be questioned, downloaded to spreadsheets or used to generate reports with built-in reporting tools. The business information can be mined to derive key performance indicators, capture comments made by teams working collaboratively and develop special alerts; for example, maverick buying exceeding a certain percentage of total purchases.

The purpose of the knowledge warehouse is to store, organize, process and disseminate knowledge. This warehouse can contain business rules, best practices, business process information and even decision support systems. Data can be in text or multi-media formats. This module can also be used to create a training and documentation database. This enterprise-wide database can be used to cut down on learning curve and training costs. Another building block of SRM tools is the SAP exchange infrastructure. This exchange infrastructure supports different standards such as XML, WSDL and SOAP, along with different communication protocols. The objective is to enable collaborative business processes by cutting across various systems and protocols used within the organization. In the absence of such support, costs of integrating different systems may become prohibitive.

The final base component is the SAP enterprise portal, which strives to provide a consistent navigation environment for corporate users. The ERP system can be run on mainframes, minis or microcomputers and on a variety of operating systems. Thus, a typical organization, even if hosting a single ERP system, is likely to have numerous user interfaces. The enterprise portal integrates applications, data and metadata, and Internet information. This integrated information can then be used to provide reports as specified by users or can be shared across the organization. This module is used in what SAP calls financial insight, procurement insight and sales insight, which essentially are pre-packaged business intelligence tools. Enterprise portals and business intelligence tools are discussed in depth in the general ledger cycle.

The next step investigates tools used to manage the SRM process. The SAP enterprise buyer module is the nexus for SAP SRM tools. This module interfaces with employees, purchase professionals, managers, suppliers and content managers. Employees can search electronic catalogs, order required goods, check status of inventory and ordered goods, and confirm goods delivered or services performed. Purchase professionals can create bid invitations, manage received bids, create purchase contracts and process incomplete purchase orders. Managers can use this module to set up workflows for approving shopping carts or purchase requisitions. Suppliers can enter delivery of goods or services and, if authorized, invoices into the system. Content managers can manage electronic catalogs by importing and structuring content from suppliers, creating new product catalogs or organizing existing product catalogs. SAP uses Open Catalog Interface (OCI), the Internet-based protocol for managing electronic catalogs. The enterprise buyer has numerous other features for administration, security and integration with back-end systems that are not discussed here.

The SAP bidding engine supports RFQs and reverse auctions. This engine can be used to monitor the consequent flow of information and changes in prices. This engine also includes a decision support system that eases determination of winning bids and automates the follow-up PO process. The SAP supplier self-service module enables document exchange, product content management, analytics and administration for suppliers. Document exchange involves exchange of requisition, PO, receipt of goods, invoicing and payment details. These documents are XML based and do not require third-party intervention. Suppliers can upload, change, modify or delete product information from their electronic catalogs. Analytics involve various pre-packaged reports, such as PO history, payment history and contract analysis. Suppliers can also create their own reports. Administration of an account can also be accomplished by suppliers by using this module and may involve changing IDs and passwords, enabling and limiting access for their own employees, changing contact information and adding other desired information to their home pages.

The supplier self-service module, as seen earlier, enables content management by suppliers. It is supported by content management tools, Requisite BugsEye and Requisite eMerge. BugsEye is a search engine, and SAP claims that this engine can accommodate variations in content presentation, user experience and user requirements. eMerge is a content management tool that can be used to create, maintain and manage electronic catalogs. This tool is especially useful for creating a description of products and materials that are not integrated with the product master information. The demands on SRM tools are enormous, and these change per business and industry. As such, it is not surprising that software supporting these business processes is also large and complicated.

Expenses and Payroll

Expense management was mentioned in discussing SRM tools, though the focus was on direct and indirect materials and services. SRM tools and procurement cards both are used to record, monitor and control expenses. Additionally, Web-based solutions from independent vendors, add-on products from ERP vendors and software offerings from credit card companies are available in these areas. As such, online management of expenses and online payroll areas have matured enough to merit a separate discussion, which follows.

Online Management of Expenses

The online management of expenses generally focuses on managing travel and entertainment expenses. Travel and Entertainment (T&E) expense can be the second- or third-largest controllable expense in the corporate world, and has significant processing costs associated with it. Accounting systems, with their emphasis on aggregating costs, cannot answer the questions that require breakdown of expenses; for example, what is the cost of reimbursing one expense report? How many people are involved processing expense reports? Are vendors complying with contractual terms? And, what is the detailed analysis of spending categories? These questions are similar to those discussed in the SRM area.

Employees can be on the road — in a different state or country — and need to file expense reports. Expense processing systems in most of businesses involve a hybrid of paper, spreadsheets and e-mail usage. The paper-based forms take time to fill out and route to managers, who approve them. Auditing of such claims can consume considerable resources of the accounting department. This process is rife with data-entry errors, since manual data entry takes place in at least a couple of places. Estimates for manual processing of T&E expenses range from $25 to $35 per report, which may translate into millions of dollars per year for a large corporation. For example, a Microsoft report on expenses states that Microsoft processed 200,000 reports in a year and spent $21 processing each expense report, prior to developing an in-house expense reporting solution.

The other aspect of T&E expenses is actual travel arrangements. The prices of tickets for business travelers have been traditionally high. Travel arrangements, if not consolidated and handled properly, can quickly become expensive. Don't forget that maverick buying, even if it is buying airline tickets, is costly. Apart from the direct costs of travel, there are indirect costs, such as time spent by employees and administrative assistants in hunting deals, booking flights and paying for travel. The other policy issue is how will an organization ensure that travel policies are being uniformly followed across the business? The travel aspect of T&E has come under a great deal of scrutiny, and different measures have been devised to streamline and reduce travel expenses.

Online management of T&E expenses can be categorized in two ways: first, managing expenses using Web-based tools; and second, online travel centers and alternatives to

Exhibit 12. Online management of T&E expenses

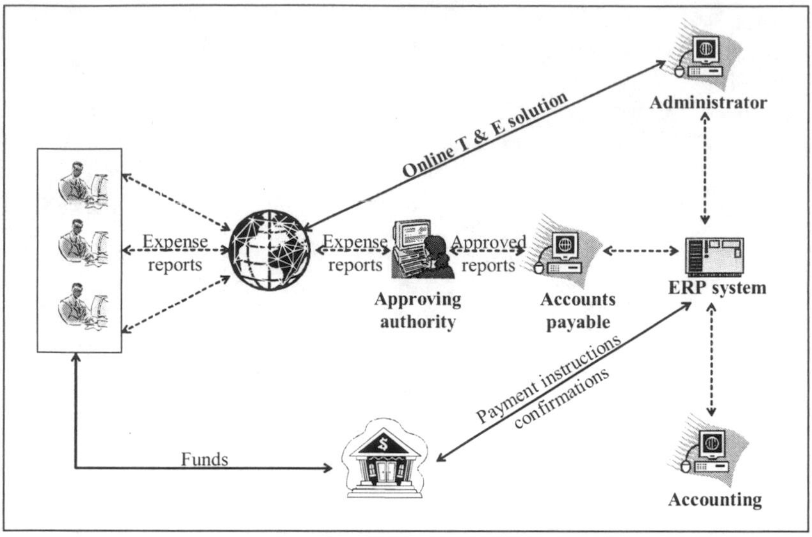

travel using Web-based technologies. DuPont in the early 1990s developed the first T&E expense management system. Now, vendors offering T&E solutions are numerous. There are Web-based solutions for small- and mid-sized organizations; the majority of ERP vendors, such as SAP and Oracle, have T&E add-ons; and a number of corporations have developed in-house solutions. American Express also offers a suite of online expense management tools. The Web-based solutions can be hosted by the provider and offered for a fee to corporations. On the other hand, a corporation can deploy a Web-based solution — whether developed internally or purchased from outside — on its networks and make it available to employees.

The basic mechanism and components of these solutions, whether internally developed or purchased from outside, are similar. Let us look at these functionalities; what follows is a general description of the process. As the user logs in, he/she may be taken to a personalized home page. This home page has links to prior expense reports, payment of those expense reports and status of the expense reports, and the user can also access relevant corporate policies and procedures. If there are any policy changes, policy alerts can inform the user. The interface with the user is either in a familiar spreadsheet format and/or has some resemblance with the paper-based voucher. The screen provides for date, name of the supplier, nature of the expenses and amount, among other things. Employees can assign project numbers and account codes. Help facilities are also available for reference purposes. Note that some T&E tools allow for offline entry of expense reports via client-side tools installed on the user's machine; some tools make it mandatory to log on to the network to fill in the report.

The T&E tools generally allow direct access to online credit card bills. The credit card bills can be directly added to the expense report. If integration between online reports and the T&E software is done properly, the fields in the expense report are automatically populated, thereby saving manual entries. If the data fields are locked and cannot be changed by the user, the Internal Revenue Service (IRS) will dispense with the requirement for paper-based receipts. Such integration depends on the cooperation between the credit card issuer and software developer. In the case of disputed transactions, direct links with credit card companies can be provided so a formal report can be filed immediately. The T&E software can also alert the employee via e-mail at the end of the month, reminding him/her that an expense report on a particular card is due.

There can also be wizards to simplify entries. For example, MS Expense 6.0 provides a hotel wizard that helps split the hotel bill into different line items, such as room charge, taxes, parking, phone and room service. Cash and out-of-pocket expenses need to be entered manually, though support for PDAs and Pocket PCs for offline expense entry is becoming common. Employees can also enter income tax-related information when filing reports concerning gifts and entertainment. In some cases, the IRS allows digital images of receipts instead paper receipts, and such receipts can be archived. These reports can also force users to enter certain information, such as tour details and itinerary, required by the back-end accounting systems for further processing.

Once the report is complete, it can be viewed online or printed for personal record of the employee filing the report. The report can be stored for further entries or completed and routed to the manager. Before the report is routed to the next level, the employee must approve the report. The employee may reject the report and provide reasons, and the report will be stored with no further action. The employee may also forward the report to a manager who does not have approval authority but who may review the report and offer comments. This utility can be useful for new employees. If the employee approves the report, it will be forwarded to the requisite manager for approval.

The approval process depends on workflow specified in the software. The administrator of the T&E program sets rules for approval workflows. The administrator can add, modify or delete employees and approval managers. The administrator designs and updates corporate policies, such as spending limits for employees, set up of special alerts and management of online expenses. The expense reporting process can change based on growth of the organization, changes in corporate objectives or for any other reason. The administrator ensures that configuration of the reporting solution changes with changes in the organization.

The security of online transactions is ensured by the administrator through standard procedures such as intrusion detection systems, firewalls, Virtual Private Network (VPN), SSL, digital certificates and multiple data backups (these security issues are covered in detail in Chapter 10). Security becomes complicated when the Web solution hosted by a provider is used. In this case, the security of the provider needs to be assessed and may involve a comprehensive review of the vendor's Web site. Many small organizations lack resources for such scrutiny and may have to accept the vendor's word for security purposes. Hacking of T&E systems is not reported in the press, but that does not mean that potential problems do not exist.

The manager who approves expense reports gets an automatic notification when the report is submitted. The report is scanned by pre-programmed business rules and any expense items that do not conform to the corporate policy are flagged. The manager can now approve the report, reject the report or ask for modification. In case of approval, the report is forwarded to accounts payable. If the report is rejected or needs to be modified, the report goes back to the employee with appropriate comments.

Accounts payable reviews the transaction and makes appropriate entries by crediting various suppliers and debiting expense accounts. Generally, the T&E software has direct links with the ERP system, and making entries is merely a matter of clicking at the appropriate places. The majority of T&E tools provided by independent vendors come with a flat file capability. The database of expense reports can be used to create a flat file that can be used to interface with accounting software. Approved expenses are then paid via different methods such as ACH, direct deposit and checks. Microsoft saved approximately $1 million by making prompt payment to American Express and receiving special discounts.

Approved expense reports are periodically analyzed by accounting. Accounting can review expense reports and establish pre-programmed rules for sampling and auditing. Audits and reviews can be conducted online, since most automated auditing tools can interface with T&E databases. The T&E software also provides a number of reporting features. Expenses can be analyzed based on time period, employee, type of expenditure, name of supplier or any other required criteria. Documents supporting the expense reports can be tracked, either in a digital or paper-based format. Tracking is easier compared to a purely paper-based system.

The T&E tools can also be used to manage other expenses. A few corporations have used these tools for managing educational costs. The employee submits receipts for fee payments and grade reports through the online system. The manager approves educational expenses online by reviewing grades and compliance with corporate policies. Expenses are then forwarded to accounts payable and can be paid via direct deposit or payroll. Any expense where the employees are physically dispersed can be effectively managed using T&E-type tools. The advantages of these tools can be summarized as follows.

- Reduced costs associated with processing transactions
- Help tools provide reduced need for expensive manual inquiries
- Increased accuracy due to reduction in manual entries
- Prompt reimbursement to employees for incurred expenses
- Prompt payments to suppliers and maximization of discounts
- Automated approval, reporting and auditing workflows
- Ability to slice-and-dice data
- Report facilities
- Enforced compliance with corporate policies

Let us not forget costs associated with the T&E software, lest the discussion sound like advertising copy for the software. Upfront costs associated with the software include programming, developing interfaces with the ERP system and installing the software. In case of external vendors, there are license fees. The upfront costs are followed by maintenance costs for the software. The users, such as the administrators, managers and employees, need to be trained and educated in use of the software. There are other intangible factors, as well, such as user resistance, alignment of workflows with corporate objectives and usefulness of information. In short, all the factors that cause problems in introducing a new piece of software are present in introducing T&E software.

Online Travel Centers

The management of T&E expenses can be taken a step further.ERP systems can now support online travel centers or e-travel capabilities. The T&E software described earlier streamlines the recordkeeping and payment of travel expenses, but does not deal directly with other substantive issues; for example, optimizing travel plans for an employee or class of employees, negotiating with airlines for best deals, reservation process and suggesting travel alternatives. The development of online travel centers or travel management addresses these areas of concern. This area is important for accountants and finance professionals as a cost containment or cost reduction strategy that has direct effects on the bottom line.

Online centers can be independently hosted and operated or can be part of the ERP system, such as SAP or Oracle. There are also consultants who comprehensively review the T&E processes of a corporation and suggest solutions. The travel business involves different entities, such as airlines, corporations, employees, travel agencies and other suppliers, such as hotels, rental cars and cruise companies. In a corporation, travel policies need to be implemented and monitored across the organization. Online travel centers or e-travel should have the capability to interface with these constituents and should also have reporting and intelligence capabilities. The structure of these software suites is similar to ones seen in the case of T&E expense solutions.

Employees log on to an online travel portal, similar to Expedia.com, a consumer travel portal on the Web. The travel portal provides self-booking capabilities, travel planning

Exhibit 13. E-travel solutions for corporate travel (Source: www.e-travel.com)

e-Travel Aergo	Brower based self-booking tool for the employees
SAP travel management	Links the travel agent, travel manager, and the accounting function
Broadvision e-Travel	This is a multi-function module. • Booking engine to provide international travel service • Tools to create and customize web sites • XML-based interface to connect with online databases
e-Travel Web Fares	Comprehensive access to the web fares -- including non-traditional and low web fares
e-Travel workflow	Specification of workflows
e-Travel reporter (US)	US specific reporting capabilities
e-Travel reporter (Global)	Global reporting capabilities
e-Travel mobile	Wireless access to the Internet based travel services

tips, city guides and maps, and references to corporate travel policies, among other things. The portal also identifies preferred airlines and travel suppliers with whom contracts have been negotiated. An employee can book airline tickets, hotel and rental cars at the same time and can obtain negotiated rates. There are several helpful utilities, such as the ability to view airline seats and maps, alternative itineraries according to cost or preferred airports, templates for frequent trips and connectivity using mobile devices. The services can be charged to corporate accounts, credit cards or smart cards.

E-Travel, an online company, partners with SAP to provide some interesting functionalities. The employee accesses the online service via SAP. The human resources module of SAP provides the travel profile for the employee. The travel profile identifies travel policies applicable to the employee, travel preferences and frequent flier details. Information concerning appropriate cost centers and bank accounts of the employee for reimbursement can also be identified. If the system is set up, the reservation can be transferred to the corporate travel office for issue of electronic or paper-based tickets.

Online travel software also automates record keeping of expenses. The mechanism is similar to the T&E software. Travel expenses can include air, hotel and rental charges; additionally, there can be per diem charges, mileage and adjustment for travel advances. The list can vary for each company. The software can also populate expense fields depending on charges received electronically from travel suppliers. Online expense vouchers can be filled and routed to the appropriate authority for approval. The software also comes with reporting or intelligence capabilities. There can be pre-defined reports and custom report abilities. Information regarding tracking travel cost and destination, booking preferences, preferred suppliers and compliance with contractual terms can be generated and routed to managers. Travel information can also be aggregated according to department, business unit and cost center, and can be compared with budgets.

Online travel may also provide *meeting management* abilities. These include selecting appropriate locations for meetings, negotiating with different suppliers for the best price, creating budgets, registering attendees and group travel planning and purchasing. These functionalities are enabled through online databases of suppliers for meeting places and electronic abilities to circulate requirements, accept answers and analyze those answers. Employees attending meetings can use the same tools to register and book tickets. These tools monitor compliance with company policies and ensure that employees use preferred suppliers and negotiated prices.

The online travel software also comes with workflow and administrative modules. These workflows can automate functions, such as requesting pre-approval for travel outside of corporate policy from an appropriate authority, notifying team members concerning the trip, and routing requests as per standard approval procedures. The system keeps users updated regarding their requests and status of expense reports in real time. Approvals, rejections or requests for modifications are automated and the employee can be alerted when these arrive. Administrative tools enable pre-configuring the software for a company's travel policy, entering information about preferred suppliers and keeping the site updated for negotiated rates. Employees authorized to use the service can be added, deleted or modified based on corporate policy.

This is a broad overview of capabilities of online travel centers or e-travel software. The software is similar to T&E tools. The primary difference is in travel planning and ensuring compliance with the travel policy, since these are more complex than merely automating or Web-enabling recording of expenses. Advantages of the software are uniform implementation of the travel policy; leverage with suppliers to negotiate prices, since volume discounts can be taken; and reduced costs of processing transactions. The tangible and intangible costs of the software are similar to those discussed earlier.

Online Payroll[1]

Payroll outsourcing is not a new phenomenon. Payroll preparation services have been in existence for a long time. These services include employee data entry and payroll calculations, direct deposits, cutting and mailing checks and 401(K) plan transfers. Many small- and mid-sized businesses have found it cost-effective to outsource payroll due to onerous federal and state tax requirements. Payroll processing companies have been in the market for decades. CPA firms have recommended payroll outsourcing services, and businesses have used these services with confidence. This established business model has found easy acceptance in the Web environment. Online payroll services have been quite successful despite general dot-com failures.

A number of established payroll services offer Web capabilities along with new dot-com arrivals. Web-based services are similar to offline payroll services, though the Internet introduces quite a few interesting twists. The prime advantage of Web-based services is 24/7 access and the ability to enable employees, employers and administrators to view and self-serve their own payroll accounts. Web-based services range a full spectrum. At one end, these services will provide an organization with software. The approved person(s) from the organization will remotely operate the software and generate payroll. In this case, accounting chores such as data entry, tax calculations and check printing are handled by the organization.

Exhibit 14. Online payroll processing

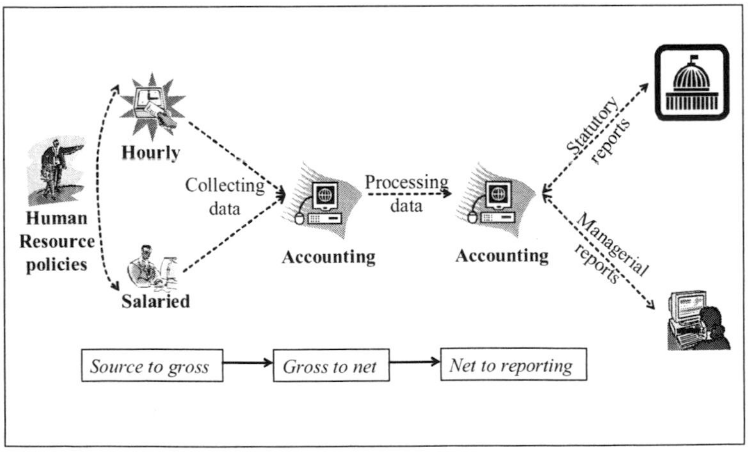

Human Resource policies
Hourly
Salaried
Collecting data
Accounting
Processing data
Accounting
Statutory reports
Managerial reports
Source to gross
Gross to net
Net to reporting

On the other end, the organization can simply submit initial data and the payroll service will take care of calculations, checks, record keeping and 401(K)-type arrangements. Employees can access payroll-related information, such as viewing and printing paycheck stubs; changing contact information; and tracking vacation time, sick time and paid time off. A number of payroll services also offer ancillary functions, such as managing insurance services, retirement plans and human resource functions. The decision regarding the extent of payroll outsourcing is unique to each company, and a wide range of practices exists in the real world.

Payroll activities can be classified into three stages: First, collection of data and calculations of gross salary, referred to as source to gross. Human resource policies are established or referred to determine hourly rates and salary levels. Then labor data is collected, managerial approvals are taken and gross pay is calculated. Second, calculating deductions and net payroll is referred to as gross to net. Third, funds are directly deposited or checks are printed and mailed, and tax and managerial reports are generated. This stage can be called net to reporting. All or part of these stages can be outsourced. Let us take a look at a comprehensive online solution.

The business user needs to register with the online payroll company before utilizing payroll services. Registration procedures require certain documentation mandated by federal regulation. An illustrative list is as follows:

- Payroll services EFT agreement
- State power of attorney
- IRS Form 8655
- Additional documents requested by online services, including copies of quarterly or annual returns, tax deposit coupons and copies of state registrations, among other things.

These documents enable the online service to fulfill legal obligations and process payroll. Generally, the user needs to appoint a payroll administrator who will be in charge of payroll. Such a person is authorized to change payroll information and add, delete or modify employee information. Additionally, a payroll approver is also needed. The payroll approver reviews the final payroll and approves the printing of checks or direct deposits.

Next is setting up the account of the business user. Payroll information can be entered via Web, PC, phone or fax. The Web-based entry generally needs only a browser and Internet connection. PC entries require client-side tools; that is, software needs to be installed on the user's machine. Data entries can be done offline and then loaded to the online software using the Internet connection. Phone entry means simply calling the online company and reading the information over the phone; and fax entry involves faxing over the required information.

A number of online companies provide tools that automate and enable remote entry of labor-related data; generally, they are referred to as time and labor management solutions. The employee checks in and either punches a card or scans a card through the clock. This is a required step in the automation of labor data collection. The scanning machine automatically captures details regarding employees and hours worked. This information is transmitted to a PC, which generally runs software provided by an online service; for example, eTime by ADP software. This software is programmed to apply business policies and procedures to the collected data; for example, rates for various employee categories, rates for overtime and hazard pay rates.

There are two issues, not Web related, of interest to accountants. A number of solutions that collect hourly data at the shop floor can also be configured to collect additional data, such as time spent on particular jobs, quantity produced and work order numbers. This data can be used in job costing or productivity analysis. A second application of these devices is in the area of scheduling. Employee hours can be matched to the production schedule, and labor shortages or excesses can be forecast. The area of job costing interface and scheduling is very complex and outside the scope of this book; however, realize that labor data collection can have alternate uses.

Reports such as total hours worked, vacation time and sickness time for a quarter or year can be generated using this software. Automatic reports for punching in and out of employees are also generated, which are statutorily required. These reports can highlight problems of absenteeism, late arrivals and departures, and missed punches. The actual data can be compared to budgeted data and exception reports can be generated. Collected labor rates and other data are directly transferred to the online payroll service. The data can also be archived and stored at a user location. This data can be reviewed, analyzed and forwarded to appropriate managers.

Online services generally send an e-mail informing the business that payroll information is due at a particular date. The authorized employee can log on to the online service and, after appropriate authentication, perform different functions; for example, running payroll, running reports, making salary payments or other administrative functions.

Exhibit 15. Payroll data entry (Source: www.surepayroll.com/, used with permission)

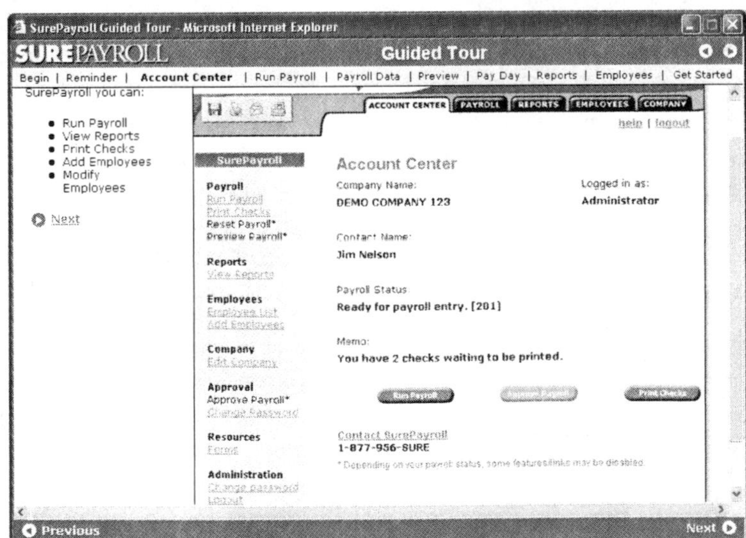

Payroll information for employees, such as hours worked, changes in salary, deductions and changes thereof, and other pertinent information, can be entered and viewed. Extra data fields may include department, cost center or business unit number. Payroll processing is generally very fast and done in a matter of minutes. The payroll, when processed, is ready for review. The review may be conducted by the data-entry employee or an authorized manager, depending on the separation of duties in a particular organization.

The next phase is payment to the employees, which can be done in a variety of formats. A paper check can be printed and mailed to employees based on their addresses in the database. The checks should have security features, such as watermarks, fading ink, company logos or micro printing. Additional internal controls can be introduced for paper checks. As the checks are being mailed, an electronic file containing details of all checks is forwarded to the bank. The bank will match every presented check with the electronic file and transfer funds only after a match is confirmed. Most online services support direct deposit, as direct deposit is mandatory for some employees. The direct deposit transfers funds to the employee-designated bank account at the end of the month. Some online payroll services offer to fill stored value cards. These cards work similar to debit cards and are useful when employees do not have bank accounts. Several variations of the payment methods described so far are available in the online world.

The most beneficial feature of payroll processing companies, online or offline, is handling of federal, state, and local taxes. These taxes are calculated and deducted at the time of payroll processing. Then, the taxes are paid and appropriate filings with government departments are completed. A number of online companies provide guaranteed performance in the area of tax payments. Certain contractual formalities need to be completed before these services are operational.

The payroll data is archived and stored. A number of reports can be generated from this data. The standard report is, of course, payroll register for the month. A list of employees with gross pay, deductions and net pay can be generated, printed and reviewed. Other reports may include year-end W-2s and 401(K)-specific reports for the employee and employer contributions. Payroll can be analyzed according to department, project or cost center, and customized reports can also be generated. Reporting facilities depend on the data details entered at the initial stage, and are generally sufficient for standard reports. This data can also be exported to Excel or Access if further analysis is desired.

Online payroll services have branched out with a number of value-added services. Online services may provide a portal that offers a database of laws and regulations applicable to salary, contain employment forms and have labor law posters and compliance tools. These portals are useful for payroll professionals. A few online services offer Internet-based employee screening and drug testing. Managing insurance — medical, dental, vision, Section 125 benefit plans and life insurance — offering and managing retirement plans, and time and attendance systems are additional services offered by online companies. The offered services are quite comprehensive and cover the entire gamut of the human resources field. They are mentioned here to highlight the fast-changing nature of the online payroll business.

Fixed Assets

Fixed assets are purchased, managed and ultimately disposed off. Fixed-asset accounting involves calculating cost of the asset, making periodic depreciation entries and accounting for disposal of fixed assets. Other accounting areas involve extraordinary repairs, additions and betterments. There is not much use of Web-based solutions in this area, since most in-house accounting software can handle fixed-asset accounting. However, there are few a Web-based twists in this area.

Fixed assets can be automatically created from accounts payable and purchasing modules. If the asset is purchased at a location different than a recording location, then Web-based application of this utility can come in handy. The purchase requisition, PO and receiving report can be generated and entered in accounting software. The software can then automatically create the fixed asset based on programmed business rules and inform the fixed-asset department. The fixed asset then can be reviewed at a central location and processed further.

Fixed assets in Web-enabled accounting software can also be managed remotely. Depreciation expense entries are generally calculated automatically and posted to the general ledger. Remote access can be used to verify these depreciation calculations; make entries for extraordinary repairs, additions and betterments; and account for gain or loss on disposal of assets. These functionalities are available in most accounting software packages, and are mentioned here for completeness. However, basic fixed-asset accounting processes have not changed dramatically due to Web enablement.

Summary

The expenditure cycle has changed considerably due to the advent of SRM, e-procurement tools, online management of expenses and online travel centers. Accounting activities of matching documents such as purchase requisition, PO, receiving report and invoice to create a voucher package and consequent payments have changed considerably. The creation of liabilities, posting of expenses, matching of documents, internal controls, workflows and payments has been automated. The changes have simplified life of accounting professionals and at the same time have demanded new skills, such as understanding SRM tools.

The changing business processes and detailed analytical requirements of modern management accelerated the ascent of SRM software. SRM tools have integrated sourcing and procurement activities and have created a single process that controls supplier-related activities. The process begins with a supplier selection strategy, which requires hard analytical data and soft strategic and political inputs. SRM tools provide a slew of analytical reports and collaborative tools to coordinate these activities. Identification of suppliers is facilitated by online trading directories, historical knowledge bases, structured electronic way to forward and receive information, and collaborative tools.

The Internet, coupled with SRM tools, has allowed businesses to negotiate and manage supplier contracts without paper. Contract templates are maintained in a central repository and can be filled online to generate customized contracts. These contracts can be automatically monitored for compliance and gathering of intelligence data. Supplier self-service abilities include changing contact information, creating Web pages, posting information on Web pages, managing electronic catalogs and limited programming abilities. Supplier self-service abilities reduce administrative burden on the purchase departments. SRM tools also facilitate auctions, the contemporary popular variant being *reverse auctions*. Reverse auctions allow buyers to host the auction and watch as suppliers post bids and drive the price down; the lowest bidder is the winner. SRM tools provide Web space, security and electronic tools to conduct reverse auctions. Automated analytical tools allow analysis of bids on dimensions other than price.

Invoicing and settlement have become embedded in the purchase process. The purchase requisition is generated by an employee or from a shopping cart. The generation of a PO is automatic and delivery of the PO is accomplished via supplier portals. The goods in transit and on the receiving docks are monitored by ASNs. The ASN is matched with the incoming shipment by using bar codes, and is automatically routed to the proper location in the warehouse or to the ordering employee. Incoming invoices are confirmed by the system by matching and reconciling PO and ASN. Invoices are electronically routed for approval and paid at the due date. SRM tools also support ERS, wherein the invoices are dispensed with or generated from the PO and ASN.

Electronic catalogs are sustained by SRM tools. These catalogs, essential to electronic purchasing, can be created, hosted, modified and searched by the SRM tools. Employees can search these catalogs from their desktops and order the required items without routing the order through the purchase department. Approvals of these purchases are specified in the workflows and can be carried online. The receipt of goods can be confirmed by the employee or a special central authority. If goods arrive at the shipping docks, those goods can be routed directly to the ordering department or employee. Payment can be approved by the employee or handled via automated procedures.

Procurement cards are used to purchase low-value items, such as office supplies. These cards have become popular in industry, government and university settings as cost-saving measures. The electronic statement coming from credit card companies can be directly posted to the general ledger; the SRM tools can facilitate such interfacing. There are Web-based services that enable administration of procurement cards from the Internet. A number of internal controls can be instituted for procurement cards, though research has shown that too much control is counterproductive in the usage of procurement cards. SRM tools can support employee procurement cards as well as supplier procurement cards.

SRM tools also provide a space or sourcing cockpit to deal with unforeseen situations. The intelligence and reporting abilities of SRM tools enable slicing and dicing of supplier data every which way. Supplier performance, purchase expenses, quality analysis and financial analysis are supported. Key performance indicators can be captured and communicated for managerial purposes. The SRM tools come with a number of pre-defined reports, and additional reports can be created using built-in tools. These supplier databases can be exported and analyzed via spreadsheets and query languages.

Online management of expenses includes managing T&E expenses, since these expenses are incurred all over the country or the globe. Online management of these expenses involves providing Web-based tools for entering of expenses, help facilities, automatic routing to an approval authority and prompt reimbursement through direct deposit. On the accounting side, a database of these expenses can be used to create various reports, perform sampling and automatic audits, and post expenses directly to the general ledger. Online travel centers take this concept a step further. They enable enforcement of travel policies throughout the organization and streamline reservations, issues and payments of tickets. Travel centers can be helpful in planning and optimizing travel across the organization.

This chapter ended with a brief coverage of fixed assets. The Web has not changed the basic fixed-assets accounting process. Remote entries and automatic creation of assets based on PO and invoice enables managing assets at far-flung locations through a central site. Depreciation entries, reports on additions and betterments, and disposal of assets can also be managed remotely, making the accounting process simpler.

References

Ala, M., & Brunaczki, B. (2003, Spring). Online benefits solutions – A new trend in managing employee benefits programs. *Journal of Health Care Finance*, 29, 61-66.

Apicella, M. (2000, June). The ABCs of enterprise procurement. *InfoWorld*, *22,* 47-49.

Campbell, J. (2003, April). Evaluating corporate travel automation. *Business Travel News*, *20,* 87-93.

Chandra, A. (2003). *Supplier Relationship Management: What is SRM? What does it do? How can it work for your company?* (SRM white paper). Oracle. Retrieved May 8, 2003, from www.oracle.com/

Copacino, W. (2001, January). Auctions expand e-procurement menu. *Logistics Management & Distribution Report*, 39.

Datex. (2002). *Datex: Supply chain – Warehouse Management System* (data sheet). Datex. Retrieved May 8, 2003, from www.datexcorp.com/

eSourcing: Enabling the strategic sourcing process from end-to-end with Internet technology (white paper). (2002). A.T. Kearney. Retrieved May 10, 2003, from www.ebreviate.com/

eTravel, Oracle product description. (2002). Oracle. Retrieved May 10, 2003, from www.oracle.com/

Federation of Tax Administrators. (2001). *Procurement cards and tax compliance: Bridging the gap*. Retrieved May 15, 2003, from www.taxadmin.org/fta/pcards.pdf/

Fixed Assets, product description. (2002). Intacct Corporation. Retrieved May 11, 2003 from www.intacct.com/

Gibley, T. (1999, July/August). A guide to purchasing card success: Overcoming 8 key hurdles. *TMA Journal*, 47-50.

Gilbert, A. (2000, November). E-procurement: Problems behind the promise. *Information Week*, 48-62.

Hallett, T. (2002). *The automation of travel and entertainment management* (white paper). Retrieved May 12, 2003, from www.cfoproject.com/

i2 procurement SRM solution. (2002). I2. Retrieved May 9, 2003, from www.i2.com/

IBM expense reporting solutions (data sheets). (2003). IBM. Retrieved May 12, 2003, from www.ibm.com/

Informatica strategic sourcing analytics (data sheet). (2003). Informatica. Retrieved May 12, 2003, from www.informatica.com/

Knaster, B. (2002, March). Payroll thrives on the Internet. *Accounting Technology*, 30-35.

Kopp, S. (2001, January/February). Reengineering your purchasing card program. *Financial Executive*, 50-51.

Martinson, B. (2002, February). The power of the P-card. *Strategic Finance*, 31-35.

Merson, I. (2000). *Reverse auctions: An overview* (white paper). Wifron. Retrieved May 15, 2003, from www.wifcon.com/analasirev.pdf

Mulhem, M., & Modesitt, L. (2004). How to make purchasing cards a key to company-wide savings. *AFP Exchange*, *24*, 32-35.

mySAP Supplier Relationship Management (white paper). (2003). SAP. Retrieved May 10, 2003 from www.sap.com/

Office of Foreign Assets Control. (2003). U.S. Treasury. Retrieved May 13, 2003, from www.ustreas.gov/offices/enforcement/ofac/

Oracle Internet procurement, an Oracle application (white paper). (2001). Oracle. Retrieved May 10, 2003, from www.oracle.com/

Oracle iProcurment 11i (data sheet). (2003). Oracle. Retrieved May 10, 2003, from www.oracle.com/

Oracle Purchasing Intelligence (data sheet). (2003). Oracle. Retrieved May 10, 2003, from www.oracle.com/

Palmer, R. (1996, September). Are procurement cards for you? *Management Accounting*, *78*, 22-29.

Porter, A. (2000). *A purchasing manager's guide to the e-procurement galaxy*. Retrieved May 15, 2003, from www.manufacturing.net/

Procurement cards. (2003). ExpensePath. Retrieved May 15, 2003, from www.p-card.com/

Product and solution description. (2003a). Concur. Retrieved May 15, 2003, from www.concur.com/

Product and solution description. (2003b). ExpensAble. Retrieved May 15, 2003, from www.expensable.com/

Product description and FAQ. (2003). ExpensePath. Retrieved May 16, 2003, from www.p-card.com/

Pruter, R. (2001, April). Vendors offer single portal Web sites to integrate benefits communications and administration. *Employee Benefit Review*, 16-20.

Purchasing. (2001, December). *Bayer Corporation beefs up its procurement card program*. Retrieved May 5, 2003, from www.purchasing.com/

SAP bidding engine, SAP help. (2003). SAP. Retrieved May 23, 2003, from http://help.sap.com/

SAP customer success story. (2003). SAS. Royal Dutch/Shell Group. Retrieved May 23, 2003, from www.sas.com/

SAP travel management (data sheet). (2003). SAP. Retrieved May 23, 2003, from www.sap.com/

SAS supplier relationship management (white paper). (2003). SAP. Retrieved May 24, 2003, from www.sas.com/

Self-service procurement slashing costs and saving time (white paper). (2003). SAP. Retrieved May 24, 2003, from www.sap.com/

Strategic sourcing and Supplier Relationship Management solution (white paper). (2003). Commerce One. Retrieved May 25, 2003, from www.commerceone.com/

Supplier enablement with mySAP Supplier Relationship Management (white paper). (2003). SAP. Retrieved May 24, 2003, from www.sap.com/

Taking charge, Ericsson, the Swedish phone giant, shows how corporate credit cards – or purchasing cards – can become a cornerstone of e-procurement strategies (2000, December/2001, January). CEO Europe. Retrieved May 26, 2003, from www.cfoeurope.com/200012e.html

Tausz, A. (2001, November). Easing expenses. *CMA Management*, 48-49.

Thompson, C. (2004, June). Inappropriate P-card practices. *Internal Auditor*, 61, 97-99.

Endnote

1 The information in this section is collected from *www.payroll.com/*, *www.adp.com/* and *www.surepayroll.com/*.

Chapter VII

The Conversion Cycle

Conversion Cycle Activities

The conversion cycle spans a range of activities — product design, production planning and control, and cost accounting. Product design is a collaborative activity and can involve a number of specialists from different functional areas. Production planning and control involves planning production by optimizing factors such as customer demand, availability of materials and labor, capacity constraints, distribution constraints and storage constraints, to mention a few. Planned manufacturing activities are carried out by processing raw materials though a combination of machines and humans and creating a finished product. The cost accounting system provides data useful for evaluating production function, determining product costs and generating information for inventory valuation for external reporting purposes.

The twin objectives of quality and cost reduction have been a holy grail for manufacturing organizations. The last few decades have seen a number of methodologies, such as material requirements planning (MRP), manufacturing resource planning (MRP II), Just in Time (JIT), Robotics and Six Sigma, which strived to achieve these objectives. The conversion cycle is most visible in manufacturing organizations; however, the service industry has also benefited from conversion cycle concepts and theories. The conver-

Exhibit 1. The conversion cycle

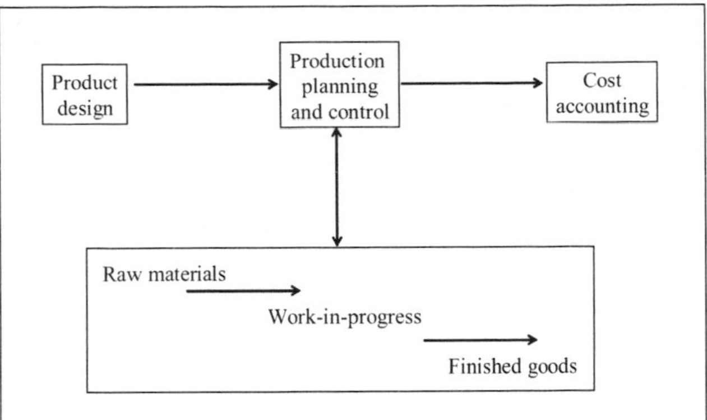

sion cycle interfaces with different functions and departments in the organization, such as purchasing, marketing and finance. Initial efforts for quality and cost management focused on connecting different departments and streamlining internal operations of organizations.

As organizations succeeded in squeezing costs from internal operations and improved product quality, their attention turned to activities and entities external to the organization. Suppliers who supplied raw materials, carriers who moved goods, distribution networks who distributed goods and customers who fueled demand; all of these external entities came under intense scrutiny. The field of SCM that comprehensively deals with all these activities was born in the 1970s, but gained prominence during the 1990s. SCM deals with the entire gamut of sourcing, production planning and control, and distribution activities to begin with! SCM, a complex field, has many definitions, many interpretations, many perspectives and no single departmental owner.

The role of accounting in the production cycle has also changed over the years. Initial involvement of accountants with the conversion cycle was primarily in determination of product costs and inventory valuation. Changes in the conversion cycle caused changes in cost accounting systems. Accountants grappled with devising measurements that align incentives of the production department with corporate objectives. Cost accounting systems evolved to measure activities (Activity-Based Cost accounting, or ABC), product costs at the design stage (target costing), quality of products and defect rates, and effects on inventory due to JIT philosophy, among other things. Financial measurements for determining relative profitability of products and advising on product mix, product pricing and special decisions such as make or buy have also seen accountant involvement.

So what are exact changes due to digital accounting in the production area, especially as they intersect accounting? The Internet has been used as an enabler or facilitator in implementing accounting processes; however, the Internet has not been used to substantively alter cost accounting processes in the conversion cycle. However, there has been a number of significant developments in managing the production function due to Internet-based SCM software. The focus of cost management and cost accounting has shifted from a single organization to the entire supply chain. Studying the field of SCM is crucial to understanding digital accounting and supply chain cost accounting.

First, a conceptual view of SCM is presented, since conversion cycle activities are best studied under the umbrella of SCM. Second, changes in different areas, such as product design, production planning and control, and product life cycle management, are investigated, with particular emphasis on SAP SCM software. Third, changes in cost accounting due to SCM are explained. Finally, a summary of the chapter rounds off the discussion.

Supply Chain Management

SCM is not a new concept; in fact, managing supplies and suppliers can be traced back to the vertical integration undertaken by the automotive industry in the 1930s. Modern origins of SCM could be traced to the 1960s, when systematic efforts to increase operational efficiency and inventory reduction were undertaken by corporations. Preliminary efforts were in the areas of optimizing warehousing and transportation functions. The concepts of SCM crystallized in the 1970s and 1980s, especially under the onslaught of JIT inventory management from Japanese automotive companies. However, the state of information technology at the time did not provide implementation capabilities. Theoretical SCM concepts continued to evolve and, by the 1990s, they embraced the entire supply chain.

ERP systems ushered in an era of integrating internal functions of the organization. Businesses have become relatively sophisticated in making internal production operations efficient and cost-effective. SCM was the next step, wherein outside entities were integrated in internal operations of the company. So what is this supply chain? The supply chain, also known as value chain or demand chain, refers to the chain of suppliers

Exhibit 2. Supply chain

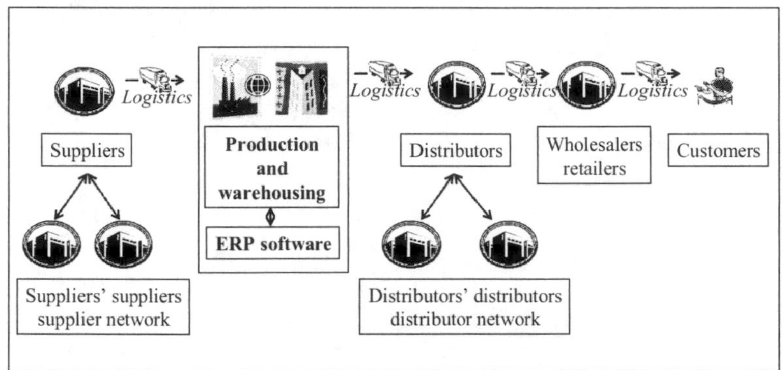

and their suppliers, manufacturers and subcontractors, warehouses, transporters and, finally, customers. Basically, the supply chain encompasses the process of sourcing, procurement, manufacturing and logistics until the product is delivered to the customer; and may even include the process of discarding or recycling products.

SCM, as the term implies, involves managing the supply chain. Management of the supply chain involves a range of complex decisions, strategic to operational. These decisions revolve around the right product, right price, right cost, right quality, right quantity, right location and right customer. Historically, supply chain constituents had adversarial relationships. Suppliers wanted long-term commitments, manufacturers wanted quality supplies at low cost and flexibility, retailers wanted fewer empty shelves; and even internal functions of the organization had conflicting objectives. The supply chain operated with inherent contradictions. SCM promises to replace such contradictions by connecting and harmonizing the supply chain; at least in theory. Decisions involved in SCM can be categorized as follows — sourcing and procurement, logistics, production, inventory and customers.

- **Sourcing and procurement:** The business needs strategies for selecting, identifying and nurturing suppliers. Quality, location, financial stability, reputation and past performance are some factors that go into these decisions. Once the supplier is chosen, then its performance needs to be measured and monitored. The process of managing inventory, receiving goods, quality control, invoicing and settlement needs to be standardized and automated. This area overlaps with SRM functionalities seen in the expenditure cycle.
- **Logistics:** Logistics refers to the process of moving raw materials from the supplier to the manufacturer, and moving finished goods from the manufacturer to the customer. There are interim processes of storage, warehousing and selecting carriers to complete movement of goods. Logistics involves decisions regarding shipment size, modes of transport, location of distribution centers, order processing costs, optimization of transport routes and a host of other variables. Logistics models can get very complex very quickly.
- **Production:** Strategic production decisions include location of manufacturing facilities; make-or-buy decisions; capacity of manufacturing facilities; and strategies concerning the product, such as low-cost or niche products. Operational details are concerned with production planning and scheduling, quality control, packaging, routing, labor management and day-to-day management of the plant.
- **Inventory:** Inventory management choices include JIT or MRP, safety stock, raw material order policies, finished goods stock level, warehousing locations and WMS, among other things.
- **Customers:** Managing customer orders, order entry, invoicing, settlement, customer service, policies regarding sales returns, resolving customer problems and creating efficient processes for disposal of returned goods are also considered part of SCM. These areas obviously overlap with CRM.

The primary objectives of SCM are to maintain the desired service levels and minimize costs across the supply chain, sometimes referred to as global optimization. An effective SCM also results in improved profit margins and increased manufacturing throughput. There is nothing new in these objectives; in fact, almost all tools we have seen so far strive for the same results. The effective SCM, however, provides *visibility* — all trading partners can view each other's requirements and can collaboratively plan, produce and meet customer expectations.

What parts of business can be considered non-SCM? SCM covers internal operations and external connections — chain — and most business activities fall under SCM. As such, SCM can be considered a strategy or management philosophy. The different techniques and philosophies we have studied so far, such as ERP, CRM or SRM, have overlapping objectives with SCM. The software suites for ERP, CRM, SRM and SCM all require each other's functionalities and databases to operate successfully; the differences are getting blurred.

SCM gained real prominence in the 1990s. Information technology has been the true enabler of SCM due to data availability and universal communication protocols. The advent of the Internet, globalization of business, an installed and operational ERP base, and increasing competitive pressures have accelerated the metamorphosis of SCM from a theoretical concept to real-world applications. SCM applications are still evolving, and may take many years to mature. The promise and performance of new technologies has a spotty record, and SCM is no exception.

How is SCM implemented? SCM is an extremely complex process, and its implementation is akin (or perhaps more complex) to ERP installation. SCM will involve installation of complex software modules, often on top of an ERP system, changes in corporate policies, redesign of workflows, changes on the shop floor; and it may extend all the way to preparing trading partners for changes through investment and education. The implementation of SCM includes suppliers, wholesalers, distributors, customers, consultants, software vendors, system developers and system integrators. SCM also needs support from the top leadership, willingness of suppliers and partners to share information and maintain confidentiality, and sharing of rewards by the dominant partner. SCM is generally an incremental, not a big-bang, process. The list of required functionalities for SCM implementation is lengthy, and is reviewed in the context of SAP SCM software.

SAP SCM Capabilities

SAP SCM capabilities fall under four categories: supply chain planning, supply chain execution, supply chain collaboration and supply chain coordination. Due to the fast evolving nature of SCM and SCM software, there is considerable terminological confusion in these four areas. The functionalities are not clearly defined, and similar functionalities are marketed under different names. The following discussion follows SAP software specifications, though SAP white papers are not entirely consistent, either. Remember the oft-repeated cautionary note: Focus on functions, not on terms.

Exhibit 3. SAP supply chain management capabilities

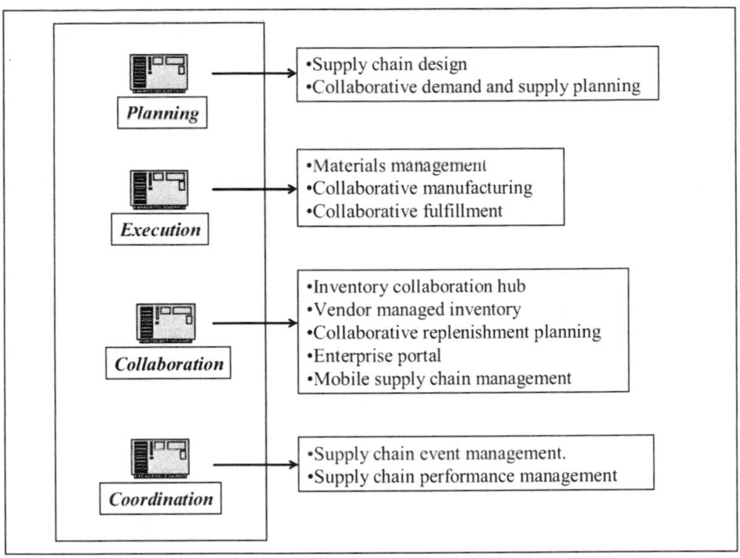

SAP SCM functionalities are enabled by SAP SCM tools, such as advanced planner and optimizer, product life cycle management, enterprise buyer and CRM. In this section, SAP SCM capabilities are conceptually discussed, and in the next section, specific SAP software modules are discussed.

Supply Chain Planning

Supply chain planning involves two functionalities — supply chain design and collaborative demand, and supply planning. Supply chain design refers to strategic decisions regarding location of the suppliers, operational decisions concerning optimizing logistics network and analytical capabilities to provide supply chain intelligence and perform what-if analyses. The geographic location, size and number of suppliers in a given location are long-term strategic decisions. These decisions affect access to customer markets and customer service levels and, hence, are of strategic significance. SAP provides an optimization model that considers different factors, such as capacity constraints, production costs, taxes and local content. These models can be used for determining and selecting location. The location decision influences transportation costs and modes, vehicle utilization, carrier selection and inventory carrying costs, among other things. The optimization model in the SAP SCM tools can also be used to optimize transportation costs across the entire logistics network. Analytical tools in the supply chain design enable: analysis of the entire supply chain to pinpoint weak points, simulation capabilities to run scenarios to strengthen weak points or work up alternate scenarios and a variety of key performance indicators available in graphical and numeric format. Supply chain design results can be connected to other supply chain modules for consequent execution.

Collaborative demand and supply planning deals with matching actual or forecasted customer orders with the supply chain network to fulfill these orders timely and profitably. Demand planning involves forecasting customer demand via statistical techniques, analysis of customer behavior, effect of marketing events on sales and performance analysis. Statistical forecasting is effective if data is cleaned of missing values, outliers, seasonal changes and unique variations. The SAP SCM tools offer standardized methods for cleaning data for statistical use. Statistical forecasting techniques include univariate models, causal analysis and composite forecasting models. Univariate models include historical data for forecasting and a range of forecasting techniques, such as moving average, linear regression and time series models. These techniques can be used for forecasting and planning demand. Such forecasts can be for a single product, a group of products, region, country or for a particular time period, such as next week or month.

Causal analysis includes estimating effects of causal variables such as price, number of displays, type of displays and number of stores, among other things on customer behavior. Composite forecasting allows for combining results of a variety of forecasting techniques and creating a composite forecast. Comparison of forecasts with actuals and subsequent analysis of deviations is also possible. Marketing events, such as promotions, are expected to spike the organization's sales. Forecasting techniques can be used to isolate effects of such marketing events on sales. These incremental sales from promotional events and incremental costs of promotions (from accounting records) enable profitability analysis of promotions. Product life cycle management can also be integrated with demand forecasting. Questions such as whether, when and how a new product should be launched or an existing product be discontinued can be asked and answered. The variety of statistical techniques in this area is mind-boggling; however, forecasts are still a combination of art and science. Performance analysis involves a number of key performance indicators that are discussed under supply chain coordination.

The purpose of demand planning is to plan the supply. Supply planning involves streamlining flow of materials across the supply chain and optimizing purchasing, transportation in and out, manufacturing and inventory. Constraints that need to be considered are: transportation costs, production capacities, warehouse limitations, financial requirements, quotas and a host of other factors. Decisions that are made in this phase include supplier choice, product mix, inventory build-up across the supply chain, and transportation in and out channels, among other things. Costs involved in this process are material costs, production costs, transportation costs, inventory costs, warehousing and handling costs, lost sales and penalties for unfulfilled contracts. SAP SCM tools provide approximately a dozen optimizing algorithms, such as simplex-based, branch and bound methods, and constraint-based optimization. If incoming customer orders differ in priority, then capable-to-match functionality can be used. This function can establish customer order priority, search the supply chain for raw and intermediate products, route production through desired manufacturing locations and fill the orders in a timely fashion.

The purchasing and production plan is followed by a distribution plan. Distribution planning involves supplying products to distribution centers. This supply may be based on raising stock levels in all distribution centers proportionately, the demand faced by each center or the priority of customer orders. The next step is transportation planning — to the distribution centers and then to the ultimate customers. Transportation decisions are complex, and variables such as types of carriers used, types of vehicles used, maximum and minimum capacity of the vehicles, routes used, costs on different routes, and current and expected demand. SAP SCM tools use these variables to optimize transportation decisions; that is, minimize transportation costs and maintain service levels.

Supply Chain Execution

Supply chain execution involves managing materials for production, manufacturing and fulfillment of orders in collaboration with trading partners. Materials management strives to procure the right raw materials at the right time, right place and right cost. SRM tools, seen in the expenditure cycle, can be used in buying direct materials — that is, raw materials — and these purchases are called planned sourcing. The ERP system determines raw materials requirements based on a production schedule, and the resulting purchase requisitions are forwarded to the central purchasing system. The purchasing system refers to the sourcing rules and forwards those requisitions to the preferred suppliers as POs. The invoicing and settlement process is identical to the one in the expenditure cycle. SRM tool functionalities, such as supplier self-service, auctions, contract management and purchasing intelligence, are also available in planned sourcing. If the final product or parts of the product are to be outsourced, then such subcontracting can be automated through materials management. The rest of the functionalities are inventory management and VMI, which are seen later.

Inventory management involves maintaining the required inventory quantity and value. The quantity on hand, quantity in the receiving department, quantity on order and quantity at different locations can be seen at any point in time. As materials are requisitioned to production, the inventory levels — that is, inventory quantity and inventory value — are updated. Designated cost accounts and general ledger accounts are also updated simultaneously. Inventory valuation using moving average price or standard costs is available for external reporting purposes. Inventory can be separated into two categories — standard and special — for efficient management. The standard category includes inventory ready for issue, undergoing quality control and reserved for special uses. The special category includes inventory that is valued, owned or managed under different criteria; for example, consignment inventory, packaging materials to be returned by customers after receipt of order and inventory earmarked for subcontractors.

Collaborative manufacturing encompasses mechanisms for sharing production information across the supply chain to coordinate production activities. Production strategies vary based on industry and business, and include engineered-to-order, configure-to-order, make-to-order and make-to-stock. Engineered-to-order products may involve complex projects and product design and development activities. Configure-to-order products allow customers to choose from various product options and customize the product. Make-to-order decisions involve making products based on customer orders; and make-to-stock entails making products based on a demand forecast. These production processes and associated procurement and product design activities must be supported to enable collaborative manufacturing.

The current status of a product should be visible to customers, production personnel and suppliers. Changes in the design, quality and quantity of raw materials, product specification and product order need to be communicated quickly across the supplier chain. Such communication allows partners to change their production schedules and manage their supply chains more efficiently. SCM tools are used in optimizing production schedules once production strategy and procurement processes are in place. Production schedules are inherently uncertain, and the optimization algorithms need to constantly adjust for changing constraints. These algorithms can be standard mathematical techniques, user-specified heuristics or a hybrid thereof. The final step in collaborative manufacturing is actual production. For a manufacturing organization, production activities are a core process, and these activities interface with cost accounting, time and labor management, warehouses and materials management, to mention a few. The information that flows across these departments should be synchronized, and changes need to be captured in real time. SAP SCM tools, as an integrated package, enable these functionalities.

Collaborative fulfillment consists of fulfilling customer orders on time, reacting to changes in customer orders in real time, adjusting for changes in customer order priorities, and avoiding expensive inventory buildup or shortfall. The achievement of these objectives depends on the extent of integration and collaboration across the supply chain. Online product configuration and design functionality enable designing products in collaboration with geographically scattered suppliers and design teams, and these functionalities are supported by SAP SCM software. Another feature is Available-To-Promise (ATP), which enables a local and global search for finished good, parts, machine availability and capacity, or accessibility of intermediate products across the supply chain. Based on this analysis, the ATP feature provides expected date of delivery to the customer. ATP helps manufacturing by coordinating procurement and production, and helps sales by faster delivery and product substitutions.

Collaborative fulfillment is also supported by intelligent allocation of products to different distribution centers and customers based on demand and customer order priorities. However, priorities of customer orders can change or unexpected new orders may arrive, which may disrupt fulfillment schedules. In such cases, all suppliers and internal functions of the organization can be informed of production schedule changes and allocation of products using the SCM software. Finally, logistics management and warehouses are also integrated to ensure low cost and fast movement of materials for effective fulfillment of customer orders.

Supply Chain Collaboration

Supply chain collaboration is required in the context of all supply chain activities; however, in this section, the focus is on inventory- and demand-related collaboration.

A few areas have been covered earlier, though additional details and a few new collaborative areas are discussed here. SAP ICH (Inventory Collaboration Hub) is the Internet-based solution, and its purpose is to increase inventory visibility and enhance collaboration across the supply chain. The primary functions of SAP ICH are listed below.

- **Communication with suppliers:** Suppliers can see the status of their parts and materials by accessing ICH via Web, e-mail or other mobile devices. Suppliers can also get special reports from the organization, which can provide aggregate and disaggregate information regarding inventory. The suppliers can review these trends in the inventory buildup and consumption, and adjust production accordingly.
- **User designed alerts:** ICH enables suppliers to design customized alerts, which are triggered based on pre-defined events, such as quantities, percentages and consumption. These alerts can be delivered through a variety of electronic methods.
- **Integration with backend accounting systems:** ICH comes with an XML-based interface, which SAP claims can be integrated with any back-end accounting system, including legacy systems.

VMI is another collaborative application in this area. VMI is also known as supplier managed inventory, consignment inventory and consignment stores. Traditionally, the customer placed an order with the vendor (or supplier) as per inventory requirements. The supplier had no idea concerning the customer's needs and had to hold safety stock or expedite the orders to fulfill demand. In VMI, the customer's inventory levels, consumption patterns and demand forecasts are integrated into the supplier's inventory

Exhibit 4. Vendor managed inventory

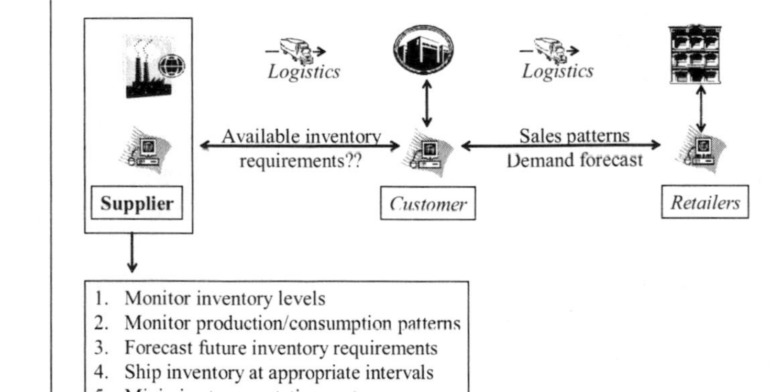

management system. VMI shifts responsibility of maintaining and managing (certain) customer inventory levels from the customer to the supplier. As the customer needs inventory, the supplier's system will automatically generate POs and produce and ship the necessary products. The most famous example of VMI is the agreement between Procter & Gamble and WalMart in the late 1980s.

VMI involves three distinct phases. First, customer inventory requirements must be estimated by continuous monitoring of customer inventory levels and sophisticated forecasting techniques. Second, required inventory should be shipped to customer locations by minimizing transportation costs. Finally, the customer's shelves must be stocked once goods reach the desired location, be it may a retail store, a parts room in the factory or shelves in the warehouse. The agreement between the supplier and customer is negotiated at the front end. The agreement deals with division of responsibilities, transportation modes, carrier selection, required service levels, key performance measures and penalties for non-fulfillment, among other things. Despite agreements, VMI requires a high level of trust and collaboration between the supplier and customer.

VMI implementation methods differ, and almost each VMI application is unique in some way. VMI can be vendor controlled. Vendors remotely monitor and manage customer inventory and usage patterns and fill in the shelves as needed. VMI can also be customer controlled; for example, if the customer has multiple locations, logistics and transportation may be handled by the customer's personnel. VMI is also not one single methodology; there are several VMI models, and the applicable model needs to chosen carefully. In any case, VMI needs electronic transmission of information, often using the Internet. VMI installations also use EDI transmissions if both parties are EDI capable.

VMI can be viewed as a value-added service activity. VMI provides inventory visibility across the supply chain, decreases inventory levels for the supplier and the customer, reduces logistical complexity and transportation costs, optimizes manufacturing and increases services levels — all the way up to the retail level. Additionally, procurement and administrative costs are lowered due to reduction of paperwork. Currently, hundreds of software vendors are supplying VMI software, and scores of consulting firms specialize in VMI implementation. The success of VMI can be inferred from the fact that almost every large corporation has some form of VMI in place.

VMI also has limitations. VMI contracts have been canceled by numerous customers due to implementation failures. First, VMI is a strategic decision, and VMI's success largely depends on support from top management. Second, the level of collaboration is limited. If the disaggregation of data is not carried to the necessary level, the strategic benefits of VMI may not materialize. Third, the internal objectives of the customer and the objectives of VMI should be aligned. The procurement staff of the customer may resist introduction of VMI and may put forth roadblocks as VMI rolls. Fourth, the customer may have high expectations, and these may not be fulfilled immediately, resulting in disappointment. Finally, performance measures must be clearly specified and quantifiable.

Another concept that is closely tied to VMI is called Collaborative Planning, Forecasting, and Replenishment (CPFR). CPFR builds on a number of practices such as VMI, Jointly Managed Inventory (JMI), Continuous Replenishment Planning (CRP) and Efficient Consumer Response (ECR). CPFR standards are established by Vendor Interindustry Commerce Standards (VICS) and can be found at *www.cpfr.org*. CPFR strives to align

Exhibit 5. Collaborative planning, forecasting and replenishment

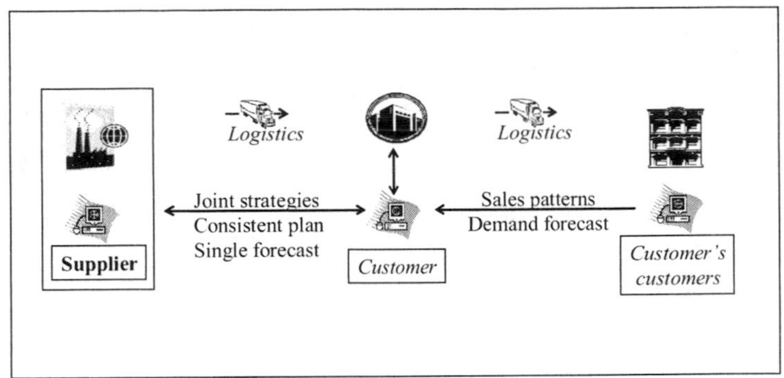

demand and supply through trading partner data interchange, exception-based management and collaborative work on problems that impede such alignment.

CPFR in terms of objectives sounds similar to the number of techniques seen so far, and it is. The primary difference is in implementation of the CPFR methodology. The CPFR process creates a joint strategy and consistent vision for supply chain partners. Such strategy then drives the operational concerns of production, marketing and distribution. The detailed process of CPFR can be described as follows.

- **Collaborative arrangement and planning:** The supplier and customer jointly devise a strategic plan. This plan may consider demand forecasts, promotional activity, production patterns, product data and any other requisite information. The strategies regarding what products to sell, how those will be merchandised and promoted, and the time period are specified. This results in a consistent plan for both the supplier and customer. By focusing on the flow of materials to the customer, this plan helps unearth constraints and bottlenecks in the process, which are then managed or neutralized. This understanding is made legal via agreements and contracts. A sample CPFR contract is available at www.cpfr.org,
- **Forecasting sales:** A single forecast is developed based on sales data, production capacities and promotional activities. This forecast is an iterative process and each partner must fully commit to the forecast before it is finalized. This single forecast is split in two parts – order forecast and sales forecast. The order forecast represents demand between the supplier and the customer, and sales forecast represents demand from the customer's customers. The forecast process considers bottlenecks and constraints in the execution of the plan and devises measures to overcome those weaknesses.
- **Production and distribution plans:** Based on the single forecast, production, shipping and replenishment plans are developed. CPFR claims that most of added value results from a single forecast, which is based on the shared information and is much more accurate than other forecasting methods.

CPFR is enabled by electronic exchange of data, primarily over the Internet. CPFR standards enable open and secure communications, flexibility, support for different data types and interoperability across differing protocols. Many organizations also use EDI in CPFR. The CPFR scenario discussed so far includes two partners, or two tiers — the supplier and customer. The CPFR that deals with the entire supply chain or, in a vertically integrated industry that deals with more than two partners, is called *n-tier* CPFR. Though more complex, the core ideas behind n-tier CPFR are similar to the two-tier CPFR.

The primary advantages of CPFR are removing bottlenecks and constraints to fulfill customer expectations, optimizing production and distribution facilities, and streamlining administration and operations. Problems in CPFR are maintenance of trust and confidentiality between partners, continuing dynamic data interchange, joint resolution of unforeseen problems and continuing support from top management. The financial results of CPFR can be measured in terms of increased revenue, decrease in production and distribution costs, and return on assets.

SAP supports CPFR standards and enables exchange of sales forecasts, exchange of order forecasts and generation of production orders. SAP SCM capabilities include support for standards from XML to EDI. SAP also supports measurement of key performance indicators and sharing of this intelligence between the partners. Actual fulfillment can be monitored using other SAP tools, and exceptions can be handled in real time.

Another important supply chain collaboration tool is mobile supply chain management. This tool basically deals with connecting to the network using mobile and remote devices. The mobile SCM capabilities of interest to accountants include automation of

Exhibit 6. Steps in CPFR

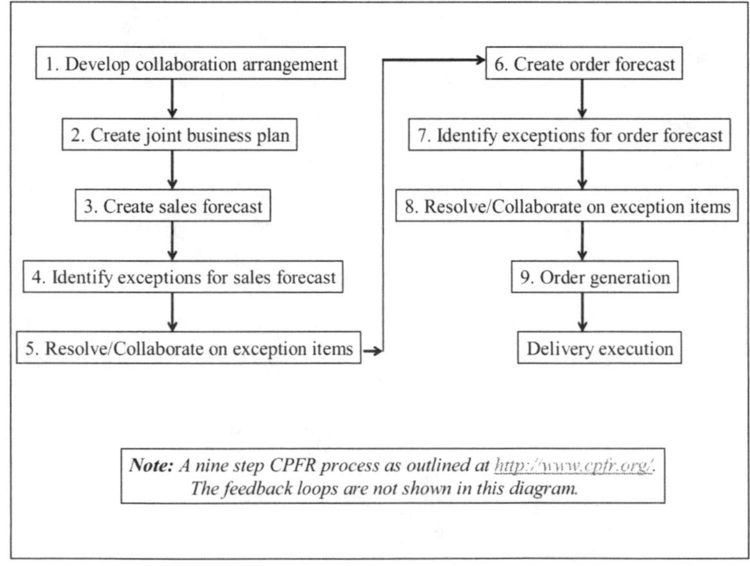

data collection activities on the shop floor and warehouses. Bar codes and other methods can be used in data collection activities that are useful in tracking raw materials, work in process and finished goods. Additionally, bar codes also enable accurate collection of product costs.

Supply Chain Coordination

SAP SCM coordination capabilities consist of managing events such as issuance of materials or shipment of goods and evaluating performance of the supply chain using key performance measures. Supply Chain Event Management (SCEM) monitors supply chain activities, such as procurement, production and sales order processing, and makes information available to supply chain constituents. Suppliers need to know status of shipments, payment of invoices and POs in the pipeline. Manufacturers require informa-

Exhibit 7. Oracle supply chain intelligence performance measures (Source: www.oracle.com/)

Bookings	Booking ($) Booking margin % Billing ($) Cancellation % Return %
Backlog	Shipping backlog ($) Billing backlog ($) Unbilled shipments backlog ($) Delinquent backlog ($)
Shipping	Number of orders shipped Number of orders fulfilled Number of orders fully shipped % of orders one day book to ship (SCOR) Number of orders one day book to ship % of orders one day pick to ship Number of orders one day pick to ship
Order to cash	Order entry cycle time (SCOR) Book to ship cycle time (SCOR) Book to fulfill cycle time (SCOR) Book to pick cycle time Pick to ship cycle time
Procure to pay	Order to pay cycle time Order to receive cycle time (SCOR) Receive to pay cycle time
Operational costs	Product sales Cost of goods sold Product gross margin % Product sales revenue growth %
Inventories	Inventory value ($) Inventory value % On hand inventory value On hand inventory quantity WIP value Inventory turns

tion regarding status of intermediate products, finished products and inventory levels. SCEM can supply information to these constituents, though the extent and depth of information for external constituents depends on the authorization granted to them.

SCEM not only monitors supply chain activities, but can flag problems based on the business rules programmed into the system. If incoming shipments are short or late, standard operating procedures will be invoked. Authorized managers will be contacted and informed regarding problems with shipments. The production schedule may get adjusted automatically, alternate suppliers may be requested to provide goods, and customers might be informed of problems with finished products delivery. SCEM provides exception-based management abilities using three mechanisms described below.

- **Notification:** The authorized manager, set of managers or trading partners are notified. Problems then can be solved individually or in collaboration with partners.
- **Simulation:** The system can simulate alternate scenarios for the problem activity and suggest alternatives. For example, if the shipment is short by a certain number of units, alternate suppliers having a ready supply may be identified and suggested. The analysis also comes with costs associated with each action.
- **Collaboration:** SCEM enables collaboration by learning from past events. If shipments from certain region are consistently delayed, such delay is factored into every activity that relies on shipments from that region. SCEM may spot patterns and suggest revising standards or fixing certain problems. The efficacy of SCEM solutions depends on the knowledge programmed into the system, and may vary according to the industry and business.

The final component is Supply Chain Performance Management (SCPM). Unless there are quantifiable, reliable and understandable performance measures, the whole edifice of SCM will be dysfunctional or may crumble altogether. SAP provides the following guidelines concerning SCPM.

- Align metrics with strategic objectives of the organization
- Assign owners (individuals or teams) to all measures
- Provide precise definition — metrics must be unique and comprehensible
- Use few parameters (less than five per process)
- Ensure that performance measures are easy to collect and reproducible
- Avoid conflicting goals

If you remember the FedEx guidelines for SRM performance measures from the expenditure cycle, you will see remarkable similarities in SAP and FedEx guidelines. The importance of performance measures is even more critical in SCM, since we are dealing with external partners who may have different internal incentive systems. Supply Chain Council (*www.supply-chain.org/*) has developed a model called Supply Chain Operations Reference model (SCOR) that provides guidance on supply chain performance measures.

The SCOR model is organized according to following processes — plan, source, make and deliver. The model covers interaction under each process; for example, customer interaction (order to payment), physical material transactions (supplier to factory, in the factory, factory to warehouse and warehouse to customer) and market interactions (demand to fulfillment of orders). The model is specified for multiple industries and businesses. SAP SCPM capabilities support the SCOR industry standard. SCPM comes with hundreds of pre-configured performance measures that can be used in SCPM.

SAP SCM Tools

The primary issues of interest for us are functionalities of the SCM software and its connections with ERP, CRM, SRM, and other tools we have seen so far. SCM software is supplied by numerous software vendors. This software ranges from add on modules from the independent software vendors, integrated packages offered by the ERP vendors, specialized pieces of software, for example, supply chain intelligence module, and a number of combinations thereof. SCM software itself has a number of modules, and different software vendors package different modules under the garb of SCM. This section looks at the SAP SCM modules as SAP is the preferred software in this book.

SCM software generally runs on top of ERP software. Theoretically, ERP software is not a pre-requisite; you can even manually feed data to the SCM software. In practice, unless the business in integrated internally via some type of ERP system, successful operation of the SCM software is well nigh impossible. Apart from the ERP system, the SCM software may need additional supporting modules. The extent of supporting modules depends on the capabilities of the SCM software and the expectations of the business from the SCM software. SAP SCM software provides a comprehensive view of the myriad of these requirements for SCM software. A word of caution: Many businesses may not need such an elaborate suite of products, many businesses may need more functionalities offered by the software, and the suitability of the software will vary depending on the industry, type of business, size of business, depth and breadth of supply chain, and a number of other factors.

Supporting modules for SAP SCM software are as follows: enterprise portal, business information warehouse, knowledge warehouse and exchange infrastructure. These components are also enablers for SRM functionalities. These modules were reviewed in the revenue and expenditure cycle and are not discussed here.

SAP SCM modules that run on top of the preceding supporting modules are advanced planner and optimizer, product life cycle management, enterprise buyer and customer relationship management. SAP Advanced Planner and Optimizer (APO) is the core module in SCM. APO is a set of software or a package of tools that supports a variety of SCM functions, such as planning, scheduling and real-time decision support. The core modules of APO and their functionalities are discussed below.

- **Demand planning:** This tool provides for structured demand planning methodology and provides forecasting algorithms. The process starts with historical data, building forecasts, refining forecast models, monitoring forecast errors, and performing historical comparisons of forecasts with actual sales. Forecasts can be created for products, a class of products, regions, time periods, and even for characteristics of configurable products. For example, if a red car with six-cylinder engine sells better than cars in other colors, this fact can be incorporated in the forecast. The forecast can be integrated backwards with a bill of materials to derive requirements for raw materials.
- **Supply network planning:** The demand plan is used to plan for sourcing, procurement, transportation and production activities. A single consistent model for the entire supply chain can be developed with appropriate constraints and penalties and can be optimized using powerful optimization methods.
    - *Deployment function:* This function determines inventory deployment to distribution centers, warehouses, VMI accounts and production lines. This deployment is based on business strategies, such as minimization of transportation costs, required safety stocks and replenishment strategies.
    - *Transportation builder:* This function can be used for maximizing capacity and minimizing costs of transportation fleets.

Exhibit 8. Details of SAP SCM tools

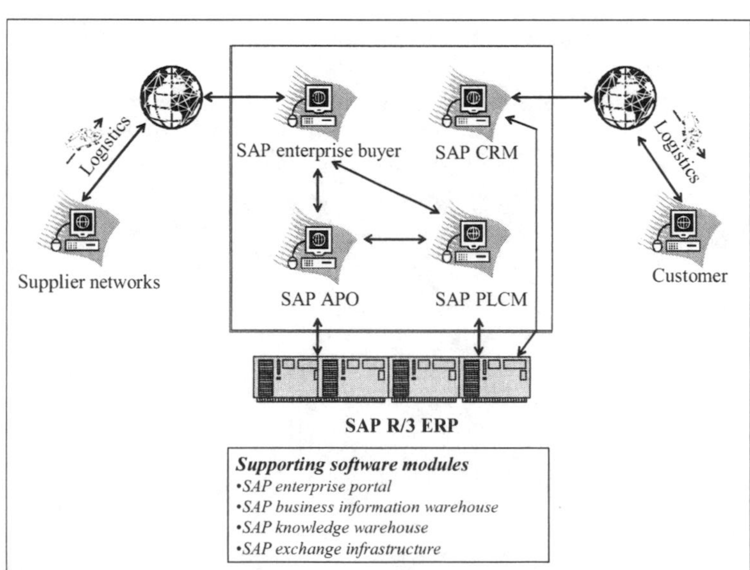

- **Global available to promise:** This tool is used to provide expected delivery dates to customers. APO uses a global multi-level search to assess the list of existing orders, current production schedule, production capacity at different locations and any other programmed factors, and provides an expected delivery date on a particular order. Availability check methods include basic, advanced or rule-based methods. These methods also provide explanations for results and simulation capabilities. The simulation capabilities can be used to vary production locations, warehouse locations and transportation methods, to mention a few. This feature also has a shipment and transportation facility that automatically schedules shipping of promised deliveries.
- **Production planning and detailed scheduling:** This tool is useful in planning production in multiple facilities and then optimizing such production by considering inventory availability and production capacity. Such facilities are useful in planning critical products with long replenishment lead times or requiring bottleneck sources. This tool enables reduction of lead times, improvement in lead times, increase in throughput and decrease in inventory costs.
- **Network design:** This planning tool has strategic and operational applications. At the strategic level, network design can be used to analyze the existing or proposed supply chain; variables such as positioning of locations, territorial divisions, transportation costs and carrier selection can be evaluated. This function comes with a what-if ability to analyze different configurations of the supply chain. Simulations can be carried out for different demand-and-supply patterns and different cost and production capacity constraints. At the operational level, this same analysis can be carried out to minimize costs and maximize service levels for the existing supply chain.
- **Transportation planning:** The transportation planner enables optimal use of transportation fleets, helps vehicle scheduling and route determination that can be adjusted in real time, decides transportation mode, selects carriers, maximizes loading of different vehicles and allows for lowering of costs.
- **Supply chain collaboration:** The purpose of this tool is to enable collaboration amongst supply chain partners via collaborative engine and ITS. This tool allows for exchange of information between trading partners, use of a browser to access and modify data, security by means of authorization and authentication, and support of exception-based management by monitoring and real-time alerts.
- **Supply chain monitoring:** The supply chain is monitored using three sub-tools: alert monitor, plan monitor and supply chain cockpit.
  - *Alert monitor:* The alert monitor watches demand plans, production plans and vehicle schedules, and alerts if actual activity deviates from the plan. An alert is routed to an approved manager, enabling management by exception.
  - *Plan monitor:* The plan monitor can be used to assess an individual production plan, compare a plan with different plans, assign scores and provide advice on the soundness of the plan. Key measures, which can be configured by the planner, can be displayed in tables or graphs.

- *Supply Chain Cockpit (SCC):* SCC provides a graphical interface that can be used to manage and control the entire supply chain. SCC can be used to perform the following functions.
  - View the entire supply chain at various detail levels
  - View, investigate and experiment with supply chain component relationships
  - Query data in the APO system
  - Provide key performance measures
  - Track alerts and respond to them.

  SCC can be divided into individual work areas. Different decision makers can work on different supply chain areas. SCC can be used by strategic planners, demand planners, supply network planners, production planners and production schedulers.

SAP APO is a complex module; in fact, the eight sub-areas of APO listed above are complex in themselves. APO has an open standard interface, and SAP claims that APO can interact with heterogeneous software environments and can seamlessly integrate even with non-SAP systems. The tools in the APO can be used at strategic, planning and operational levels.

The next module to enable SAP SCM capabilities is SAP Product Life Cycle Management (PLCM). The PLCM module can manage products and assets from the design phase to retirement phase. PLCM supports evaluating existing product portfolio, identifying market threats and planning new products for the future. New products can be designed, developed and evaluated online. The changes in existing products can be executed and production schedules changed. Finally, maintenance of existing products, after-sales service and management of long-term assets can also be performed. Detailed functionalities in these areas are briefly discussed below.

- **Life cycle data management:** Life Cycle Data Management (LCDM) involves managing data for products and assets from design to retirement phases. LCDM integrates with a wide range of CAD tools to support online and offline design of products. LCDM also supports Supervisory Control and Data Acquisition (SCADA) tools, Geographic Information Systems (GIS) and Microsoft Office applications. LCDM has an XML interface to quickly connect with third-party tools.

  LCDM offers handling of different product features and requirement documents, bill-of-materials, routing of materials, CAD models and other technical documentation over the Internet and intranet. These functionalities can be used for online design of products, managing changes to existing products, releasing product changes to engineering and production lines, and supporting decisions concerning discontinuation of products.
- **Program and project management:** Classic project management techniques, such as controlling project structures, scheduling activities, estimating costs and resources, and Critical Path Method (CPM) are supported by this function. Projects

can be monitored online, a global view of current projects can be derived, and aggregate tools that support cross-project management can be used in management of programs and projects.

- **Life cycle collaboration:** This function uses an XML-based interface and the Internet to connect development teams and engineers. External parties such as contractors, suppliers and customers can exchange data such as drawings, service bulletins, product manuals and parts information.
- **Quality management (QM):** QM provides support for the quality loop specified by ISO 9004. This quality loop consists of planning (market research, concept, design, testing and production planning), implementation (production, inspections, storage and shipping) and usage (maintenance and disposal). Employees in charge of quality can access the services and quality-related documents through the enterprise portal.

  The QM module is connected to the enterprise buyer for supporting procurement activities. Historical quality records of a supplier, quality requirements for a new product and changes in existing quality requirements can be communicated to interested parties for further action.
- **Asset life cycle management (ALCM):** ALCM is used to manage physical assets and equipment from investment to retirement phases. ALCM can be used to rank assets according to cost, maintenance and support in the purchase phase. Once installed, the ALCM can be used to monitor equipment malfunctions, manage

Exhibit 9. SAP APO components

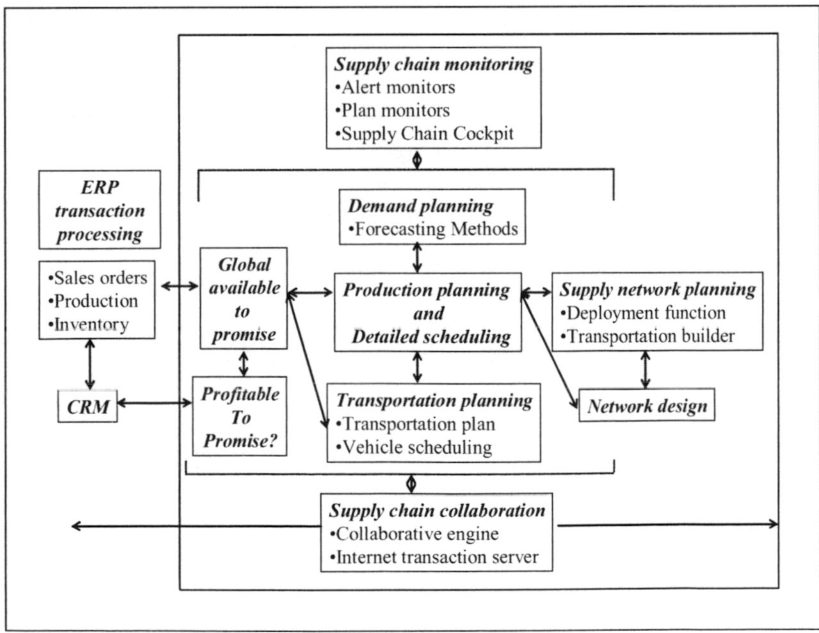

equipment modifications and upgrades, and design and execute maintenance schedules. Asset costs are available on an individual and aggregate basis; and related calculations, such as depreciation, can be automated. Asset replacement decisions are aided by analyses of compatibility of new machines with existing machines, maintenance schedules and costs for new machines, comparison of capacity and cost and other pertinent factors.

- **Environment, health and safety:** Environment, health and safety issues include product safety, hazardous materials management, dangerous goods management, industrial hygiene, occupational health and waste management. Federal and state regulations in these areas mandate collection of certain data and require standardized work procedures. Such records can be kept and other ancillary functions can be performed with the PLCM module.

The SAP Enterprise Buyer module is the nexus for SAP SRM tools, which was discussed in the expenditure cycle. Enterprise buyer is also used in planned sourcing; that is, purchases of direct raw materials. Purchasing can be done in an automated mode and also by employees as self-service. This module interfaces with employees, purchase professionals, managers, suppliers and content mangers. Employees can search electronic catalogs, order required goods, check status of inventory and ordered goods, and confirm goods delivered or services performed. Purchase professionals can create bid invitations, manage received bids, create purchase contracts and process incomplete purchase orders. Managers can use this module to set up workflows for approving shopping carts or purchase requisitions. Suppliers can enter delivery of goods or services and, if authorized, invoices into the system. Content managers can manage electronic catalogs by importing and structuring content from suppliers, creating new product catalogs or organizing existing product catalogs.

Exhibit 10. SAP PLCM components

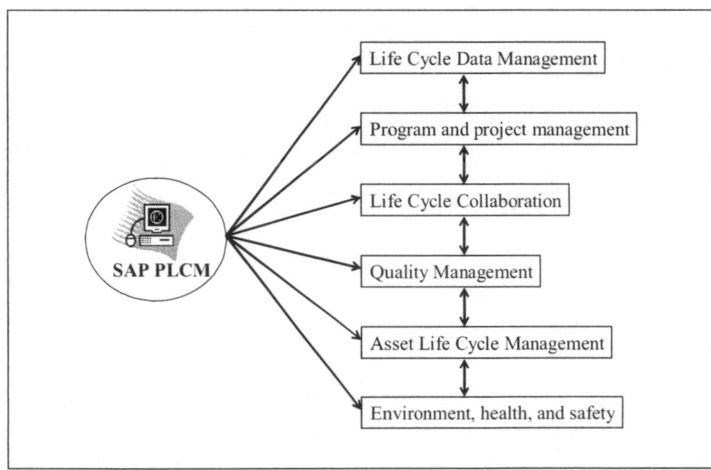

The final module included in SAP SCM is SAP CRM. CRM is primarily used in forecasting sales. APO requires information regarding incoming sales orders to plan back-end activities. If sales orders are managed in the CRM module, then APO must have access to such data for planning purposes. Thus, the CRM module should also be connected to the ERP system or to APO for feeding sales-related data. Another interesting application of integration of SCM and CRM capabilities is extension of Global ATP. The extension involves the ability to answer the question — is it Profitable to Promise (PTP)?

Incoming customer orders specify quality, quantity, delivery dates and service requirements, if any. If the item is in stock or if production capacity exists, then answers to order-filling questions are easy. If the plant is running at capacity, should such an order be accepted? The costs involved now are not only product costs, but also extra costs, such as disrupted production, delayed shipments to other customers, and rescheduled logistics. The decision still seems fairly easy to make. But wait! What if the customer is important to us? If maintenance of a long-term relationship with this customer is more important than making money on the order, the order should be filled. The CRM software helps quantify the customer value and match it with expected costs. Alternatives, such as accept order, accept order but raise price, outsource production or reject order, can explored by combining SCM and CRM capabilities.

APO, PLCM, enterprise buyer and CRM modules enable SAP SCM capabilities, and all of these modules generally run on top of an ERP system. The types of modules used, the configurations of these modules and the deployments of various modules depend on the size of the organization, nature of the industry, financial considerations and a number of other factors. The demands on the SCM tools are enormous, and these change per business and industry. As such, it is not surprising that software supporting these business processes will also be large and complicated. Practical problems in implementing such a package are not discussed here.

Supply Chain Cost Accounting

The integration of functional areas via ERP and intra-business collaboration due to SCM and CRM has led to merging of cost accounting in organizational information flows. The cost accounting focus is not only on internal costs, but now are also on supply chain costs. Typical internal cost accounting functions supported by ERP packages include support for traditional cost accounting techniques, such as standard costing, variable costing, application of overheads and inventory valuation for external reporting purposes. Additionally, advanced cost accounting techniques, such as activity-based costing, activity-based cost management, balanced scorecard, resource-consumption accounting and customized-cost accounting techniques are also supported by ERP packages. Cost accounting simulations and what-if abilities are also included in the toolset. These are useful in optimizing supply chain costs. The rest of this section is as follows: First, costs involved in the supply chain are reviewed. Second, cost accounting features of the ERP/SCM software are introduced. This is a general, brief review and not restricted to effects of the Web and Internet.

Exhibit 11. Supply chain costs

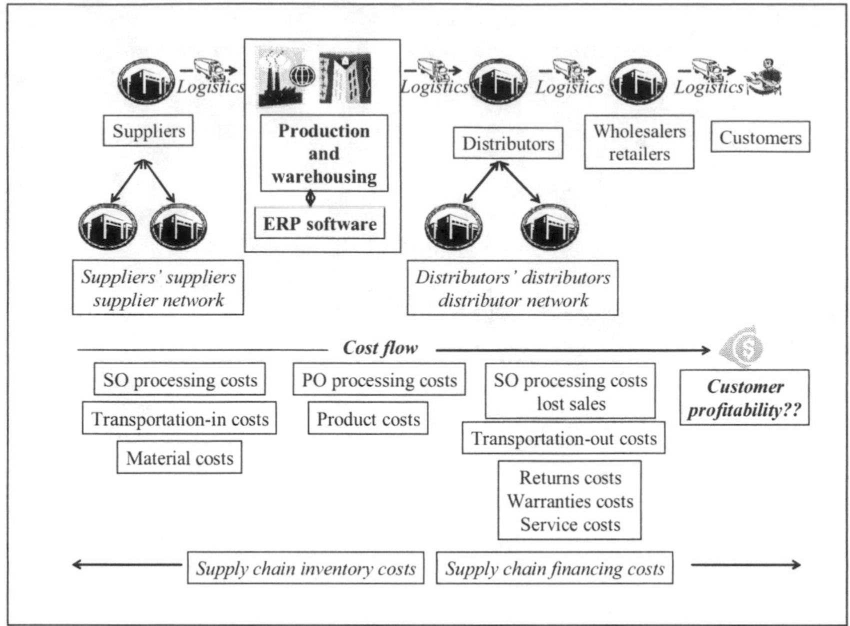

Supply chain costs by definition include costs across the supply chain, including order processing costs, transportation-in and -out costs, material costs, product costs, warehousing, and supply chain-wide inventory and financing costs. These costs are described below.

- **Order processing costs:** Order processing costs include processing of POs for raw materials and sales orders for finished goods; order capture, validation, sourcing and distribution. The time and effort of the staff assigned to handle these orders, paperwork, searching for lost orders, order expediting, order confirmations, order pickings, billings and invoice reconciliation are all examples of costs incurred in order processing. Order processing costs are incurred by suppliers and by sellers. These costs can be lowered by automating orders, EDI or eliminating orders such as in VMI or CPFR.
- **Transportation-in and -out costs:** These costs comprise a large portion of supply chain costs. The measure for transportation-in costs is ratio of total transportation-in costs to total material purchases. Transportation-out is measured by a ratio of transportation-out costs to cost of goods sold, sales revenue or total fleet operating costs. Transportation costs and inventory costs are generally related; for example, transportation costs can be reduced by building inventory and vice versa. Transportation optimization models that consider these different costs are used to manage transportation-in and -out costs.

- **Material costs:** These are easily quantifiable as prices paid for materials. However, we need to factor in quality of materials. Materials not up to standards can cause shortages due to rejections, production problems and sub-par finished product. SRM and SCM tools specially pay attention to quality metrics in deciding among approved suppliers.
- **Product costs:** These costs include costs of materials, labor and allocated overheads. Quality initiatives and activity-based management techniques are routinely used to control product costs and improve quality.

  The costs of returned products, warranty costs and after-sales service costs also need to be considered. These may be calculated as the total cost of ownership and must be minimized, since these may be borne by the producer.
- **Supply chain inventory costs:** One of the objectives of SCM is to decrease inventories throughout the supply chain, since inventories are costly. Inventory costs include financing costs, handling costs, wastage and storage costs, among other things.
- **Supply chain financing costs:** These costs capture funds invested in managing the supply chain. Collaborative activities must be planned and appropriate software purchased and operationalized — these activities consume money and time, along with time invested by management. Inventory carrying costs are sometimes included in this category. SCM software strives to make these costs visible, and then optimizes those costs through different techniques.

In the ERP and SCM software world, cost accounting tools can be grouped under three headings: traditional cost accounting tools, analytical and reporting tools, and proactive tools. Traditional cost accounting tools are the tools for various methods for measuring product costs, different techniques for allocating overheads and inventory valuation methods. Analytical and reporting tools enable simulating different cost scenarios, what-if analyses, comparison of budgets and standard costs with actuals, and other reports useful to the organization. Proactive tools permit costing in a dynamic environment, estimating costs across the supply chain and simulating planned scenarios. The primary effect of these tools on cost accounting is that cost accounting can perform both reactive and proactive roles.

Traditional cost accounting focuses on product costs and involves cost accumulation, cost allocation and inventory valuation. ERP packages support cost accumulation in real time, and costs can be observed for each batch, overhead expenses can be automatically allocated and unit product costs can be calculated. If standard cost accounting is used, then variances can be calculated at pre-defined intervals. Inventory can be valued using LIFO, FIFO or average costing methods. As materials are issued, cost of goods sold and inventory entries can be created automatically. Cost accounting calculations are linked to the financial accounting module, and inventory values can be transferred to those modules for financial reporting purposes.

Activity-based costing and activity-based management is supported by most ERP systems; Oracle has an add-on module, whereas SAP has an external partner to supply the necessary software. Managing profits centers by defining cost objects, such as

Exhibit 12. Oracle traditional cost accounting features (source: www.oracle.com/)

Product costing	• Use multiple cost elements with unlimited sub-elements, resources, and activities to define cost item structure • Report and view assembly costs by level • Assign multiple material overheads to items • Assign multiple resources to routing operations • Apply overhead costs on a fixed or variable basis • Roll up costs for engineering prototypes • Roll up costs for a single level or multiple levels in bills of material • Copy a current bill of material to an alternate bill when you perform a cost rollup • Roll up costs by cost type • Roll up costs based on alternate bills and routings • Update standard costs any time to revalue inventory and work in process
Allocation of overheads	• Fixed amount per lot • Percent of item value • Percent of resource value • Amount per resource unit • Automatically create all work in process accounting entries • View work in process account balances by transaction, job, or schedule • Automatically revalue work in process after standard cost changes • Variance reporting and control
Inventory, manufacturing, and maintenance costing	• Use standard, average, LIFO, or FIFO costing • Maintain perpetual inventory costs • Automatically create all inventory accounting entries • Analyze accounting transactions online • Track asset, expense items, and locations • Use rule-based accounting for revenue and cost of goods sold • Automatically revalue inventory after standard or average cost changes • Maintain perpetual balances, discrete jobs, and schedules

products or customers, or allocation of indirect costs by identifying activities, resources and objects, is generally supported. Activity-based management can be carried out by using activity-based cost accounting data and analyzing cost drivers, activities and performance.

A number of studies have shown that for SCM, the traditional cost accounting focus on internal costs is not adequate; activity-based costing and target-costing approaches are more useful. The analytical, reporting and proactive tools support these functions.

- **Target costing:** Changes in product cost due to changes in sourcing, product design and manufacturing facilities can be simulated. Cost elements such as material, labor and overhead, and effects of outsourcing on product cost can be estimated and different scenarios evaluated. Overheads can be allocated using activities, resources and cost drivers, and if standard costing is used, variances can be simulated and incorporated.

Exhibit 13. Oracle activity-based cost accounting features (source: www.oracle.com/)

Cost assignment and mapping	• Assign costs four ways: o *Department account to Department* o *Department account to Activity* o *Activity to Activity* o *Activity to Department* • Compute cost assignment distribution using statistical or account methods • Assign costs using multi-stage mapping-allows cost assignments to flow through multiple sets of departments and activities • Create multiple mapping calculations and effective rule sets
Hierarchies	• Assign activities, materials, and cost objects to bill hierarchies • Define activity hierarchies to facilitate activity cost rollup calculations • Define an unlimited number of bill and activity hierarchies
Cost drivers	• Import cost drivers from external systems • Compute drivers based on statistical or account data • Assign multiple drivers to the same activity
Calculations	• *Mapping* - Assign costs to departments and activities • *Activity rates* - Compute rates based on activity costs and related drivers; use local or rolled up rates • *Material unit cost* - Compute material unit cost based on total cost and usage data • *Activity cost rollup* - Sum up activity data based on a defined activity hierarchy • *Cost object unit cost* - Sum all activities, materials, and sub components based on consumption quantities for a selected bill type • *Extensions* - Extend material unit costs and cost object unit costs based on related statistics
Visual tracing	• Trace cost components back to their source department accounts • View online in trace stack window • Trace by stock consumption or by total amounts

- **What-if analysis:** What-if analyses include estimating changes in raw material costs, transportation costs and products due to changes in SCM. Cost changes due to engineering changes, new products and classic make-or-buy decisions can be analyzed and evaluated. These cost changes can be compared with the sales price, and gross margin reports can be generated.

  Reports: A plethora of reports can be generated using ERP- and SCM-type software. These reports can be centered on item, time, period, cost elements, cost activities, operation or department, or can be user specified. Transaction analysis reports for these items, and comparisons between actual and standard or budgeted costs, are also available. The reports are generally supported by drill-up and -down abilities for aggregated or detailed information.

Cost accounting, managerial accounting, cost management and most other cost approaches are generally supported by higher-end ERP systems. Financial and cost data is stored in a repository or a database, and is connected to other organizational databases. Such integration permits a high level of analytical flexibility, enables sophisticated simulation capabilities and supports management techniques such as Balanced Scorecard or the SCOR model. The benefits of these systems are considerable; however, software costs, implementation problems and failure rates are also formidable.

Summary

The conversion cycle consists of product design, production planning and control, and cost accounting. Traditionally, cost accountants have been involved in determining product costs. This cycle has seen many innovations in the last few decades. Techniques such as MRP, MRP II and JIT have been successfully employed to reduce costs and improve quality. Cost accounting has also changed, and new techniques to track activities, quality and defect rates have been discovered and applied. As internal improvements stabilized, the focus of businesses turned to their trading partners — SCM. The effect of the Internet in the area of SCM is most pervasive and a new frontier for accountants.

The concepts of SCM can be traced to the automotive industry of the 1930s and World War II. SCM decisions revolve around right product, right price, right cost, right quality, right location and right customer. SCM involves managing sourcing and procurement, logistics, production, inventory and customers. SCM connects with front-end customer-centric systems, back-end accounting systems and supplier networks. The advent of the Internet, globalization of suppliers, installed and operational ERP base, and increasing cost pressures have accelerated the dominance of SCM in organizations.

SCM capabilities, which were seen in the context of SAP SCM tools, include supply chain planning, execution, collaboration and coordination. Supply chain planning deals with designing the supply chain for optimizing costs and service levels, and collaborative demand and supply planning. Demand is planned using forecasting techniques, and supply is planned in collaboration with internal manufacturing facilities and supplier networks. Supply chain execution executes plans devised during the planning phase by managing materials for production, manufacturing and fulfillment of orders by collaborating with partners. Remember, the watchword is collaboration — collaboration with suppliers and customers.

Supply chain collaboration includes a number of techniques, and two — VMI and CPFR — were reviewed. VMI integrates the customer's inventory levels, consumption patterns and demand forecasts into the supplier's inventory management system. As the customer needs inventory, the supplier's system will generate POs and produce and ship necessary products. CPFR takes the concepts of VMI a step further. CPFR merges the supplier's and customer's strategies and objectives into one forecast. The entire supply chain is coordinated as one organism. CPFR.org claims that such forecasts are more accurate than forecasts that depend only on the sophistication of algorithms. The primary advantages of CPFR are to remove bottlenecks and constraints in fulfilling customer expectations.

Supply chain coordination is the hands-on activity that monitors the supply chain for problems and bottlenecks, and alerts the proper authority if deviations are detected. Exception-based management capabilities are enhanced by simulation and learning algorithms programmed into the system. In this phase, supply chain intelligence is also provided. Supply chain intelligence metrics generally are based on SCOR, provided by the Supply Chain Council.

SAP SCM software tools that allow for these functionalities were also reviewed. Enabling modules, such as SAP APO and SAP PLCM, were explained in detail. The connections between SCM and CRM, such as global available to promise and profitable to promise, were explored. This interacting set of modules is complex — as it should be, since enormous demands are placed on this software.

Finally, cost accounting functionalities in the new era were surveyed. Apart from supporting traditional and activity-based cost accounting techniques, the SCM/ERP era also supports target-costing approaches and provides simulation and what-if abilities. Changes in supply chain costs due to changes in sourcing and production; changes in product costs due to changes in design, engineering and materials; and make-or-buy decisions can be modeled and simulated by the new software. However, do not confuse availability of functionalities with successful implementation of the software, which is another story — not covered in this book.

References

Bowersox, Closs, D., & Cooper, B. (2002). *Supply chain logistics management* (international ed.). New York: McGraw-Hill.

Cloud, R. (2000, August). Supply Chain Management: New role for finance professionals. *Strategic Finance*, 29-32.

Cooke, J. (2002, March). Why Ace is becoming the place? *Logistics Management*, 34-36.

Coordination with mySAP supply chain management (white paper). (2003). SAP. Retrieved July 7, 2003, from www.sap.com/

Creating a networked value chain with Oracle supply chain management (white paper). (2003). Oracle. Retrieved July 8, 2003, from www.oracle.com/

E-business solution for financial management (white paper). (2003). Oracle. Retrieved July 8, 2003, from www.oracle.com/

Ganeshan, R., & Harrison, T. (2002). *An introduction to supply chain management.* Pennsylvania State University. Retrieved July 8, 2003, from http://silmaril.smeal.psu.edu/misc/supply_chain_intro.html/

Improving corporate governance: A balanced scorecard approach (white paper). (2002). Oracle. Retrieved July 8, 2003, from www.oracle.com/

Koch, C. (2002). The ABCs of supply chain management. *CIO*. Retrieved July 10, 2003, from www.cio.com/research/scm/edit/012202_scm.html

mySAP product life cycle management, key capabilities. (2003). SAP. Retrieved July 12, 2003, from www.sap.com

mySAP product life cycle management (white paper). (2003). SAP. Retrieved July 12, 2003, from www.sap.com

mySAP SCM supply chain planning, SAP solutions in detail. (2003). SAP. Retrieved July 12, 2003, from www.sap.com

mySAP supplier relationship management (white paper). (2003). SAP. Retrieved July 12, 2003, from www.sap.com

mySAP supply chain management (white paper). (2003). SAP. Retrieved July 12, 2003, from www.sap.com

Operations Management Roundtable. (2001). *Optimizing costs along the supply chain* (white paper). Retrieved July 12, 2003, from www.omr.executiveboard.com/guest/OMR/SampleOptimizing.pdf

Oracle activity based management 11i (data sheet). (2003). Oracle. Retrieved July 15, 2003, from www.oracle.com

Oracle cost management 11i (data sheet). (2003). Oracle. Retrieved July 15, 2003, from www.oracle.com

Oracle process manufacturing cost management 11i (data sheet). (2003). Oracle. Retrieved July 12, 2003, from www.oracle.com

Oracle supply chain intelligence (data sheet). (2003). Oracle. Retrieved July 15, 2003, from www.oracle.com

Planning with mySAP supply chain management (white paper). (2003). SAP. Retrieved July 16, 2003, from www.sap.com/

Process view mySAP product life cycle management (white paper). (2003). SAP. Retrieved July 16, 2003, from www.sap.com/

Product life cycle management, solutions map. (2003). SAP. Retrieved July 16, 2003, from www.sap.com/

Production planning and detailed scheduling with SAP advanced planner and Optimizer (white paper). (2003). SAP. Retrieved from www.sap.com/

Profitable-to-promise: The next step in the evolution of order promising (white paper). (2003). SAP. Retrieved July 16, 2003, from www.sap.com/

Quality management, SAP solutions in detail. (2003). SAP. Retrieved July 16, 2003, from www.sap.com/

Quantifying the impact of supply chain glitches on shareholder value (white paper). (2003). SAP. Retrieved July 16, 2003, from www.sap.com/

Reddy, R. (2002a). *Supply chain intelligence: Know what to expect and how best to achieve it.* Intelligent Enterprise. Retrieved July 16, 2003, from www.intelligententerprise.com/030513/608infosc1_1.jhtml

Reddy, R. (2002b). *The evolution of supply chain technologies*. Intelligent Enterprise. Retrieved July 16, 2003, from www.intelligententerprise.com/020114/502infosc1_1.jhtml

SAP Solutions Brief. (2003). *Asset management with mySAP product life cycle management*. SAP. Retrieved July 5, 2003, from www.sap.com/

SAP Solutions in Detail. (2003). *Materials management with mySAP SCM supply chain execution*. SAP. Retrieved July 12, 2003, from www.sap.com/

SAP advanced planner and optimizer, Release 3.1 (white paper). (2003). SAP. Retrieved July 20, 2003, from www.sap.com/

SAP advanced planner and optimizer, SAP help. (2003). SAP. Retrieved July 20, 2003, from http://help.sap.com/

SAP APO – Supply chain cockpit (white paper). (2003). SAP. Retrieved July 20, 2003, from www.sap.com/

Seuring, S., & Goldbach, M. (2002). *Cost management in supply chains*. Heidelberg: Springer-Verlag.

Simchi-Levi, D., Kaminsky, P., & Simchi-Levi, E. (2003). *Designing and managing the supply chain: Concepts, strategies, and case studies* (2nd ed.). New York: McGraw-Hill.

Supply chain cockpit, SAP help. (2003). SAP. Retrieved July 21, 2003, from http://help.sap.com/

Supply chain coordination with mySAP SCM (white paper). (2003). SAP. Retrieved July 21, 2003, from www.sap.com/

Supply chain event management with mySAP supply chain management (white paper). (2003). SAP. Retrieved July 22, 2003, from www.sap.com/

Supply chain execution with mySAP supply chain management (white paper). (2003). SAP. Retrieved July 22, 2003, from www.sap.com/

The inventory collaboration hub in mySAP supply chain management, SAP solutions brief. (2003). SAP. Retrieved July 23, 2003, from www.sap.com/

Transportation management with mySAP SCM, SAP solutions in detail. (2003). SAP. Retrieved July 23, 2003, from www.sap.com/

Visibility with mySAP supply chain management, SAP solutions brief. (2003). SAP. Retrieved July 24, 2003, from www.sap.com/

Chapter VIII

The General Ledger Cycle

General Ledger Cycle Activities

The general ledger cycle consists of posting of entries from special journals, subsidiary ledgers, and general journal to general ledger; as well as generating financial, managerial and special reports. Accounting transactions are first recorded in special and general journals from source documents and posted to subsidiary and general ledgers. At the end of the accounting period, an unadjusted trial balance is prepared. Then adjusting entries are made based on information from the controller and treasurer. The general ledger can then be used to generate required reports. Once the financial statements are finalized, accounting books are closed via closing entries, and a post-closing trial balance is prepared. The traditional use of a general ledger has been for generating financial reports for investors. Every student of accounting knows this.

Computerized accounting systems used s chart of accounts for capturing and classifying accounting data. Data classified according to the chart of accounts can then be used to generate financial, managerial and special reports. Reporting demands placed on the chart of accounts continually grew. As a result, charts of accounts became very complex in many organizations. The complexity of chart of accounts soon hit a roadblock. Instead of facilitating flexible reports, charts of accounts became a monster to maintain and

Exhibit 1. The general ledger cycle

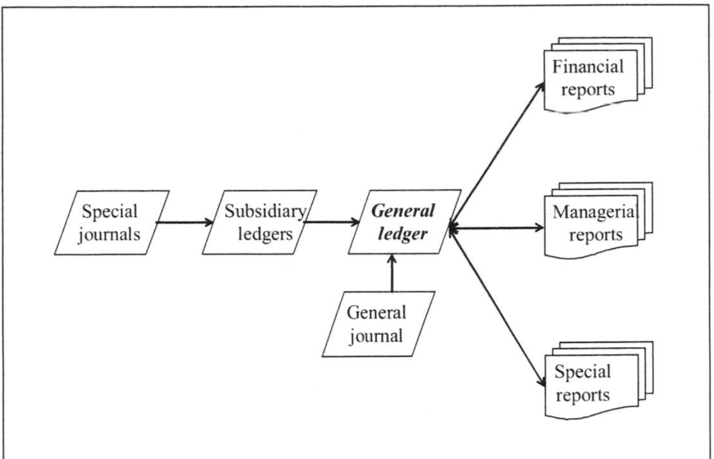

manage. The problem still persists in many organizations. Charts of accounts exist in all ERP/accounting systems; however, customization and implementation of charts of accounts and consequent reporting capabilities are more of an art than a science.

The general ledger in the first automation phase was maintained as some form of indexed file organization. Many entry-level accounting systems still rely on Btrieve-type environments. Relational databases offered more flexibility and, when coupled with the client server architecture, could perform far better reporting tasks. Software such as Crystal Reports, which specialized in reporting and analyzing data, became commonplace. These tools extracted subsets of data from corporate databases and used those data sets to meet varied reporting and analytical demands of the organizations. The ERP systems changed the nature of the general ledger by merging financial and non-financial information; data warehouses, business information warehouses and knowledge warehouses ushered in a new era of financial analytics.

The Internet increased functionality of ERP software. Closing of the books, which took weeks or months for many organizations, was reengineered using Web-based tools. Financial analytics extended beyond standard financial reports and included performance measures spanning customers, suppliers, manufacturing, human resources and stakeholders. Data mining tools operated underneath and provided statistical analyses of corporate data. Executive dashboards enabled executives to monitor vital signs of the organization almost instantaneously. Planning and budgeting changed as far more information and tools to manipulate corporate information became available to managers. Enterprise portals that organized and disseminated the fragmented organizational information came on the scene. These portals provided easy navigation and drill-down capabilities to explore corporate databases. Remember, these tools promise a lot, but implementation has not always been successful; these are not substitutes for managerial vision and common sense.

Exhibit 2. Changes in general ledger

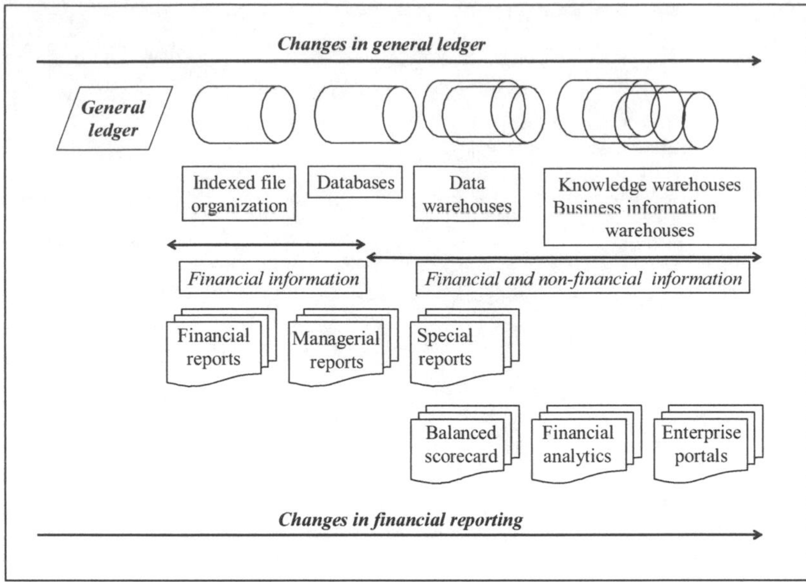

Let us take a look at these changes in the general ledger cycle. First, reengineering of closing of the books to shorten the time required for closing of the books is examined. Such reengineering is often refereed to as *virtual close*. Second, new financial analytics tools are investigated. Third, changes in planning and budgeting due to simulation capabilities and what-if analyses are explored. Fourth, enterprise portals are explained, and advantages and disadvantages of these tools are discussed. Finally, a summary rounds off the chapter.

Closing of the Books[1]

Closing of the accounting books refers to a process that starts with posting entries to the general ledger and results in a post-closing trial balance. The process begins with posting entries to the general ledger, preparing a trial balance, making adjusting entries, preparing an adjusted trial balance, preparing financial statements, preparing closing entries and, finally, preparing a post-closing trial balance. The prior year's books are closed or computerized accounts are sealed and cannot be altered — sometimes referred to as *hard close*. The organization carries balances from the post-closing trial balance to the next year and the process begins again. The books are also closed for quarterly reporting and issuance of quarterly financial statements; this close is sometimes called *soft close,* since accounting records are not sealed and can be altered.

What is the significance of the closing process? The primary issue is getting a handle on financial results. Unless the closing process is complete, a clear understanding of financial results is not possible. The financial results are matched with management forecasts, and corrective actions, if required, are undertaken. The initial push for faster closing of the books came in the 1990s, as markets criticized companies who did not have visibility into their financial statements. Cisco achieved closing of the books in less than 24 hours and became a symbol of the new economy of financial management. The intervening years saw a decline of the importance of virtual close, since formidable difficulties were encountered in this endeavor. However, now the days of pro-forma financial reporting are over, and GAPP-based reporting is valued again. New SEC requirements specify that 10-Ks must be filed within 60 days (instead of 90 days) after the close of the fiscal year and 10-Qs must be filed within 35 days (instead of 45 days). The virtual close and its variations are beginning to receive attention again.

What is the status of the closing process in business, and does that pose a problem? Surveys done in the U.S. and Europe indicate that the range to close the books spans from 4 to 75 days. Organizations in the U.S. are more efficient, with the average closing and reporting process being close to 12 days. The closing process is closely tied with the quality of information. However, the length of the closing process is not associated with the quality of information. For example, if the books are closed over a longer period, management may expect more accurate financial information. However, a longer process of closing of the books may indicate a chaotic state of accounting systems. Underlying causes can be fragmented legacy systems or sloppy financial procedures. On the other hand, the mere existence of quick close does not guarantee the quality of information, either. Cisco, a poster company for virtual close, claimed that it possessed a godlike ability to peer into every nook and cranny of the business, which enabled proactive measures to control and steer the company. However, in the third quarter of 2001, sales declined 30%, 2 billion dollars worth of inventory was written off and approximately 8,000 people were laid off. Many analysts commented that Cisco's financial systems contributed to the management's inability to make correct decisions. As always, technology and Web-enabled virtual or fast close is merely a tool, and not a substitute for managerial thinking.

Virtual close is considered to be the ability to close the company's books quickly and generate financial statements. Virtual close can also be viewed as a minimum distance between business activity and reporting of such an activity. The quickness or distance has not been defined precisely. According to various analysts, closing of the books in less than 5 days can generally be considered a virtual close; however, John Chambers, CEO of Cisco, may disagree, since he has defined virtual close as the ability to close the financial books with one hour's notice. The time elapsed in closing of the books is often times considered a symptom of underlying problems. Many organizations have undertaken the virtual close process as a way to streamline the financial reporting process. This effort involves a number of important decisions concerning relevance and reliability of accounting information.

Closing of the books, though tidy on paper, can be a nightmare in the real world. Problems in closing of the books can be classified into four broad categories: accounting problems, technology problems, organizational problems and environmental problems. This classification is helpful in conceptualizing problems, though the classifications are not entirely independent. The provided list is illustrative, and each organization faces a unique set of problems in the closing process. Let us take a look at these problems and the methods used to overcome them.

The primary accounting problem is the lack of standard accounting procedures across the organization for data collection, recording and reporting. Data collection processes can be a mélange of automated processes, manual processes and spreadsheet-based processes. Adjustments, reclassifications and reconciliations can also be a mix of manual/spreadsheet/automated functions and can be time consuming. Organization can have more than one chart of accounts. This problem is more acute with multinational organizations, who must comply with local and head-office accounting requirements. Closing of the books can also be used to generate managerial reports or correct immaterial errors, causing distractions from the core process. These problems generally go hand in hand with the complex charts of accounts. Detailed accounting codes need additional validation during closing, since these fields need to be verified before the books are closed, though all of them are not required for financial reporting. In many organizations, once the financial statements are prepared, they are reviewed by some sort of financial planning group. If the results are not acceptable, the statements might come back and additional processing may take place to achieve desired results. Such obvious manipulation of results adds to the closing process.

The fragmented accounting or financial systems cause a major problem in the closing process. Data from disparate systems need to be collected, which may be in the form of paper entries, spreadsheets or databases. Such data have to be validated and entered into the main accounting system. Data for consolidation purposes may also include budget

Exhibit 3. Problems in closing of the books

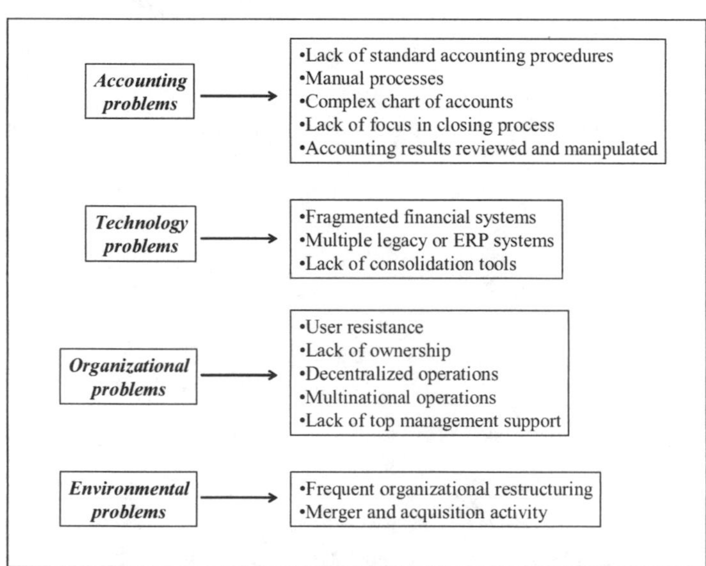

data, human resource data, inventories and shipments. The collected data needs to be normalized to conform to a common set of definitions and entered into the accounting system. The consolidation of financial statements also requires currency translation, elimination of intercompany transactions, accrual adjustments and minority ownership calculations, which, if not automated, can consume a large block of time. The consolidation process is iterative and calculations may need to be repeated; all in all, such requirements are not conducive to virtual close.

Organizational problems start if top management is not committed to the process. If top management is not committed, problems such as user resistance and decentralized operations become even more acute. The closing process should also have a clear ownership for accountability. Decentralized and multinational organizations may have a variety of ERP or accounting systems in operation and can face consolidation problems. Finally, even if the closing process is efficiently organized, it may have to undergo revisions if there is continuing merger and acquisition activity. The existing closing process also needs to be revised as the organization grows and expands, adds markets and products, restructures businesses and segments, or contracts by shedding markets and products. As such, the closing process is always a work in progress.

The initial rush to reengineer the closing process has slowed considerably. Organizations realized formidable barriers in such an effort. Now, the focus is not merely on time required to close the books, but also on the quality of financial reporting, process improvements and proper use of technical infrastructure. There have been some successes in this area, notably in the technology sector. For example, Microsoft's financial reporting system consolidates 340 statutory companies in 4 days, handles 3,000 queries per month from 1,200 users, and has an uptime of 99.25%. The reengineering efforts led by Cisco, Motorola, Dell and Microsoft have led to development of guidelines in these areas. The main lessons learned are summarized below.

- **Standardize accounting procedures:** The first step in standardizing accounting procedures is to have a common chart of accounts. This chart should be detailed enough at the unit level and should allow quick consolidation at the higher corporate level. The organization should have a standard method of collecting, presenting and measuring transaction data. Cutoff dates for subsidiary ledgers should be clearly specified, and a closing calendar should be synchronized. Other helpful activities are as follows:
    - Regularly close subsidiary ledgers and journals that feed data into the general ledger.
    - Reconciliations, whether subsidiary ledger to general ledger or intercompany transactions, should be continuous or at frequent intervals, not at the end of the quarter or the end of the year.
    - Make sure that a powerful consolidation system exists for consolidation purposes. Use Web-based applications or interfaces in consolidation, which have been found to be cost-effective. At minimum, the consolidation package should offer submission and consolidation workflow management,

multicurrency management, intercompany and allocation processing, and journal entry processing.

- Have a clear and coordinated closing schedule and make sure it is communicated clearly across the organization. Establish clear checkpoints for the closing process.
- Simplify the chart of accounts.
- Focus on material items such as sales, accounts receivable and inventory; and reduce judgments in the entry process.
- Beware of problems in standardizing transactional data. The definitions of order, raw material and finished good can vary per user. Janelle Hill of META Group says — *"Winning semantic agreement over transactional data is even harder than gaining semantic agreement over data for the data warehouse"* (Decker et al., 2002).

- **Integrate and automate financial systems:** The organization should be standardized on a particular ERP system. Unless the ERP system is in place, the process of virtual close is next to impossible. Data should be captured at the source and entered only once. Adjustments, reclassifications and reconciliations should be standardized and automated. Manual entries should be minimized.
- **Tie in operational systems:** Operational systems should be closed before the financial systems or, at least, the results should be available to the financial system in real time. Operational data, such as shop floor data, needs to be integrated into the financial system, if possible.
- **Use the Internet:** Enable self-service features using the Web to reduce administrative overhead in accounting. Distribute reports via the Web, use XBRL to transmit reports to external stakeholders, send flash alerts to line managers using the intranet to enable exception-based management and publish key performance measures on the Web for immediate access.

  End users should be trained in Online Analytical Processing Tools (OLAP) or enterprise portals so that they can acquire needed information. Such education reduces administrative overhead on the Finance and IT departments.
- **Automate workflows:** Routing of entries for approval, the approval process and posting should be automated. Business rules should be developed to deal with formula-based accruals, standardized month-end entries and standard transactions. Any deviation from the rules should result in an alert to the appropriate manager.
- **Use Key Performance Measures:** Key performance indicators should be standardized and distributed to line managers in real time. Such performance measures can provide alternate information to managers in the absence of full-blown financial statements.

A complete reengineering of the closing process is supposed to take approximately 5 years. Even after 5 years, the target may be elusive due to changes in business and accounting systems. The benefits of virtual close primarily accrue due to improvements

Exhibit 4. Microsoft key performance measures

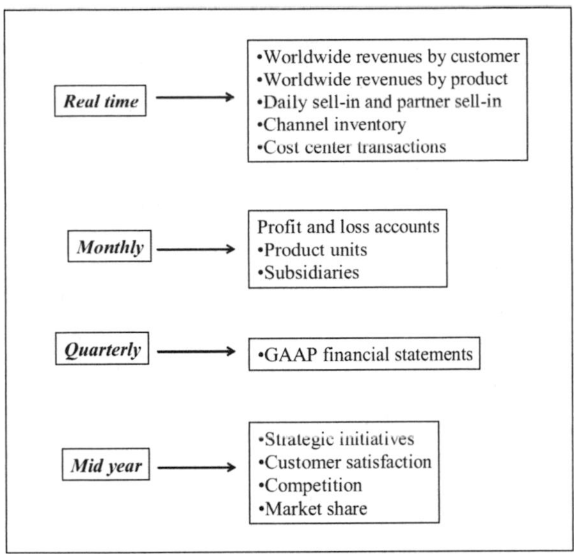

in the underlying accounting systems and not only by faster closing. For example, Microsoft lists the following benefits of virtual close.

- Batch processing of transactions is significantly decreased
- Estimates and accruals have been reduced
- The accounting process is aligned with accounting systems
- Users find the system useful and use it more
- Finance is a value-added partner and not a transaction-processing machine

Virtual close is not pursued by many corporations, and for good reasons. First, the cost benefit analysis may indicate that costs of virtual close outweigh benefits. Costs such as disruption of work, new workflows, new systems and standardized accounting procedures may be more than benefits due to real-time access to financial statements. Second, the quality of accounting information may suffer due to virtual close. Many organizations have pursued virtual close at the cost of detailed verifications and controls, and the resulting financial information has followed the ancient law of information technology — garbage in, garbage out. Due to recent accounting scandals and Sarbanes Oxley, 2002 requirements, many CEOs and CFOs are not interested in accelerating the closing process if there is even the slightest doubt that the quality of information might suffer. Finally, the added business value of such an effort may not be significant.

Financial Analytics

Financial analytics refer to analyses of financial data; financial analytic tools, generally software, are any tools used for analyzing financial data. General ledger as a repository of financial data has always been the source to be mined for information. Before machine accounting, paper-based trial balances – a torturous process of balancing the trial balance and preparing financial statements — was in place. In the mainframe era, financial reports could be generated by submitting requests to the IT department. The era of PCs and the advent of spreadsheets led to the rise of the end user. The types of tools used to explore financial databases/data warehouses have exploded; consequently, the types of available financial reports also have mushroomed.

The time-tested tool of financial analyses is spreadsheet. The revolution started by VisiCalc and Lotus 1-2-3 continues unabated. Currently, there are dozens of spreadsheet software packages, though the market is primarily dominated by Microsoft Excel. Spreadsheets have been used and are being used in preparing financial statements, preparing budgets, performing ad-hoc analyses and even for consolidation purposes. Spreadsheet functionalities have expanded exponentially and now include the following.

- **Data management:** Spreadsheets provide unsurpassed flexibility in managing data. Data can be arranged in different ways and analyzed using numerous mathematical and statistical functions; attractive charts can be prepared and printed or electronically distributed. Advanced functionalities such as multidimensional pivot tables for data analysis, solver for constraint optimization, auditing features and linking of files have made accountants' lives easier throughout the world.
- **Statistical analysis:** Spreadsheets have become increasingly sophisticated in statistical analysis. Initial tools for descriptive statistics have given way to advanced statistical techniques such as Analysis of Variance (ANOVA), forecasting and Fourier analysis.
- **Macro language:** Macros can be used to automate repetitive tasks in the spreadsheet. Microsoft Excel comes with in-built Visual Basic for Applications (VBA) that can be used to customize the spreadsheet by changing appearance or adding functionality.
- **Add on:** There is a flourishing industry that creates add-ons for spreadsheet software. Illustrative examples of functions that can be added are given below.
    - Genetic algorithms for solving complex optimization problems
    - Data mining and advanced statistical applications, such as *survival analysis*
    - Applications in finance, such as bond analysis, derivatives analysis, portfolio analysis, foreign exchange options and credit analysis
    - Specialized applications in Chemistry, Pharmacology and Engineering.

Exhibit 5. Financial analytics

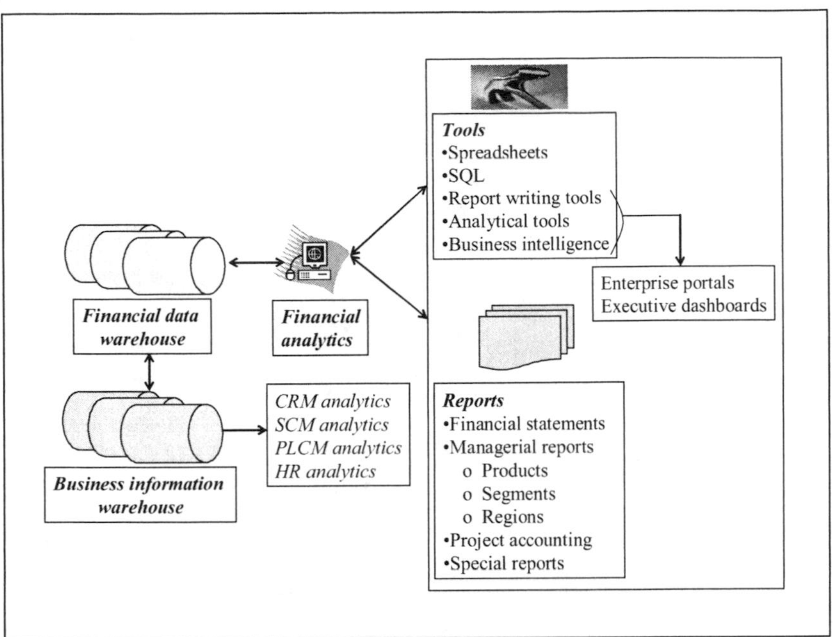

The influence of spreadsheets is pervasive. Excel is being taught at the high school level and copies of spreadsheet software have reached most households. Spreadsheets are now used by accountants, economists, engineers, managers and even in personal money management. The spreadsheet footprint can be seen in most reporting software, where the user interface is invariably in the row/column format of a spreadsheet. Spreadsheets will continue to be used in financial analytics for the foreseeable future. The expertise in spreadsheets is almost a given for entry-level accountants. Spreadsheets, however, have limitations. Spreadsheets cannot handle large amounts of data, a problem especially in a terabyte corporate environment. The interfaces of spreadsheets with ERP and accounting systems need to be programmed and configured, or else manual entries become inevitable. These limitations, of course, spawned alternatives.

As client-server and relational databases became prevalent, the use of database query tools also increased. These databases can be queried using SQL, which is relatively easy to learn. Initially, databases also came with database report writing tools. These tools can perform vital accounting functions, such as formatting documents like checks and invoices, collecting required data from the database and generating financial statements, formatting financial statements and creating special reports such as aging accounts receivable analysis. Databases such as Microsoft Access and Lotus Approach offer these functionalities. These databases and SQL are used by many accounting departments in small- and mid-sized organizations.

Exhibit 6. Business intelligence tools

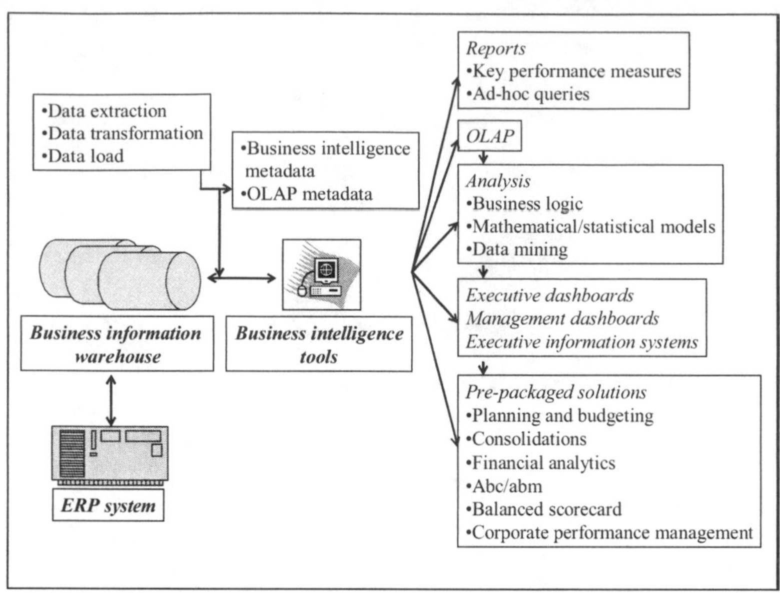

These tools were soon superceded by specialized report writing tools and analytical tools, which now have evolved to a new category of Business Intelligence (BI) tools; Crystal Reports/Business Objects and Cognos are examples of leading software vendors in this area. This BI software can handle report writing, data analysis and consolidations, and support ad-hoc queries. This software extracts data from disparate data sources, such as relational databases, legacy systems and flat files. The extracted data can have different data structures so it is transformed to conform to requirements of the BI tools or according to the business rules defined by the system administrator. Then, data is loaded typically into data marts, which are subsets of the data warehouse that focus on a desired topic. The loaded data can be put to reporting and analytical use. The Extract, Transform, and Load (ETL) process is generally handled by separate components, which enable defining and implementing of the ETL process by system administrators. The software is Web enabled and can interact with a variety of ERP systems; in fact, BI software vendors have developed strategic alliances with ERP vendors. Note that there are legions of software vendors offering separate software for supporting ETL processes, reporting information, analyzing data and for BI. Crystal/Business Objects and Cognos are, however, integrated environments and support all stages. The functionalities of BI software follow.

- **Reports:** Reports can be designed using reporting software. The software comes with designer module that generally has a drag-and-drop interface and operates in the Windows environment. The report design can be extremely complex, and data-rich reports can be created. Data can be sorted, mapped, grouped, charted and hyperlinked. Reports can be saved and exported in a variety of formats.

- Reports can be streamed over the Internet at pre-defined intervals to authorized parties. Crystal incorporates a utility called report streaming that delivers reports to the user's browser in real time.
- Reports can be scheduled for delivery at periodic intervals.
- Users can interact with reports and modify them through ad-hoc queries.
- Reports can also be delivered to users based on happening of a certain event, called event-driven reporting.

- **OLAP:** OLAP processing enables multidimensional analysis. The transformation phase of the ETL process creates data structures, which can be explored dimensionally; Cognos calls such data PowerCubes. What is the meaning of dimension? In business parlance, a dimension can be time — week, month or year; product — product groups or individual products; or location — county, city, state, region or country. Dimensional analysis refers to connecting these disparate dimensions to answer questions such as: What are sales in Erie in March for product X? What salesperson in the northeast region sold the highest units of product Y? Such questions are extremely difficult to answer using a general ledger.

  Data captured in multidimensional cubes can be manipulated in different ways; that is, different questions can be asked to understand data. The numbers can be drilled down; for example, if sales in a particular region are below target, then sales for each product can be examined. If that does not answer the questions, then sales per salesperson or territories in that region can be explored. Data can be sliced and diced, meaning dimensions can be changed to view data from different angles. Data can also be graphed for better understanding or presentations.

  The data capacity of OLAP tools is much higher than spreadsheets, and can be measured in billions of rows and columns. Data can be viewed over the Web or in a Windows environment, or can be downloaded to Excel. Excel can read OLAP cubes directly and manage multidimensional data sets by using pivot tables. OLAP tools can automate business calculations, such as percent changes in revenue and market share. Users can design alerts; for example, if sales decline more than 1% in region Z then the manager will be notified immediately.

- **Analysis:** Users not only want to view data but also to crunch it. Analytical tools provide these abilities via mathematical functions and statistical procedures. These are similar to functions encountered in Excel. There can also be data mining tools that automatically analyze data and provide hidden information in the absence of priori hypotheses. This analysis can be carried on the multidimensional cubes and other data structures, depending on the capabilities of the software.

- **Pre-packaged solutions:** BI software now provides a number of pre-packaged solutions that can operate on top of an ERP system and perform the required service. Solutions range from planning and budgeting tools to CPM. The BI software collects data from disparate corporate sources and can manipulate it using in-built mathematical and statistical capabilities. These abilities can be easily transformed to perform budgeting, consolidations, financial analytics, or to support ABC and ABM.

- **Executive dashboard, management dashboard, metrics driven management or executive information systems:** The term dashboard indicates continuous monitoring of vital indicators of the business and taking corrective actions, just as you control your car. The concept behind Executive or Management Dashboards (EDs) is not new; earlier versions of accounting systems implemented Executive Information Systems (EIS) that were similar to EDs. The concept of SAP cockpit seen earlier is another version of ED. Cognos implements the same concept as metrics driven management.

  The BI software can provide ED-type solutions; these can be pre-packaged or custom-designed by the company. EDs generally use a browser-based interface and provide pre-specified Key Performance Measures/Indicators (KPMs/KPIs). These KPIs are defined by management and are tied to industry benchmarks and best practices. Data can be viewed at the aggregate level and displayed in numbers and graphs. Some EDs may even show the graphics as fuel or speedometer gauges to compare performance against budgets or benchmarks. The why behind the indicators can be further explored due to drilldown capabilities. An illustrative list of ED characteristics is provided below.

  - The user interface can be customized
  - Exception-based reporting is achieved via colorful graphics, such as red traffic lights
  - User-defined alerts can be designed, which can come to the user via e-mail, PDAs or as on-screen alert messages

  EDs are not limited to top management. The BI software has extended the concept. Top-level managers are provided with scorecards, critical business metrics and visualizations of the required data. Mid-level managers can receive more detailed information, which can be sliced, diced and analyzed. Operational data can be delivered on the shop floor. Reports can vary from a multi-page detailed report to a one-page summary. Pros and cons of EDs have been discussed in the literature. The only lesson is that the ED is only as good as the manager who makes decisions based on its output.

The framework for BI software that enables these functionalities will now be discussed by using Cognos BI tools for illustrative purposes. Users interface with BI tools via Cognos Upfront. This is a Web-based point of access or portal to Cognos tools and has a zero footprint on the user's desktop, meaning the contents can be accessed through a browser and do not require any resident software on the desktop. This portal has a graphical interface and reporting and analytical tools, and can be personalized. A user can change the look and feel of the portal, change settings and create new boxes with personalized content. The portal also standardizes the user interface, and every user in the organization sees the same interface. Users can share and transfer reports and collaborate on projects.

Exhibit 7. Examples of Cognos reporting and analytic applications (Source: www.cognos.com/)

Area	*Capabilities*	*Analytical measures*
Sales	Questions > 500 KPIs (*Key Performance Indicators*) > 200 Reports > 45	• Functional performance • Customer sales • Product sales • Channel sales • Sales organizational effectiveness • Distribution functional performance • Distribution organizational effectiveness
Accounts receivable	Questions > 600 KPIs > 60 Reports > 35	• Performance • Customer credit • Corporate self-Appraisal • Cash Inflow • Organizational effectiveness
General ledger	Questions > 500 KPIs > 60 Reports > 35	• Financial performance • Budget • Key financial ratios • Operational performance
Accounts payable	Questions > 700 KPIs > 65 Reports > 35	• Performance • Vendor account • Cash outflow • Organizational effectiveness
Inventory	Questions > 500 KPIs > 80 Reports > 30	• Stock overview & valuation • Material movement activity • Inventory demand • Material reservation • Physical inventory • Inventory forecast • Organizational effectiveness
Procurement	Questions > 200 KPIs > 170 Reports > 30	• Material expenditure • Material demand • Vendor • Process effectiveness • Organizational effectiveness
Production	Questions > 120 KPIs > 170 Reports > 45	• Work order material usage and cost • Time-to-delivery • Quantity and yield • Organizational effectiveness

Cognos Web Services uses an XML-based interface. This service can be used to deliver business intelligence in different computing environments having a software and hardware mix via Web-based protocols. For example, such protocols can be used to deliver data to mobile phones or visual programs, such as Macromedia Flash. Cognos tools come with pre-packaged reports, analyses and ad-hoc query routines. Cognos Web service can be used as an adapter (a device that allows one system to connect to and work with another) for such packaged reports. This service also provides a visual test studio environment that can be used to test and verify business intelligence applications.

Cognos Access Manager centralizes security functions for reports, analyses and queries. The access manager maintains user classes and applies authorization and authentication rights to these classes. Security can be applied across multidimensional

Exhibit 8. Business objects dashboard manager (Source: www.businessobjects.com/products/dashboard_manager/, used with permission)

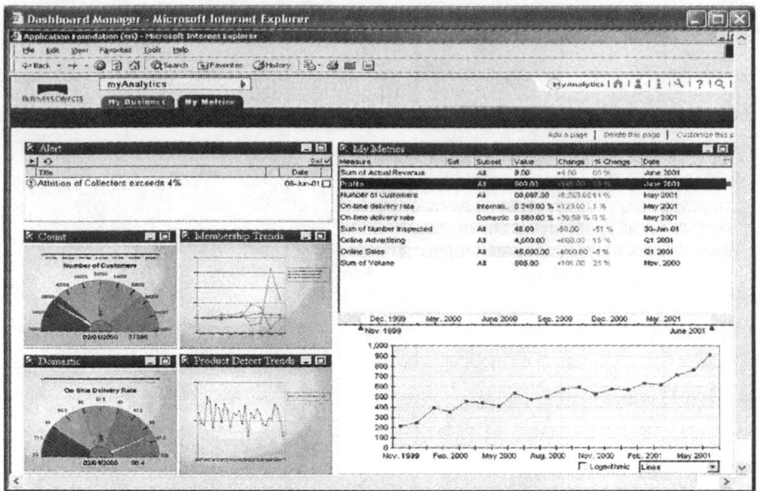

cubes, tables, rows or columns. Cognos Administrator handles standard functions, such as configuration, deployment and administration. The configuration manager allows configuration of BI servers, and these configurations can be saved and re-used. The deployment manager allows deploying applications or parts of applications for users across the enterprise. Administrative functions, such as monitoring the system, ensuring security, managing users and troubleshooting, are also carried out in this component.

Cognos Architect manages BI metadata and business rules. Architect gathers data collected from corporate sources and creates metadata — data that describes data — and creates a consistent data view for BI applications. This metadata is used to provide reports and analysis. The advantage of having a BI framework is ease of installation and configuration. Ease is a relative word; there is an industry of consultants, trainers, implementers and programmers that has developed around BI tools.

ERP vendors are also aggressively integrating reporting and analytical capabilities in their software. Lawson Software, for example, uses OLAP to create separate data marts that serve different users in different functional areas. These data marts are essentially multidimensional cubes. Advantages of these data marts include reliving burden on the general ledger, providing pre-packaged calculations and enabling user self-service. These financial data marts perform the following functions.

- **Financials data mart:** The general ledger is transferred to the OLAP environment and can be analyzed on different dimensions such as segments, account periods, fiscal year and products. This data mart obviously can be used to generate GAAP-compliant financial reports.
- **Daily financial data mart:** The focus of this data mart is on the short term. Daily integration of point-of-sale information with consumer buying patterns can be achieved in the retail environment. The dimensions of analysis are similar to the financials data mart.

- **Project and activity accounting data mart:** Designated projects, such as construction of a fixed asset and activities such as services deliverable to customers, can be monitored..
- **Strategic ledger mart:** This data mart provides strategic information, such as profitability or business performance, along required dimensions. Regional managers can view performance of the region, profit centers can monitor their profit and loss statements, and transactional data can be viewed in a format desired by the user. Users can essentially monitor their slice of business on a pre-defined metrics. Ad-hoc analyses can also be performed.
- **Assets data mart:** Assets information, such as book value, location, depreciation methods, lease costs and accumulated depreciation, can be obtained instantaneously. The assets can be viewed by segments, departments, costs centers or locations. Changes in policies can be administered from this central location, making policy compliance easier.
- **Lease management data mart:** This data mart contains information on operating and capital leases and related assets. Payment schedules, rent and lease obligations, and related calculations can be done in this data mart.

SAP, on the other hand, uses mySAP BI to deliver business analytics, of which financial analytics is a part. These tools are supported by technologies seen earlier — SAP exchange infrastructure, SAP knowledge warehouse, SAP business information warehouse and SAP enterprise portal. MySAP business Intelligence consists of a BI platform, BI tools and measurement and management. The BI platform provides a foundation for

Exhibit 9. Cognos architecture

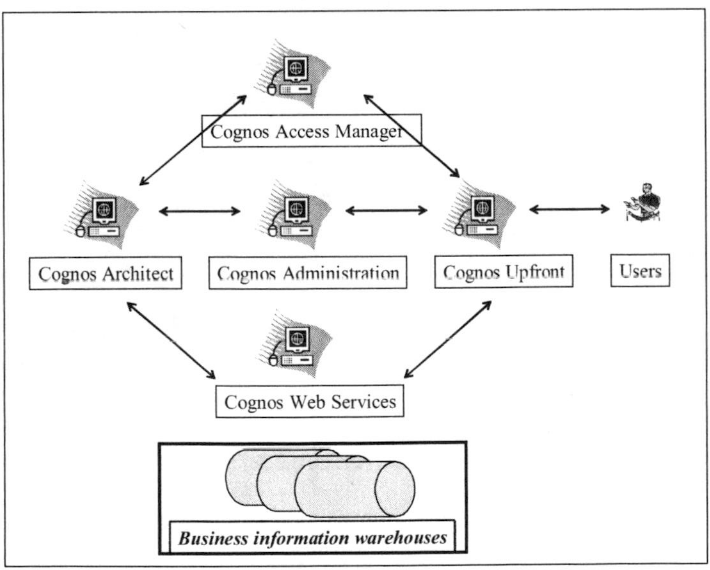

Exhibit 10. Lawson financial data marts

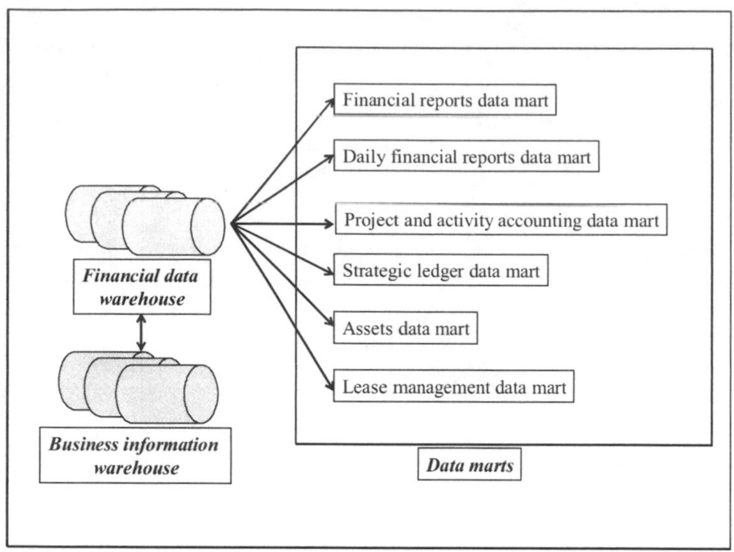

OLAP, data mining tools and user alerts. BI tools provide for a Web-based or ad-hoc query design, reporting and analytical functionalities, and the ability to create Web-based reports and dashboard for dissemination of information. Measurement and management tools allow for measuring and monitoring of business performance based on packaged and user defined KPIs, management of metadata to maintain consistent data and collaborative business intelligence. Additional capabilities of mySAP BI include Web-based reporting and analysis, different modes of delivering information to the end user, integration with Microsoft Excel, multidimensional analysis, mathematical and statistical functions for analysis, and support for mobile means of access. SAP also provides best practices as per industry to guide new installers of mySAP BI tools.

The mySAP BI tools use these supporting technologies and interact with the SAP ERP system to provide business analytics. The advantage of this package is that it is tightly integrated with SAP ERP and is transparent with respect to data warehouses, middleware (software that serves as an intermediary between systems software and an application) and BI software. The mySAP BI tools function similarly to the Cognos and Business Objects tools. The basic building block of mySAP BI tools is called InfoObjects. These objects contain data concerning customers, sales orders, settlements and other business information. InfoObjects are created by pulling information from different data sources and are used in BI applications. InfoObjects are used to create data marts and multidimensional cubes for further analysis. These BI tools can also be integrated with Crystal Reports for specialized needs of various departments.

SAP also provides packaged BI solutions — sales insight, procurement insight and financial insight. These packages have built-in reports, analyses and displays for important measures in sales, procurement and financial areas. Financial Insight Package is a Web-enabled analytical cockpit that centralizes financial analytics at one place. This package is an advanced version of EDs. The abilities provided in this package are similar to those of BI tools and the Lawson ERP system. Financial statements required under GAAP, details of general ledger and subsidiary ledgers, revenue and cost accounting, order and project accounting, and product and service cost calculations are the primary general ledger-based reports. Multidimensional analysis is available; for example, in the revenue cycle, customer paying habits, overdue payments and days of sales outstanding can be monitored using built-in data marts. Similar to BI tools, analytical capabilities to crunch the numbers are available, user alerts can be designed and reports can be streamed over the Internet or Web to users.

Spreadsheets skills are a must and BI skills will soon be required. Financial analytics seen so far and business analytics discussed in the next chapter obviously indicate that reporting and analytical requirements of the coming age are far more detailed and complex than the spreadsheet era. Accountants are involved in a number of reporting issues, including design and generation of reports. A number of ABC and ABM models are run using data warehouses. If you want to explore such data warehouses for cost accounting reports, you need to understand names and definitions of data elements in the warehouse. Specifying data marts requires defining the areas of interest, again, by understanding data elements in the data warehouse. Data mining software and embedded tools are quite user friendly, and if you need to get a deeper understanding of, say, customer behavior and profitability, then you should be capable of specifying the required models. The basic idea is to understand what is possible using these tools. Accountants need to understand the possibilities, or they may fail to exploit the tremendous power of these tools.

Exhibit 11. SAP business intelligence

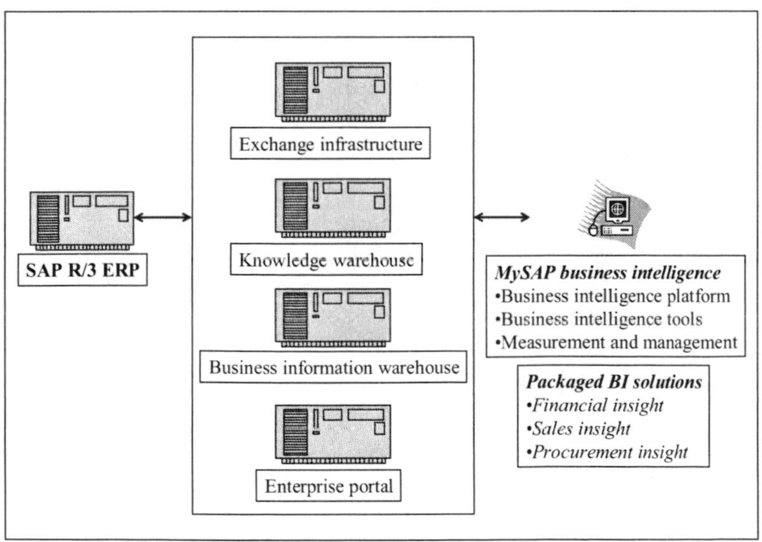

Planning and Budgeting

Budgeting has been used as a control tool for many decades. The budget philosophy developed in the slow-growth and stable environment, primarily as a means of controlling costs. The objectives of budgeting and performance measures have evolved in modern times. Business is more dynamic and budgets are not confined to long time frames; dollar amounts and net income are not the only things measured; and budgets are used for purposes far more creative. Research indicates that today the annual cost of planning and budgeting is 1.5% to 3% of revenue, and managers and controllers spend between 20% and 50% of their working hours on planning and budgeting. Costs involved in the planning and budgeting process are substantial. Are the benefits worth these costs? The answer depends on the handling of the budget process by an organization. The Internet, data warehouse and multidimensional analysis, among other things, all play a role in a world-class planning and budgeting system.

The budget process in many companies is still based on the general ledger and supported by extensive use of spreadsheets. Many accounting systems and ERP systems restrict the budgeting process to general ledger, in spite of having a central relational database system. Budget functionalities may allow for creating budget codes that can be used to post budget numbers to the required budget, such as planned budget, forecasted budget or revised budget. Budgets can be created using budget-entry sheets and imported (or exported) to spreadsheet software. The budget can be posted to general ledger accounts for specified accounting periods, and percentage and monetary variances can be calculated. However, such a process does not support the needs of managing budget submission workflow, creating models, simulating various scenarios and viewing real-time changes in results.

If the budget process is managed using spreadsheets, then such a process is inefficient, ineffective and expensive, even for a mid-sized corporation. Spreadsheets can multiply rapidly — product, segments, departments, locations and regions. The number of spreadsheets may spiral into triple digits. Consolidating these spreadsheets may take weeks, never mind the verification, validation and auditing of them. A survey conducted by the International Association of Financial Executives Institute (IAFEI) found that data collection and validation, consolidation of information and production of meaningful reports took a long time, making budget numbers obsolete. Financial executives were also concerned with their inability to link business strategies with operational plans and budgets.

Software vendors recognized needs of planners and budgeters, and now a slew of vendors is offering planning and budgeting software. These solutions range from standalone simulation tools and budgeting software, integrated tools offered by ERP vendors or standalone tools offered in a package with an ERP system. New planning and budgeting systems have the following features.

- **Roll up and Roll down:** Budgets should be easy to roll up to the macro level and connect with corporate financial metrics that represent business objectives and strategies. The budgets should also be easy to roll down to individual operational or departmental managers.

- **Web-enabled:** Budgeting tools that are browser-based enable collaborative budgets. Bottom-up and top-down forecasting, real-time information from the field, revision of targets and changes in business strategies, among other things, can be incorporated rapidly.
- **Integration with back-end systems:** Planning and budgeting software needs to be integrated not only with the accounting system but also with multiple applications, such as CRM and SCM, across the enterprise. Most high-end budgeting applications use data or business information warehouses.
- **Flexibility:** Planning and budgeting software should come with built-in analytical applications and permit analysis across multiple dimensions. Consolidations should be done immediately and revisions to the budget should be easy. Users should be able to see changes in the entire budget due to changes in tparts of the budget or budget assumptions.
- **OLAP:** Multidimensional analysis is generally possible in the OLAP environment. The OLAP component is a requirement for good budgeting software.
- **Security:** Budgets are sensitive, and security should be established at the user, departmental and each managerial level. Input data should be validated, user activity should be audited and a system administrator should be able to manage the security from a centralized location.

The required capabilities are similar to those offered by BI software. As such, many BI vendors offer planning and budgeting software. A BI vendor not seen so far is a company called SAS. SAS has origins in statistical analysis, and using that as a base, the company has made strong offerings in the BI area. The corporation, in recent years, has also diversified into offering business software such as CRM, financial management and SRM; planning and budgeting software being a part of their financial management solution.

The first requirement in budgeting software is planning facility. The term *planning* used hereafter is not merely restricted to financial planning, though discussion centers on financial planning. The planning facility must enable collaborative planning. The people involved in planning, tasks allotted to those people, timelines and designated workflows should be visible to planning participants. For larger corporations, a Web-enabled planning process is a necessity. Browser-based processes can be widely used, irrespective of software and hardware platforms. The different types of planning functions, such as top-down, bottom-up, currency translations, rolling budgets and activity-based budgeting, should be supported. The user interface should be customizable; for example, rows and columns, visualization techniques or other data presentation techniques need to be supported for wider user acceptance.

The planning facility should have simulation capabilities. Changes in assumptions of the plan; running of multiple scenarios; factoring in changes in external variables, such as economic growth; and what-if analysis should be supported by the planning software.

Budgets are no longer static, and simulation capabilities are especially useful for rolling forecasts. Plans for income statement, balance sheet, profit centers or cost centers should be capable of being independently set while being connected with each other. Plans and budgets can be capable of being aggregated, disaggregated and drilled down for further details. If the supply chain is integrated, the plans need to be visible to supply chain participants. Portals or other mechanisms should be in place to share plan information with trading partners.

SAS's planning and budgeting solution comes with similar planning abilities. A formulated plan must be mapped to dollars and cents, which is budgeting. The budget administrator or responsible manager sets the objectives and defines the budget criteria. The budget criteria specify planning period, entities involved in planning, types of budgets required and persons responsible for the budgets. SAS also incorporates what it calls *business drivers* in the planning solution. These drivers are either fixed values or formulas similar those seen in the spreadsheet. Examples of these drivers may include a given dollar figure for fixed overhead or formula for calculating sales commissions. These business drivers can be tracked, defined and changed on a system-wide basis. These drivers represent organizational policies and budget assumptions, and help align budgets with organizational objectives.

The first step in SAS solution is the creation of data entry forms. These forms can be used to capture financial and non-financial data. Data can be captured on the desired dimensions and subjected to what-if analyses. The desired data fields can be pre-populated but cannot be altered by the user. Automated features such as increment and spreading expedite filling in correct data. These forms are distributed, reviewed, filled and submitted over the Web. A centralized location saves completed forms. Budget partici-

Exhibit 12. SAS planning and budgeting solution

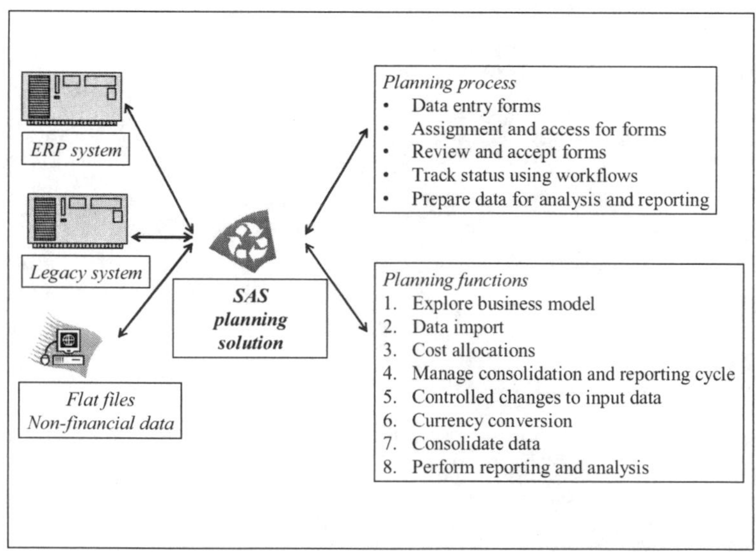

pants can be notified via e-mail that these forms are available to set the budget process rolling. These forms support both top-down and bottom-up budgets. In the case of top-down budgets, the forms can be populated with desired numbers and sent downward. For bottom-up budgets, the budget numbers can come from the lower levels of the organization. The iterative process can be then carried out.

The forms are subject to strict ownership and access requirements. The budget director establishes the ownership and accountability for each form by defining authorization for user groups. Authorization rights include read, write, modify and submit. The systems administrator manages access controls and issuance of passwords. Internal control over forms is established by using these rights. Authenticated users can log in and perform the necessary functions to complete the forms. As users submit the forms, the budget director or department reviews those forms and accepts or rejects them. If the form is accepted, it moves to the next approver as specified in the workflow. Upon final approval, the form is submitted to the central administrator. In the case of rejection, the user gets an e-mail notification of rejection along with the reasons. At the completion of this process, the central administrator can consolidate the forms. The planning solution comes with a financial data warehouse that stores the data and can be used for reporting and consolidation purposes.

This planning solution also provides workflow and auditing capabilities. Workflow features enable the administrator to track the forms and provide information such as: Who has finished the forms? Who has finished and submitted the forms? Who has not opened the forms? E-mails can be automated and sent to laggard users at periodic intervals. User activity is logged and a detailed record of users, forms, changes and approvals is kept. Illustrative additional controls are as follows: First, when files change or new journals are created, the process is flagged and details of the events are recorded. Second, data can be managed by setting up batch processes with stringent controls. Third, users can define their own data validation procedures for incoming or imported data. Fourth, if the budget form is not approved, it cannot be used in budget consolidations. Finally, users can exercise control over consolidations and reconsolidations for correcting errors.

The SAS planning solutions supports extraction of data from a variety of sources. Users can build data validation routines to ascertain data integrity and automatically add new dimensions during the data-importing phase. Costs can be allocated to departments, products or customers by using different methods, such as percentage split, equal split, and proportional and fixed values. ABC and ABM capabilities are provided by a third-party vendor and can be used, if needed. The consolidation and reporting cycle is dynamic; that is, data arrives in batches and budgets get revised with the incoming data, data can change and be resubmitted thus changing the budgets again. Top management can also change budget assumptions, triggering a new round of budget calculations. The consolidations can be repeated and reports regenerated. The SAS planning solution provides for a Web-enabled workflow to view these changes and incorporate them in a timely fashion. Reports can be scheduled and executed at pre-determined intervals.

The original data for intercompany transactions, goodwill, minority interest or similar transactions is not altered, but changes are kept in a separate file, providing an audit trail. Currency conversion can be carried out based on user-defined tables and business rules.

The collected financial data can be analyzed and explored in a multidimensional mode. SAS also provides various mathematical and statistical functions to analyze data, if desired. The reports can be distributed in the form of electronic booklets, and actual performance can be measured against budgeted norms. The usual facilities of graphical visualization, dashboards, drill downs, user-defined and programmed alerts, and user-defined reports are available. The SAS planning and budgeting solution is a typical solution, and most competing vendors offer similar functionalities.

Enterprise Portals

The word *portal* refers to a door, gateway or entrance, especially the one that is imposing. Internet portals are gateways to information stored at different locations. You have probably visited Yahoo.com, which is a portal that provides organized information on various topics. There are also various search engines called Search Portals, such as Google and AltaVista, that can search for information based on terms and descriptions. These portals are referred to as *public portals,* because they are available to all users and only need connection with the Internet for use. The portal concept has been transported to the corporate world. These portals are called enterprise portals, Enterprise Information Portals (EIPs), business portals and corporate portals. These portals are *private*, meaning their use is restricted to authorized users.

The primary function of portals in the corporate world is similar to public portals — organization and dissemination of information or content. However, enterprise portals cannot merely focus on content; the corporate world requires and demands far more functionalities than public portals. Software vendors and consultants have produced multiple definitions and interpretations of enterprise portals. These definitions revolve around organization of information, collaboration among users, technical infrastructure and business intelligence capabilities. As the enterprise portal technology evolved, all these functionalities have converged, and now comprehensive software offerings have emerged in this area. So, what are the characteristics of enterprise portals?

- Enterprise portals provide consistent user-friendly interface across the organization and can be accessed from the intranet, Internet or mobile devices.
- Enterprise portals use push-and-pull technologies to disseminate information. Users can pull information via the portal, and the portal can push (or send) information to users based on pre-programmed criteria, similar to *alerts*.
- Information sources can be internal and external. Enterprise portals are capable of retrieving data from different computing environments, application packages and Web-based sources.
- Enterprise portals, as opposed to public portals, provide interactivity, often called bi-directional flow of information. The users not only drill for information but can also analyze, format and transfer information.

- Enterprise portals come with pre-packaged applications or packages targeted at functions or industries. For example, an enterprise portal aimed at CFOs will be different than one aimed at CEOs.

The integration and analytical functionalities of the enterprise portal may seem similar to the CRM, SRM, SCM and BI packages discussed earlier. The functionalities are similar, and Enterprise portals and these packages do interact with each other. Enterprise portals are useful if the organization has a mix of computing systems; the fragmentation of

Exhibit 13. Business objects Infoview XI portal (Source: www.businessobjects.com/products/platform/enterprise.asp, used with permission)

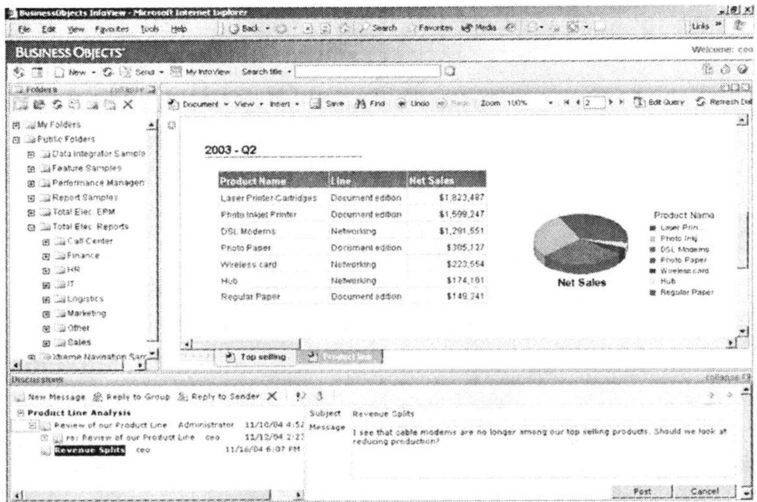

Exhibit 14. Information fragmentation in organizations

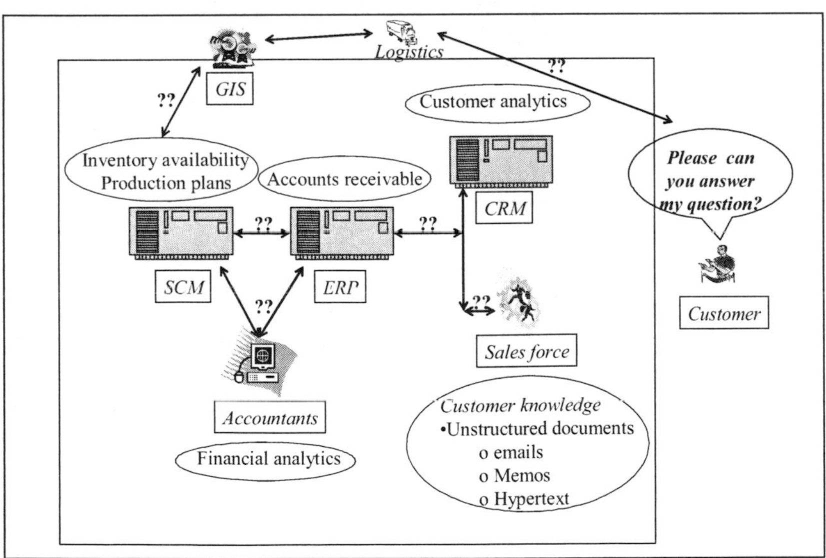

information is more of a problem. Even if the organization uses software packages from the same vendor, complete integration of structured (data stored in relational databases) and non-structured (documents, hypertext, e-mails, news, etc.) information is not possible. The ERP system can collect the information, but enterprise portals are needed to extract and deliver such information.

The SAP white paper "*Business Unification with mySAP Enterprise Portal 2003*" describes the use of portal by a sales manager as follows:

> *"The sales manager receives an alert from the portal detailing all outstanding orders. The manager simply drags an order from the alert to the Web component of the ERP application to display details of the order. To check on its progress, the manager then drags the order onto the shipping carrier's Web site icon, which automatically displays the order status." (Source: www.sap.com)*

The sales manager in this case does not need to remember which system to use, does not have to log in using separate IDs to different systems, and does not have to manually synthesize the information. The enterprise portal brings together the required information from different sources such as CRM, EDI, data warehouse, document management or the Internet, to mention a few. If the sales manager needs to analyze data, the embedded analytical and data mining tools can be used. The enterprise portal pulls information from different sources in a seamless fashion; at least, that is the promise.

Components of an Enterprise Portal

Conceptually, the major components of an enterprise portal are as follows: functionalities, interface and infrastructure. The functionalities of enterprise portals should include BI tools, collaboration tools, knowledge management tools, search facilities and workflow management tools. BI tools such as report generation, analytical capabilities, OLAP and data mining are generally provided in an enterprise portal. These tools can come with the enterprise portal package, or existing tools such as Cognos can be integrated with the enterprise portal package. Enterprise portals generally support collaborative tools, such as discussion boards, document sharing, chat, instant messaging, virtual conferencing and video. The analytical and collaborative abilities of the portals separate private portals from public portals.

Knowledge management tools are absolutely necessary, since enterprise portals promise to access information in any format from any location. Sources of information can be transactional systems, databases and data warehouses, the Internet and documents. This information can be further classified into two categories — structured and unstructured. Structured information, such as data stored in databases, can be effectively searched, since databases already come equipped with search tools and mechanisms. The data organization in structured databases is already standardized, and search and

Exhibit 15. Components of enterprise portals

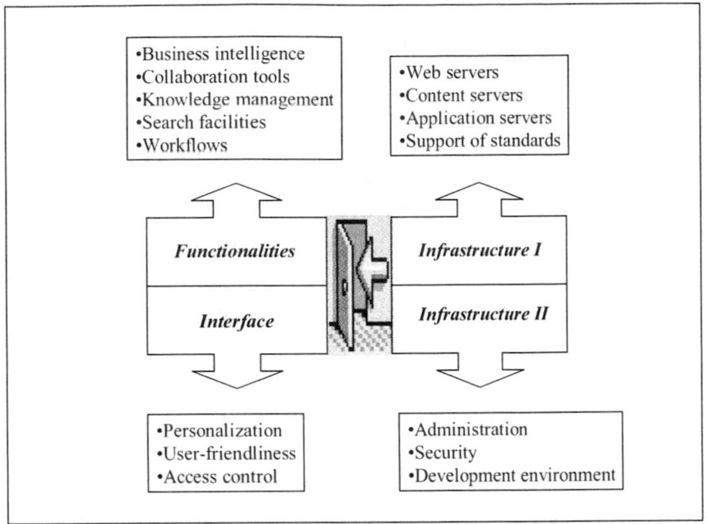

retrieval mechanisms are easy to devise. Organizations also generate massive amounts of unstructured information that may be stored in documents, memos, newsgroups and discussion boards, which need to be indexed and categorized for effective use. Organizations also acquire new businesses, and in the process acquire new and inconsistent sources of data and information.

Knowledge management tools provide different ways to manage unstructured data and information from disparate sources. These tools have a repository that maintains indexes that point to the documents stored throughout the organization. The documents can also be categorized so users can find them without knowing the exact content of the document. The interface standard for knowledge management solutions is called Web Based Distributed Authoring and Versioning (WebDAV), which is an open standard. This standard specifies document-locking protocols, metadata standards, deletion and retrieval functions and searching for resource location on the Web, and also supports copy-and-move operations. These are merely illustrative examples; WebDAV can also provide a front end for knowledge management solutions.

A searching facility is the capability to access, browse and retrieve information based on the user's requirements. Search facilities are enabled by search-and-retrieval engines. These are similar to Google or AltaVista. Different types of queries, such as simple queries (one word), term queries (search for a term such as enterprise portals), Boolean queries (words connected by *and* or *or*) and linguistic queries (different forms of the word), are supported by these search engines. Advanced searches, such as searches based on *author* or *date*, are also possible. An enterprise portal provides access to various applications on the corporate system. As such, the portal should be capable of interacting with workflows contained in these different applications. enterprise portals have the ability to interface with existing workflows so the user can access and interact with the workflows. Additionally, users can receive alerts through e-mail, PDAs or directly through the portal.

The enterprise portal interface uses a Windows-type environment and the portal can be accessed via browser over the Internet or intranet. The user can customize the portal by changing the setting, fonts and colors, and choosing the content to be displayed after log in. The user interface needs to be user-friendly to shorten the learning curve. Navigation across the portal can be achieved in a number of ways. For example, the user can move through pages that are hierarchically arranged, click on links to drill down for information, click on a link to change some aspects of the page, or drag and drop the information. The portal should also offer help facilities for new and experienced users. Help features come in various formats, such as general help, context-sensitive help, interactive help or help wizards. Portal access is governed by standard authentication and authorization procedures. Security procedures are important, since portal access generates further access to various applications and corporate intranets.

The infrastructure for enterprise portals consists of different servers to accomplish various functions and software for the administration, security and development environment. The servers contain the logic to perform functions such as business intelligence, knowledge management, interfacing with databases and document repositories and portal management. Enterprise portals also come with software for administering and securing the portals, and a development environment for developing and customizing portals. The architecture, that is, mix of hardware of software for portals, is different for each vendor; as usual, claims, definitions and terminologies are confusing in this area. A detailed discussion of the architecture is beyond the scope of this book.

SAP Enterprise Portals — A Business View

The SAP enterprise portal is a suite of software modules that comes with the capabilities described earlier. These functionalities include unification of information from different sources, BI, knowledge management, and access to internal and external databases. This software connects with the underlying ERP system, applications, databases, data warehouses, unstructured documents, and Internet and intranet content to become operational. The focus of discussion in this section is on the abilities and users of the enterprise portal, not on the technical infrastructure.

At the heart of the SAP enterprise portals is software called iView. This program integrates information from the ERP system, applications, databases and data warehouses, and also provides search functions. Additionally, users can access content from Microsoft Outlook, Oracle database, Yahoo! and similar programs. SAP calls iView a unification technology. iView can add windows to a user desktop that integrate external Web-based sources of information with the desktop. If the user wants a continuous feed of information from the stock market, the related Web site, such as Bloomberg, will always be available on the desktop without the need to fire up the browser and navigate to the

Exhibit 16. SAP enterprise portal

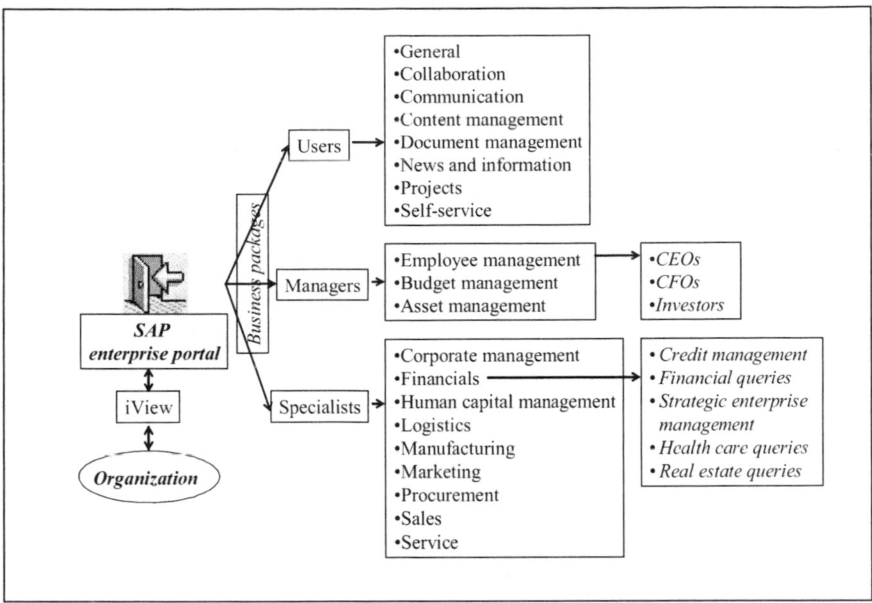

site. The user can use the capabilities of iView to organize and arrange the required information for a personal view.

SAP provides what is called *business packages* to complement its enterprise portal. Business packages are pre-assembled content for certain tasks, and can be used either out of the box or to shorten custom development of applications. Business packages essentially package required information, analytical tools and tasks geared to satisfy specific users. The primary business constituents at whom Business packages are aimed are users, managers and specialists. The packages aimed at the user include tasks common to all users, whether managers or functional specialists. Standard tools include e-mail, task lists, calendars, travel management, benefits management, e-learning and search engines. Users can manage documents using industry standard platforms, get news and information from Yahoo!, manage projects and access their own data in the human resources department for self-service. Information and workflows can be managed using collaborative tools. The business package provides all the necessary tools to conduct enterprise portal activities.

Business packages aimed at managers perform a variety of tasks that should help them manage the enterprise. Employee management tasks include monitoring attendance, reviewing employees, recruiting employees and compensation planning. Budgets can be planned using cost centers and profit centers, and costs can be allocated using various allocation mechanisms. Assets can be monitored according to costs centers or profit centers, depreciation and useful life can be viewed, internal service requests can be generated, and maintenance schedules can be reviewed. Workflows for various activities, such as requisitions, can be viewed and changed. The basic idea is to reduce time spent on routine administrative tasks and support strategic work. Enterprise portals and related business packages specifically targeted at top management or stakeholders/investors are also available.

- **Enterprise portal for CFOs:** This portal provides a single access point for the CFO to access data required on a day-to-day basis. The portal uses information from internal financial systems and also incorporates information supplied by external news and content providers. BI tools are used, data is analyzed and information is provided regarding strategic management and performance management, business planning and consolidation, and risk and treasury management.

  The portal is similar to executive dashboards. What is the difference? The difference depends on the capabilities of the underlying system and implementation; conceptually, there is very little difference in this portal and executive dashboards. The way SAP describes this portal apparently makes it an advanced version of executive dashboards.
- **Enterprise portal for investors:** This portal provides information to investors and prospective investors. Information includes analyst estimations; financial calendar; stock information; newsletter subscriptions; and names, addresses and photos of the investor relations team. This portal can be useful in disseminating information, reacting to market information and disinformation, and damage control.

The term specialist refers to functional specialists, such as people in accounting, marketing and finance. These packages deliver operational and analytical tools and functionalities appropriate for each department. Illustrative business packages for financials include customer credit management, financial queries and strategic enterprise management. Customer credit management is useful for credit managers and provides payment analysis, payment history, customer details, details of overdue invoices and credit memos, changes in customer credit and analysis of customer credit, among other things. This package allows for end-to-end analysis of customer credit and interfaces with SAP FI/CO module or the underlying ERP system. The financial query package interfaces with SAP Business Information Warehouse and provides a list of prepared queries. These queries can be used to analyze financial data according to cost center, profit center, period, budgeted vs. actuals, financial statements or projects. The business package for strategic enterprise management provides financial and non-financial analytics, which is covered in the next chapter. Business packages can also be designed for an industry; for example, SAP offers health care queries and real estate queries, aimed at healthcare and real estate industries, respectively.

Summary

The general ledger cycle, from the accounting perspective, consists of making period-end-adjusting entries in the general ledger, preparing financial statements and closing the books by making closing entries. As accounting systems got computerized, the general ledger cycle has undergone a metamorphosis. Closing of the books, which used to take weeks or months in the real world, has been reengineered. The closing process and preparation of financial statements give a real picture of business. Managers who want to view this picture and make course corrections demand virtual close. The closing process has been shortened via standardized accounting procedures, integrated and automated financial systems, real-time connections with operational systems, use of the Internet and automation of workflows. Shortening the closing process highlights inefficiencies in the financial system and is useful even if the closing time is not reduced significantly.

Financial analytics has leaped beyond the standard financial, managerial and special-report routines of accounting departments. New tools to mine financial information include report writing, analytical and BI tools. They supplement and at the same time supplant trusty spreadsheets. Integrated environments, such as Cognos or Business Objects, offer all functionalities in one package. These tools extract data from different sources, transform it using business rules and load it in data marts. The loaded data can be formatted using reporting tools, crunched using analytical tools, even mined for knowledge, and can be downloaded to spreadsheets for analyzing in a familiar environment. These packages also provide packaged solutions, such as planning/budgeting and consolidations software. Top-level managers can use executive dashboards to monitor the pulse of the organization by looking at key performance measures in a graphical, user-friendly environment.

Planning and budgeting tools have changed the traditional process of budgeting. The functionalities of new software allow for roll up and roll down of budgets, use of the Internet in budgeting, integration with back-end systems, flexibility, use of data warehouses and strong security measures.

The SAS Budgeting solution was then reviewed. This solution starts from creation of data-entry forms that support top-down and bottom-up budgeting. These forms are consolidated in the financial data warehouse and can be used for budgeting and data analysis. The solution also comes with solid security, workflows and auditing capabilities.

The final technology changing financial reporting is enterprise portals. These portals provide user-friendly interface, use push-and-pull technologies to collect and disseminate data and information, tap external and internal data sources, provide analytical capabilities and provide pre-packaged solutions for certain functions. The functionalities of these portals, interface characteristics and infrastructure requirements were reviewed. The SAP enterprise portal for financial and managerial purposes was discussed. This discussion covered iView, business packages and portals aimed at CFOs and investors. However, do not confuse the availability of functionalities with successful implementation of the software, which is another story, not covered in this book.

References

A business person's guide to enterprise portal terms and business impacts (white paper). (2003). PeopleSoft. Retrieved August 10, 2003, from www.peoplesoft.com/media/en/pdf/PWS924SQJRC_MDA.pdf

A new dimension in financial planning and budgeting (SAS white paper). (2003). SAP. Retrieved August 5, 2003, from www.sap.com/

Anonymous. (2003). 7 ways to close the books quicker and improve reporting. *IOMA's Report on Financial Analysis, Planning, and Reporting, July,* 5-7.

Berinato, S. (2001). What went wrong at CISCO? *CIO, August*, 52-58.

Bodwell, D. *Predictive executive dashboard concepts* (white paper). (2003). PT Consulting Partners. Retrieved August 16, 2003, from http://ptcpartners.com/Art_PredictiveExecutiveDashboards.htm

Business analytics in mySAP financials (SAP Solutions Brief). (2003). SAP. Retrieved August 5, 2003, from www.sap.com/

Business package for financial queries, users guide. (2003). SAP. Retrieved August 5, 2003, from www.sap.com

Business planning and simulation with mySAP financials and mySAP business intelligence (SAP Solutions Brief). (2003). SAP. Retrieved August 6, 2003, from www.sap.com

Business unification with mySAP enterprise portal (mySAP Enterprise Portal Brief). (2003). SAP. Retrieved August 6, 2003, from www.sap.com

Caplan, J. (2001, July). What to look for in your next budgeting system. *CFO*. Retrieved August 16, 2003, from www.cfo.com/article.cfm/2998105/c_2984787?f=archives&origin=archive

Colkin, E. (2002, February). Fast-track financials. *InformationWeek*, 57-60.

Cope, J. (2001, February). Virtual close fails to work for CISCO. *ComputerWorld*, 24.

Decker, J., Alarvan, S., Sribor, V., Handler, R., Hill, J., Brand, J., & Kudnick, D. (2002). Making the "virtual close" a reality. White paper. Meta Group. Retrieved from http://www.2dnet.com/

Deshmukh, A. (2004). Virtual close: Problems and prospects. *Review of Business Information Systems*, *8*(4), 103-108.

Dougherty, K. (2003). *Web-enabled financial reporting & the virtual close* (CPE seminar). Broomall: The Center for Professional Education.

E-financial reporting (white paper). (2003). Lawson. Retrieved August 7, 2003, from www.lawson.com/

Enterprise performance management (SAS white paper). (2003). SAS. Retrieved August 7, 2003, from www.sas.com/

Firestone, J. (1999). *Have you seen KMCI knowledge management certification program* (white paper). Retrieved August 7, 2003, from www.dkms.com/

Firestone, J. (2000). *Enterprise knowledge portals and e-business solutions* (white paper). Retrieved August 7, 2003, from www.dkms.com/

Frequently asked questions, iView. (2003). SAP. Retrieved August 7, 2003, from www.iviewstudio.com/

Hafeli, J. (1999). *Analytical applications & the new millennium* (white paper). Retrieved August 7, 2003, from www.dbatoolbox.com/WP2001/appsmisc/Analytical%20Apps.pdf/

Hallett, T. (2002). *Record to report: Accelerating the close cycle* (white paper). Retrieved August 10, 2003, from www.cfoproject.com/

Incentives and commission management with mySAP financials (SAP white paper). (2003). SAP. Retrieved August 7, 2003, from www.sap.com/

Knorr, E., Udell, J., & Farley, J. (2003, January). The new enterprise portal. *InfoWorld, 26,* 42-52.

McKie, S. (2000). *Financial analytics.* Loveland, CO: Business Technology Press.

mySAP enterprise portal (SAP Solutions Brief). (2003). SAP. Retrieved August 7, 2003, from www.sap.com/

mySAP financials next-generation integration (SAP Solutions Brief). (2003). SAP. Retrieved August 7, 2003, from www.sap.com/

mySAP financials: Financial and management portals (SAP Solutions Brief). (2003). SAP. Retrieved August 9, 2003, from www.sap.com/

O'Rourke, J. (2002). *The virtual close – Myth or reality?* (white paper). Retrieved August 17, 2003, from www.cfoproject.com/

Optimizing your IT investments with SAP business packages for mySAP enterprise portal (mySAP Enterprise Portal Brief). (2003). SAP. Retrieved August 10, 2003, from www.sap.com/

Oracle performance analyzer 11i (data sheet). (2003). Oracle. Retrieved August 10, 2003, from www.oracle.com/

Profit management by pricing and profit maximization (SAP white paper). (2003). SAP. Retrieved August 10, 2003, from www.sap.com/

Roth, R. (2000, February). Capitalize on virtual close. *Financial Executive*, 45-46.

SAP: The evolution of finance and the enterprise (white paper). (2003). The CFO Project. Retrieved August 10, 2003, from www.cfoproject.com/

Saran, C. (2000, November). What transformation of budgeting and planning process. *CFO*. Retrieved August 10, 2003, from www.cfo.com/

SAS data warehousing (SAS Solutions). (2003). SAS. Retrieved August 12, 2003, from www.sas.com/

SAS financial management solutions (SAS white paper). (2003). SAS. Retrieved August 12, 2003, from www.sas.com/

SAS information delivery portal (SAS Solutions). (2003). SAS. Retrieved August 13, 2003, from www.sas.com/

Scherpenseel, C. (2003, July/August). Getting more from an ERP investment. *Financial Executive, 19,* 52-54.

Schroeder, J. (1999). Enterprise portals: A new business intelligence paradigm. *DM Review*. Retrieved August 11, 2003, from www.dmreview.com/

The SAP procurement insight package (SAP Solutions Brief). (2003). SAP. Retrieved August 15, 2003, from www.sap.com/

The SAP sales insight package (SAP Solutions Brief). (2003). SAP. Retrieved from www.sap.com/

Virtual close – A financial management solution (white paper). (2003). KPMG International. Retrieved August 15, 2003, from www.kpmg.com/

Zurell, N. (2002). Built for speed. *Intelligent Enterprise*. Retrieved August 16, 2003, from www.intelligententerprise.com/

Endnote

1 This section is based on Deshmukh, A. (2004). Virtual close: Problems and prospects. *Review of Business Information Systems*, *8*(4), 103-108.

Chapter IX

Financial Management, Strategic Management and Digital Accounting

Digital Accounting and Accounting Processes

A dominant trend in information technology is the convergence of different software functionalities. Even after the dot-com bust or, perhaps because of it, the convergence has gathered steam. Different tools and techniques get concentrated in one solution or software in a short duration. Distinct techniques and technologies, such as accounting software, Web-based businesses, supply chain management, data warehouses and artificial intelligence, are converging as the organizations move from ERP to ERP II, integration of internal functions to integration across supply chain, and the Internet to Internet 2. Today's ERP software packs all applications into one monster package and offers tremendous functionalities.

The Internet and ERP systems have created a strange amalgam of fragmentation and focus in accounting processes. Accounting processes are scattered across various xRM modules. Sales order and incoming payments can be handled in the CRM function, POs and invoices can be handled in the SRM function, and financial reports are available through enterprise portals. As such, accounting processes are not exactly centered in standard accounting modules. This effect is not uniform across organizations, but the movement of fragmentation of accounting has begun. Internal controls are also being moved with accounting processes, and we have seen numerous examples of this movement. On the other hand, due to data and information warehouses that store financial and non-financial information, accounting departments can have insights into the most remote corners of the organization. BI tools can be used to access data locked into different systems across the organization, empowering the accounting function.

These effects took us to the core accounting areas, as well as areas peripheral to accounting. Again, this is inevitable due to the convergence not only in Information Technology but also in organizational functions. This chapter is no exception. First, changes in the Treasury function due to the Internet and related technologies are explored. Treasury functions, such as cash and liquidity management, have changed due to new integrated tools, and make for a fascinating discussion. Second, the new subject of financial supply chain management is briefly reviewed. This area deals with changes in accounting and finance mainly due to the Internet, and neatly fits with the theme of this book. Third, the area of Corporate Performance Management (CPM) is reviewed. CPM pools all the new tools and technologies and puts a new spin on the ancient problems of strategy formulation, strategy execution, strategy monitoring and performance measurement. CPM is intimately connected with accounting and finance, and cannot be executed without appropriate financial tools and software. Financial supply chain and CPM highlight the emerging integrative and collaborative nature of the organization. Finally, a summary rounds off the chapter.

Exhibit 1. Whither accounting?

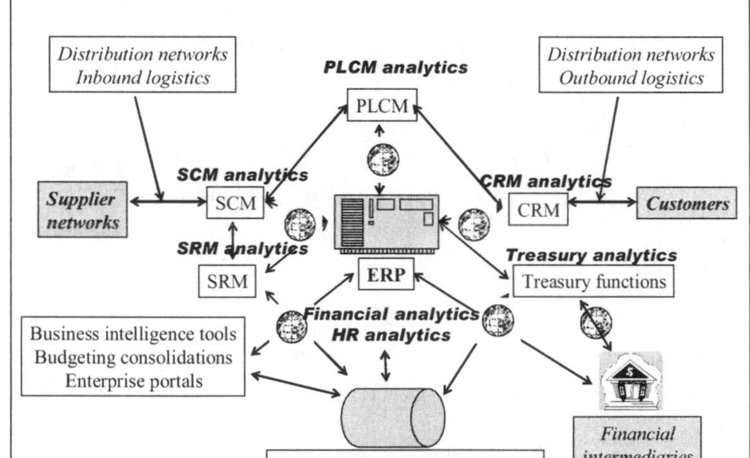

Corporate Treasury Functions

Corporate treasury functions include cash management, investment and debt management, financial risk management and investor relations. This is a catchall description, not an authoritative definition, and there is considerable overlap in these classifications. Treasury functions also deal with complex financial areas, such as foreign exchange rates, derivatives and interest rate swaps, among other things. Treasury functions also might differ between, say, a manufacturing firm and a bank. These treasury functions have changed due to Web-based tools and technologies. The pace of change is uneven; several years ago e-treasury or virtual treasury was projected to be a fait accompli for corporations. The penetration of Web-based tools has been slow; however, promised functionalities have begun to appear in most ERP packages. Independent vendors also are providing services such as electronic banking and trading market software. These areas are now briefly reviewed.

Cash management deals with liquidity management, payments and collections, and electronic banking, which are complementary areas. Liquidity management involves forecasting short-term and long-term fund requirements, arranging for financing, investing surpluses and maintaining a proper balance between assets and liabilities. The objective is to provide the required cash at minimum cost. Electronic banking, electronic lockboxes and electronic bank statements all are used to optimize liquidity. To forecast cash requirements, a detailed analysis of payments and collections also needs to be undertaken. As such, payments and collections are integral to liquidity management. Illustrative problems in liquidity management are summarized below.

- **Bank account management:** A large corporation can have a number of bank accounts spread across the globe. In this case, even obtaining a bank balance may take days.
- **Bank reconciliations:** Bank accounts need to be reconciled with the cash account to get a handle on cash transactions.
- **Payment and collections processing:** The schedule of payments and collections should be available for understanding future cash in and outflows. For multinational corporations, such data has to be collected from subsidiaries and consolidated for analysis.
- **Cash forecasts:** These include forecasts for subsidiaries and different units, and need to be consolidated into a central forecast. Time periods, such as short-term vs. long-term, need to be specified. Cash forecasting models need to be developed and vetted. These different forecasts can come in different file formats, and currency adjustments may be required. Also, cash flows may have to be appropriately classified; for example, committed, uncommitted, budgeted or financial.
- **Global problems:** Managing cash across various countries can pose problems, such as regulatory considerations, taxes, regional banking standards for minimum cash and vehicles available for investments and financing.

Exhibit 2. Treasury functions

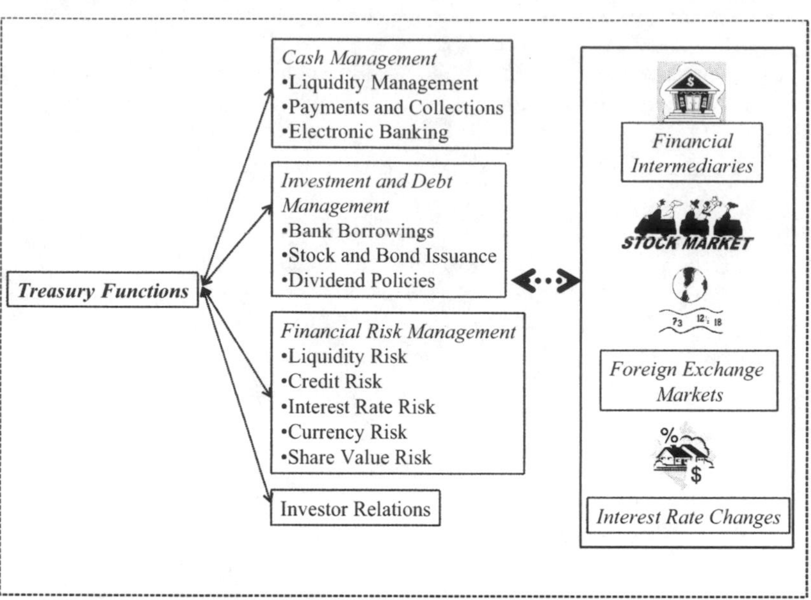

Investment and debt management deals with investments in marketable securities, issuance debt and security instruments, and sale and redemption of these instruments. These activities require access to stock market information, money markets, fixed-income securities markets, foreign exchange rates and derivatives. The treasurer also needs a view of market positions, ability to track, check and complete transactions, and back-end connections to the accounting system. Accounting standards such as Financial Accounting Standard (FAS) 133, FAS 138 and IAS 39, which provide authoritative guidance for measurement and valuation of transactions in these areas, need to be supported by accounting and treasury systems.

Risk management involves assessing liquidity, credit, interest rate, currency and stock market risks. Liquidity risk is the risk that the corporation will not be able to meet its short-term or long-term commitments. Assessing this risk is part of liquidity management. Treasury policy often specifies applicable credit rating criteria for third parties while investing in cash assets or making derivative contracts. Credit risk deals with the creditworthiness of business partners and, in the case of international transactions, may also include analysis of country risks. Interest rate risk deals with changes in the interest rate and interest margins and the consequent effects on financing costs, returns on investments and valuations of investments or debt. These changes need to be monitored and appropriate corrective actions need to be taken to minimize the risk. Currency risk is a risk that an organization's operations or an investment's value will be affected by changes in currency exchange rates. Currency risks are important for companies that derive revenues from other countries, since adverse changes in currency values can affect the bottom line. Currency and interest rate risks can be managed using different on- or off-balances sheet hedging strategies such as forwards, futures, swaps and trading strategies, among other things. Stock market risk is the risk that the market value will fluctuate and the portfolio of stocks held by the corporation will decline in value. Treasury functions may also include dealing with current and prospective investors and providing them with relevant and reliable information.

The software that manages the treasury functions, especially debt/investment and risk management, must deal with different activities — trading, back-office record keeping and accounting. Trading activities involve buying and selling of debt and security instruments. For risk management purposes, treasury often uses financial instruments such as options, futures, swaps and derivatives. As such, the trading activities involve evaluating offers, contracts, order, confirmation of orders and settlements of transactions. This front end must have access to debt, security and foreign exchange markets, and should receive information in real time. Back-office record-keeping activities involve completing the paperwork or electronic document work for purchases and sales of financial instruments, tracking various contracts, and maintaining historical and current data for all transactions. The accounting function includes recording all financial transactions in accordance with the GAAP, particularly FAS 133 and 138 in the U.S. and IAS 39 for countries following the IAS.

The preceding is a simplistic explanation of treasury functions, and these functions may vary based on industry and business. Our interest is in the Internet and Web-based tools that have evolved in this area. There is a profusion of software in this area, and most of the ERP vendors offer Web-based functionalities to a varying degree. To understand these functionalities, a Web-based treasury tool, eTreasury, and SAP CFM module are now reviewed.

SunGard Treasury System

SunGard Treasury System, a part of the SUNGARD group of companies, offers Web-based treasury management solutions. The core module in this solution is called eTreasury, and is supported by a number of complementary modules to support treasury functions. eTreasury provides consolidation abilities for intra-corporate units and interfacing ability with general ledger. A complementary product eTreasury Exchange, on the other hand, provides integration with markets and connects trade and reporting systems with corporate treasury management systems. These solutions are available on the web or as software to be installed on the corporate network.

eTreasury enables use of the Internet to manage cash, debt and investments. Cash management services include automatic consolidation of bank balances and transactions, details of cash on hand via cash worksheets and reconciliation of expected vs. actual cash transactions. The data-entry screens available on the workstation or browser ease entries for bank transactions and wire transfer requests. Debt management services include automatic calculation of interest rates and tracking of fixed and floating rate debt instruments, such as lines of credit, notes and intra-company loans. Current market positions and historical activity can be observed, and forecasts can be generated. Investment management functionalities are similar to the debt management services. Supported investment functionalities include automatic calculation of interest; tracking of fixed and floating rate investments, such as money market accounts, bonds and government issues; and viewing of market positions and historical activity. Analytical tools include online inquiries, drill-down abilities and reporting tools. Analytical tools have pre-packaged and user-defined reporting functionalities.

The modules that support eTreasury are now described. Not all companies require full-fledged treasury functionalities, and the required modules can be selectively installed. These modules have many overlapping functionalities and can be used in isolation or in combination with other modules.

- **Advanced Portfolio Systems 2 (APS 2):** APS 2 is an investment management product aimed at the financial services industry. Functionalities include securities tracking, regulatory compliance and reporting tools. Additional modules provide extra functionalities, such as cash flow, fund accounting, bank polling — connecting to different financial institutions for obtaining balance and transaction information — and investment swap analysis. APS 2 also provides an interface to connect with general ledger, vendors and accounting systems.
- **Global Treasury and Risk Management System (GTM):** This module is aimed at mid- to large-sized corporations and medium-sized financial institutions. Trading and risk management for currency, commodity and interest rates is supported by this module. Accounting standards such as FAS 133 or 138 also are supported by this module.
- **ICMS/TS treasury system:** This module manages daily cash transactions and in-house banking, and debt, investment and foreign exchange transactions. Collaborative tools, such as access to e-mail and the Web, also are included in this module.
- **Quantum™:** This module provides an integrated treasury environment for cash management, accounting and risk management, and pricing models for commonly traded instruments.
- **ResourceIQ²:** This module is aimed at corporations and governments. It can be used to manage cash positions, investments, debts, in-house banking, foreign exchange and fund accounting. A subsidiary ledger to account for treasury transactions can be created. This subsidiary ledger can be integrated with a general ledger or accounts payable ledger.
- **QRisk:** This module provides risk management and performance measurement for derivatives. Deals can be priced and captured using the software, query engines can be used to analyze deals, and historical data is stored in databases. Data can be drilled down or downloaded to Excel or Crystal Reports for further analysis.

These modules access external data by using eTreasury Exchange (eTX). eTX provides the following real-time connections.

- With banks for cash balances, prior-day debits and credits, current-day debits and credits and EFT requests

Exhibit 3. SunGard eTreasury modules

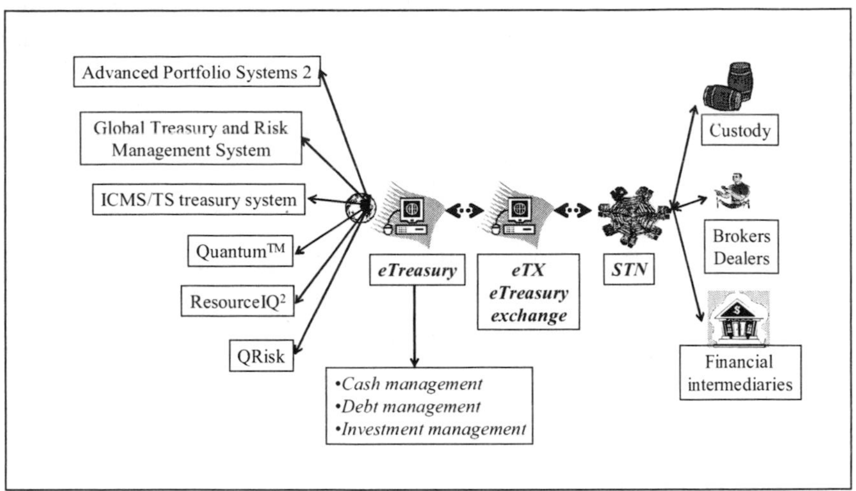

- With fund managers and brokers/dealers for price requests, trade requests, trade acknowledgment and confirmations, and position updates
- With markets for foreign exchange rates and security prices

eTX real-time connections with banks, financial institutions, and stock and foreign exchange markets enable *Straight-Through Processing (STP)*, which became a treasury buzzword several years ago. STP means automation of the entire trade cycle — authorize, request, confirm and settle. The trade process is standardized and automated. Most other treasury packages support STP. eTX provides appropriate security mechanisms to ensure generation and delivery of electronic documents to the required financial institution along with processing instructions. SunGard has developed SunGard Transaction Network (STN), which is Internet-enabled and handles NASDAQ transactions and other forms of financial market transactions. eTX uses this network to gather and disseminate information, and support functionalities of eTreasury.

SAP CFM Tools

SAP CFM is considered a comprehensive solution and can be used by large corporations and financial institutions. For funds management, SAP offers cash management, loans management, liquidity planner and in-house cash modules. Please note that the terminology used by SAP is slightly different than terminology used earlier. Risk management capabilities include three analyzers — portfolio analyzer, market risk analyzer and credit risk analyzer. Transaction manager connects front-end trading activities with back-end accounting and is the nexus of SAP CFM. These modules run on top of the SAP ERP system and are integrated with accounting and treasury modules.

The cash management module provides abilities to monitor incoming and outgoing cash flows. This module supports importing of electronic bank statements in various formats, posting and processing of bank statements, automatic bank reconciliations and conversion programs for special electronic bank formats. Other functionalities include monitoring electronic lockboxes, electronic check deposits, bank polling, presentation of bills of exchange at programmed intervals and cash payments. Financial planning in the cash management module deals with cash concentration — consolidating cash from various bank accounts to the required bank account — rule-based automatic payments and rule-based bill of exchange presentations. To summarize, this module receives data from sales, distribution and finance, and handles cash reporting, bank interfacing, transaction posting and period-end closing activities.

The loans management module manages the entire loan process from initiation through posting entries to the accounting module. The loans, such as mortgage loans, borrower's notes, policy loans and general loans can be handled in this module. Initial data, such as potential contacts, contract information, analysis of interest and repayment terms, calculated credit standing and required collateral, among other things, can be managed and entered via standardized screens. Position management functions in this module can be used to process existing contracts, change existing contracts or automatically rollover the loans. Accounting entries for loans can be maintained in the subledger and then transferred to the general ledger, either automatically or manually. Reporting tools in the module can be used to monitor deadlines and calculate interest and repayment of loans for cash flow purposes.

Exhibit 4. A conceptual schema for SAP CFM

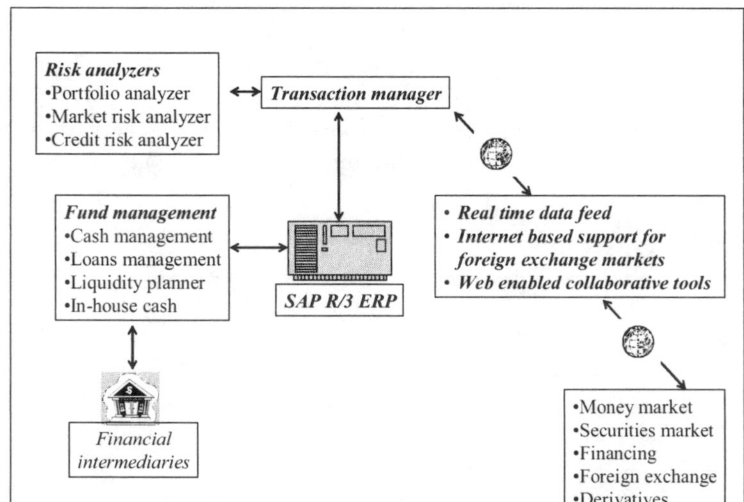

The liquidity planner aims to improve cash flow planning and the internal and external payments process. This planner can be used for short-term and long-term liquidity planning. Data entry and time schedules can be entered using standardized templates, which can be centrally administered for security purposes. Data can be captured from central databases and databases of subsidiaries and other business units. The planner can be used to aggregate data from different businesses, compare current data with historical data, and forward results and analyses to managers. Liquidity planner has workflow features that can be used to simplify entry, aggregation and reporting of liquidity and cash flow data.

SAP in-house cash, a Web-enabled tool, serves as an in-house virtual bank that can be used to manage intercompany transactions, transfer of funds to subsidiaries and payments to external partners. Cash information from subsidiaries, corporate headquarters and banking networks is centralized and monitored. Policies such as tolerated overdraft by subsidiaries, cash concentration and balance notification can be set at this central location. Using these policies, the internal payments between subsidiaries, central payments — settlement of subsidiary dues using in-house cash center — and central incoming payments where customers of subsidiaries pay to the in-house cash center, can be automated and monitored. The illustrative functionalities of this module are given below.

- Calculation of interest and other charges and posting
- Analyzing and granting current account overdrafts to subsidiaries
- Generating bank statements for subsidiaries
- Automation of intra-group payment transactions
- Automation of cash payments and cash receipts from external parties
- Transferring funds to subsidiaries

The in-house cash module is integrated with the financial accounting module. For example, cash payments are initiated using the payments program in the accounting module, or electronic bank statement information can be imported from the accounting module. This module can also be used to anticipate and manage cash crunches, reduce netting process times, reduce bank transfers and bank charges, manage currency exchange losses, decrease physical cash transfers and reduce administrative overhead.

Risk analyzers aid in managing risk associated with financial instruments — portfolio, market and credit risk — and also provide decision support systems. Portfolio analyzer calculates actual performance of the investments. This return is then compared with the targeted or budgeted return. Portfolio analyzer can break down the performance portfolio to the individual component level for control and evaluation purposes. The functionalities of this analyzer are as follows.

- Making yield calculations
- Reporting risk and yield figures

- Supporting portfolio hierarchies
- Handling portfolio audits

Market risk analyzer manages risks associated with the stock market, foreign currency holdings and fluctuations in interest rates. Stock market positions such as mark-to-market valuations can be evaluated using the built-in tools. Different calculations, such as risk and return, exposure, future values and value at risk, can be calculated using this analyzer. Accounting standards such as FAS 133 are supported. Simulation tools can be used to run valuation scenarios based on actual and simulated market prices. These tools can also be used to simulate changes in interest and currency exchange rates and run hypothetical valuation scenarios. Market risk analyzer also accesses payment information from the transaction manager, and calculates amount and due dates for payments in different currencies. This information can then be used in hedging activities to manage foreign currency exposure. Reporting tools can be used to generate graphical or tabular reports.

Credit risk is considered to be a default risk in the SAP CFM. SAP defines default risk as a risk that refers to possible loss arising from a financial transaction should the business partner not fulfill his/her contractual obligations due to economic or political reasons. Credit risks involved in treasury functions extend to the individual party — a corporation, or may extend to the country (country risk). The mechanisms of assessing credit risk — that is, decline in the creditworthiness of a business partner — in SAP CFM are similar to the Web-based methods seen in the revenue cycle. Country risk deals with getting payments from a country that has become insolvent or bankrupt, or has political problems in releasing payments. Credit risk analyzer provides the following functionalities for managing these risks.

- Online credit checks
- Setting enterprise-wide credit limits
- Managing credit limits
- Providing formulas for calculating credit exposures
- Assessing country-specific risks
- Supporting netting and collateral agreements

Transaction manager connects to all modules in SAP CFM — risk management tools, fund management tools, the financial accounting module and online sources of information. Transaction manager supports the front-end activities of trading and transactions and can transfer those transactions to the financial accounting module. Additionally, automation and workflow facilities in the transaction manager can be used to streamline business processes, and the reporting and evaluation tools can be used to analyze financial transactions, positions and portfolios. Transaction manager standardizes data entry, as well as monitoring, processing and posting of transactions across different modules and different financial instruments. SAP claims that such standardization enables STP, which is demanded by a number of users.

Transaction manager supports transaction handling for multiple financial instruments in money markets, securities markets and foreign exchange markets. Managing risks — stock market, interest rate or foreign currency — requires different strategies. Transaction manager can be used to configure these strategies based on the product types for each organization. Transaction manager manages the following functions:

- **Trading area:** This area supports tools that can be used by traders in optimizing trading. Here, offers can be entered and evaluated, and common transactions can be automated. Additionally, order limit checks, date checks, and expiration and barrier checks for options are provided. Financial calculators that calculate, for example, option price and Net Present Value (NPV) are also included. This is the front end for trading.
- **Back office:** In this area, details for transactions, such as account assignments and payment information, can be entered. Orders can be confirmed and counter-confirmed — automatically or otherwise — and securities accounts can be managed.
- **Accounting:** Transaction data can be automatically transferred and the general ledger can be updated. This area also supports processing of payment transactions, valuation procedures and accrual/deferral procedures.
- **Internal Controls:** User authorizations can enforce separation of duties in trading, back office and accounting areas. User activities are logged and monitored to enforce user authorizations. Other software-specific control functions are designed to satisfy requirements of financial accounting and treasury, which are not discussed here.

Exhibit 5. Components of transaction manager

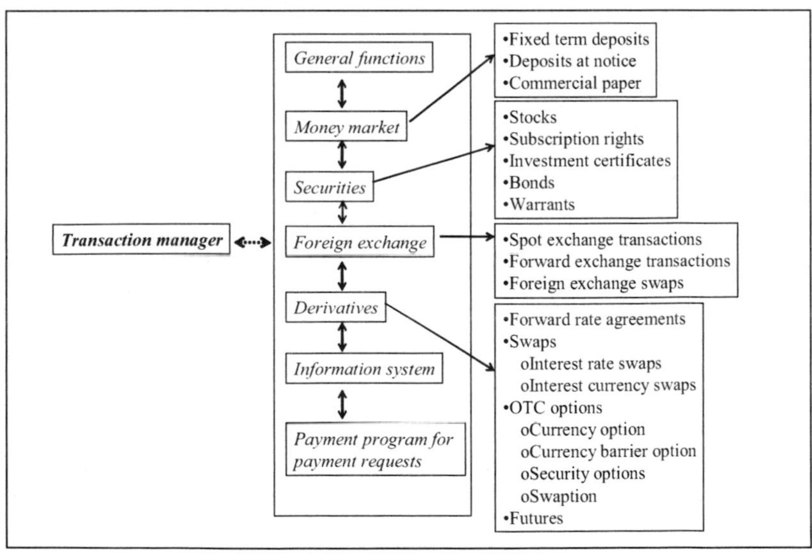

Transaction manager can receive real-time data from designated information providers. The incoming information can come from stock markets, foreign currency markets and financial analysts. Using real-time data, historical databases and analytical tools; transaction manager can be used to manage risks and the trading process. Transaction manager can connect with risk analyzers and funds management components for real-time exchange of information. SAP CFM is also equipped with Web-based collaborative tools to facilitate treasury functions. SAP CFM is capable of meeting strategic and operational treasury management, as per most ERP analysts.

We have reviewed two treasury management solutions. However, a number of vendors offer treasury management solutions, and most leading vendors offer similar functionalities. As with Internet-based tools, the promise and hype of treasury solutions far exceeded the benefits offered by such software. Surveys done a few years earlier of CFOs and treasurers indicated that they believed that the Internet will substantially change the treasury function. The treasury function is indeed changing, but in an evolutionary manner. Again, practical problems involved in installing and operationalizing these systems are not discussed here. There is precious little research in this area, and even anecdotal evidence is hard to come by.

Financial Supply Chain

Accounting and finance departments have always strived to improve the management of cash flows, reduce working capital and financing costs, track long-term indicators of solvency and contain transaction-processing costs. However, the centralized accounting function, due to intra- and inter-enterprise collaboration and integration, is no longer centralized in many organizations. Accounting processes are handled by different pieces of software, costs are not only internal but also spread across the supply chain and accounting information is contained not only in the general ledger but also is scattered in data, information and knowledge warehouses. These changes pose new challenges in dealing with old problems and offer new solutions for the same problems.

The financial supply chain, also referred to as financial value chain, is the new area emerging to deal with the new financial processes. This term has been around for at least a decade, though consultants and software vendors have put a new spin on it. Now, the area of financial supply chain, similar to SCM, has multiple interpretations, multiple perspectives and no single departmental owner. Aberdeen Group defines financial value chain as follows: *"A range of B2B, trade-related, intra- and inter-enterprise, financial transaction-based functions and processes"* (*Best practices in streamlining the financial value chain*, 2002, *www.aberdeen.com*). Killen & Associates Inc. categorizes all the services provided by financial supply chain into three categories: *"performance measurement and control, decision support and transaction processing"* (*Optimizing the financial supply chain*, 2002, *www.killen.com*). SAP, on the other hand, includes *"order-to-cash, purchase-to-pay, bank processes and relationship management, and cash management"* (*mySAP Financials: Next generation integration*, 2003, *www.sap.com*) as four processes in the financial supply chain management.

Exhibit 6. Financial supply chain

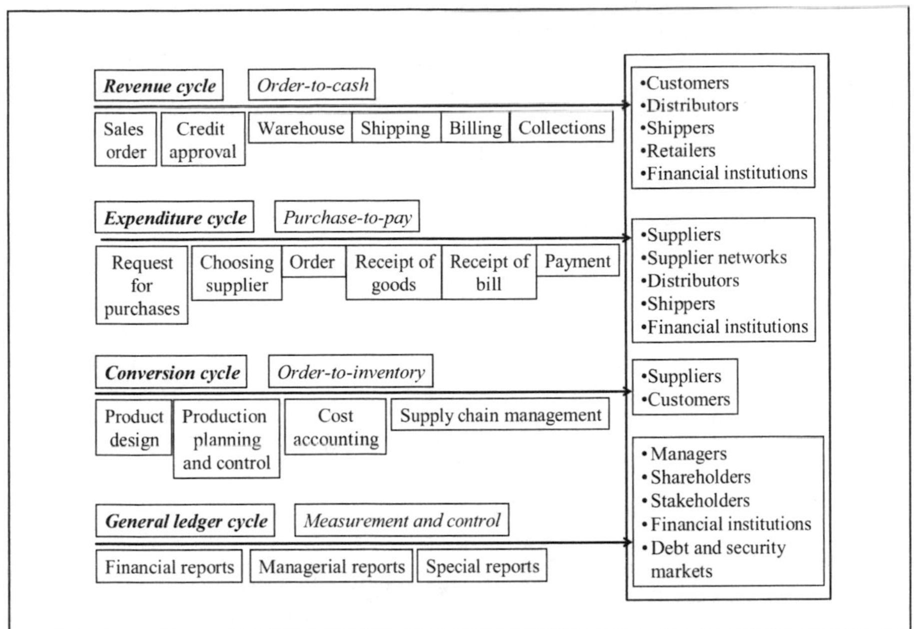

These definitions evidently cover all aspects of accounting and finance. Functionalities explored, from the revenue cycle to treasury functions seen in the last section, fall under the gamut of financial supply chain. Problems encountered by accounting departments in identifying costs, let alone controlling those costs, are formidable. Illustrative internal problems include disparate ERP systems, lack of consolidation and budgeting software, patchwork of add-on modules and absence of an organizational strategy. External problems may include establishing relationships with suppliers and customers, banking relationships, lack of access to real-time data and managing funds in an uncertain external environment. A number of these problems were reviewed earlier in the book.

Financial supply chain management tools are available, though a concerted strategy to employ those tools for optimizing financial supply chain is missing in most organizations. Aberdeen Group forecasts that optimization of financial supply chain can result in substantial savings. The savings forecasts for a *billion*-dollar company are as follows.

- Reduction in working capital by 20% to 25%
- Reduction in financing costs by $4 million per year
- Proactive warnings for delayed receivables and reduction in Days Sales Outstanding (DSOs)
- Approximately $13 million savings from transaction processing costs

According to another estimate, the cost to finance products moving through the supply chain is approximately $360 billion, or 4% GDP. If these forecasts are correct, then major corporations can achieve billions of dollars in savings by optimizing financial supply chain. But, how does a corporation optimize the financial supply chain?

Solutions offered by consultants and software vendors primarily revolve around the new tools seen so far. Suggested tools can be classified into three categories: ERP systems to integrate internal functions, Web-based tools to facilitate free flow of information with trading partners, and hybrid tools that use functionalities of ERP and the Internet. Due to the convergence of software tools, no distinction in these categories was made in this book. However, most of the tools and software that we have seen is from the second and third category. A summary of these tools for each cycle is provided.

- **Revenue cycle**
  - *CRM*
  - *Online credit checks*
  - *Web-enabled WMS for order fulfillment*
  - *Web-based tracking of shipments*
  - *Electronic invoice (bill) presentment and payment*
  - *Online management of receivables*
  - *Web-based cash collection and payment methods*
- **Expenditure cycle**
  - *SRM tools*
  - *Procurement cards*
  - *Employee self-service features*
  - *Online management of expenses*
  - *Online management of assets*
- **Conversion cycle**
  - *Supply chain planning tools*
  - *Supply chain execution tools*
  - *Supply chain collaboration tools*
  - *Supply chain coordination tools*
- **General ledger cycle**
  - *Technical and managerial requirements for virtual close*
  - *BI tools*
  - *Planning and budgeting solutions*
  - *Enterprise portals*
- **Treasury functions**
  - *Cash and liquidity management tools*
  - *Debt and investment management tools*
  - *Risk evaluation tools*

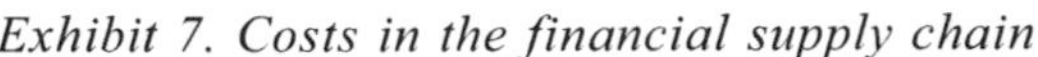
Exhibit 7. Costs in the financial supply chain

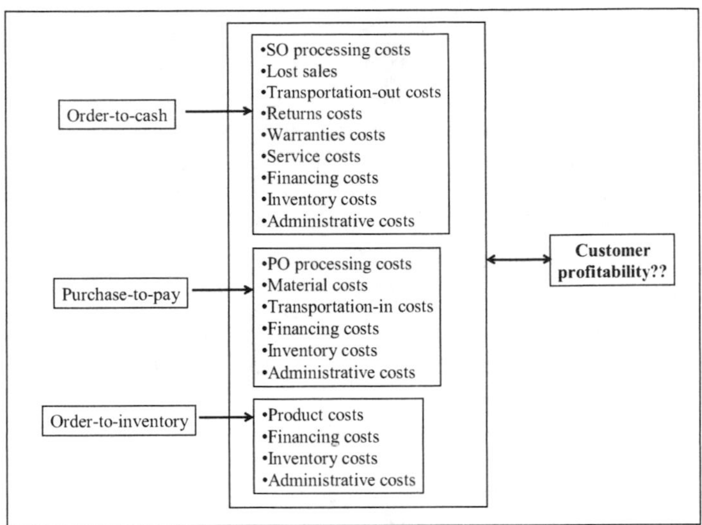

Financial supply chain management aims to reduce costs in financial management, transaction processing and financial reporting. Financial supply chain is optimized by automating, outsourcing Web enabling and rationalizing financial workflows and business processes. The tools to achieve these objectives are available. However, the cost-effectiveness and efficacy of these tools is not proven. The optimal investment in information technology for financial supply chain management is a difficult question to answer, and the answers are probably unique for each organization. It seems that consultants and software vendors will thrive in this area for a while!

Corporate Performance Management

So far, a number of philosophies and tools that manage a variety of business processes were explored; for example, ERP, CRM, SRM, SCM, BI, treasury management, and planning and budgeting software. These tools and techniques are devised to solve pressing business problems. CRM software handles customer-centric functions and provides a platform to coordinate and execute customer-related strategies and activities. SRM handles supplier relationships, SCM handles collaboration across the supply chain, and BI tools provide desired measurements. So what is the problem? The problem is how to coordinate these different techniques to ensure that corporate strategy and direction set by top management is being consistently followed. How do you provide assurance that these different initiatives are optimizing profits for the entire enterprise? Corporate strategy has to be linked with performance measures, which should be communicated to responsible managers at desired intervals and, if required, corrective action should be taken.

Enter Corporate Performance Management (CPM). CPM is neither a brand new concept nor a new suite of software modules. CPM builds on the tools seen earlier and integrates them as a cohesive methodology to manage corporate strategy, at least that how it is being sold! CPM bridges the gap between corporate strategy and different software tools and management techniques, and provides a way to steer the entire enterprise. This area has spawned numerous acronyms, such as corporate performance measurement, Enterprise Performance Management (EPM), Business Performance Measurement (BPM) and Strategic Enterprise Management (SEM). As usual, there is no unanimity in the definitions; though the description of the CPM process is fairly standard.

The CPM process consists of seven steps: strategy formulation, scenario analysis, planning and budgeting, communication, monitoring, forecasting and reporting. Strategy formulation is carried out at the top management level. This is an iterative process and different scenarios are analyzed from different angles to select a set of strategies. These strategies are converted into operational plans and financial budgets. The planning and budgeting process needs to be speedy and flexible to be useful. Key performance measures are designed for each area, and the budgets and performance measures are communicated to all levels. As the strategic execution unfolds, performance measures are monitored and forecast of future results is derived based on existing trends. Performance measures are communicated to all levels and corrective action, if required, is taken. This process is probably at least a century old; so, why the sudden interest? The technology tools now have developed to such an extent that an effective implementation of this process is possible.

Exhibit 8. CPM process and information technology tools

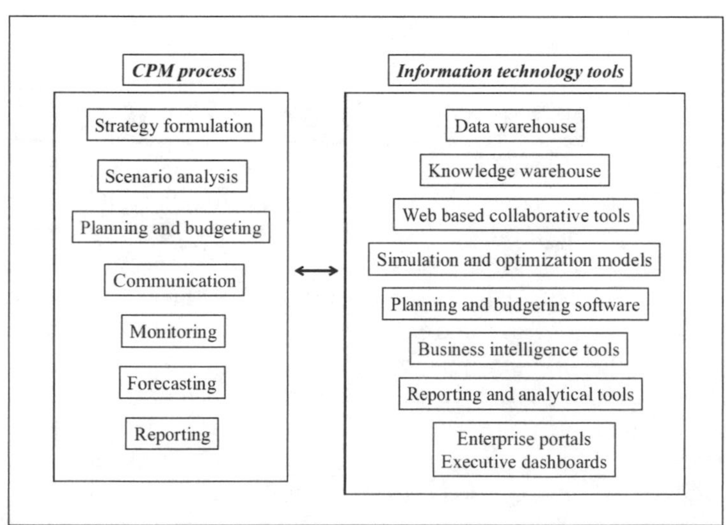

The technology tools required for the CPM process are data warehouse, knowledge warehouse, Web-based collaborative tools, simulation and optimization models, planning and budgeting software, business intelligence tools, reporting and analytical tools, and enterprise portals. These tools have been around for some time, and the applications of these tools have been investigated at various places in this book. However, what has changed is the ability of these tools to talk and work together. ERP integrated internal functions, CRM/SCM/SRM has extended the integration across the supply chain and BI tools can extract and deliver the information across the organizations. Bring these tools together, tie in the strategy formulation via performance measures, and we have CPM. This, of course, is a simplistic description, and the practical problems inherent in such effort are not discussed here. Now, SAP SEM tools are reviewed to get an idea as to how the CPM process might work in the real world.

SAP SEM Tools

SAP offers a set of SEM tools, which is integrated software that addresses areas identified in the methodology of CPM. This set of tools operates on top of the following SAP components: business information warehouse, knowledge warehouse, exchange infrastructure and enterprise portals. These are common components to most mySAP functionalities and have been discussed in earlier chapters. SAP says that SEM tools can also be used as a stand-alone application or can interface with an existing third-party warehouse. The core components of SAP SEM are SEM Business Planning and Simulation (BPS), SEM Business Consolidation (BCS), SEM Corporate Performance Monitor (CPM), SEM Business Information Collection (BIC), and SEM Stakeholder Relationship Management (SRM). The SAP white paper, *Translating Strategy into Action* (2003), enumerates the following functions of SEM tools.

- *"Structure your strategy (strategy map or balanced scorecard)*
- *Communicate your goals throughout the entire organization and to stakeholders*
- *Value your strategy through scenario planning and activity-based planning*
- *Link strategy with operative targets and resource allocation*
- *Support integrated planning, budgeting and forecasting process*
- *Collect unstructured information from external and internal sources*
- *Consolidate actuals*
- *Monitor the performance of strategic key success factors using external and internal benchmarks — either online or in the management cockpit room*
- *Communicate your strategy and performance to major stakeholders and collect feedback."*

SEM BPS supports strategy formulation and planning functions. The modeling techniques can be used to model linear relationships, non-linear relationships, competitor

Exhibit 9. A conceptual schema for SAP SEM tools

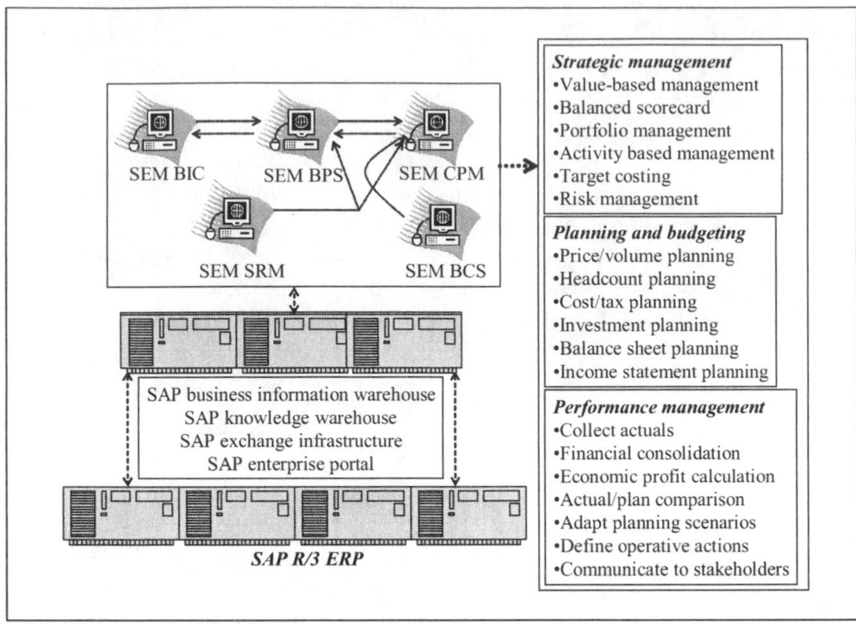

behavior and risk assessment, among other things. Illustrative simulation abilities include changes in assumptions of the plan; running of multiple scenarios; factoring in changes in external variables, such as economic growth; and incorporating of analysts' reports. Strategy scenarios can be created for worst case, best case or most likely case; probabilities can be assigned to different scenarios; and Monte Carlo simulations can be performed on required strategies. These strategy models can be optimized and analyzed for different levels of risk by using *Powersim Solver*, a powerful optimizing tool. The collaborative aspects of strategy formulation are supported by Web-based and browser-based access to these tools, management cockpit and what-if analyses functionalities. Results can be displayed in the management cockpit (SAP's version of executive dashboard), and the management team can run simulation scenarios on these results in real time.

The different planning techniques, such as top-down planning, bottom-up planning, hybrid of top-down and bottom-up planning, decentralized or distributed planning, and rolling forecasts, are supported in the SEM BPS. A user can develop customized planning methods and models and can also store those models. The plan data can be modified using techniques such as revaluation, percentage revaluation and transfer of data from other sources. The plan data can be generated using trend analysis or other statistical forecasting techniques. This data can be allocated using top-down allocations or can be consolidated. Revised or new plan data need to be posted only once to update the entire plan. The user interface for strategy and planning functions is customizable; for example, rows and columns, graphs, gauges and dials, or other data presentation techniques, which are supported for wider user acceptance.

Exhibit 10. Planning functions in SEM BPS

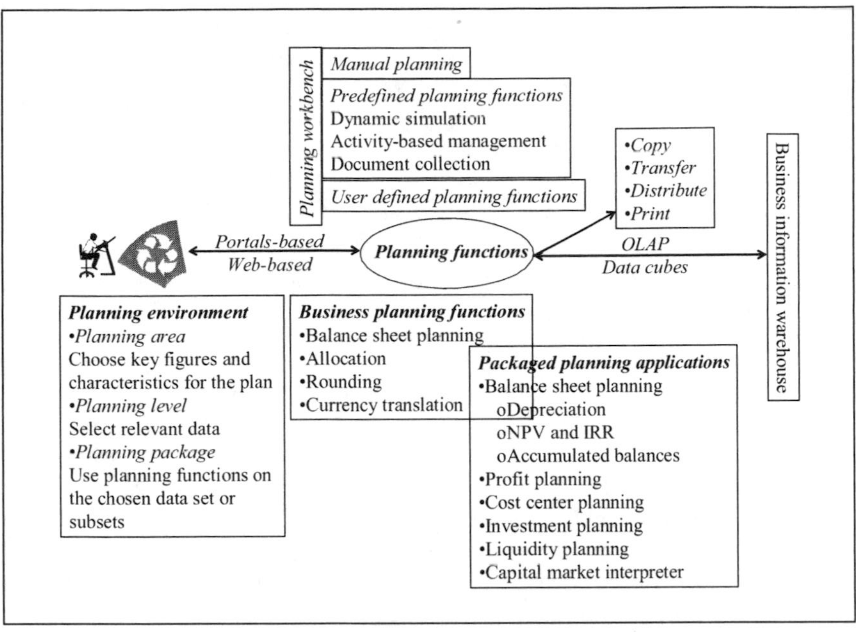

Exhibit 11. Information collection in SEM BIC

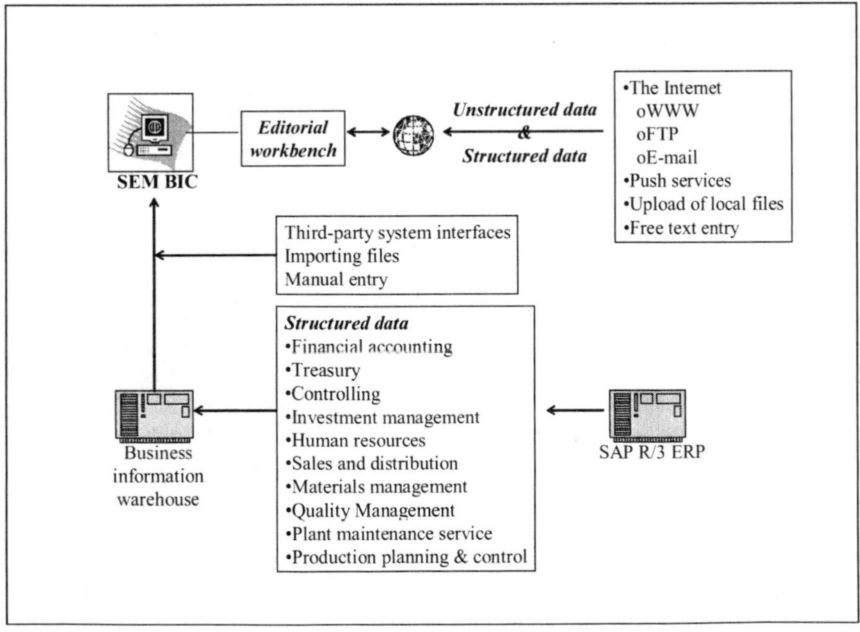

SEM BPS can also be used to create budgets or financial plans, such as sales and profit plans, financial budgets and balance sheet plans for different business units and for the entire organization. Examples of pre-packaged plans include quantity and sales planning, material requirements planning, cost planning, headcount planning, capacity planning, profit-and-loss planning and balance sheet planning. SEM BPS also comes with a function called capital market interpreter. Capital market expectations are revealed through current stock price, buy and sell recommendations by the stock brokers and financial analysts' reports, to mention a few sources. Capital market interpreter accepts these expectation inputs and forecasts financial numbers and key value drivers to meet market expectations. Activity-Based Management (ABM) activities, such as resource modeling, activity modeling, cost object modeling, budgeting and planning, simulation and decision support are also supported by SEM BPS.

Strategy formulation and planning functions need access to data and information. SEM BIC collects structured and unstructured information from internal and external sources. The structured data from different functional areas of the organization can be collected from the underlying ERP system via data extractors. SEM BIC is integrated with the SAP R/3 system; however, it also comes with third-party ERP interfaces, file uploading capabilities and even the ability to manually enter data. Unstructured information generally comes from external sources; for example, business databases, expert opinions and reports, conference papers, discussion forums and analysts' reports. A large portion of this information can be accessed using the Internet. SEM BIC comes with an editorial workbench, which is used to collect and organize information collected from the Internet and other sources. Editorial workbench can be used to store numerical, textual or multimedia information, or to point to such information. This information is then linked

Exhibit 12. SEM CPM for performance measurement

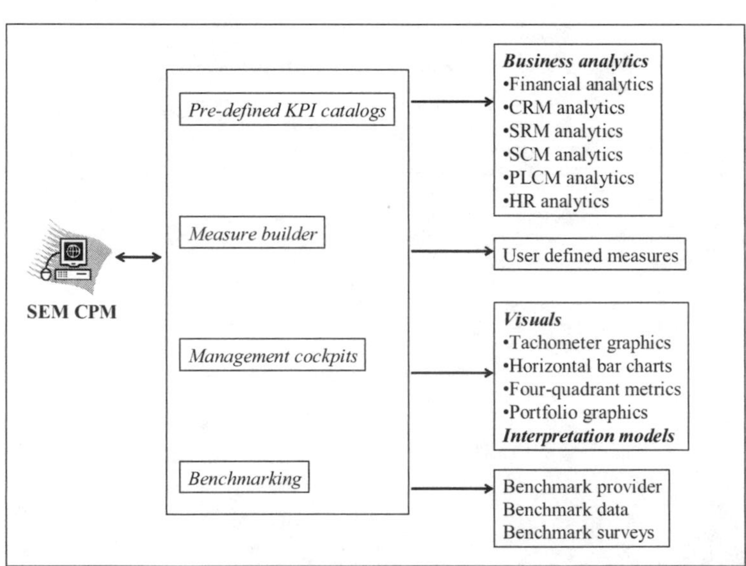

with SEM BIC; for example, a sales estimate from the broker's report can be linked with actual sales figures for the same period. Users can also post queries to the workbench and such queries can be answered using existing information, or a search to identify relevant information may be initiated. Currently, research is going on regarding automatic collection, indexing and linking of information from external sources.

Information collection and strategy/plan formulation are followed by strategy execution. There are severe problems in connecting strategy with operational measures. For example, if top management decides that shareholder value will be the guiding principle in conducting business affairs, how do you explain this measure to other stakeholders and how do you measure whether the organization is working toward maximizing shareholder value? There are two parts to this problem: the first is to design appropriate key performance indicators, and the second is to make those available to stakeholders for continuous monitoring and corrective action. SEM CPM helps in designing, displaying and disseminating key performance indicators and operational indicators. The functionalities of SEM CPM are described below.

- **Pre-defined KPI catalogs:** Approximately 200 pre-packaged financial and non-financial measures exist. These measures span all functional areas of business, such as accounting, finance, sales and distribution, production and human resources. Collaborative areas, such as CRM, SCM and SRM, are also covered. Industry-specific KPI templates are also available.
- **Measure builders:** This function can be used to generate user-defined KPIs. Existing KPIs can be modified, or entirely new ones can be created.
- **Management cockpits:** These cockpits are similar to executive dashboards and enterprise portals, though aimed at management. The KPIs can be displayed numerically or visually. Visual representation includes graphics, such as bar and pie charts, gauges and dials, or matrix format. KPIs displayed depend on the user level; for example, KPIs displayed for the CEO will be different than those for the plant manager.

  There are a number of interpretation models to aid understanding of KPIs. For example, KPI figure trees reveal individual values and mathematical relationships in the KPIs and also enable sensitivity analyses by changing those values and relationships. KPI driver trees, on the other hand, display causal relationships between measures. Balanced scorecards are also supported at this level. Industry-specific, balanced scorecards can highlight strategic themes, strategic objectives, KPIs and causal relationships between strategic objectives.
- **Benchmarking:** This function helps in selecting a benchmark provider, accessing benchmark data and participating in benchmarking surveys, which is useful for organizations involved in benchmarking efforts.

Consolidation abilities are useful in closing of the books and generating financial reports. SEM BCS can be used to perform legal consolidations and user-defined consolidations across desired dimensions. Since SAP software is used by large corporations, SEM BCS supports U.S., international and country-specific GAAP requirements. Different charts of accounts that support different GAAP requirements are built into the software. User-defined consolidations can be carried out across world zone, country, division, strategic business units or profit centers. SEM BCS can also be used to consolidate actual and budgeted figures, carry out simulations, say, for different currency exchange rates, and generate reports.

SEM SRM is used to manage stakeholders of the corporation and can include stockholders, employees, customers, suppliers, partners, federal/state/local governments and the general public. SRM involves understanding stakeholder expectations, evaluating appropriateness of such expectations, incorporating appropriate expectations in corporate strategy, devising and monitoring performance measures and communicating those measures to stakeholders to close the loop. SEM SRM comes with the following functionalities to manage stakeholders.

- **Stakeholder map/Relevance matrix:** This tool can be used to map different types of stakeholders, objectives and interests of stakeholders, power of the stakeholders to influence the corporation and risks posed by each group.
- **Stakeholder questionnaire generator:** This function can be used to design surveys to assess stakeholder expectations and interests, automate delivery and acceptance of forms, and automate statistical analysis.
- **Stakeholder database:** This database contains information regarding stakeholder groups, such as expectations, interests and power structure; and individual stakeholders, such as name and contact information.
- **Stakeholder value proposition modeling:** This tool can be used to develop models of stakeholder relationships and similarities and differences in their expectations. These models can be mathematically optimized for deciding the course of action.
- **Stakeholder communication processor:** This processor enables two-way communication with stakeholders via print, fax, telephone, Web and e-mail.
- **Stakeholder report builder:** This report-generation tool can be used to generate various reports targeted at different stakeholder groups.

This is a nutshell description of SAP SEM tools. A closer look at these tools will reveal a strong connection with accounting and finance functions. Accounting functions, such as financial consolidation and reporting, budgeting and planning, financial performance measures, and even closing of the books, are closely connected with effective CPM. It is also instructive to note that SAP SEM tools are marketed as a part of *mySAP Financials* and integrated with FI, CO and Treasury models. Aberdeen Group's white paper, *The Financial Implications of Corporate Performance Management*, states that the primary role of accounting in CPM is to provide the answer to the question: *How far along the way are we*? Remember, measurement of strategies, plans, and initiatives must be linked with financial objectives. As it is often said, you get what you measure.

Summary

This chapter completes coverage of digital accounting by reviewing treasury functions, financial supply chain and CPM. The introduction reiterates changes in accounting due to the Internet and ERP. Accounting processes are scattered across various modules and can even be handled by customers and suppliers. At the same time, data and information warehouses have centralized financial and non-financial information, allowing insights into nooks and crannies of the organization. BI tools can be employed for controlling accounting processes, such as consolidations, planning and budgeting, and report generation.

Treasury functions, such as cash management, investment and debt management, and financial risk management, have changed considerably due to Web-based tools. The primary advantage is access to real-time information from across the globe. Such information can be leveraged to effectively manage the treasury function. Two tools — SunGard Treasury tools and SAP CFM — were reviewed. These software tools facilitate front-end trading by accessing real-time market information, transaction and document management, and automated back-end accounting functions. Accounting standards, such as FAS 133 and 138, are supported by most of these treasury tools.

Financial supply chain or financial value chain is a new term that refers to the management of financial functions across the enterprise and even beyond for cash management and cost reductions. Billions of dollars of savings have been forecasted for corporations that effectively manage their financial supply chain. Financial supply chain concepts are similar to the theme of this book. Proposed financial supply chain tools can be classified into three categories: ERP systems to integrate internal functions, Web-based tools to facilitate free flow of information with partners, and hybrid tools that use functionalities of the Internet and ERP. A number of these tools were explored in earlier chapters.

Finally, the topic of CPM was reviewed. The CPM process consists of seven steps: strategy formulation, scenario analysis, planning and budgeting, communication, monitoring, forecasting and reporting. This is not a new process; however, an effective implementation of this process is now possible due to advances in Information Technology. CPM packages different technology tools, such as ERP systems, CRM, SCM and SRM, to name a few, and uses business intelligence tools to extract and deliver performance measures across the organization. The SAP SEM solution and its support for CPM were explored in-depth. However, do not confuse the availability of functionalities with the successful implementation of the software, which is another story, not covered in this book.

References

Banham, R. (2003, March). *Performance* is its middle name – Can new software help companies link past, present, and future? *CFO*. Retrieved September 3, 2003, from www.cfo.com/

Best practices in streamlining the financial value chain. (2002). *The abridged report.* Boston: Aberdeen Group. Retrieved from www.aberdeen.com/

Beyond budgeting (white paper). (2003). SAP. Retrieved September 5, 2003, from www.sap.com/

Corporate finance management with mySAP Financials (SAP Solutions Brief). (2003). SAP. Retrieved September 5, 2003, from www.sap.com/

Crane, A. (2003). Actionable e-metrics. *Intelligent Enterprise*. Retrieved September 6, 2003, from http://intelligententerprise.com/

Empowering finance for e-business (white paper). (2003). SAP. Retrieved September 7, 2003, from www.sap.com/

Enterprise performance management (white paper). (2003). Business Objects. Retrieved September 7, 2003, from www.businessobjects.com/

Financial supply chain management with mySAP financials: Biller direct (SAP Technical Brief). (2003). SAP. Retrieved September 8, 2003, from www.sap.com/

Financial supply chain management with SAP in-house cash (SAP Financials Brief). (2003). SAP. Retrieved September 8, 2003, from www.sap.com/

Improving corporate governance: A balanced scorecard approach (white paper). (2003). SAP. Retrieved September 10, 2003, from www.oracle.com/

Kersnar, J. (2001, December). STP: Is it the racer's edge? *CFO*. Retrieved September 12, 2003, from www.cfo.com/

Lloyd, M. (2002). Enterprise commerce: The new paradigm for treasury management (white paper). Retrieved September 12, 2003, from www.cfoproject.com/

mySAP financials: Next-generation integration (SAP Solutions Brief). (2003). SAP. Retrieved September 13, 2003, from www.sap.com/

mySAP financials: Strategic enterprise management with the balanced scorecard (SAP Solutions Brief). (2003). SAP. Retrieved September 13, 2003, from www.sap.com/

Optimizing the financial supply chain (white paper).(2002). Palo Alto, CA: Killen & Associates. Retrieved from www.killen.com/

Oracle 9i application server: Business intelligence technical overview (white paper). (2003). Oracle. Retrieved September 14, 2003, from www.oracle.com/

Osterland, A. (2002, January). Virtual treasury: Any day now. *CFO.* Retrieved September 16, 2003, from www.cfo.com/

Product information and description. (2003). SunGard Corp. Retrieved September 15, 2003, from www.treasury.sungard.com/

Release 11i Multi-Org Today (white paper). (2003). Oracle. Retrieved September 15, 2003, from www.oracle.com/

SAP strategic enterprise management – Enabling value based management (white paper). (2003). SAP. Retrieved September 20, 2003, from www.sap.com/

SAP strategic enterprise management – Translating strategy into action (white paper). (2003). SAP. Retrieved September 22, 2003, from www.sap.com/

SAP strategic enterprise management with mySAP.com (white paper). (2003). SAP. Retrieved September 22, 2003, from www.sap.com/

SAP strategic enterprise management, The functions – A closer look. (2003). SAP. Retrieved September 22, 2003, from www.sap.com/

Talbot, I. (2002). *Questioning the future for outsourcing the financial supply chain* (white paper). (2003). The CFO Project. Retrieved September 23, 2003, from www.cfoproject.com/

Taub, S. (2001, October). Internet will have big impact on Treasury, say finance execs. *CFO.* Retrieved September 12, 2003, from www.cfo.com/

The financial implications of corporate performance management (white paper). (2002). Boston: Aberdeen Group. Retrieved from www.aberdeen.com/

White, C. (2003). *Corporate performance optimization guide* (white paper). Oracle. Retrieved September 16, 2003, from www.oracle.com/

Wright, J. (2002). *Order-to-cash: Unlocking corporate value* (white paper). Retrieved September 11, 2003, from www.cfoproject.com/

Chapter X

Controls, Security, and Audit in Online Digital Accounting

Internal Controls: What and Why?

Internal controls have existed since the dawn of business activities. Internal controls are basically systems of checks and balances. The purpose is to keep the organization moving along desired lines as per the wishes of the owners and to protect assets of the business. Internal controls have received attention from auditors, managers, accountants, fraud examiners and legislatures. Sarbanes Oxley Act 2002 now requires the annual report of a public company to contain a statement of management's responsibility for establishing and maintaining an adequate internal control structure and procedures for financial reporting; and management's assessment of the effectiveness of the company's internal control structure and procedures for financial reporting. Section 404 of the Act also requires the auditor to attest to and report on management's assessment of effectiveness of the internal controls in accordance with standards established by the Public Company Accounting Oversight Board (PCAOB).

Internal controls are also affected by changes in business and information technology. As such, the sophistication, scope and interpretations of internal controls have evolved

Exhibit 1. Perspectives on internal controls (Source: A Comparison of Internal Controls: COBIT, SAC, COSO and SAS 55/78, by Janet Colbert and Paul Bowen; www.isaca.org/)

	Definition:	**Components:**
ISACA	The policies, procedures, practices, and organizational structures are designed to provide reasonable assurance that business objectives will be achieved and that undesired events will be prevented or detected and corrected.	Planning and organization Acquisition and implementation Delivery and support Monitoring **Focus**: Information technology
IIA	A system of internal controls is a set of processes, functions, activities, subsystems, and people who are grouped together or consciously segregated to ensure the effective achievement of objectives and goals.	Control environment Manual and automated systems Control procedures **Focus**: Information technology
COSO	A process effected by an entity's board of directors, management, and other personnel, designed to provide reasonable assurance regarding the achievement of objectives in the following categories: • Effectiveness and efficiency of operations • Reliability of financial reporting • Compliance with applicable laws and regulations	Control environment Risk management Control activities Information and communication Monitoring **Focus**: Overall entity
AICPA	A process effected by an entity's board of directors, management, and other personnel, designed to provide reasonable assurance regarding the achievement of objectives in the following categories: • Reliability of financial reporting • Effectiveness and efficiency of operations • Compliance with applicable laws and regulations	Control environment Risk management Control activities Information and communication Monitoring **Focus**: Financial statements

over the years. However, internal controls do not have a standard definition, standard objective nor one owner. The basic questions tackled in this section are: What are internal controls? What function do they serve? Answers to these questions, of course, depend on who is answering the question.

The major U.S. organizations that have articulated concepts of internal controls include Information Systems Audit and Control Association (ISACA), Institute of Internal Auditors (IIA), Committee of Sponsoring Organizations (COSO) and AICPA. These efforts are not independent, but borrow from each other in an evolutionary spiral. Internal controls are viewed as an amalgam of business models, organizational processes, organizational procedures, people and information technology. These controls are used in safeguarding assets of the business, providing relevant and reliable information, promoting operational efficiency and complying with managerial policies and procedures.

The responsibility for instituting and maintaining internal controls rests with management. In the real world, involvement of various layers of management in internal controls varies widely. Internal controls provide reasonable, not absolute, assurance. Internal controls are subject to cost benefit analysis. And all internal controls have limitations, such as collusion by personnel to overcome controls, override by top management and human error. Internal controls ideally should evolve in tandem with changing business conditions; thus, the need for continuous management monitoring.

Each organization defines components of internal controls differently, though there are a number of similarities. Components defined by COSO and adopted by the AICPA are comprehensive and briefly discussed below.

- **Control environment:** This is the foundation of internal controls, since it deals with the people aspect. Control environment signifies attitudes of the people in charge of the organization toward the controls. The tone set at the top soon permeates the entire organization. As such, no system of internal controls is effective unless actively supported by top management. The different elements of control environment are as follows:
  - Management's commitment to integrity and ethics
  - Management's philosophy and operating style
  - Complexity of the organizational structure
  - Oversight exercised by the board of directors, audit committee and internal auditors
  - Procedures for delegating authority and responsibility
  - Human resource policies and procedures
  - External influences, such as requirements of the Sarbanes-Oxley Act
- **Risk management:** All businesses face internal and external threats. Risk analysis involves analyzing these threats and taking proactive and reactive steps to mitigate risks. The steps involved in the risk analysis are given below.
  - Identify threats in financial, operational and strategic areas
  - Estimate risks involved in each threat
  - Assess cost of loss due to the risk; that is, likelihood of the occurrence of the risk multiplied by possible loss
  - Manage risk by designing appropriate controls
  - Make sure that all controls undergo cost/benefit analysis
- **Control activities:** These are policies and procedures that ensure that management's directives are carried out. The five classes of these policies and procedures are given below.

- Appropriate authorization of transactions
- Separation of duties
- Proper design and usage of documents and records
- Safeguarding of assets and records via adequate access controls
- Independent verification; for example, internal and external audits

- **Information and communication:** Internal controls should identify, capture, process and report appropriate information, which may be financial or operational.
- **Monitoring:** Internal controls should be evaluated, periodically or continuously, to assure that they are functioning as intended by management. The methods of evaluating internal controls depend on the type of controls being evaluated; for example, the evaluating tone set at the top will be different from evaluating separation of duties.

How does this discussion help understanding internal controls in the online world? Surprisingly, or, perhaps not surprisingly, the theoretical framework advocated by COSO fits well to the controls on the Internet. In the context of internal controls over business transactions over the Internet, risk management, control activities and monitoring aspects of the COSO framework are useful and applicable. Use of the Internet and Web-based tools, as seen so far, permeate almost every functional area of the business. Problems regarding information flowing in and out of the organization via the Internet are similar to the problems encountered in EDI. Add to that a unique mixture of disparate

Exhibit 2. Internal controls and the networked world

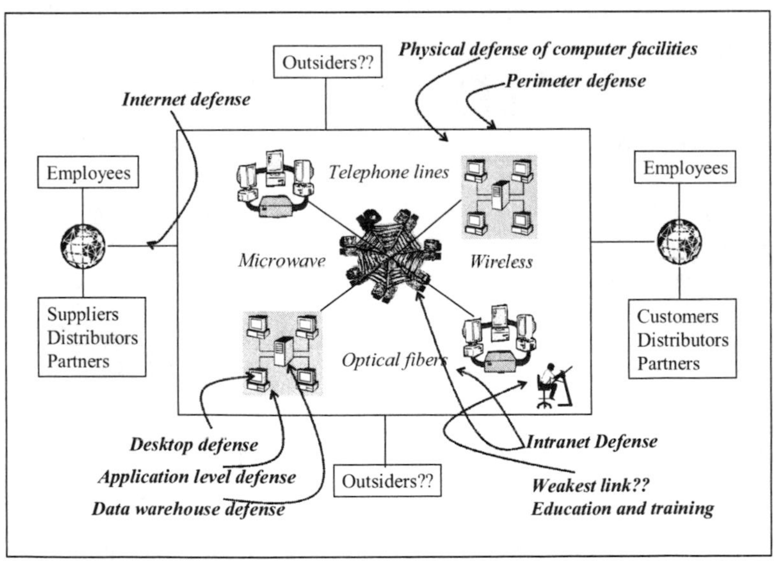

technologies, networks and computing systems, along with people collaborating — perhaps from across the globe — who may not have ever met face to face. No wonder security is considered to be one of the prime problems for businesses and consumers already on the Internet or wishing to move processes to the Internet.

The objective of this chapter is not to list every internal control in the online world. You should be able to ask intelligent questions regarding the controls — What is being protected? Why? How? How effectively? Conceptual discussions of these issues are more important than the details, which can get very complicated very quickly. To that end, this chapter is structured as follows. First, the technical, human and legal dimensions of security issues in the online world are investigated. Second, a conceptual framework to evaluate controls in the online world is presented. Third, standard online control techniques that should be known to accountants and auditors are explored. Fourth, a taxonomy of network anti-intrusion techniques, which provides proactive, reactive and interactive defenses against network intrusion attempts, is discussed. Fifth, since millions of transactions are being processed in minutes due to automation, manual controls are not very useful in Internet transactions. This section looks at a couple of software tools that can be used in automating internal controls and complying with new laws. Sixth, privacy issues and assurance services in the online world are discussed. Finally, a summary rounds off the chapter.

Security Issues in the Online World

The objectives of internal controls in the online world are similar to internal controls in the physical world — protect assets and information, provide reliable and relevant information, promote operational efficiency and comply with managerial policies. The online environment presents a mix of technological, human and physical elements, and threats to business can arise from any of these elements. Generally, in the security literature, technical solutions have received the most attention. However, there is no technological silver bullet to solve security problems, since technology is but one piece of the problem. Security solutions and internal controls must cover every aspect of the online environment.

The Internet is a global collection of networks and connects myriad operating systems, applications, databases and machines. The explosive growth of the Internet and commercial applications has sidelined security issues; and to begin with, the Internet was designed to promote communication, not security. A white paper published by the CERT® Coordination Center (2003) gives the following reasons for security problems on the Internet.

- *"The Internet was never designed for tracking and tracing user behavior.*
- *The Internet was not designed to resist highly untrustworthy users.*
- *The addresses of information packets over the Internet is untrustworthy, which hinders user tracking.*

- *Today's risk levels far exceed the Internet's design parameters.*
- *The expertise of the average system administrator continues to decline.*
- *Attacks often cross administrative, jurisdictional and national boundaries.*
- *High-speed Internet traffic, tunneling of information and anonymizers hinder tracking of errant users.*
- *The Internet links networks, so a well-protected network can be attacked from a connected but less-secure network."*

Additionally, the Internet has a large user population that is accessing a large and dynamic pool of computer services and resources. Programs can be accessed, transported and executed by remote and anonymous users. Numerous protocols run Internet transfer of data and are difficult to debug and monitor. Authentication and authorization mechanisms are different at each Web site; users may have multiple IDs and can be geographically scattered. Security, a late-comer to the party, has become a serious problem. A popular belief in the security community: If you want to truly secure your system, unplug it and pour concrete over it!

The efficiency and effectiveness of internal controls in the online environment encompasses technical, human, legal and audit considerations. Technical considerations consist of protecting against physical threats and logical attacks directed at networks and information technology assets. This area encompasses network infrastructure, operating systems, application programs, browsers and communication methods, just to mention a few. To avoid technical complexities, a conceptual view of technical problems will be taken in the ensuing discussion. The human element arguably is the weakest link in internal controls, and unless users are adequately educated and trained, no control system will function as desired. The legal element deals with validity of transactions. Federal and state commercial laws have different requirements for enforceability of the commercial transactions; for example, the UCC requires that a contract must be signed and in writing if it involves a sale of goods for more than $500. Several new laws to facilitate e-commerce are in place, though there are many unanswered questions in implementation and acceptance of these laws. Audit considerations include storage of transactions and maintenance of audit trails. The problem of internal controls on the Internet, as expected, is multidimensional.

Technical problems can be classified in two parts: physical security and logical security; these parts are not entirely independent. Physical threats to the network and information technology facilities should be identified and controlled. These threats include natural hazards, such as fire, flood, and hurricanes; and man-made hazards, such as riots, terrorism and sabotage. Physical facilities should be located away from hazardous areas, have solid construction that can withstand certain levels of stress and have uninterrupted power supply. Access to the facilities should be controlled and appropriate heating and air conditioning installed. Inventories for hardware, software and supplies should be established and maintained. Storage, access and usability policies for data should be established. A team of security professionals should handle the physical security. The security system should be periodically audited and corrective actions taken, if required.

Exhibit 3. U.S. Department of Defense security levels, circa 1987 (Source: www.fas.org/irp/nsa/rainbow/tg003.htm; this summary appears on various Web sites)

D1	***No Security – Minimal Protection***
C1	***Discretionary Protection*** • Discretionary Access Control, for example ACLs (Access Control Lists), User/Group/World protection. • Usually for users who are all on the same security level. • Username and password protection and secure authorizations database. • Protected operating system and system operations mode. • Periodic integrity checking of TCB (Trusted Computing Base). • Tested security mechanisms with no obvious bypasses. • Documentation for User Security. • Documentation for Systems Administration Security. • Documentation for Security Testing. • TCB design documentation. • Typically for users on the same security level • C1 certification is rare.
C2	***Controlled Access Protection*** • Object protection can be on a single-user basis, e.g. through an ACL or Trustee database. • Authorization for access may only be assigned by authorized users. • Object reuse protection (i.e. to avoid reallocation of secure deleted objects). • Mandatory identification and authorizations procedures for users, e.g. Username/Password. • Full auditing of security events (i.e. date/time, event, user, success/failure, terminal ID) • Protected system mode of operation. • Added protection for authorizations and audit data. • Documentation as C1 plus information on examining audit information. • This is one of the most common certifications.
B1	***Labeled Security Protection*** • Mandatory security and access labeling of all objects, e.g. files, processes, devices etc. • Label integrity checking (e.g. maintenance of sensitivity labels when data is exported). • Auditing of labeled objects. • Mandatory access control for all operations. • Ability to specify security level printed on human-readable output (e.g. printers). • Ability to specify security level on any machine-readable output. • Enhanced auditing. • Enhanced protection of Operating System. • Improved documentation.
B2	***Structured Protection*** • Notification of security level changes affecting interactive users. • Hierarchical device labels. • Mandatory access over all objects and devices. • Trusted path communications between user and system. • Tracking down of covert storage channels. • Tighter system operations mode into multilevel independent units. • Covert channel analysis. • Improved security testing. • Formal models of TCB. • Version, update and patch analysis and auditing.
B3	***Security Domains*** • ACLs additionally based on groups and identifiers. • Trusted path access and authentication. • Automatic security analysis. • TCB models more formal. • Auditing of security events. • Trusted recovery after system down and relevant documentation. • Zero design flaws in TCB, and minimum implementation flaws.
A1	***Highest level of security – Verified Protection*** • Formal methods and proof of integrity of TCB.

Logical attacks against the network can be broadly classified into three categories: client-side attacks, server-side attacks and attacks on transmission of information. Client-side security, also called browser-side security, deals with protecting the end user. The end user's system can be crashed or damaged by active content (programs) that executes on the user's computer with or without authorization. The user's privacy may be breached and personal information, such as bank account numbers, might be used for unauthorized purposes. Server-side security is concerned with protecting the Web server — hardware and software. The idea is to prevent unauthorized access to confidential information by remote users, changes in content or format of Web site information, and the use of the hardware and software to break into the host system. Secure transmission of information protects from interception of data traveling on the network – from Web browser to server and vice versa. Such data can be accessed from the network on the browser's side, on the server's side and on the ISPs on the browser or server side — all of these access points need to be guarded.

Logical attacks are possible due to network and computer system vulnerabilities. These include faulty architecture of the system, improper configuration by inexperienced administrators or built-in programming flaws in the operating system or application programs. Some systems are not designed for the Internet, but are rushed to it for business reasons. System configurations, such as setting up a firewall, network components and network services may not be done in accordance with security guidelines. Security features may not be configured or may be turned off. Security fixes may never be installed. Today's software is designed at breakneck speed with scant attention to security, and may be shipped with poor code, inadequate testing or design problems. Users may not follow security policies of the organization with respect to setting of passwords, log-in and log-off procedures, downloading of files and running of anti-virus software. These fault lines are then exploited by hackers. Remember, malicious hackers can be insiders, outsiders, trading partners or anyone in between!

How can hackers exploit these problems to attack or gain access to the network? There are numerous methods for such access, and new ones are being regularly developed. Any successful attempt or security breach wherein a network is used without authorization for whatever purpose is called a network security incident. Such incidents can be used to steal information, damage a compromised system, infiltrate other systems or launch attacks on other networks. The standard technical methods of such attacks are described below.

- **Probes and scans:** Probing involves checking access points to the network to collect information regarding the network; for example, network layout, operating systems, types of services offered on the network and users of the system. Scanning, also called *footprinting*, refers to simultaneously conducting a large number of probes using automated tools. The objective is to determine points of vulnerability for the network, which can later be used to infiltrate it.
- **Compromises:** An account compromise refers using an authorized user's account without permission. Generally, the users' accounts have limited privileges, but once an account is compromised it is used to burrow deeper into the system. In

account compromise, the damage is contained to the specific user(s); however, the victim may suffer from theft, loss or unauthorized use of data.

A root compromise is unauthorized use of the system administrator's (or an equivalent) account. Generally, system administrators are considered superusers, meaning they have special privileges on the system. Once the root account is compromised, the hacker can take over the entire system or network, run his/her programs and cover traces of intrusion. The damage caused by a root compromise is far more severe than an account compromise.

One way to compromise a user account is to obtain the user ID and password for that account. Getting a user ID is relatively easy; however, getting user passwords is difficult. Password crackers are programs that crack passwords using a brute force approach or using dictionaries of frequently used passwords. This, of course, necessitates password policies that regulate formation and deployment of passwords. User passwords are stored on computer or network systems in encrypted files. These files can also be stolen and decrypted to obtain passwords.

- **Packet sniffer:** The purpose of sniffer programs is to monitor network activity, diagnose the network, generate traffic and help troubleshoot problems. These programs can be used by hackers to capture data or information packets as they travel over the network; that is, data is sniffed. Data may include private information, user names or user passwords. This information can then be used to launch further attacks against the network.
- **Malicious code:** These programs, once executed, are designed to damage or compromise the user's system. The malicious code can be used for different purposes; for example, it may simply display a message, can destroy data on the user's machine or can transfer command of the machine or network to the remote

Exhibit 4. Dimensions of online controls

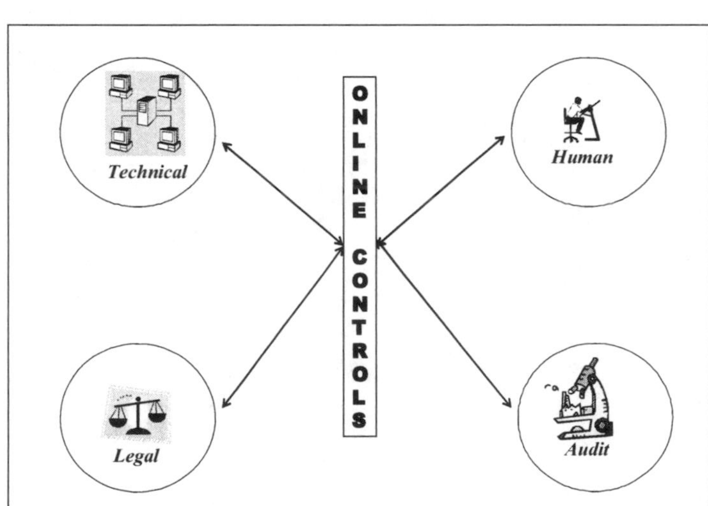

hacker. Malicious code includes viruses, worms, Trojan horses and logic bombs. Computer viruses are programs that replicate themselves and spread from computer to computer. These viruses spread when infected disks or files are shared or downloaded from the Internet. E-mail is a favorite method to spread different types of malicious code. E-mail can spread viruses not only via attachments but also through embedded HTML, pictures or sound files. Computer viruses are operating-system specific and exist in most operating system environments, such as Windows, DOS, OS/2 and UNIX. These computer viruses can be broadly classified into four categories:

- *Macro viruses*: Macros automate functions such as keystrokes or commands and are written in special-purpose command language in a particular application. Since macro viruses are written in macro language, they are platform independent and can spread to any machine that runs that particular application. For example, if the virus is written in Microsoft Word macro language, any machine running Word can be infected.
- *File viruses*: These viruses attach themselves to executable files and are activated when the file is run or executed. There are different types of file viruses. Terminate and Stay Resident (TSR) viruses, once activated, stay active in the memory and attach themselves to other programs. Direct-action file viruses load themselves in the memory and infect other files and then unload themselves. Companion file viruses create false .COM (Command) files that invoke a virus code when a program is used.
- *Boot viruses*: These viruses write over or move the disk's (floppy or hard-drive) boot sector data and replace it with malicious code. As the disk is shared and used, the virus loads into memory and performs assigned tasks.
- *Multi-partite viruses*: These share characteristics of file- and boot-sector viruses; they can infect .COM and .EXE (Executable) files and also have the ability to infect the boot sector.

The development of new viruses is an ongoing process; every year, hundreds of viruses are developed. The software code for viruses is also getting sophisticated. Stealth viruses attach themselves to the file, do not change the file length and try to stay invisible to anti-virus software. Polymorphic viruses change their identifying signatures every time they infect a new system. Such change makes it harder for anti-virus programs to detect them.

Worms, another type of malicious code, are programs that replicate themselves. In the process, the worm consumes computing resources and eventually slows or shuts down the attacked system. Worms move through the networks, scanning it for security holes. If it finds one, the worm copies itself to the new machine, and so on. Trojan horses are programs that simulate legitimate programs; for example, a free game. The free game may work, but in the background, assigned illicit activities are carried out. These may include stealing passwords; stealing information for fraud, embezzlement or espionage; destroying data; or transferring local control to a remote location. A logic bomb performs certain acts when certain conditions are met. For example, a logic bomb might erase data exactly 6 months after the software programmer, who wrote the bomb, was fired.

- **Active content (spyware, adware, software microbes, electronic moles and electronic latch-keys):** Active content has different definitions; however, generally, active content refers to any information transmitted over the Internet that modifies the behavior of the recipient computer. The most common examples of active content are Java applets and Active X controls. Not all active content is bad; in fact, active content is required for many routine functions carried over the Internet. These programs are routinely used to download Web pages containing, say, animation, and play it on the user's computer.

  Active content programs are based on macros and scripts, share program libraries and other executable objects, and can be used to remotely control infected PCs. These programs can be used to steal customer lists, conduct industrial espionage, capture e-mail addresses and capture user keystrokes, among other things. Active content can also be modified to acquire worm or Trojan horse capabilities described earlier. Some programs can be used to kill the antivirus software and firewalls, and also to launch Internet Infrastructure attacks (see the next bullet point). These programs were called by various names, but now the term "spyware" seems to be taking hold. In spite of these threats, a recent survey showed that only 25% businesses acknowledge spyware as a major problem.

  A White Paper on *www.pestpatrol.com* has this to say about spyware:

  "[It is] any product that employs a user's Internet connection in the background without their knowledge, and gathers/transmits info on the user or their behavior. Many spyware products will collect referrer info *(information from your Web browser, which URL you linked from),* your IP address *(a number used by computers on the network to identify your computer) and* system information *(such as time of visit, type of browser used, the operating system and platform, and CPU speed). Spyware products sometimes wrap other commercial products, and are introduced to machines when those commercial products are installed."*

  The problem is that traditional anti-virus software and firewalls could not identify and filter spyware. Spyware can hide in files downloaded from the Internet. It can also download itself on the person's computer if the person merely visits certain Web sites. A new breed of software tools, such *PestPatrol* and *Spybot Search and Destroy*, is being developed and employed to secure systems against active content. Many traditional anti-virus software suites are also being re-tooled to detect and neutralize active content.

- **Internet infrastructure attacks:** These attacks target the Internet infrastructure, such as network name servers, network access providers and major archival sites, to disrupt the smooth functioning of the Internet. These attacks are not targeted at a particular corporation, but can cause problems to a large number of users.
  - *Denial of Service (DNS) attack:* The objective of a DNS attack is not to gain entry in the network but to deny network services to legitimate users. This attack may be carried out by flooding the target network with a large volume

of data, or a critical resource may be overloaded to crash the network. Initially, this attack compromises the Internet infrastructure. Then the compromised infrastructure is used to launch further attacks.

- **Steganography:** Steganography means *covered writing*, and dates back thousands of years. In the digital age, steganography has been used to hide messages by embedding them within other harmless messages or images. Steganography is similar to encryption; however, steganography does not create unintelligible messages, it makes them vanish altogether. Steganography uses unused space in images and hides information and data in those spaces.

  Steganography can be used for theft of information. An engineering firm suspected an insider of passing of proprietary information to outsiders. A complete forensic audit did not discover anything abnormal; however, the consultants found two outgoing e-mails with attached images. These images were analyzed and were found to contain the firm's vital engineering specifications.

Hackers can be teenagers, criminals, insiders, industrial spies or foreign government agents. Insiders may include company employees, trading partners who have access to company networks and other users who have limited privileges on the network. If hacking attacks are launched by insiders, industrial spies or foreign government agents, then the level of sophistication and probability of damage are high. Frauds carried out by insiders using networks and information technology generally go on much longer before being detected. Motives may include psychological rewards, such as vengeance, curiosity or attention. The attacks may also be launched for competitive advantage, money or disruption of the target's computing resources. The political side of hacking has given rise to a new area of *Information Warfare*, which deals with attacking a nation by attacking the core information infrastructure that holds the nation together.

What tools carry to out these attacks? How do these tools and programs get distributed? The hacker community is getting sophisticated. There are number of easy-to-use hacking scripts for newbie hackers, many of them available on the Internet. A number of talented persons have devoted their lives to develop effective hacking programs. If insiders or foreign agents are hackers, they can be legitimate, motivated and highly educated individuals, well-versed in the art and science of programming. The development and dissemination of hacking tools is also carried out via telephone, Internet Relay Chat (IRC), anonymous FTP services, publications and even conferences such as DEF CON (www.defcon.org). Advanced hacking tools are automated, discover security loopholes faster, use firewall- and wireless-friendly packets (for easy penetration of networks) and employ distributed server and client agents. However, hacking is not merely an arena of technical expertise but intersects the human element of security. Medina (2002), in his article *Profile of Sophisticated Hackers*, provides the following characteristics of a sophisticated hacker.

- *"Understands the business culture of their targets*
- *Recognizes potential security holes*
- *Exercises patience and collects pertinent information*

- *Plans and organizes the attacks*
- *Manages the hacking process and controls details*
- *Applies new techniques to combat security measures*
- *Evaluates attack outcome and performance*
- *Enhances technical skills and defines new objectives"*

The human element of the hacking side also includes behavior of internal employees. A technique employed by the hackers to obtain information from employees is called *social engineering*. The idea behind social engineering is to deceive legitimate employees and gain proprietary information that can be used for hacking purposes. Social engineering is an application of a very old idea to the technological age. Social engineers can use any psychological tools, such as flattery, friendliness, intimidation, name-dropping, ridicule or impersonation. Contact with the employees can be on the phone, through e-mail, over the Internet or face to face. A few typical methods employed in social engineering are described below.

- **Over the phone:** The hacker calls the employee over the phone and pretends to be someone in authority. The discussion will be aimed at drawing sensitive information out of the employee. Help desks are easy prey in this scam, since they exist to help. Hackers can obtain information regarding names, telephone numbers and recent projects going on in the company, which can then be used for contacting those employees and obtaining further information. Hackers will also shoulder-surf near pay phones or ATMs and steal credit card numbers and other identification information.
- **Dumpster diving:** This activity involves going through company dumpsters and collecting discarded information. Things discarded by a company may include directories, organizational charts, computer disks, system manuals, security policies and printouts. These things may be used to glean information about personnel on duty, computer system, default passwords and security environment. A hacker gave the following illustrative guidelines on dumpster diving: Park your car a couple of blocks away, do not carry ID or wallet with you, carry a trash bag filled with cans to claim that you are collecting cans, and wear dark-colored clothes.
- **Using the Internet:** A computer is used to gather sensitive information. For example, a hacker may install a pop-up window with a company logo that might ask for user IDs and passwords, Web-based forms might be sent asking the same information, or e-mail questionnaires or forms may be circulated. The hacker might pretend to be a network or system administrator while asking for the information.
- **Physical contact:** Hackers can disguise themselves as repairman, IT support specialists, employees from other departments or managers. Fake identity cards can be used to gain entry. Information then may be collected by looking for passwords taped to the computer, stealing documents and assuming role of a new employee and eliciting passwords. There are many variations on this theme. The hacker may also use this initial information to gain a deeper acceptance in the organization.

The defense against social engineering tactics is difficult. Sloppiness on the part of network personnel and employees aids social engineering. For example, if network administrators have not applied the latest security fixes, changed default factory passwords for the software or set security policies for the organization, social engineering is that much easier. Employees also need to be aware of security and should not leave important documents and offices unlocked or keep passwords taped to their workstations. A general security awareness, constant training and education, and standard and consistent security protocols may minimize social engineering instances. Appropriate physical security for computing facilities also prevents social engineering attempts. Standard security precautions are simple, though are frequently ignored in favor of expediency. Standard security techniques against social engineering are examined in a later section.

A global information security survey carried out by *InformationWeek* in 2002 found the following reasons for network break-ins. The reasons are arranged in descending order of importance. The listing of reasons highlights the role of human error in network break-ins.

- Known operating system vulnerability
- Known application vulnerability
- Use of valid user account
- Unintended misconfiguration or human error
- Poor access control
- External denial of service attack
- Exploited unknown vulnerability
- Guessed passwords

The validity of transactions over the Internet is a legal issue. The UCC is a primary federal commercial law in the U.S., is accepted by every state and governs business transactions. There are numerous other commercial laws at the state level. Most of these commercial laws have been designed with paper-based transactions in mind. How do you interpret and apply these laws to electronic transactions? This question is an important internal control issue. In general, existing commercial laws apply to e-commerce transactions. However, e-commerce also raises a few novel legal issues not addressed by existing laws. These issues in the online world can be stated as follows.

- Can you consider electronic records and paper documents as equivalent?
- Can you enforce the online sale if the customer denies that he/she ever placed the order?
- Are electronic agreements legally valid?
- What is the role of electronic signatures vis-à-vis pen and ink signatures?

There are three primary acts that govern the electronic transactions. The first two acts, Uniform Electronic Transactions Act (UETA) and Uniform Computer Information Transactions Act (UCITA), were drafted by the National Conference of Commissioners on Uniform State Laws in 1999. The third act, Electronic Signatures in Global and National Commerce Act (E-SIGN) was passed by Congress in 2000. UETA validates electronic signatures and establishes an equivalence of electronic documents and paper-based documents. The majority of states in the U.S. have adopted this act. UCITA is primarily aimed at computer information transactions and applies to computer software, digital databases, digital music and digital storage devices, such as CDs and DVDs. This act, in essence, provides a commercial contract code for digital information transactions. The majority of states in the U.S. have *not* adopted this law, as some provisions have been controversial. E-SIGN, on the other hand, is a federal statute that provides legal validity and enforceability to electronic contracts and electronic signatures across the entire country. E-SIGN defines electronic signature as an electronic sound, symbol or process, attached or logically associated with the contract or other record, and executed and adopted by a person with the intent to sign the record. This definition is broader than, but includes, digital signatures.

Does that mean these laws have resolved our e-commerce concerns? The answer is a qualified yes. These laws, in general, make electronic documents and paper-based documents equivalent. The use of electronic signatures now has a legal force of paper-based signatures. Electronic contracts are now legally enforceable. Electronic contracts can come in various formats; for example, in case of intangible goods, such as sale of software (or rather licensing of software) there are clickwrap, shrinkwrap and boxtop licenses. Clickwrap licenses are clickable, the types you encounter when you are installing software and the agreement pops up and will not allow you to proceed until you click the *I Agree* button. Shrinkwrap licenses apply to digital products that are shrinkwrapped, and breaking the shrinkwrap indicates acceptance of the agreement. Boxtop licenses are generally enclosed in the boxes that contain the software or digital products. All of these contracts are enforceable. The courts have upheld these contracts as long as these agreements were consistent with general contract principles.

The primary concerns in these areas are drafting of electronic contracts, methods of acceptance, and compliance with the letter and spirit of the law. The laws also shift the burden of proof to the corporation if the customer denies ever having ordered the goods. For such a situation, the online corporation must establish electronic controls that will enable tracing of each order to a specific customer (refereed to as non-repudiation). In B2C transactions, standard controls may ask the customer for name, address and credit card number, and assign password-protected areas before the order is finalized. UETA, UCITA and E-SIGN have rationalized conduct of online transactions, though this is an emerging legal area, and not all questions are answered: a fact to remember as internal controls are designed for online transactions.

The USA PATRIOT (Uniting and Strengthening America by Providing Appropriate Tools Required to Intercept and Obstruct Terrorism) Act of 2001 has specific provisions to combat money laundering and financing of terrorist activities. This act is applicable to financial institutions, and also to entities such as broker-dealers, insurance companies, credit unions, mutual funds, credit card companies and money service bureaus. The act will eventually apply even to travel agents and car dealers. Money laundering refers to funds that were illegally acquired, generally through criminal activities, and then routed through a financial institution to make them look legitimate. The act also adds funds that are legitimately moving through financial institutions but have the ultimate purpose of financing illegal activity to the definition of money laundering. The act requires financial institutions to detect, deter and report all money-laundering activities. Financial institutions need to watch financial transactions from a money-laundering perspective and should have compliance programs in place. Non-compliance with the act may result in severe civil and criminal penalties; for example, eBay's PayPal was charged with violating provisions of the Act on March 31, 2003, by the U.S. Attorney's office. The next day, eBay's shares went down by $4 per share, a total loss of approximately $1 billion in market capitalization.

Another important issue on the Internet is privacy of customer information. Privacy has been an important issue for a long time, though it becomes even more urgent in the online world. The Internet makes collecting, storing, analyzing and selling of customer information very easy. Additionally, such information can be collected without the consumer's knowledge or consent. The Gramm-Leach-Bliley Act (GLBA) deals with privacy issues in the context of financial industry, banks, securities firms and insurance companies. GLBA provides guidelines for protecting customer and member information. The objectives of GLBA are to ensure security and confidentiality of nonpublic personal information and to protect against destruction or unauthorized access of such personal information. GLBA does not provide specific guidance on how to achieve these objectives; it is left to individual organizations. However, since GLBA deals with privacy and control issues, it must be factored in while designing internal controls. A number of automated solutions have come to the market to manage risks associated with compliance of these new laws, which are explored in a later section.

Finally, design of internal controls should also cover auditing concerns. Internal controls in this area deal with tracking, validating, recording and maintaining audit trails for online transactions. The storage of past transactions, backups for the storage and easy access to disputed past transactions are some areas that need to be addressed. The audit trail needs to be maintained for valid and invalid transactions, especially if invalid transactions indicate security violation or inappropriate user activity. This area assumes importance due to the ease with which electronic records can be erased and intrusion tracks or fraudulent activity can be covered. The personnel who handle online auditing duties need to be qualified, have clear responsibilities and be supported by management. However, technical solutions are only the first line of defense. The Sarbanes-Oxley Act of 2002 mandates documentation of internal controls over financial reporting by management. If networks are used for financial transactions, and that is the purpose of networks in business, then management needs proper understanding of controls and should be able to assess the adequacy of documentation.

A Conceptual Framework for Online Internal Controls[1]

Internal controls, no matter the exotic terminology, have standard objectives. The objectives of online controls can be classified as validity of transactions, mutual authentication of identity, authorization, end-to-end data integrity and confidentiality, non-repudiation and auditability of transactions. These areas are not mutually exclusive, but provide a way to conceptually organize and discuss internal controls in the online world. Let us take a detailed look at elements of the conceptual framework. Some of the controls mentioned below are covered in detail in a later section.

- **Validity of transactions:** The primary question in online transactions is its legal status. Transacting parties in EDI take care of this problem by using trading agreements. New laws, such as UETA, UCITA and E-SIGN, have facilitated validity of transactions in the online world, though compliance with these laws remains an important internal control issue.
- **Mutual authentication of identity:** Authentication is a process of verifying identities of the transacting parties. It involves determining whether someone or something is, in fact, who or what it is declared to be. Authentication of identity has two facets: identity of the machines and identity of the humans operating the machine.

  Such authentication can be carried out by means of static or dynamic passwords or PINs, passwords or PINs and security tokens, automatic callbacks and biometric

Exhibit 5. A conceptual framework for online controls

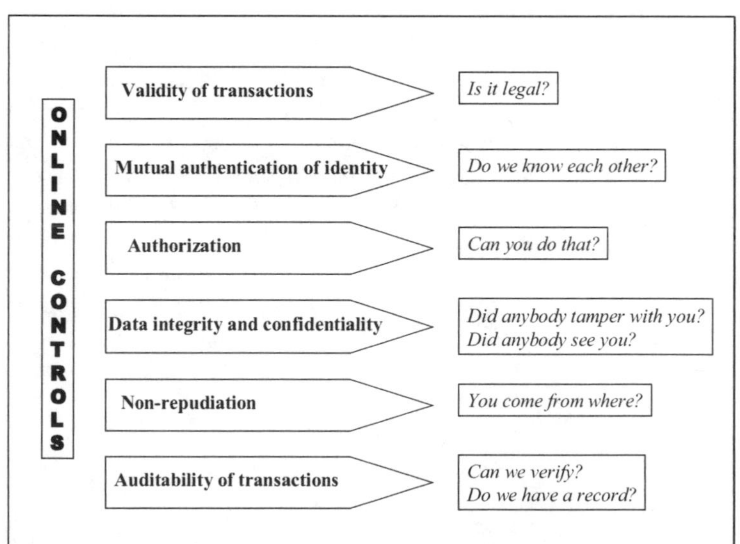

techniques. The use of digital certificates is also increasingly common. Establishing identity of a human at the end of the machine is primarily a matter of intra-organizational controls. It requires review of access controls and separation of duties within the organization. The human user is identified by something the user knows or carries. These criteria include passwords, ID cards or biometric measures, such as fingerprints.

- **Authorization:** Authorization is the step after authentication. The machine and user are identified and allowed access to the computer system in the authentication phase. Then, the authorization phase deals with granting rights to the user to perform certain functions. These rights define types of resources and actions allowed to the user; for example, the user can read, write or modify but cannot delete files. The rights can be assigned via Access Control List (ACL).

  Accounting, which may follow authorization, involves collecting statistics and usage information for a particular user or class of users. This information is used for authorization control, billing, trend analysis, resource utilization and capacity planning.
- **Data integrity and confidentiality:** Data integrity refers to transfer of data without any modification, intentional or unintentional, in the transit. Data confidentiality refers to inability of unauthorized parties to access data. Standard controls in this area include encryption, security algorithms and communication protocols such as SSL.
- **Non-repudiation:** Non-repudiation refers to proof that the electronic document was sent by the sender and received by the receiver. The three aspects of non-repudiation are: non-repudiation of origin, non-repudiation of receipt and non-repudiation of submission. Non-repudiation covers the problem of post-facto denial of an electronic transaction by transacting parties. First, it proves that the transaction took place, and second, it establishes identity of the transacting parties. Controls such as digital signatures and digital certificates address non-repudiation.
- **Auditability of transactions:** Auditability of transactions refers to the existence of an audit trail and the ability to verify past transactions. The transactions should be validated, controlled and recorded properly. A log of users, resources used by the users, and various system functions is also required for auditability. Audit trail problems can be solved by maintaining backups, time stamps and file linkages.

This classification does not cover every dimension of the internal control problem, though it helps ask the right questions. For example, if you want to evaluate internal controls over e-mail, you can ask the following questions based on the conceptual framework:

- How do you know the e-mail is valid?
- How do you know the e-mail came from the person identified in the e-mail?
- How do you grant permissions for users of e-mails to do e-mail-related activities?

- How do you know the e-mail was not altered in the process?
- How do you know that no one has seen the e-mail?
- How can we trace earlier e-mails?

These questions do not need any technical understanding of internal controls for the Internet. The framework simply enables us to ask intelligent and logical questions. These areas are not mutually exclusive, and a control technique can perform several or more functions, such as validity, authorization and authentication, at the same time. The identified characteristics of internal controls and COSO framework are now used to discuss standard internal controls in the online world.

Standard Online Internal Control Techniques

Internal control techniques must address technical, legal, human and audit dimensions of security in the online world. A well-designed internal control system should be supported by top management and cover a wide range of technical and managerial strategies and tactics. No single method provides reasonable, absolute — it is never absolute — protection. A mix of security mechanisms needs to be in place to protect information assets. Security and internal controls are an ongoing and evolving process.

Exhibit 6. The COSO framework and online controls

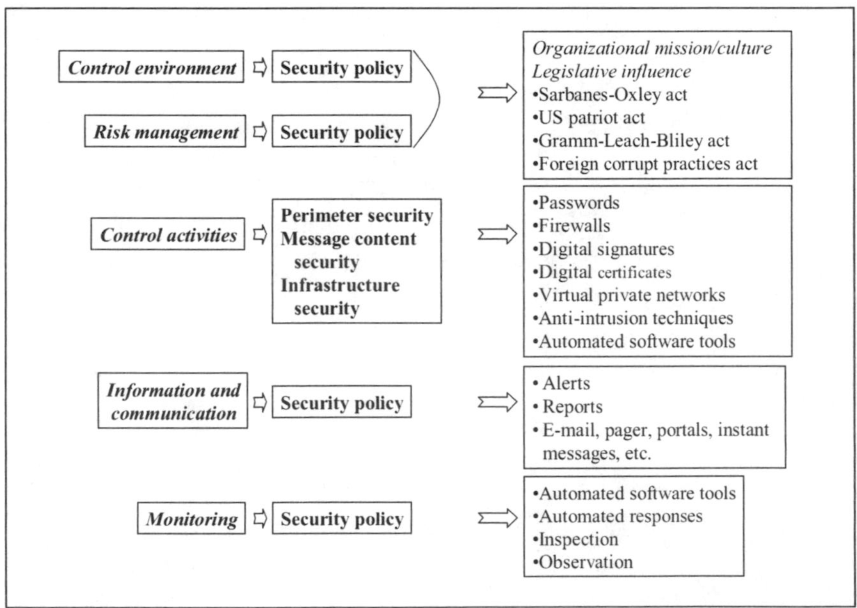

This process must be monitored as business situations change. The consensus of experts in this area indicates a layered approach to security. The different layers of a security system are given below. This is but a broad classification, and these areas intersect at various levels.

- Security policy for the organization
- Perimeter security
- Message content security
- Back-end infrastructure security

Security policy is a pervasive element of the security architecture. Security policy captures business issues and relates them with technical requirements. Perimeter defense refers to the defense of all contact points between the corporation's internal network and external public/private networks. Perimeter defense has become more difficult due to collaborative activities with trading partners and new technologies, such as wireless networks. The perimeter has now become amorphous. Message content security refers to maintaining integrity and confidentiality of a message, whether the message is traveling over the Internet or internal private networks. Finally, back-end infrastructure security refers to security of the hardware and software used by the organization to carry out its routine activities. This topic is only tangentially covered in this book, since it is not specific to the Internet. The ensuing discussion covers security

Exhibit 7. The conceptual framework and online controls

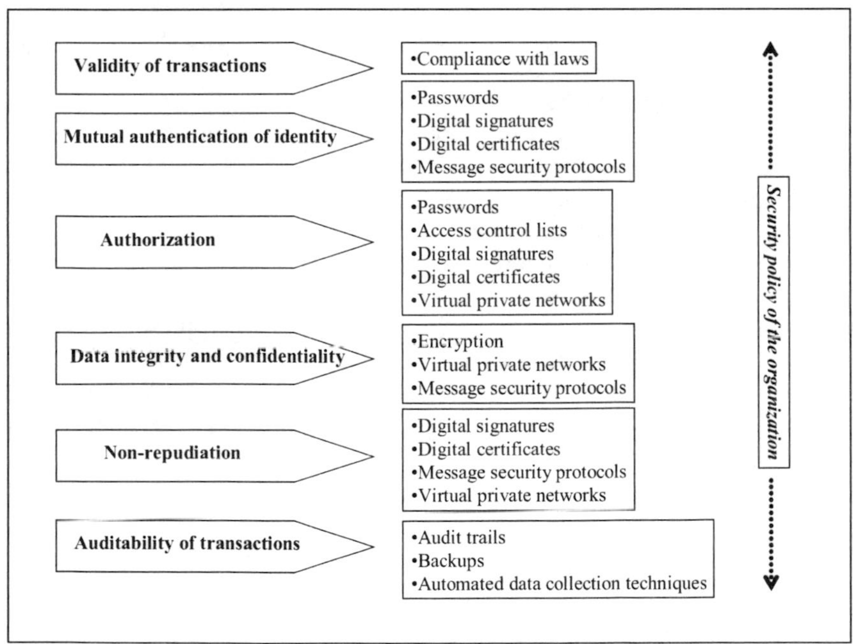

Exhibit 8. Classification of online controls

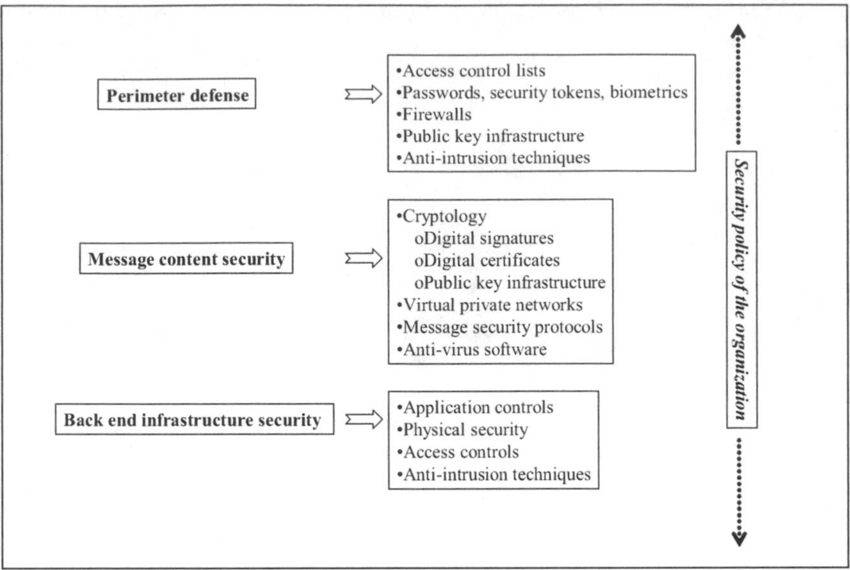

policies and standard internal controls employed in perimeter defense and message content security.

Security Policy

Security and internal controls are not technological issues; they are business issues. The security architecture for any organization begins with a clear plan of action: If you do not know what you are supposed to protect and from whom, the latest technological gizmos are of little use. Security procedures and internal controls must embody strategic, cultural, political and technological aspects of an organization. Security policy is the place where these factors are integrated to develop a comprehensive framework for security. Security policy contains goals and objectives of the security system, defines overall purpose of the security system and provides direction for implementation of the security system. Security policy is generally designed for the entire information system, not only the online component. However, the ensuing discussion focuses on the online component. Questions addressed by the security policy can be simplistically stated as follows.

- Who will use the system?
- What will be the rights and responsibilities of the users?
- How will remote and local users access the system?

- When the system can be accessed?
- Who will decide and grant user rights?
- How is user activity tracked and recorded?
- What disciplinary actions will be taken for errant users?
- What are the procedures for responding to security breaches?

Designing a security policy is a multi-disciplinary process. As the COSO report states, involvement of top management is crucial. Senior management knowledge, operational management knowledge, information technology knowledge and financial knowledge is required to complete the assessment necessary to design a security policy. The process is interdisciplinary and iterative. The designed policy is not set in stone, but changes as the organization changes, and it needs constant updating and maintenance. The steps in development of the security policy are outlined below.

- **Identify and classify organizational assets:** Information assets of the organization may include hardware, software, network infrastructure, data and information, people, documentation and supplies. These assets should be classified according to importance, more important assets being more stringently protected; for example, the resulting asset protection categories may be public use, confidential, restricted or administration use only.
- **Assess the risk:** Risk refers to probability of loss. Online examples of risk are unauthorized access to the network, stealing of data and information, denial of service, damage to hardware and loss of reputation. In mathematical terms, risk can be defined as the cost of damage to an asset multiplied by probability of an event that can damage the asset. Asset values are generally identified in the identification and classification phase. Then, probability of the undesired events for these assets must be identified. Risk analysis should answer questions such as, what should be protected? From whom? and By what?
- **Determine acceptable use:** Permissible business uses of information assets are identified in the acceptable use policy. These policies will tell users what they can and cannot do, what might be construed as an abuse of privileges, and privacy and confidentiality positions of the organization. In specific terms, these policies may tell the user how to set a password and how often to change it, what kind of backups are the user's responsibility, which content can and cannot be downloaded from the Internet, and whether e-mail is property of the organization.
- **Create security awareness:** Having a security policy document will not in itself create security awareness among stakeholders of a corporation. These policies should be communicated to new and continuing employees, suppliers, customers and trading partners. Training and education activities should be outlined and provided.
- **Monitoring and auditing:** Security policies are worthless unless monitored for execution and performance. Fortunately, security policies in the networked environment can be monitored using in-built tools or automated auditing tools available

in the market. Monitoring and auditing activities are designed to spot intentional and unintentional misuse of the system by users. Such a misuse needs to be detected, preferably in real time, and corrected. The collected information, at least a summary, needs to be forwarded to appropriate managers.

- **Security breach policies:** In a security-related incident, perpetrators can be insiders or outsiders. Security breach policies prescribe actions in case of a discovered security breach. The conduct of the investigation to determine the nature and causes of breach should be outlined. If the perpetrators are identified, then the question is whether to contact authorities and proceed with prosecution or simply fire the employee and plug security loopholes. A large percentage of security violations are *not* reported to authorities, since prosecution of offenders, collection of evidence, possibility of copycat attacks and loss of reputation are considered too costly. In any case, whatever the course of action, the system must be restored to a safe state by correcting security flaws.

Depending on the organization, the security policy can be a two-page statement or an elaborate document that may span several binders. The security policy offers many advantages. First, system administrators know what is and what is not permitted on the system. This baseline can be used to determine whether a security violation has occurred. Second, the policy can be used for user training and education. Security awareness spreads through the entire organization, since users know their rights and responsibilities. Such a policy also demonstrates that the organization is committed to security. Third, the security policy can be used as a guide in devising technical solutions. For example, technical requirements for guarding nuclear missile command codes will be different than the requirements for guarding a university network designed to facilitate

Exhibit 9. Automated security policy tools

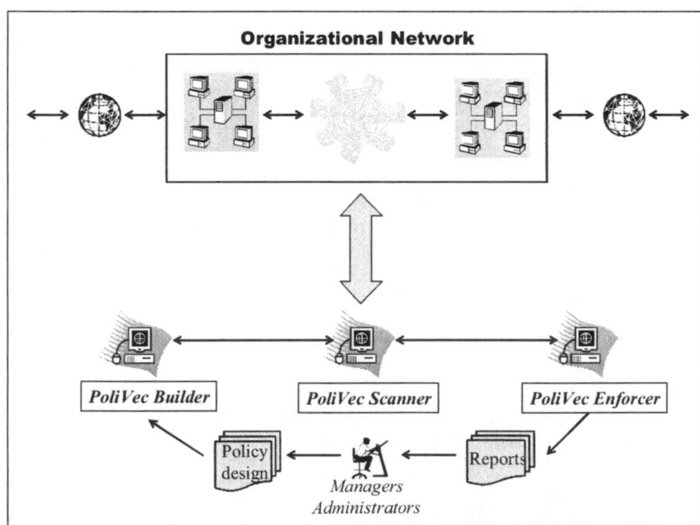

Exhibit 10. PoliVec security policy management console, used with permission

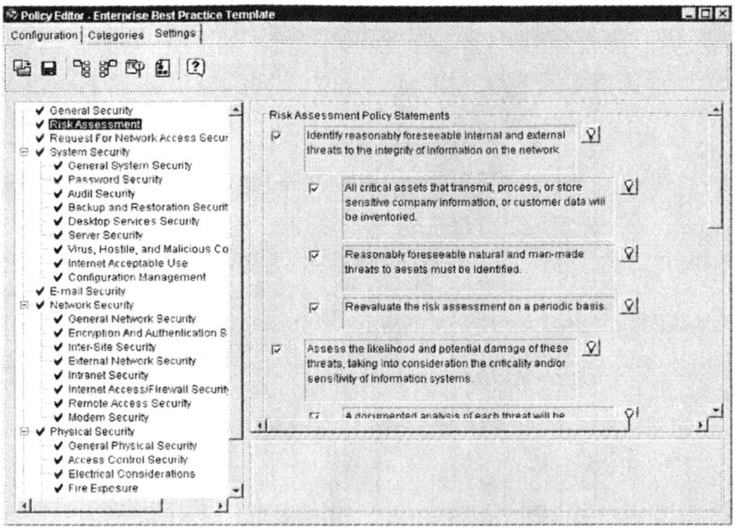

a free-flow of information. These rules can also be used to perform cost benefit analysis of various technical products on the market. Finally, it provides a legal foundation for taking action against offenders.

Development and implementation of security policies do not have to start from scratch. Many automated tools can be used to customize canned security policies for an organization. The Security Policy Automation (SPA) market consists of scores of vendors providing SPA solutions. The entire security policy cycle, from development to deployment, monitoring and change can be managed using these tools. As is the trend in the last decade, these tools have a graphical interface and do not need a deep programming knowledge. PoliVec software, a typical SPA solution, is now reviewed.

PoliVec software consists of three modules: Builder, Scanner and Enforcer. PoliVec Builder, as the name implies, partially automates development of the security policy. The software comes with built-in, industry-specific templates; for example, banks or credit unions. These templates cover different facets of security, such as regulatory, general, systems, network and physical security. These templates can also be operating-system specific, such as Windows or Linux. The templates serve as a starting point and are customized to develop organization-specific policies. The developed policies are then converted to XML files, which are passed on to the Enforcer module for automatic implementation. HTML filescan also be created, for publication and distribution purposes. PoliVec aids formulation of security policies using the following features.

- **Policy configuration:** This feature can be used to set global variables repeated throughout the policy document; for example, company name, address and organization structure.
- **Policy categories:** This feature enables the user to add categories or subcategories such as legal or computer systems, and provides an illustrative policy for each category or subcategory. These policies may be customized, if desired.

- **Policy settings:** These settings can be used to accept the best-practices policy built into the product or customize the policy for the organization.
- **Policy details:** This feature enables viewing of all security categories and policies, and displays rationale for each policy. This feature may be useful to auditors in evaluating network security.

PoliVec Scanner scans the network to assess security configurations and compare those to the security policy for conformance and exceptions. Scanner automates discovery of weaknesses in the security setting; recommends remedies for those weaknesses; and, after authorization, applies changes to the network systems. Security settings that can be analyzed include password management, account management and audit trails. This feature is also equipped with a password cracker that hackers use to crack passwords. Password cracker can be used to detect ineffective passwords set by users. Scanner is essentially an analytical and audit tool, and is designed to be used by system administrator from a central location. Additional illustrative features of Scanner are user authentication, security auditing and event logs, trust relationships, user and group management, system rights, system services and scheduled audits.

PoliVec Enforcer enforces security policies designed and contained in the builder. As the security policy evolves, Enforcer automatically changes enforcing mechanisms based on the new policy. Enforcer deploys small software agents on the network and host computer systems, and these agents constantly monitor security settings. Moreover, these agents also run security-related tests on the computer systems. These agents report to the agent manager, which is designed to manage the agents. A component named *controller* manages the Enforcer system, and a GUI can be used by the system administrator to administer and manage the components of the Enforcer. The software agents evaluate the actual system configuration settings and transmit that information to the agent manager. Incoming information is evaluated by the agent manager against expected configurations, as defined by the security policy. Exceptions are passed on to the controller for further processing. Security policy infractions are reported to designated managers using designated methods at designated intervals or in real time. Compliance reports can be evaluated to ascertain performance of security policies to support the core business, and strategic and legal objectives of the organization.

Passwords, Security Tokens and Biometrics

The standard authentication technique is passwords. Users logging remotely or from inside the corporate network are expected to enter a user ID and password to get on the network. User IDs are assigned by the administrator, and passwords are set by users. The problem with passwords is that most users set simple passwords that can be guessed easily; for example, "bulls" and "Jordan" were favorite passwords in Chicago at one time. If users are forced to set difficult passwords, users tend to write them down on paper and put the papers in their drawers or, worse, stick them to their computers. Passwords still continue to be the first line of defense in many organizations. Passwords are easy to deploy and can be maintained cheaply. Many corporations have policies as to design, expiry and storage of passwords; the critical issue is, of course, in monitoring adherence with these policies.

The standard password is called *one factor authentication*. Passwords can be strengthened by using a *two-factor authentication*. In two-factor authentication, users have to present some form of identification either before they are allowed to enter passwords or concurrently with the passwords. For example, security tokens can be used along with passwords. Some security tokens display a number on the token that is synchronized with the network computer; this number changes after a fixed interval, such as 60 seconds. In a two-factor authentication, a user will have to type in this number and his/her password to access network resources. However, the management of these security tokens remains an implementation issue. Smart cards can also be used as security tokens. Smart cards can even allow storage of digital certificates and can provide stronger authentication for remote users.

A *three-factor authentication* can use biometrics in conjunction with passwords and security tokens (or smart cards). Biometrics refers to physical characteristics unique to the user; for example, fingerprints or eye retina patterns. Now the user has to use three factors before being allowed to access network resources. Such stringent security requirements are needed only for the most critical resources, since these requirements are expensive. Numerous commercial products manage storage, comparison and validation of biometric measures. However, implementation of biometrics is a tricky issue, since some biometric tools are not completely ready for real-world use; if valid users get rejected or invalid users are accepted, user resistance to these techniques will be very high.

The additional control technique for remote access to the network, especially using modems, is a call-back technique. The remote user calls in, connects and is then asked to provide the designated authentication. The system breaks the connection, verifies the user authentication and then dials back to the user. The system uses a phone number stored in the system for that particular user. If the user is not using that number or is being impersonated from another line, the connection will not be established. The user, after the connection is established, can have access to the network. This technique is useful against a hacker dialing in at random, guessing passwords or using brute force methods to break the passwords. This technique, however, slows down network access for the user; especially if the user is calling long distance or from another country.

Access Control List (ACL)

ACL, which is commonly used in database security, is also routinely used in network security. ACL specifies the rights of users within the network. ACL maintains a list of users and a list of available resources and assigns those users specific resources. For example, user X might be able to read the Web page, user Y might be allowed to read and write, and user Z might be authorized to read, write and modify content. ACL can be used in the Web environment by analyzing incoming user requests, matching those requests with resources and granting appropriate rights to users. For example, most visitors will have read rights whereas read, write and modify rights will be reserved for Web administrators. ACLs are also used in firewalls to analyze incoming traffic and assign appropriate rights to incoming messages and users.

Anti-Virus Software

Ant-virus software probably resides on the majority of computers and perhaps most corporate, government and academic networks. You may have scanned files on your hard drive using anti-virus software or received messages that a certain e-mail was carrying a virus that has been neutralized. Anti-virus software automatically scans resident files, incoming and outgoing network traffic, and incoming and outgoing e-mails for suspected viruses. The anti-virus software can also monitor instant messages for viruses and take appropriate action. Anti-virus software depends on a database of known viruses, called signatures, and if a match is found for an incoming file then either an alert is sounded or an automatic action — such as deleting or isolating the file — is taken. Other variations of anti-virus software provide real-time defense against viruses. Some techniques are listed below.

- **Sandbox:** This technique identifies every program that arrives from the Internet using monitoring agents. Sandbox uses a set of rules to identify the intent of the program that is downloaded or arriving as an active content. If the program is identified as a malicious code, that program is neutralized.
- **Heuristics:** This technique analyzes the program code to determine whether it is malicious. This technique is useful against script- or macro-based viruses.
- **Blocking:** Incoming files can be blocked based on pre-defined rules. The rules may be based on file signatures, file length or even an analysis of the actual content of the files before the files are cleared or blocked.

Since new and improved viruses are continuously being developed, anti-virus software also needs to be updated continuously. Anti-virus software, though ubiquitous and prosaic, is an important element in the overall security architecture.

Defense Against Social Engineering

The defense against social engineering starts with a security policy that offers guidelines on providing information to the public and colleagues. The next factor is controlling access to physical facilities. The buildings and other entry points should be guarded, and entry should be provided based on verified identifications. All visitors should be logged at a central location. Employees should be trained to question unescorted guests, not to type in passwords in the presence of strangers or give out passwords on the phone. Vacant offices should be locked, and computers that are on while owners are absent should at least have password protection. Important documents, letterheads and security badges should not be lying around, but should be well guarded. The trash should be secured, and all documents should be shredded before dumping. Hard disks, floppy disks and CDs — all magnetic storage media — should be wiped clean or physically destroyed before being trashed.

Employees should be assigned a positive identification before the help desk can help them via phone or in person. For potentially sensitive questions, the help desk should be instructed to call back the (alleged) employee, or they should have caller ID facilities on their system. The persons managing the phone system should investigate all international and overseas calls and should not transfer calls unless positively identified. The corporation should have a clear modem policy, since modems bypass firewalls. Generally, modems should not be permitted. In some corporations, the mere presence of a modem on an employee desk can be reason enough for dismissal. The company should also have a policy regarding formation, use and expiry of passwords. If the organization deals in sensitive information, two- or three-factor authentication may be considered.

Finally, if a social engineering attempt succeeds, then the corporation should have a response policy. The incident should be investigated, damage ascertained and lessons learned should be disseminated. Security loopholes that caused the incident should be plugged, and if the perpetrators are identified, legal action may be initiated. The defense against social engineering is neither easy nor static. Hackers also learn, and try new and unexpected attacks. As such, continuous user training and education are necessary.

Cryptology

Cryptology can be approximately described as the art and science of hiding data and information, to shield it from unauthorized eyes and still keep it accessible to legitimate recipients. Cryptology consists of two branches: cryptography and cryptanalysis. Cryptography deals with cryptosystems, which convert plain text or data into text or data that is unintelligible — called ciphertext. Cryptanalysis is the study of legal *and* illegal methods to crack such unintelligible text and access the hidden message. Cryptography can be called encryption and cryptanalysis can be called decryption. The primary objective of cryptography is to keep sensitive communications private. The conversion of readable data or text into nonsensical gibberish using coding techniques has been practiced since time immemorial. The field of cryptology expanded exponentially when digital computers arrived on the scene, and have become even more important due to the advent of the Internet. Cryptology can achieve the objectives of authentication, data integrity, data confidentiality and non-repudiation in e-commerce.

Let us use the terms encryption and decryption to keep the ensuing discussion simple. Encryption transforms plain text or data into something that seems like gibberish and makes no sense. How can this transformation be achieved? A method allegedly used by Julius Caesar replaced every A by D, B by E, C by F and so on. The code now can be broken using *shift alphabets backwards by three* rule. The age of computers brings a great deal of processing power to our desktops, not to mention the computing power of networks and supercomputers. Unless the encryption scheme is strong enough, it will not hide data very well. Today's encryption schemes are based on complex mathematical techniques. The harder the technique is to crack, the stronger the encryption system will be.

The mathematical techniques or formulas used in encryption schemes are called encryption algorithms. Encryption algorithms use a string of bits to perform a transformation, and such a string is called a *key*. The larger the string of bits used , the larger the potential encoding patterns will be; as such, a larger key is harder to break. Thus, a key that uses 128 bits is harder to break than the key that uses 64 bits. The historical problem with encryption is that of key management. Based on the type of key management, there are three types of encryption schemes in practice.

- **Symmetric encryption (private key):** In this case, the sender and receiver both have the same key. The sender encrypts the message and forwards it to the authorized recipient. The receiver uses the same private key and decrypts the message. This method of encryption and decryption is computationally very fast. This key management method is useful when keys are shared by a small circle of people, such as in the defense sector. This key management method is not suitable for the Internet, where the user population is large and the chances of a key being compromised are high. There are various private key algorithms, and a few common ones are listed below.
    - *The Data Encryption Standard (DES)*, having a 56-bit key
    - *DES variants*, such as 3DES and DESX, having a 168-bit key
    - *The IDEA*, a basis for PGP (a famous algorithm used for encryption), having a 128-bit key.
- **Asymmetric encryption (public/private key):** In this system, the recipient has a pair of keys – private/public key. The public key, as the name says, is available to all. Anyone can see and access it. The sender will encrypt the message using the public key of the recipient. The message encrypted using the public key can only be decrypted by using the associated private key. But if the key with which the message is encrypted is known to everyone, why can't everyone decrypt the message? The answer lays in the mathematical functions involved; they only work one way. The public key cannot decrypt the message that is encrypted using the very same key! The recipient now only has to guard his private key, which is a relatively easier task. The common asymmetric algorithm is the Rivset, Shamir and Adleman (RSA) algorithm and can have keys up to 1024 bits.
- **Hash functions:** A hashing algorithm is used to calculate a hash value or message digest from the message that is being encrypted. Hash value or message digest generally refers to the generation of a fixed string of numbers using the text in the message. If the text in the original message is altered, the resulting hash value is different from the original. This hash value is then forwarded to the recipient, along with the message. The recipient independently recalculates the hash value; if the two values match, the message has not been altered in transit. If the two values do not match, the message has been altered. The hash values, if properly calculated, can be as unique as fingerprints. Message Digest Hash Functions (MD4 and MD5) are the common hash functions that produce 128-bit hash values.

The basics of encryption schemes covered now can be applied in the framework of internal controls. Encryption techniques can be used to create digital signatures, digital envelopes and digital certificates or digital IDs. These techniques are used in e-commerce for various authentication, integrity and confidentiality purposes. Digital signatures are used to confirm data integrity, data confidentiality and non-repudiation. Digital signatures can be implemented using a variety of methods. A standard method based on private/public key or asymmetric encryption will be described.

A digital signature can consist of a unique data string designed by the sender, a hash value (or message digest) of the message and/or any other mutually acceptable data. If a unique data string is used as a digital signature, then either the recipient knows what it is or it can be attached as plain text with the message or sent separately. The unique data string or hash value of the message is encrypted using the sender's private key. The original message is also encrypted using the sender's private key. The digital signature and original message are joined and again encrypted using the receiver's public key. The message is then forwarded to the receiver. The receiver now uses his/her private key to decrypt the entire message. The decryption yields two messages — the digital signature and the original message, both of which are still encrypted (by the sender's private key). The recipient can now decrypt the digital signature and the original message using the sender's public key. The digital signature, if verified, indicates that the message has originated from the sender. If the digital signature contains the hash value, recalculation and comparison of this hash value confirms that the message has or has not been tampered since its origination.

Asymmetric encryption is computationally slower, and hence, can cause bottlenecks in the fast-paced Internet environment. Digital signatures can also be implemented using a combination of symmetric and asymmetric encryption. The sender creates a symmetric

Exhibit 11. Applications of cryptology

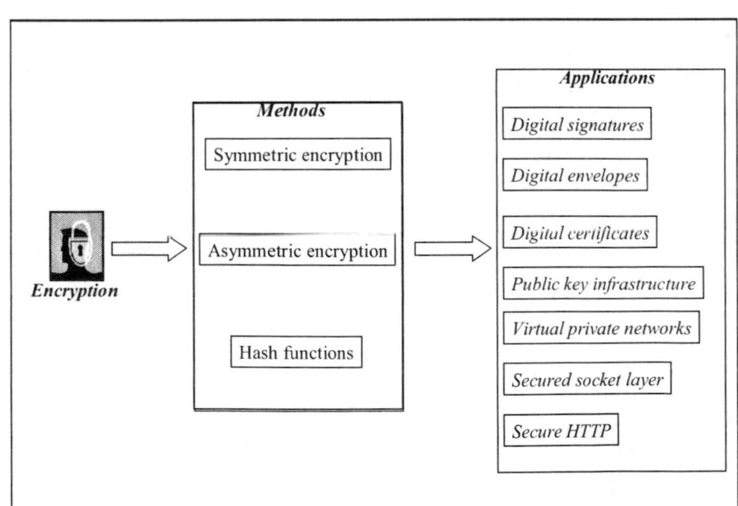

private key for a particular message and encrypts the message with that private key. This private key is generally created and used only for one session. Then the private key is encrypted using the public key of the recipient, which is called a digital envelope. The encrypted message and the digital message are forwarded to the recipient. The recipient decrypts the symmetric private key for the message using his/her private key. This key is then used to decrypt the original message. This process is faster than purely asymmetric encryption.

Digital certificates, also called digital identifications or digital IDs, are similar to passports or drivers licenses in the physical world. Digital certificates carry identifying information that is validated and guaranteed by a trusted third party —CA. Digital certificates use the framework of asymmetric encryption. The CAs are generally Internet-based companies; for example, the most famous trusted third party is VeriSign (*www.verisign.com/*). Digital certificates perform two functions. First, they authenticate the holder of the certificate. The holders can be Web servers (site certificates), individual persons (personal certificates), software publishers or CAs. Second, digital certificates provide data integrity and confidentiality. Digital certificates are used in e-commerce, e-mails and EFT.

The business or entity that wishes to use digital certificates applies to CA. The CA issues a digital certificate that generally contains the following digital information.

- Details of the certificate owner, such as name, address or e-mail
- Certificate owner's public key
- Serial number of the certificate
- Validity dates for the certificate
- Name and digital signature of the CA who issued the certificate

The CA also creates a hash value or message digest and encrypts those using its private key. The hash value or message digest is now called signed certificate. The public key of CA is made available to all. Digital certificates have in-built security and cannot be captured online and altered. VeriSign offers different types of digital certificates, from Class 1 through Class 4. These types are differentiated by assurance levels; the Class 4 certificate carries the highest level of assurance.

The customer who wishes to deal with the business requests the signed digital certificate from that business. Digital certificates can be delivered via e-mail or can be embedded in the Web pages. The signed digital certificate is then decrypted using the public key of the CA. The customer calculates the hash value or message digest independently. The hash values are compared; if these values match, the identity of the business is confirmed. Generally, these tasks are automatically done by the customer's browser and/or the server. When the secure session is established, the browser will indicate a lock at the bottom of the screen. If you click on the lock, you will be able to see the digital certificate. The customer now has the confidence to conduct business knowing that he/she is dealing with a legitimate business on the Internet. The same assurance is available for persons, software publishers and CAs who hold digital certificates.

Exhibit 12. Encryption mechanisms

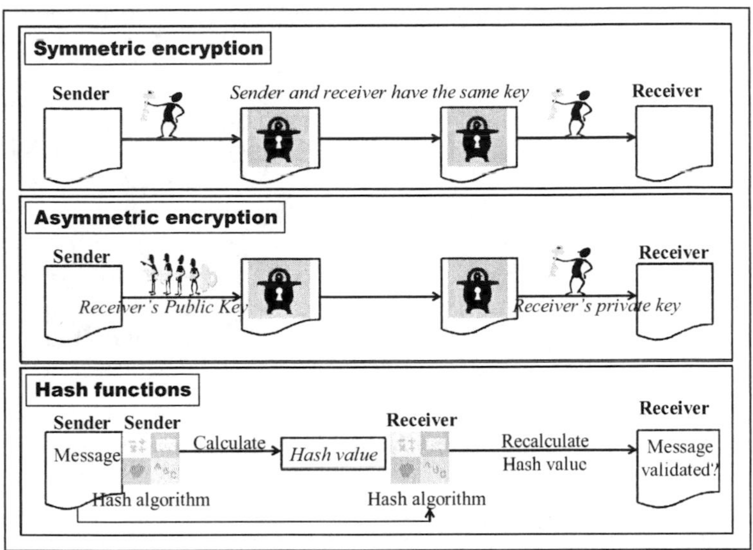

The mass implementation of digital certificates in the Internet environment is done via PKI. PKI is in an evolving phase, and different solutions are offered. PKI establishes a framework or system to use digital certificates, encryption and digital signatures as an authentication mechanism and devises management methods for such usage. The basic idea behind PKI is to integrate the use of digital certificates, CAs and other security mechanisms to provide an infrastructure that can be used to validate each party involved in e-commerce; thereby making e-commerce more secure. PKI should consist of a CA to issue and verify digital certificates, Registration Authority (RA) to verify the digital certificates before they are issued, appropriate storage places for digital certificates and public keys and a certificate management system. PKI can offer services such as issuance of new certificates with public keys, obtaining public keys of a trading partner or customer, cancellation of certificates, validation of certificates and recovering private keys under exceptional circumstances. A number of developments are in progress in PKI standards and architecture, PKI-enabled applications and PKI security requirements. Currently, Entrust (*www.entrust.com*) is one of the leading PKI providers.

Digital Watermarks

A digital watermark is an application of steganography. Watermark is a pattern or design; paper watermarks have been used for a long time to provide authenticity to paper documents. For example, the new U.S. $20 bill contains watermarks that make copying the bill almost impossible. Watermarking can also be used in digital media, now called digital watermarks. Digital watermarks are generated by adding extra data to the digital file that does not make any difference to legitimate users. However, if the digital material is copied, the watermark will not get copied and such material can be identified as a copy. A few digital watermarks will also corrupt a copy so that copy becomes unusable. Numerous software vendors exist; for example, DigiMarc Corporation, which provides digital watermarking software.

Digital watermarks shot to prominence due to the music industry's campaign to stop downloading of music on the Internet. Digital watermarks can also be used to protect materials posted on a Web site. Digital watermarks can provide protection to images, audio files and video files. The protection format can vary. First, such images cannot be copied to a hard disk, even after using the print screen feature. Other Web sites cannot provide links to such images. Second, audio and video files can be streamed over the Internet and played without storing data on the user's hard drive. Third, audio and video files can be downloaded, but will expire after a certain number of uses or days.

Digital watermarks and related technologies that strive to prevent copying and reproduction of digital material are called Digital Rights Management (DRM) Technologies. DRM technologies are intrusive, and can have fair use and privacy implications for users. For example, if you buy a music CD, you may not be able to make a backup copy, or, if you are allowed, such information might flow to the owner of the music copyrights. This area is currently mired in congressional bills and legal fights. From the internal control perspective, remember, digital watermarks can be used to maintain confidentiality and integrity of digital images and digital audio/video files.

Firewalls

A firewall is a fireproof wall used to prevent spread of fire. The purpose of an electronic firewall is to prevent spread of unauthorized data packets in protected private networks and limit damages. Traditionally, firewalls have been a foundation for perimeter defense. In the networked world, a firewall is generally a hardware/software system that sits at the intersection of the private (corporate or personal) network and the Internet or public network. A firewall interfaces with both private and public networks. It scans incoming data packets, which are either accepted and forwarded to the private network or rejected and denied access. For outgoing data packets, the process is reversed. Some methods used in scanning data are illustrated below.

- **Packet filtering:** Data packets are analyzed using pre-set rules, referred to as filters, which are set by system administrators or users. Filters can look at the source and destination addresses; protocols, such as HTTP or FTP, used by the data packets; or any other designated information; and can make a decision regarding the acceptance or rejection of the data packets. Critical message characteristics include traffic direction, network address, port (a pathway in or out of the computer or network) address, protocol type and service type.
- **Proxy servers:** Proxy servers sit between the real server and the application and intercept all requests directed at the real server. If the proxy server can fulfill a request, then it is not forwarded to the real server. Proxy servers improve performance and can be used in firewalls to direct incoming and outgoing traffic. A proxy

server can also be used for filtering; for example, a corporation can block undesirable Web sites and make them inaccessible.

- **Stateful inspection:** This method not only uses pre-set rules but also looks at prior packets to establish context for incoming information. The incoming or outgoing information is analyzed for its characteristics. These characteristics are then compared with stored and acceptable characteristics. If they match, then messages are forwarded, or else they are discarded.

Firewalls can be used to protect at network and application levels. Applications such as e-mail, FTP and remote logins can be managed by limiting access to the network. Only authorized users are allowed to pass through the firewall, thus providing a certain level of assurance. The unauthorized login can be effectively blocked and trigger alarms. Logging features can be used to track and analyze user records, thus providing a valuable diagnostic tool, even in case of a successful breach. Private network addresses can be masked by converting them into different addresses, as messages carrying those addresses travel over the public network. Firewalls are being embellished by new functionalities, such as encryption and VPN. Finally, firewalls provide a single point for security and audit purposes.

Firewalls do not protect against attacks that bypass firewalls. This may seem like a truism, which it is, though there are many corporations having strong firewalls but no policies on modems that dial in and out of the organization. Firewalls also do not protect against careless employees, social engineering, dumpster diving and failure to apply the latest security patches. Firewalls will not protect against theft of information if CDs are used to copy and take the information out of the corporation. Viruses are also hard to stop

Exhibit 13. Firewalls

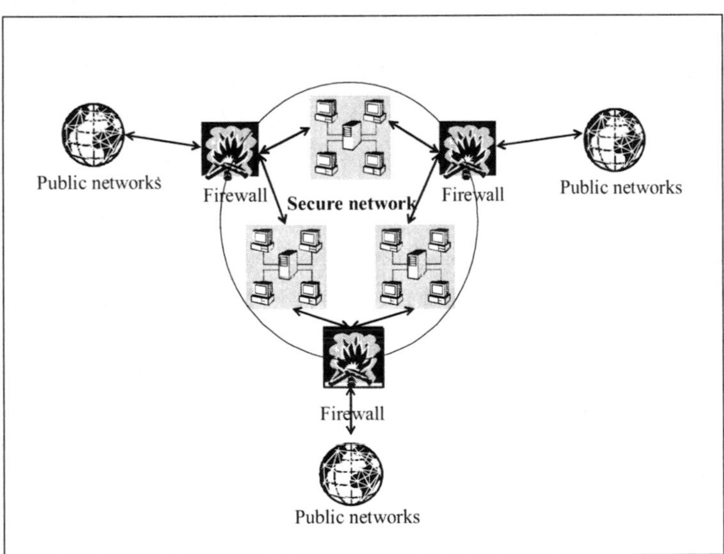

using only firewalls. There are far too many types of viruses, and firewalls cannot replace anti-virus software. Firewalls can cause traffic bottlenecks on the network; the more complex the method for scanning, the more computing resources are required. If a firewall is the only security point, the failure of the firewall can be catastrophic. Firewalls, in essence, are no substitutes for security policy, security awareness and common sense.

Web Content Filtering

Numerous commercial products provide Web content filtering or URL filtering services. Proxy servers can block traffic to undesired Web sites. However, if the employee browsing is a major concern, then a commercial product may be deployed. Web-filtering solutions work in the following way.

- **Capture:** Browser requests are captured before Web pages are delivered to the employee
- **Evaluation:** The request is evaluated for acceptance against the Web access policy
- **Action:** Based on the policy, the request is accepted, rejected or delayed.

How does the filtering software know the Web content of the requested pages? It uses a variety of techniques to distinguish between acceptable and unacceptable Web sites. The four commonly used techniques are: platform for Internet content selection (PICS), URL blocking, keyword filtering and intelligent analysis of Web site content.

The World Wide Web consortium created a set of specifications that can be used to construct a platform for content rating systems. Web publishers can associate labels or metadata with their Web pages to identify the nature of the Web site. However, PICS is not mandatory, and mislabeling of Web sites is possible. URL blocking works by comparing URLs with a database of unacceptable URLs, and then by denying access to the URL for which there is a match in the database. Another variation of this method is to only allow access to acceptable Web sites. Keyword filtering works by comparing words and phrases on a Web page with a keyword dictionary of prohibited words and phrases. If a match is found, the Web site is blocked. Intelligent content analysis, on the other hand, strives to achieve a semantic understanding of the context of the words and phrases on the Web pages. Statistical methods are then applied to this semantic understanding to categorize Web pages into acceptable and unacceptable categories.

Corporate policy decides what Web sites can be inappropriate given the corporate mission, sensitivity of target audiences and risk to the organization due to legal liability problems. The choice of filtering software, thus, depends on corporate policy. The software can also be customized for a particular organization. The trick is to find the commercial product that is a best fit for the organization.

Virtual Private Network (VPN)

VPN technology allows secure and confidential transmission of data and information over the Internet or public networks. VPN cannot exist without the Internet. Internet transmission is unsecured and can be intercepted using automated tools; however, using the Internet is a cost-effective way to transfer data. Major corporations sometimes use expensive dedicated communication lines, which in the long term are not cost effective; and small- and medium-size businesses generally cannot afford dedicated lines. VPN provides a cheaper and safer way to transfer data over the Internet.

The VPN is operated through a combination of hardware and software. The VPN server can be a piece of hardware or software that accepts VPN connections from VPN clients. This server is perpetually on and listens to VPN clients calling in to connect. A VPN client is generally a computer with loaded VPN client software. A client uses this software to initiate a call and establish a connection with the VPN server. VPN clients can use a variety of channels, such as corporate networks and telephone and satellite communications, to establish a connection with the VPN server.

The idea behind VPN technology is to create a private network over public networks. VPN creates a private network by establishing a secure and private communication channel between two machines across the public network. The secure links are established using *tunneling*. Tunneling does not mean establishing a fixed path through the Internet, though VPN users feel as if they have established a point-to-point connection. Tunneling refers to the fact that only the authorized users at both ends can see inside the message and obtain information. VPN also uses encryption of user data to shield it from prying eyes.

The data flows over the Internet using TCP/IP. TCP performs transportation functions for data and makes sure that the correct message reaches the destination. IP manages network addresses and routes messages over the networks. The IP Packet of data, created using tunneling, contains three elements: passenger protocol, encapsulating protocol and carrier protocol. The passenger protocol contains user data sent by the user, such as credit card number, addresses or other confidential information. The encapsulating protocol is the protocol wrapped around the passenger protocol or user data and can be specific to the network hardware and software used by the corporation. This information can contain addresses of the ultimate user on the corporate network. If accessed, this information can be used by hackers to attack Web sites. The carrier protocol contains the source and destination addresses using IP protocol so the data can travel over the Internet.

VPN generally uses IP Security (IPSec) protocol for tunneling. IPSec is a standard developed by the IETF that defines a set of protocols and encryption algorithms that create secure communication links. These standards apply at the packet level. IPSec is developed to serve the following goals.

- **Authenticity:** Each data packet contains a unique digital signature that identifies the sender. If such data packets are forged and passed on to the network, they will be identified and rejected. Authentication is a two-way process — the VPN client and the VPN server mutually authenticate each other.

- **Confidentiality:** Data is encrypted and transported over the Internet privately; unauthorized uses are not allowed to see or sniff data. The IPSec can be configured even to hide source and destination addresses, so no one knows whom you are communicating with.
- **Integrity:** If the data packets are altered without proper authorization, authorized users are able to detect such modification. This protection is applied to each data packet. An illustrative technique to ensure integrity is the use of hash functions. This function calculates a unique number based on the characteristics of data. This number is attached to data and the data is encrypted. These numbers can also be sent via different message, if desired. These hash numbers cannot be recalculated unless the specific mathematical functions are known, and thus, cannot be altered by the hacker. The recipient, after receiving the message, decrypts the message and calculates the hash number independently. If the two hash numbers do not match, data has been altered in transit.

If a denial of service is initiated using duplicate data packets copied from the original, they can be identified and rejected before the services get overloaded and shut down. Such identification is possible due to message counting features enabled by the IPSec protocol.

Exhibit 14. Architecture of VPN

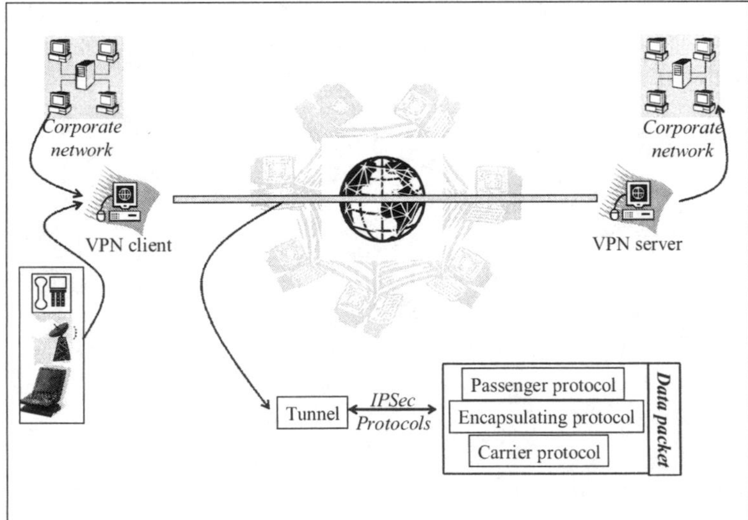

VPN serves different groups. First, remote, traveling or telecommuting employees can avail the corporate computing resources. This is referred to as remote VPN, which uses the Internet to establish cost-effective communication links. Second, branch offices and subsidiaries can establish a secure network to conduct business. This is referred to as Intranet-based VPN, which uses TCP/IP and authentication mechanisms, such as passwords. Finally, stakeholders and trading partners can be given controlled access to the corporate network. This is referred to as extranet-based VPN, which connects the networks of the stakeholders or trading partners to create the Extranets.

The primary benefit of VPN is cost reduction due to the elimination of leased lines, reduction in long-distance and international calls, deployment of cheaper VPN equipment as compared to other remote access solutions and simpler network administration, since part of the network is the Internet. VPNs also provide adequate security to conduct business over the Internet. Moreover, VPNs can be scaled cheaply as the business grows, as opposed to, say, leased lines, which increase exponentially as the business grows. The global reach provided by VPNs is generally unmatched, considering the cost benefit. Costs of VPNs include hardware, software, installation, changes in workflows, defining and managing security policies, and buying or outsourcing required expertise. Additionally, the improved security requires high-speed computers and high bandwidths, which should be considered in deploying VPN.

Message Security Protocols

Numerous security protocols ensure message integrity. Two common protocols are discussed here. SSL is a protocol or technique to secure communications between two computers communicating over the Internet. For example, if a customer buys books on the Internet, he/she needs a secure way to send personal information over the Internet. SSL enables such secure communication. SSL can be used if supported by the customer's browser. Nowadays, most browsers support SSL, and the SSL connection is exemplified by a lock at the bottom of the screen. SSL establishes secure links via encryption, digital certificates and authentication algorithms.

The SSL process consists of four steps. First, the client computer (a computer that is initiating the SSL session) makes a request to the server computer (a computer to whom the request is being made) to establish a secure connection. Second, mutually acceptable methods for establishing such a connection are established by the client and server computer. Third, a secure link is established and data is exchanged; however, tests that verify security of the connection go on constantly. Finally, the communication is completed and the session is terminated.

Initiation of the SSL session is done after the request is made by the client computer. The request is handled by the server using a special port. Standard requests for information and requests to establish SSL connection are generally handled by different ports. A choice of special port by the server signals preparation for negotiating procedures for establishing an SSL session, which is called SSL Handshake. SSL Handshake begins with the client saying Hello to the server. Remember, the client computer is accessing the server using a browser, and there are different types of browsers and different versions

Exhibit 15. SSL protocol

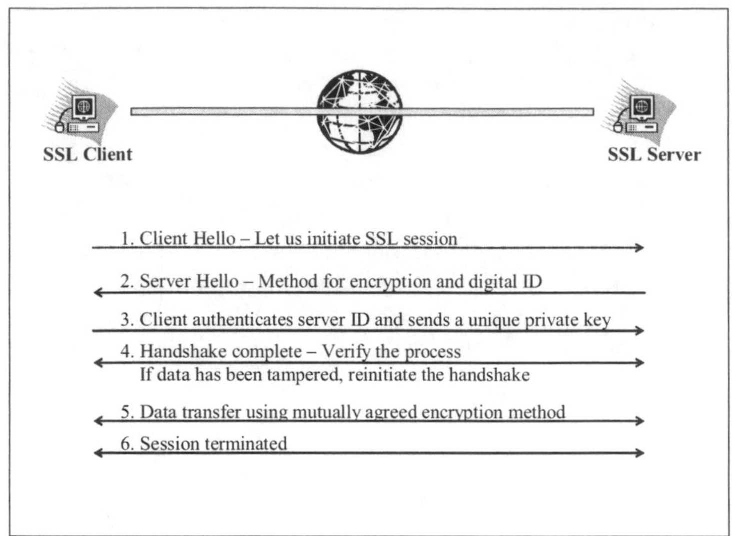

of each browser. Each type and version supports different encryption protocols and algorithms. The initial Hello tells the server supported encryption protocols and data compression algorithms; and also sends a random number. This random number is used to establish a secure connection in a rare case where the server does not have a digital ID. At this point, no private information is being passed; merely, the ways of exchanging information and the methods of encryption acceptable to the browser are being conveyed to the server. Finally, the browser also asks the server for identification.

The client Hello is followed by the server Hello. The server now sends its digital ID (including public key) for authentication or identification purposes. Additionally, another random number and the chosen encryption method and data compression algorithm are sent back to the client; the method chosen is generally the strongest method supported by the client. The server may request the client's digital ID. The client now validates the digital ID of the server by decrypting it with the public key. Then validity checks are conducted to ensure that the decrypted digital ID contains a digital certificate from a trusted authority, dates are correct and the Web site URL matches with the certificate. The client, if assured, generates a private key, encrypts the private key with the server's public key and the encryption method suggested by the server. The encrypted key is compressed using the chosen data compression algorithm and sent back to the server. This encrypted key can now only be opened with the private key of the server.

The entire process is now verified. The client and the server know the private key. A copy of previous transactions is recreated and encrypted using the client private key and exchanged to confirm that it has not been tampered with in transit. If the answer is no (the information has not been tampered), the handshake is completed and both parties are ready for transmittal of data on a secure link. If the answer is yes (the information has been tampered), the handshake is not completed but re-initiated. The client-generated private key is used only for one session and discarded; a new session requires generation of a new key.

Data transmission after the handshake is carried out using the previously agreed encryption method. The messages are encrypted, digitally signed and forwarded by the server and the client during the session. The encryption also extends to the URL of the requested document and cookies sent from server to browser and vice versa. The encrypted data are verified for authentication, integrity and confidentiality. As in the VPN, SSL also establishes a secure tunnel through the Internet using encryption. When data transmission is complete, the session can be terminated. At termination, the client computer is warned (Are you sure you want to leave the secure connection?), and the session then terminates.

Secure HTTP (S-HTTP) is another way to secure messages over the Internet, though SSL is more prevalent and enjoys wider support. Do not confuse S-HTTP with HTTPS. HTTPS is a browser-specific application of SSL to HTTP. S-HTTP has different design goals and can be used in conjunction with SSL. S-HTTP provides authentication, integrity and confidentiality features for data flowing on the Internet. The basic functioning of S-HTTP is similar to SSL. During the initial negotiation, the client and server computer set the security requirements, such as a preferred method of encryption. Then the client sends the private key encrypted with the server's public key. This key can be used for encryption purposes by both the client and server. The primary difference in SSL and S-HTTP is that SSL sets up a secure session. S-HTTP does not set up an entire session, but sets up packet headers for each data packet that specify the security requirements. Thus, if a customer is viewing a product description on Web pages, the session will be unsecured. But if the customer moves on to the payment page for payment, a secure transmission is established. S-HTTP can be used in conjunction with SSL to provide a stronger security for sensitive information.

A Taxonomy of Network Anti-Intrusion Techniques

This section is based on an excellent white paper by Halme and Bauer, titled *AINT Misbehaving: A Taxonomy of Anti-Intrusion Techniques,* found at *www.sans.org/resources/idfaq/aint.php*. Anti-intrusion techniques are used to identify and prevent network intrusion attacks. These techniques evolved as technology and misuse of technology evolved. Anti-intrusion techniques now include proactive defenses, such as attacking hacker bulletin boards and spreading misinformation; reactive defenses, such as intrusion detection; and interactive defenses, such as intelligent programs that continuously monitor network traffic. Anti-intrusion techniques can be classified into six categories: prevention, preemption, deterrence, deflection, detection and counter-measures.

Exhibit 16. Network anti-intrusion techniques

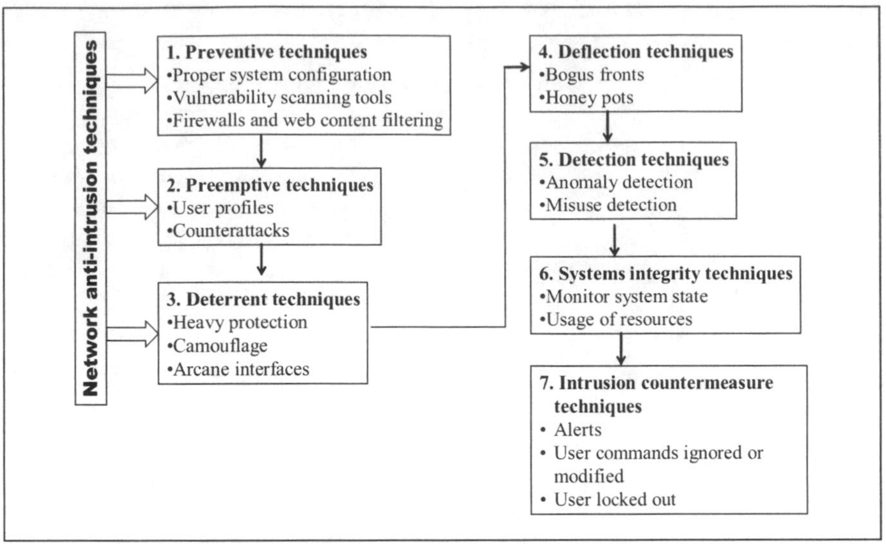

Preventive Techniques

Preventive techniques strive to prevent network attack. Prevention of a network attack refers to either foiling a network intrusion attempt or preventing serious damage to the system. Security techniques include proper configuration, vulnerability scanning tools and firewalls. Proper configuration of computer and network systems include following the software vendor's directions, installing appropriate security patches, developing physical and logical security routines for the system, and continuous update and maintenance of the system. Given the plethora of operating and network software systems, wide variations in security training and spotty organizational security awareness, proper configuration is not as easy as it sounds. Security policy and user education are non-technical but important components of preventive techniques.

Vulnerability Scanning Tools scan the network and identify possible vulnerabilities for network attacks. These tools scan networks computers, operating systems, applications and attached peripherals. Examples of common vulnerabilities include unauthorized software, unauthorized computers on the network, unauthorized user accounts, weak passwords and compromised valid user accounts. These tools also look for intruder activity, may have a database of known vulnerabilities that can be used to investigate weak network points and even check for dormant viruses. Vulnerability scanning services, if outsourced to a security company, may also include ethical hacking to test the network. The scanning tools can be used periodically or in real time to continuously monitor the network. Scanning tools can automatically fix security flaws, create alerts and pass on reports to authorized persons. Numerous vulnerability scanning tools are available, and vulnerability scanning services are offered by different software vendors.

Firewalls and Web Content Filtering are also preventive measures. Firewalls prevent network attacks by monitoring bi-directional network traffic and stopping potentially dangerous data packets. A Web content filtering mechanism blocks access to Web sites and bulletin boards, which may be used by hackers for disseminating viruses, Trojan horses or for social engineering. Remember, firewalls and Web content filtering techniques are not foolproof. Vulnerability scanning tools complement firewalls, since firewalls can be bypassed or compromised, especially if the hackers are from inside or are knowledgeable; for example, industrial spies and foreign agents.

Preemptive Techniques

Preemptive techniques use a pro-active stance to defeat network attacks. These techniques can include real-time analysis of network traffic, profiling of users, developing contacts in the hacker community to glean information and taking appropriate preemptive action. For example, some companies have developed intelligent programs that sit outside the firewall and monitor incoming traffic. If the incoming traffic indicates a hacker attack, which may be identified by the nature of commands, such as probes and scans, then counteraction is taken. The intelligent program will respond by sending back bogus data to confound hacking efforts. Preemptive techniques may also include attacking hacker resources or planting false information; such efforts are dubious in nature, since innocent users may also be hurt. Another venue is to lobby legislatures for stringent laws; an excellent example is a campaign carried by the music industry to halt the spread of digital distribution of music. Such campaigns, of course, have their own risks; there being no free lunch.

Deterrent Techniques

Hackers, like thieves, follow a path of least resistance. If the network is heavily protected, rigorously prosecutes offenders or does not appear to be important, hackers will move on to softer systems. Deterrence techniques may be implemented by heavily protecting all network entry points. Such protection may discourage prospective hackers or may attract a few as a challenging system, though the overall rate of attacks will go down. This policy, of course, is expensive and used to guard critical resources. Other techniques might be to post warnings to prospective hackers on the Web site, swiftly punish any errant user activity, develop an aura of a highly security-conscious company, or plant false security indicators. Some systems may be camouflaged, meaning a system may appear to be plain, uninteresting, of little importance, may use arcane user interfaces or any other technique that will cause a prospective hacker to lose interest and move on.

Deflection Techniques

In this technique, a network attack is not prevented or stopped; it is allowed to succeed — under controlled conditions. As the network attack begins, the hacker(s) are lured into network systems specifically created for them. These systems can be totally separate or built into the network. These systems, called *honey pots*, are made especially attractive for hackers. The systems display all signs of protecting a vital resource and present (not insurmountable) difficulties in penetration. The intruder may think that he/she has compromised a user account, obtained supervisory rights,or successfully penetrated the network. The attacker can be fed false information, tracked for counterattack or his/her attack pattern studied for research and security purposes.

Detection Techniques

Network intrusions, either in real time or after the incident, are detected using network intrusion-detection systems. There are three types: host based, network based and hybrid systems. Host-based systems analyze network traffic data that is collected by a host computer, which is a computer that hosts a service such as a Web server. Data collected by the host system is aggregated; it can be forwarded to another location or kept locally, and then analyzed using a network intrusion detection system. A host-based system is effective in network intrusion initiated by insiders and unauthorized file modifications. A host system becomes inefficient when the network is large and has thousands of entry points; collecting and analyzing data from each host computer can become cost prohibitive. A network-based system operates on the network in real time and analyzes incoming and outgoing data packets. These systems monitor live network connections and data transfer; as such, these systems are more effective in detecting unauthorized access by outsiders and denial-of-service-type attacks. A hybrid system combines characteristics of both systems to provide better coverage from network intrusion. The choice of a particular type of system depends on the risks posed by insiders vs. outsiders.

How do these systems detect network intrusion? Network intruders obviously want to cover their tracks and will not announce successful penetration. Standard techniques for network intrusion are anomaly detection and misuse detection. Anomaly detection refers to any network activity that *differs* from the normal or expected pattern of activity. How do we define *differ*? There are a number of techniques, but they take us in the realm of statistics and computer science; for example, any activity that occurs with a frequency that is either above or below two standard deviations compared to the norm may get flagged as possible intrusion. A few methods of anomaly detection are given below; each method has strengths and weaknesses, and many of these methods are concurrently used in intrusion detection.

- **Work profiling:** In this method, the user's standard work habits and requirements are compiled. For example, a work profile of a manager may be as follows: logs in early mornings, uses e-mail regularly, browses extensively and may log in on weekends. If the manager changes his/her behavior, acts like a system administrator and tries to change a user profile, then network intrusion will be suspected. This method can be extended to a group of workers to develop group profiles. Any behavior that differs from a group profile may become target of an investigation.

- **Resource profiling:** Here, the resources in the network system, such as applications, network connections and peripherals, are profiled for usage. Each of these resources will have a usage pattern, based on usage since deployment. Any significant deviation from the usage pattern may be a suspected network intrusion.
- **Executable profiling:** Executable programs that execute certain activities to use system resources can also be profiled. If the executable programs seem to be consuming a great deal of system resources, that might indicate anomalous behavior.

Misuse detection, also referred to as *signature detection method*, on the other hand, explicitly checks for illegal, illicit or prohibited activity on the network. Instead of looking for deviations from the norm, as in anomaly detection, misuse detection scans specific patterns of activities. The illegal activity can be as simple as three failed log-in attempts or can involve analysis of data packet contents (packet content signatures or header content signatures) that indicates intentions to carry out unauthorized actions. Misuse detection methods work best when there is a historical database of network intrusion cases that can be used to develop methods to identify misuse of the network. Different methods — such as expert systems that use a series of if and then rules to arrive at conclusions, model based reasoning, or neural networks that are trained using historical cases — are used. A variety of artificial intelligence techniques, such as data mining and Bayesian networks, are also used in developing models that can be used for misuse detection. Anomaly detection and misuse detection are not mutually exclusive, and many systems use both techniques at the same time to improve performance.

To be effective, intrusion detection systems must have a low rate of false alarms and false negatives. A false alarm refers to an alarm triggered by the system when there is no intrusion (legitimate visitor classified as attacker) and false negative (attacker classified as legitimate visitor) refers to the real network intrusion that is not identified by the network detection system. The problem with many of today's systems is that there is an incredibly high rate of false alarms. An analogous problem in reducing the rate of false alarms is that one needs reliable historical data and complete audit trails, which may not be possible. A new breed of hacking tools simulates hundreds of attacks in a few seconds, thereby overwhelming the network intrusion detection system; the system can crash, overlook real attacks or operate but become dysfunctional. A test carried out by *NetworkWorld* on eight intrusion detection systems, which includes hardware and/or software, identified the following problems: repeated crashes due to a high rate of false alarms, missing real attacks, overly complex interfaces and consumption of a large amount of computing and communication resources. Another issue is the requirement of skilled and costly personnel required to operate and maintain network detection systems. Network intrusion detection systems are important in the overall security architecture, but should not be unduly relied upon.

System Integrity Techniques

These techniques monitor various vital signs of the network. The initial configuration is known, since it is set by the system administrator. These tools take a snapshot of the network system; for example, the system configuration files, systems programs or Web pages. The network system is then monitored by changes in system files and usage of system resources. Standard and expected changes are ignored and changes that seem incompatible with the purpose of the network are investigated in real time. The network system integrity tool may sound an alarm if suspicious changes are found; however, in case of an active attack, it may be too late by the time the alarm is investigated and action is taken. Sometimes responses can be automated; for example, restore the Web pages or system files using backups. These tools can operate in the background, constantly or periodically checking system status. The trick, of course, is to develop intelligent tools that will minimize false alarms and false negatives.

Intrusion Countermeasures (ICE) Techniques

Network intrusion detection is the beginning of a process; the next step is to immediately neutralize the intrusion. ICE refers to the process of taking action against the perceived intrusion. The problem with network intrusion attacks is that they are automated and done within minutes; human responses are too slow to parry such fast-moving threats. ICE automates responses and responds to network attacks in real time. Numerous retaliatory responses are possible. The severity of the response will depend on the confidence placed by ICE on the possibility of intrusion. First, the intrusion attempt might be conveyed to the system administrator using e-mail, instant messaging or even by beeper. Second, user activity may be monitored, user authenticity may be (re)verified or security personnel may be alerted to check on the user. Finally, ICE can take programmed actions, such as slow response to user commands, only pretend to execute user commands, lock out the user, disconnect the network or track back the attack to the suspected offender and counter-attack.

But which action do you take given the high incidence of false alarms? If you lock out legitimate users continuously, ICE will face resistance in the organization. If the CEO is locked out while doing important work, the chances that ICE will be put on ice are very high. On the other hand, if network intrusion attempts succeed, the very same fate awaits the system administrator and ICE. There is no one right answer to these questions. The configuration of ICE is not a science, since each organization and network is unique. As such, the correct answer is different for each organization.

A Word on Wireless Networks

Most network anti-intrusion techniques discussed so far are also useful in case of wireless networks. However, wireless networks provide new ways to attack the network. Additional vulnerabilities can be summarized as follows. First, the hackers do not need physical access to the network; attacks can be launched on any computer connected to the network. For example, an employee may be working in an office on a secure system, but if the hackers manage to get a seat outside the office window, then they may be able to hack into the wireless network. Second, wireless networks are used predominantly for laptops or mobile computing. Network nodes or laptops are constantly moving. The problem of physical security is now even more acute, since these computers can be compromised on airports, roads, motel rooms or any unknown location. The comprised node can be used to launch attacks from anywhere on the globe, which makes tracking such attacks very difficult. Third, in some cases, wireless networks do not have a centralized authority but work due to cooperation among peer nodes or connected computers. Such lack of centralized authority makes it easier to launch hacker attacks. Finally, wireless networks extensively use proxies (trusting tasks to other computers) or software agents (partially or fully automated software performing certain tasks) to accelerate processing. These proxies or agents can also be targeted for attacks.

The technical details of wireless networks are beyond the scope of this book. Standard security tools such as encryption, digital signatures and digital certificates are obviously used to secure wireless networks, but these are not enough. The vulnerabilities of a wireless network warrant additional security precautions. The standard algorithm used to protect confidentiality and for authentication purposes is Wired Equivalent Privacy (WEP); however, a number of questions have been raised about the efficacy of this algorithm. Regardless, new and improved security standards are emerging in this area. Here are some common-sense controls suggested for a wireless network.

- **Secure SSID:** SSID stands for service set identifier, which is used for identification purposes on the wireless network. Securing SSID involves a few simple things, such as change the default SSID set by the manufacturer and customize it, change SSID at frequent intervals and do not use an easily identifiable SSID. These requirements are similar to requirements for setting up good passwords.
- **Change passwords:** Change the default passwords set by the software vendor, which may be overlooked by tsystem administrators.
- **Change access point position:** Make a survey of the wireless network area and make sure that those areas do not extend outside the office or someplace where hackers can easily tap into the network.
- **Use filtering:** Network interface cards generally carry a number or address used in directing traffic by the wireless network. Use only those addresses in directing traffic, and filter out any other addresses demanded by the data packets.
- **Use security protocols:** For larger wireless networks, use security protocols such as IPSec or Remote Authentication Dial-In User Service (Radius) that provide better security.

The wireless security area is in transition, and many new security protocols and tools are emerging. For example, IBM has developed Wireless Security Auditor (WSA), which is an automated tool to audit a wireless network for proper configuration and vulnerability assessment.

Anti-Intrusion Products

The anti-intrusion product market is flooded with different types of products. There are standalone products in every category. Some of these products, such as Security Administrator Tool for Analyzing Networks (SATAN), are freely available and used by system administrators and hackers alike. These products may also come in a box, a hardware/software combination, which can be connected with the network. These products are sometimes referred to as *security appliances*. There are also numerous software-only products. As is the trend of the times, these products are converging and a number of comprehensive security software suites are now on the market. The efficiency and effectiveness of these products still remains a research issue.

Automated Control and Compliance Tools

Traditional internal controls are useful in the online environment. However, millions of transactions are processed online in minutes; illicit transactions are few, but need to be identified in real time, and the after the fact audit or knowledge of such transactions is not very useful. Privacy and security requirements imposed by new legislation are stringent and backed by stiff penalties. As a result, a number of software vendors have offered automated control and compliance tools. Research in efficiency and effectiveness of these tools has not kept pace with offerings. This area promises to grow rapidly, since only automated tools seem capable of meeting the online challenge. Automated software offerings by Searchspace and TransactionVision are now examined. The ensuing discussion will hopefully provide an understanding of this segment of the market.

Searchspace

Searchspace is a software provider of what is called intelligent enterprise systems, which refers to software that automates decisions, reduces risk and monitors compliance. Some examples of solutions offered include anti-money laundering, financial fraud, compliance with laws and assessment of operational risks to business. These products are generally tailored to a particular industry, because the external environment and applicable laws are different for each industry.

Searchspace employs what it calls Intelligent Enterprise Framework (IEF) to carry out automated duties. The IEF-based software analyzes normal *and* abnormal patterns of behavior in data. By developing both patterns, the software can remain alert to situations that conform to the norm and differ from the norm. This pattern identification is done using artificial intelligence techniques, data mining techniques and business rules applicable to a particular business and industry. This framework has certain core components to manage different functions. The IEF is structured as five different layers, each layer processing and filtering data to enable intelligent decisions. These five layers are discussed in the following list.

- **Data manager:** Data manager extracts data from the production or operational systems of the enterprise. Data manager also has abilities to transform data collected from different business systems. Data can be extracted in real time or in batch modes.
- **Adaptive profiling engine:** This part of the software develops profiles or behaviors of data extracted from the operational systems. Profiles are developed for each entity — for example, a customer, channel, account, product or country — in three dimensions. These dimensions are comparison against peers, comparison against other entities and comparison over time. The profiles capture necessary attributes or characteristics of the entity. The problem in profiling is to develop necessary models that are neither too simplistic nor too complex. Moreover, the profiles must change as complexity of the transactions changes. The actual profiling process is proprietary, it uses techniques such as statistical profiling, clustering and generic algorithms.
- **Operational data store:** Profiles are stored in the operational data store. Specific transactions used to develop the profiles may also be stored, if necessary. The profiles can be sliced and diced to examine how different transactions affect different profiles or behaviors of entities.
- **Sentinels:** Sentinels use the profiles stored in the operational data store as baselines. These tools use heuristics techniques to statistically predict behavior. Different profiles can be compared across different dimensions, and abnormal or anomalous behaviors are spotted. Sentinels derive their own rules in the process; a user can also add other desired rules to the sentinel knowledge base. These rules are used to suggest actions to the action manager.
- **Action manager:** Based on the sentinels' characterization, actions are initiated by the action manager. For example, a money-laundering alert to the manager shows reasoning, account summary, customer summary, notification status and history of the account. If needed, regulatory reports required under the U.S. Patriot Act can be automatically generated. Drill-down abilities and additional contextual details are available in the system. Every recommended action is stored for audit trail purposes.

Solutions such as Searchspace are useful in environments where millions of transactions are being processed and manual monitoring or evaluation is almost impossible. Figuring out normal behavior for customers and finding a customer who is involved in money laundering or check kiting is not possible, even using an army of employees. The primary advantage is that these systems learn and adapt from data and then automate the decision making. The incidence and costs of false alarms and false negatives, of course, assumes great importance in case of such systems and should be evaluated.

Exhibit 17. Searchspace functionalities

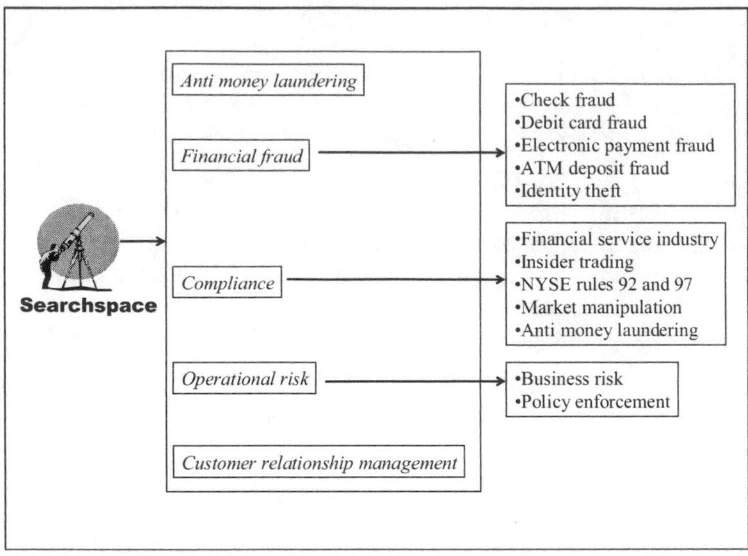

Exhibit 18. Searchspace operations

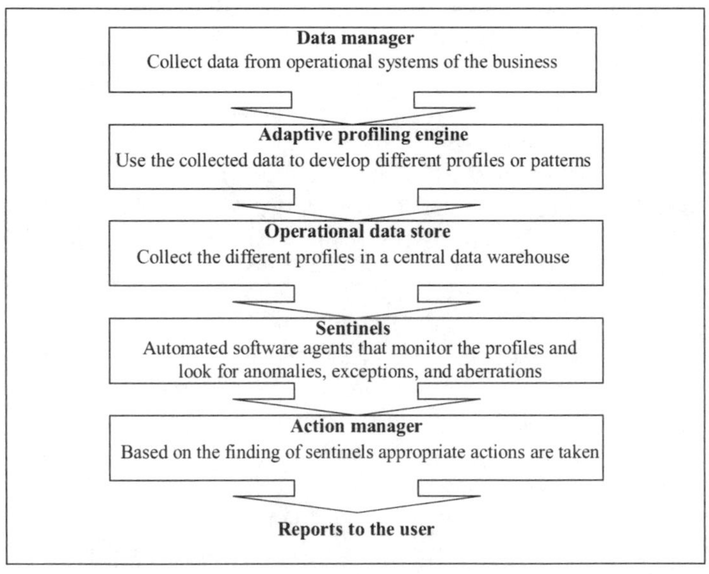

TransactionVision

TransactionVision is not exactly an automated control tool; however, this software tracks electronic transactions across systems, functions and departments, and has interesting applications in the maintenance of audit trails. This software can be used in business activity monitoring, end-to-end transaction tracking, and sales and marketing analytics; our interests are in the first two activities. Tracking transactions in the electronic environment is difficult, due to a mix of hardware and software, application-specific file formats and/or functional or departmental technology islands. TransactionVision uses the following services to track the transaction.

- **Sensors:** These are software agents, having a small footprint, installed on applications in the business process. These agents do not interfere with the applications. The transaction data is collected and forwarded to the events collection controller.
- **Event collection controller:** The transaction data that is forwarded by the sensors is now stored in a relational database.
- **Event analysis service:** This service analyzes the electronic messages and constructs a coherent business transaction. The business transaction is stored, along with the associated transaction path. For example, a PO and subsequent activities based on that PO can be assembled to figure out how the PO was processed.
- **Transaction analysis service:** The business events are analyzed by this service, and subsequent actions are initiated. For example, an action may be to contact a customer, execute a pre-defined workflow — say to process a sales order, or alert an appropriate manager. All business events and initiated actions are stored to provide a complete audit history.
- **Reports and dashboards:** Reports can be generated on business events and the actions taken based on those events. Executive dashboards provide real-time monitoring for the given objective; for example, transactions processed, transactions delayed and key performance measures.

The obvious application of such technologies is maintaining a complete audit trail. In the electronic environment, the audit trail can get broken, fragmented or untraceable very quickly. If each financial transaction is tracked, there will be an audit trail that is now independent of the applications processing the data. TransactionVision uses business rules to define normal processing of financial transactions. If the processing deviates from a normal path, then such transactions are closely monitored. Since fraudulent transactions, misuse of computer systems or override of internal controls do deviate from a normal path, such activities may get detected in real time.

To reiterate, the purpose of this section is to highlight new developments in automated control and compliance tools. The efficacy of such tools, problems in implementation or rates of false alarms and false negatives are not yet researched, and even anecdotal evidence is hard to come by. But as the past suggests, technology becomes better in performing tasks that may have been hyped in the initial phase. These tools, as they become widely available, will be definitely used by accountants and required to be evaluated by auditors.

Exhibit 19. TransactionVision functionalities

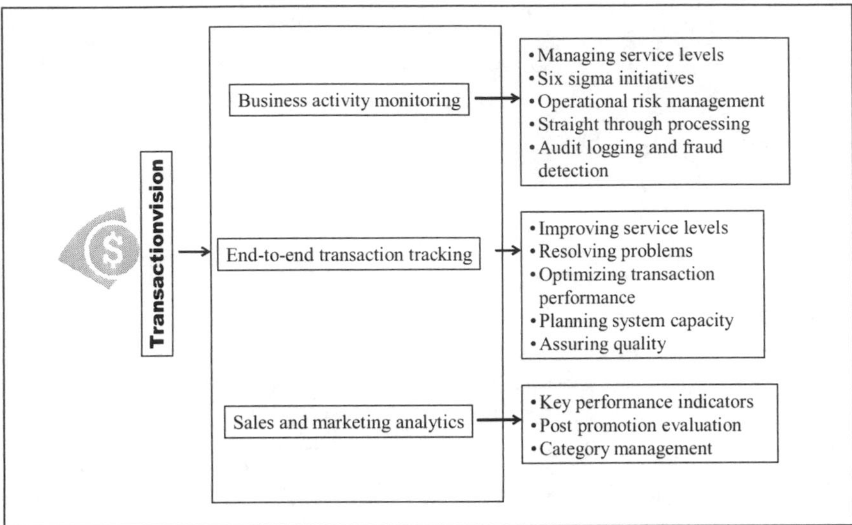

Exhibit 20. TransactionVision operations

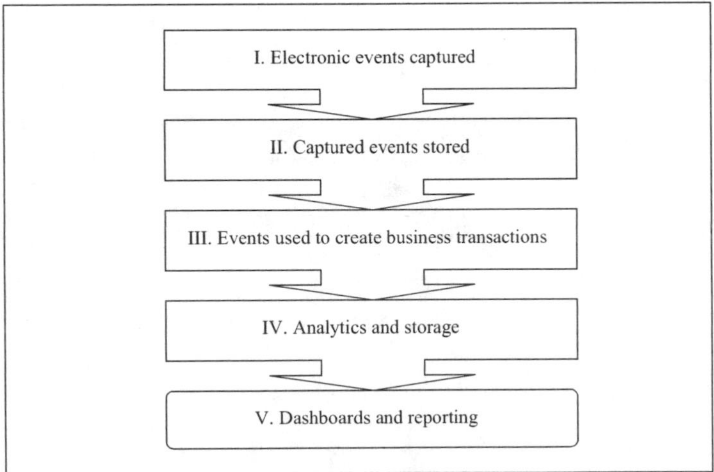

Privacy and Assurance Issues in the Online World

"In God we trust, all others ..." Fill in the blanks with your favorite — pay in cash, show identification, undergo body search or show corroborating data. Privacy and security issues are pervasive and intertwined in e-commerce. The problem is two-fold: How can Web sites trust consumers? And how can consumers trust the Web site? These questions are more acute in B2C transactions. In typical B2B transactions, a due diligence process is undertaken to certify a supplier if the supplier is unknown, and generally the payments are made upon receipt of the order. B2C transactions pose a number of problems. First, the standard method of payment is credit card, and that raises a number of security issues. Some issues we discussed in the revenue cycle are reproduced as follows:

- Credit cards are designed for face-to-face commerce. Identifiers such as name, social security number and signature are irrelevant in e-commerce. There have been efforts by some credit card companies to introduce PINs in online transactions for additional security, though enrollment is voluntary.
- Credit card data, basically name and card number, can be easily stolen. The card numbers do not change and are stored on merchant servers, an easy target for hackers.
- Credit cards are easy to duplicate.
- Credit card fraud costs run into tens of billions of dollars. There are no concerted efforts by credit card companies to create common fraud-fighting utilities.

Second, a large amount of personal customer data is collected, which raises privacy and security issues. Finally, due to the large number of Web sites, customers cannot always be certain about the legitimacy of online companies.

Online companies can be victimized due to the misuse of stolen credit cards in e-commerce. The law provides limited liability for individual consumers in case of credit card misuse, if certain conditions are followed; however, generally such protection is not afforded to businesses. They may have to absorb the losses, and many small online businesses have incurred severe losses due to the use of stolen credit card numbers. A bank can even cancel the credit card facility, thereby endangering the very existence of online business. Estimated fraud rates vary within a range of 2% to 40%. This is one business risk and needs to be managed using appropriate insurance and business policy tools. Some standard business policies used for this purpose are given below.

- Require customers to fill in all requested details and ask for all relevant information
- Scrutinize all orders where billing and shipping addresses are different
- Be wary of international orders with free e-mail addresses (Hotmail or Yahoo!)

- If the order looks suspicious, do not hesitate to call the customer
- Have special procedures in place for first-time large orders

This section, however, focuses on the risk posed to consumers, and privacy and assurance services that have risen to manage these risks.

Consumers have to provide name, address and credit card number (a preferred method of payment on the Web) to online companies for buying goods and services. If the Web site is not authentic, the information can be stolen, which is one of the methods used to commit Identity Theft. In this crime, the identity of a person is hijacked and assumed by another person. To commit this theft, a criminal needs personal information, such as social security number, driver's license number or credit card numbers. The criminal can use identity theft to take out loans, buy cars and products, or even empty the bank accounts of the legitimate owners. Even though identity theft is a federal offense, it is generally extremely hard for the victim to prove innocence and clear charges. Web sites also collect enormous customer data, such as Web viewing habits, types of sites most visited and products purchased, which is stored, packaged and sold to other companies. Illustrative questions that might be important to customers are listed below.

- Is the online operation legitimate?
- If it is legitimate, does it deliver products and services?
- Does it have appropriate controls to guard its Web site and customer information?
- Does the online business misuse private information collected from customers?

Exhibit 21. Objectives of online seals

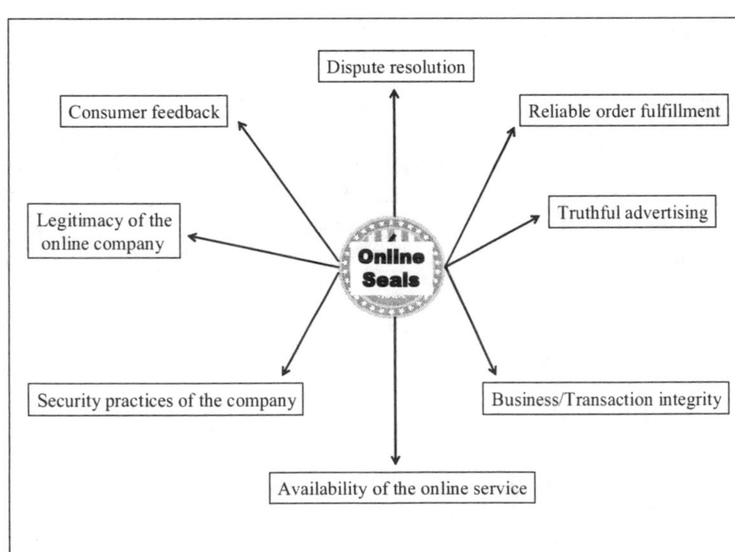

Such a state of affairs seems ripe for online assurance services. A number of initiatives have been launched to fulfill this niche in e-commerce. The standard method of operation is to display a seal on the Web site. This seal might be a symbol, logo or trust mark. A seal is a mark of assurance that the online company adheres to guidelines formulated by the organization granting the symbol. Customers can click on the seal and browse to the organization granting the seal. Here the details of seals, such as privacy, security or confidentiality requirements required, can be obtained.

The auditor's opinion on financial statements is also a type of seal. By law, financial statement audits are carried out by Certified Public Accountants or Chartered Accountants (CPAs or CAs) in the U.S. and in most other counties. The seals in the online world are not regulated by such laws, and a number of organizations issue their own seal. The purpose of the seals varies; for example, dealing with privacy issues, outlining procedures for resolving disputes between customers and online companies, or certifying veracity of the online company. A few seals simply indicate that customers can provide their feedback on the buying experience and these responses will be aggregated and displayed on the seal provider's Web site. A seal like WebTrust provides assurance on a number of dimensions. Due to the different focuses of different seals, a business might

Exhibit 22. Examples of different types of online seals

Seal	Organization	Purpose
BBB Reliability Seal	Better Business Bureau Online	Quality assurance – satisfactory complaint handling record; self-regulation in advertising; arbitration procedures in case of customer disputes
BBB Privacy Seal	Better Business Bureau Online	Privacy – privacy policies are posted on the web site and complied with; compliance assessment review; practice monitoring
Better Internet Bureau	Better Internet Bureau Association	Quality assurance – merchant agree to abide by the guidelines
BizRate	BizRate	Collection and aggregation of customer feedback; displayed on the website
Netcheck Commerce Bureau	Netcheck Commerce Bureau	Resolution of disputes between companies, companies and consumers, and consumer and companies
PublicEye	ePublicEye.com	Customers rate the online business for privacy, reliability, and satisfaction; ratings maintained by ePublicEye.com; confirms that customers received the orders
SiteCertain	American Bankers Association	Validates that the online company is a genuine financial institution
TRUSTe	Truste	Privacy policies developed according to the Truste guidelines and displayed on the website; periodic verification by Truste
WebGuardian	WebGuardian	Provides information on web sites; disputer resolution between a customer and a company; reporting of the Internet frauds
WebTrust	AICPA/CICA	Audits the online companies to provide assurance regarding – privacy, security, and business practices/transaction integrity; availability of the service; confidentiality; non-repudiation

need more than one seal. The annual prices required to acquire different seals vary widely — some seals are free, whereas seals like WebTrust may cost thousands of dollars depending on the size of the online corporation.

Given the plethora of seals, the obvious question is what makes the seal reliable? A few general rules can be cited in this area. First, look at the organization that is granting seals. Does this organization have expertise in this area? Does the organization have a trained cadre of members or other mechanisms to monitor compliance with the requirements of the seal? Second, investigate the requirements of the seal itself. Are the requirements clear and comprehensive enough to justify the goals of the seal? Third, the organization must have a sound procedure to investigate compliance with the requirements of the seal. Does the organization actually audit compliance with the seal, or is compliance based on self-reported data by members? Who does the audit and what is its frequency? Business models and methods change rapidly in the online world, and the seal administration should reflect those changes. Fourth, the objectives of the seal should be matched with requirements of customers. A customer interested in knowing whether the online company is a genuine company will not be interested in the privacy seal. Finally, even if the site displays the seal required by the consumer, the seal's authenticity needs to be verified. Each seal employs mechanisms to protect integrity of the seal, such as links to the seal-granting institution, digital signatures, digital certificates and the use of Web spiders to verify existence of unauthorized seals. However, consumers need to be alert, since authenticity of the seals are not guaranteed under all circumstances.

Such assessment, of course, takes time, and most online consumers do not have the time or expertise to conduct such investigations. Security and privacy are often cited as prime consumer concerns in e-commerce. Initial expectations were that the seals would be demanded by customers; however, the seal market has not found wide acceptance. A study on seals displayed by Web merchants found that less than half of companies selling office equipment, general merchandise and apparel had seals. On the other hand, specialty realtors, such as Amazon.com and Home Depot, had more assurance seals. The study classified the seals into three types: security (controls over the Web site and personal data), privacy (confidentiality of the information) and business integrity (truthful marketing and reliable order fulfillment). The study found that most seals fell in the security and privacy areas, and business integrity assurance seals were the least common. Researchers are still studying the reasons for lack of wide acceptance of seals in the online market.

Trust Services

One of the ambitious initiatives launched by AICPA and Canadian Institute of Chartered Accountants (CICA) in the e-commerce area is called *Trust Services*, which are offered by practicing CPAs. These services include two types of services — WebTrust and SysTrust. Note that WebTrust is a security seal to be displayed on the merchant Web site, but SysTrust is not a seal; it is a report that may or may not be displayed on the Web site. Recently, AICPA/CICA harmonized the requirements for WebTrust and SysTrust; these two services still independently exist, though the underlying requirements have become very similar.

The latest guidelines for Trust Services issued by AICPA/CICA is called *The Suitable Trust Services Criteria and Illustrations*, which is established by the Assurance Services Executive Committee of the AICPA. The new guidelines define trust services as a set of professional assurance and advisory services based on a common framework (that is, a core set of principles and criteria) to address the risks and opportunities of IT. The definition indicates that trust services is not only limited to e-commerce. If trust services result in an expression of an opinion by the CPA, then these services are assurance services. If there is no opinion; for example, the practitioner merely applies trust principles and criteria to evaluate e-commerce or IT services, then the services are of an advisory nature.

The trust services and principles are categorized into four areas. First, appropriate business policies have been devised by the business and documented. Second, these policies have been communicated to authorized users. Third, the business procedures developed by the entity are in accordance with business policies. Finally, the system is monitored by the business to assure compliance with policies. These policies address the following areas.

- **Security:** The system (defined as infrastructure, software, people, procedures and data) is protected against physical and logical attacks
- **Availability:** The system is available to users as promised
- **Processing integrity:** Processing done by the system is accurate, timely and authorized
- **Online privacy:** Personal information collected by the business is used, disclosed, and retained *only* as per privacy policies
- **Confidentiality:** Information designated confidential is treated as such

WebTrust services result in a seal awarded to Web sites. This seal is displayed on the Web site, and the consumer can click on the seal to obtain further information and assurance that the seal is valid. This seal identifies that the business has followed the guidelines issued by Trust Services in the areas of privacy, security, business practices/transaction integrity, availability, confidentiality or non-repudiation. WebTrust services can also be tailored to specific objectives. WebTrust for Consumer Protection

Exhibit 23. WebTrust seal on the AICPA Web site (Source: https://cert.webtrust.org/jhcohn.html)

primarily deals with online privacy and transaction-processing integrity. WebTrust for Online Privacy provides assurance regarding privacy protection to consumers. WebTrust for Certification Authorities includes application of a technical set of standards to organizations that issue digital certificates. The technical standards in this area are different than the earlier two areas and not discussed here. As per CPA Web Trust (*www.cpawebtrust.org*), the WebTrust seal means the following things for consumers.

- The seal has been issued by a specially trained and licensed public accounting firm
- The business has disclosed its business practices
- The Web site has been audited to confirm compliance with policies
- The online business meets the international WebTrust standards

SysTrust is the second service, which addresses concerns regarding system reliability, and is based on the Trust Services guidelines. In the case of SysTrust, these guidelines not only include assurance and advisory services guidelines, but also provide best practices for comparison purposes. The system is evaluated in the following areas.

- **Security:** The system (defined as infrastructure, software, people, procedures and data) is protected against physical and logical attacks
- **Availability:** The system is available to users as promised
- **Processing integrity:** Processing done by the system is accurate, timely and authorized
- **Online privacy:** Personal information collected by the business is used, disclosed and retained only as per privacy policies
- **Confidentiality:** Information that is designated confidential is treated as such

This description is identical with that of WebTrust services, which is expected, since the AICPA has harmonized these two services. The system is evaluated using the guidelines and best practices. If a business is in compliance with these guidelines and best practices as per the judgment of the CPA, then the attestation report is issued. This report can be displayed on the Web site at the discretion of the business. SysTrust services can also be offered in different formats; for example, a practitioner can issue a report on compliance with selected SysTrust principles or on the suitability of the controls of a system in pre-implementation phase, or certain mutually agreed-upon procedures from SysTrust principles may be performed by the practitioner.

CPAs have been trusted advisors for businesses since inception of the profession. In the general public, CPAs are well known for independence, integrity, objectivity and discretion. The AICPA expectation was that such trust can be leveraged to build new practice areas. WebTrust and SysTrust were considered to be logical extensions of the core practice areas for the profession. The acceptance of these services, though improving, has not matched the a priori expectations. Several accounting firms have developed competing assurance services, and the online world, of course, has its own

Exhibit 24. SysTrust report issued to GlobalNetXchange (Source: https://processcertify.ey.com/GNX/GNX_SYSTRUST_Independent _Practitioner's_Report.htm)

Report of Independent Accountants

To the Management of GlobalNetXchange:

We have examined the accompanying assertions by the management of GlobalNetXchange (GNX) regarding the effectiveness of its controls over the availability, security, integrity, and maintainability of the Negotiations and the Supply Chain Collaboration Suite Systems during the period November 1, 2002 through December 31, 2002, based on version 2 of the SysTrust™ Principles and Criteria established by the American Institute of Certified Public Accountants (AICPA) and the Canadian Institute of Chartered Accountants (CICA), which are available at www.aicpa.org/assurance/systrust/princip. These assertions are the responsibility of the management of GNX. Our responsibility is to express an opinion on the aforementioned assertions based on our examination.

Management's description of the aspects of the Negotiations and the Supply Chain Collaboration Suite Systems covered by its assertions is attached. We did not examine this description, and accordingly, we do not express an opinion on it.

Our examination was conducted in accordance with attestation standards established by the AICPA and, accordingly, included (1) obtaining an understanding of the controls related to system availability, security, integrity, and maintainability of the Negotiations and the Supply Chain Collaboration Suite Systems; (2) testing and evaluating the operating effectiveness of the controls; and (3) performing such other procedures as we considered necessary in the circumstances. We believe that our examination provides a basis for our opinion.

Because of inherent limitations in controls, error or fraud may occur and not be detected. Furthermore, the projection of any conclusions, based on our findings, to future periods is subject to the risk that the validity of such conclusions may be altered because of changes made to the system or controls, changes in the processing requirements, or the failure to make changes to the system when required may alter the validity of such conclusions.

In our opinion, management's assertion that GNX maintained effective controls over the availability, security, integrity, and maintainability of the Negotiations and the Supply Chain Collaboration Suite Systems to provide reasonable assurance that:

- The systems were available for operation and use at times set forth in service-level statements or agreements,
- The systems were protected against unauthorized physical and logical access,
- The systems' processing was complete, accurate, timely, and authorized, and
- The systems could be updated when required in a manner that continued to provide for system availability, security, and integrity

during the period November 1, 2002 through December 31, 2002, based on the SysTrust™ Principles and Criteria established by the AICPA and the CICA, is fairly stated in all material respects.

Ernst + Young LLP

February 5, 2003

Exhibit 25: Interested in the security field? (Source: SC Security Magazine, 2002, July, 38). This is a partial list, and the number of existing security certifications is quite large and increasing.

Certification	Organization	Area
BNS – Brainbench Network Security Certification	Brainbench	Network security
CCISM – Certified Counterespionage and Security Manager	Espionage Research Institute	Counterespionage and information security
CIA – Certified Internal Auditor *CCSA – Certification in Control Self-Assessment*	Institute of Internal Auditors	Internal auditing Control self-assessment
CFE – Certified Fraud Examiner	Association of Certified Fraud Examiners	White collar crime
CISA – Certified Information Systems Auditor	Information Systems Audit and Control Association	IS audit, control, and security
CISSP –Certified Information Systems Security Professional *SSCP – System Security Certified Practitioner*	$(ISC)^2$ – International Information Systems Security Certification Consortium, Inc.	Network and system security
CPP – Certified Protection Professional	American Society for Industrial Security	Technical and procedural security topics and technologies
CWP – Certified Web Professional	International Webmasters Association	Web security
GIAC – Global Information Assurance Certification	SANS Institute	Technical knowledge of information systems and networks
SCNA – Security Certified Network Architect	Security Certified Program	Network security
SCNP – Security Certified Network Professional	Security Certified Program	Network security

logic. For example, PricewaterhouseCoopers' BetterWebSM Services include assessing the Web site from customer and competitor view points, analyzing prospective and existing customer contact points and suggesting ways to build trust in the Web site. Another PWC service called WebCPO offers a complete Web site privacy management solution. In any case, this is the beginning of a long journey, and these services may yet emerge to be winners for the profession.

Privacy Audits

A number of accounting firms offer privacy audit services. These services are also offered by other service firms and even done by businesses internally. Privacy — the ability to keep designated information safe from prying eyes — is a problem for both organizations and individuals. The U.S. Constitution does not specifically mention *right to privacy*. Historically, law has protected an individual from intrusive efforts to collect personal information. As automation became widespread, collection, aggregation and dissemination of personal information became easier. Privacy issues are beginning to be taken seriously by individuals, organizations and legislatures.

Personal information collected at various Web sites can be personally identifiable or not identifiable. Personally identifiable information can contain items that are publicly available, such as name and phone number, or it may contain sensitive information. Sensitive information can be financial, medical or collected from children (under age 13). U.S. and international laws apply to such information. Other information that can be collected by Web sites relates to the Web viewing habits of the customer/user, types of browsers used, dates and times of the visit, and type of information viewed.

This information can be voluntarily provided by the customer/user via registration forms, filling in of order forms or for e-mails. The information can also be automatically extracted using log files or cookies. Cookies are text-only strings sent by the Web site to the customer/user computer. Cookies can be used to personalize information, help with online sales and service, or collect demographic information. The information can also be purchased from third-party organizations that specialize in collecting and selling of consumer information. The information format can change rapidly; for example, it can be stored in a digital format, printed or maintained in an audio/video format.

This information can be and has been abused by online companies. The privacy policies posted on the Web site are often legalistic in nature and difficult to understand. Privacy policies are often flouted since a consumer cannot find breaches easily. A few examples of findings of a study done by Annenberg Public Policy Center at the University of Pennsylvania and reported in *The Wall Street Journal*, are described in the following list.

- Approximately 60% of users know that Web sites collect information about them, even if they do not register
- Approximately 60% believe that a Web site with a privacy policy will not share their personal information
- Approximately 50% of users think Web policies are difficult to understand
- Approximately 50% of users have searched information on how to protect personal data

These findings show that user awareness as to what happens on the Web is increasing, but still has a long way to go. There has been an outcry from informed consumers and organizations such as the Electronic Frontier Foundation. Consequently, various laws have been passed or are progressing thorough the legislative process. If organizations want to earn consumer trust, they must have a privacy policy. Many organizations have developed privacy policies and displayed them on the Web site. The question is, how do the consumers know that privacy policies are being followed? What if such data is stolen due to the lax control procedures of the organization? Privacy audits serve these particular concerns.

Privacy audits not only evaluate the online company's compliance with privacy policies but also evaluate areas such as data security and access controls, password administration, database administration, personnel security, network administration and physical security of the Web site. The requirements of WebTrust and SysTrust clearly underscore the interconnected nature of privacy and security issues. Privacy deals with confidentiality of information; however, it must also deal with security, since unsecured information is not private information. As such, privacy audits have to deal with internal controls and actual organizational behavior. *Privacy Knowledge Base* (*www.privacyknowledge base.com*) provided the following objectives for the privacy audit.

- **Notice and disclosure:** What does the company's privacy policy promise consumers as to its information practices? How does the company collect, capture, use and disseminate personal information?
- **Access:** Does the company provide consumers with access to data collected about them?
- **Choice (opt out/opt in):** Does the company give consumers a clear choice with respect to using information supplied through visits to Web sites?
- **Enabling technology:** Does the company have the proper technology to ensure anonymity of consumers' information?
- **Security:** Does the company ensure that consumers' data is safe and secure?
- **Redress:** Does the company provide due process for consumers that have grievances or are harmed?

The privacy audit market is fragmented among various service providers. The demand for privacy audits may increase as customers and users become more aware about how personal information is being collected, used and abused. Currently, due to legislative requirements such as the Health Insurance Portability and Accountability Act (HIPPA) and the U.S. Patriot Act, many corporations are paying close attention to the privacy and security of information. Hopefully, there will be progress in this area in the near future.

Summary

The controls, security and audit area on the Internet is a vast field. This chapter is but just a brief overview of the complicated control requirements on the Web. First, the concept of internal controls was reviewed. Internal controls are important for accountants, auditors, managers and legislatures for different reasons. Internal controls have been defined differently by different organizations; however, there are common themes in those definitions. The COSO framework was discussed in detail, since it is applicable to the online world.

Security and control issues on the Internet are multidimensional and not only restricted to technical areas. The Internet is inherently an unsecure environment, used by millions of users around the globe, and is created to facilitate the free flow of information. Technical problems in this area include protections against physical and logical attacks directed at networks, facilities and people. Logical attacks include malicious code, active content, or probes and scans to penetrate the network. Social engineering is often used to illegally acquire information from legitimate employees. Human error generally plays a larger role in successful hacking. Also, various laws, such as UETA, UCITA, E-SIGN and the U.S. Patriot Act, which affect e-commerce transactions, were investigated. Finally, auditing considerations, such as maintenance of audit trails and backups, were discussed.

A conceptual framework for internal controls was presented to aid our understanding of controls on the Internet. The objectives of internal controls were stated as validity of transactions, mutual authentication of identity, authorization, data integrity and confidentiality, non-repudiation and auditability of transactions. This framework enables us to ask intelligent questions regarding internal controls, even if we do not have a full technical understanding of them.

Then, standard controls employed in e-commerce were covered. Controls reviewed were security policies, passwords and biometrics, ACL, cryptology, digital watermarks, firewalls, VPNs and security protocols. These controls were also classified according to the COSO framework and into four classes — security policy, perimeter security, message content security and back-end infrastructure security. Then, various network anti-intrusion defenses were reviewed. Remember, these defenses are not only reactive, but can also be proactive and interactive.

Automated software tools are increasingly being deployed to carry out control duties in the online world. Searchspace and TransactionVision solutions for financial fraud and audit trail purposes, respectively, were examined. Finally, privacy and security issues, which are intertwined, were reviewed primarily for B2C transactions. Different types of seals were discussed, and the Trust Services offered by the AICPA were reviewed in detail. A number of assurance and advisory services, such as privacy solutions, are offered by accounting and other firms. Consumers are more aware of privacy issues, and new laws are in progress to protect the privacy of personal information. As such, these areas may witness positive developments in the near future.

References

A review of federal and state privacy laws (white paper). (2003). BBB Online. Retrieved May 5, 2004, from www.bbbonline.org/UnderstandingPrivacy/library/fed_statePrivLaws.pdf

Arthurs, W. (2001). *A proactive defense to social engineering*. Retrieved May 7, 2004, from www.securitydocs.com/library/2230

Baumer, D.L., Maffie, R.L., & Ward, A.L. (2001, November/December). Cyberlaw and e-commerce: An internal audit perspective. *Internal Auditing*, *17*, 24-31.

Bernstein, G.L., & Campbell, E. (2002, September). Electronic contracting: The current state of the law and best practices. *Intellectual Property & Technology Law Journal*, *14*, 1-11.

Boncella, R.J. (2000, November). Web security for e-commerce. *Communications of the AIS, 4,* 1-43.

Cale, D., & McGinnis, T. (2002). *Partners share responsibility for marketplace security.* Retrieved May 7, 2004, from www.informationweek.com/813/prmarketplace.htm

CERT Coordination Center. (2003). *CERT/CC overview incident and vulnerability trends* (white paper). Pittsburgh, PA: Software Engineering Center, Carnegie Mellon University. Retrieved May 10, 2004, from www.cert.org/present/cert-overview-trends/module-7.pdf

Colbert, J., & Bowen, P. (2002*). A comparison of internal controls: COBIT, SAC, COSO, and SAS 55/78*. Retrieved October 3, 2003, from www.isaca.org/bkr_cbt3.htm/

Combating check fraud with Searchspace (Solutions Brief). (2003). Searchspace. Retrieved October 4, 2003, from www.searchspace.com/

Combating debit and credit card fraud with Searchspace (Solutions Brief). (2003). Searchspace. Retrieved October 4, 2003, from www.searchspace.com/

Combating fraud with Searchspace (Solutions Brief). (2003). Searchspace.Retrieved October 4, 2003, from www.searchspace.com/

Combating wire payment fraud with Searchspace (Solutions Brief). (2003). Searchspace. Retrieved October 4, 2003, from www.searchspace.com/

Command center: Policy awareness and vulnerability management for long-term, cost-effective risk reduction (white paper). (2003). META Group. Retrieved October 15, 2003, from www.metagroup.com/

Cryptography FAQ. (2001). Internet FAQ Archives. Retrieved October 20, 2003, from www.faqs.org/

Deshmukh, A. (2004). A conceptual framework for online internal controls. *Journal of Information Technology Management*, *3-4*, 23-32.

Developing a security policy (white paper). (2002). Retrieved October 21, 2003, from www.sun.com/blueprints/

Dreazen, Y. (2003, June 25). Consumers are in the dark on Web-site privacy. *The Wall Street Journal*, *Personal Finance Section*, D2.

Dubin, L. (2002). *The Enemy within: A system administrator's look at network security.* Retrieved May 7, 2004, from www.sans.org/rr/papers/51/530.pdf

Duh, R., Jamal, K., & Sunder, S. (2002, October). Control and assurance in e-commerce: Privacy, security, and integrity at eBay. *Taiwan Accounting Review*, *3*(1), 1-27.

Electronic fund transfer fraud with Searchspace (Solutions Brief). (2003). Searchspace. Retrieved October 4, 2003, from www.searchspace.com/

Entrust. (2001.) *The concept of trust in network security* (white paper). Retrieved November 18, 2003, from www.entrust.com/

Everhardt, N. (2002). *Meeting the AML (Anti Money Laundering) compliance challenge* (white paper). Retrieved October 4, 2003, from www.searchspace.com/

Givens, B. (2001, June). A checklist for responsible information-handling practices. *Business Credit*, *103,* 47-52.

Gordeev, M. (2001). *Intrusion detection techniques and approaches* (white paper). Retrieved November 21, 2003, from www.forum-intrusion.com/archive/Intrusion%20Detection%20Techniques%20and%20Approaches.htm

Gragg, D. (2003). *A multi-level defense against social engineering*. Retrieved October 21, 2003, from www.sans.org/rr/papers/51/920.pdf

Granger, S. (2001). *Social engineering fundamentals, part I: Hacker tactics*. Retrieved January 7, 2004, from www.securityfocus.com/infocus/

Granger, S. (2002). *Social engineering fundamentals, part II: Combat strategies*. Retrieved January 7, 2004, from www.securityfocus.com/infocus/

Greenfield, P., Rickwood, A., & Tran, H. (2001). *Effectiveness of Internet filtering software products*. CSIRO Mathematical and Information Sciences. Retrieved September 23, 2004, from www.aba.gov.au/internet/research/filtering/filtereffectiveness.pdf

Halme, L., & Bauer, K. (2002). *AINT misbehaving: A taxonomy of anti-intrusion techniques* (white paper). Retrieved January 10, 2004, from www.sans.org/resources/idfaq/aint.php

How to develop a network security policy: An overview of networking site security (white paper). (2002). Sun. Retrieved January 10, 2004, from www.sun.com/software/whitepapers/

Intrusion detection FAQ. (2002). SANS. Retrieved January 11, 2004, from www.sans.org/resources/

Kazienko, P., & Dorosoz, P. (2003, April). *Intrusion detection systems part I, WindowSecurity*. Retrieved January 11, 2004, from www.WindowSecurity.com/

Lee, P., Hui, S., & Fong, A. (2003). A structural and content-based analysis for Web filtering. *Internet Research*, *13*(1), 27-37.

Lipson, H. (2002). *Tracking and tracing cyber-attacks: Technical challenges and global policy issues* (white paper). Pittsburgh, PA: CERT Coordination Center, Software Engineering Center, Carnegie Mellon University. Retrieved January 15, 2004, from www.cert.org/archive/pdf/02sr009.pdf

Medina, L. (2002). *Profile of sophisticated hackers*. Retrieved October 15, 2003, from http://searchnetworking.techtarget.com/

Merkow, M. (2000). Bathe your site in seals of privacy assurance. *Insights-EC Outlook, September*. Retrieved October 23, 2003, from http://ecommerce.internet.com/news/insights/

META Group. (2002). *Making information security policy effective* (white paper). Retrieved January 15, 2004, from www.metagroup.com/

Network security policy: Best practices white paper. (2002). CISCO. Retrieved October 24, 2003, from www.cisco.com/

Newsletter. (2004, September). IT managers believe Spyware is not a problem - report. *Telecomworldwire*, Coventry, 1.

Northcutt, S., Zeltser, L., Winters, S., Frederick, K., & Ritchey, R. (2003). *Inside network perimeter security*. Indianapolis, IN: New Riders.

SAS anti-money laundering solution (SAS white paper). (2003). SAS. Retrieved October 23, 2003, from www.sas.com/

Saunder, K., & Zucker, B. (1999, August). Counteracting identity fraud in information age: The Identity Theft and Assumption Deterrence Act. *International Review of Law, Computers, & Technology, 13,* 183-192.

Schneider, P., & Perry, J. (2001). *Electronic commerce* (2nd ed.). Course Technology: Thomson Learning.

Searchspace: Enabling the intelligent enterprise (white paper) (2003). Aberdeen. Retrieved October 4, 2003, from www.aberdeen.com/

Security policy automation: An introduction (white paper). (2003). Polivec. Retrieved January 15, 2004, from www.polivec.com/

Shimonski, R. (2003, April). Wireless security primer (part II). *WindowSecurity*. Retrieved January 11, 2004, from www.WindowSecurity.com/

Shinder, D. (2003, March). Understanding the role of PKI. *WindowSecurity*. Retrieved January 11, 2004, from www.WindowSecurity.com/

Shopping on the Internet – Facts for the consumers. (2002). Australian Government, The Treasury. Retrieved January 11, 2004, from www.dcita.gov.au/

Sivasailam, N., Kim, D., & Rao, R. (2002, June). What companies are(n't) doing about Web assurance? *IEEE IT Professional*, 33-40.

Suitable trust services criteria and illustrations for security, availability, processing integrity, online privacy, and confidentiality (including WebTrust and SysTrust). (2003). Retrieved February 17, 2004, from www.cpawebtrust.org/download/final-Trust-Services.pdf

Taylor, L. (2001). *Seven elements of highly effective security policies*. Retrieved November 10, 2003, from www.zdnet.com/

The World Wide Web security FAQ (2003). The World Wide Web Consortium. Retrieved November 22, 2003, from www.w3.org/Security/Faq/

TransactionVision, end-to-end transaction tracking (white paper). (2003). Bristol Corp. Retrieved November 29, 2003, from www.bristol.com/transactionvision/

Understanding virtual private networking (white paper). (2003). AdTran. Retrieved November 25, 2003, from www.adtran.com/

VPN security and return on investment (Solutions white paper). (2003). RSA Security. Retrieved November 25, 2003, from www.rsasecurity.com/

Web services security (Solutions white paper). (2003). RSA Security. Retrieved November 29, 2003, from www.rsasecurity.com/

Zhang, Y., Lee, W., & Huang, Y. (2003). Intrusion detection techniques for mobile Wireless networks. *ACM WINNET*, 1-16.

Endnote

1 A substantial part of this section is taken from Deshmukh, A. (2004). A conceptual framework for online Internal controls. *Journal of Information Technology Management*, *3-4*, 23-32.

About the Author

Dr. Ashutosh Deshmukh is an associate professor of accounting and information systems at the Pennsylvania State University – Erie. He received his MBA from the University of Alabama and PhD from the University of Memphis. His research and teaching interests are in accounting information systems and auditing. He has published more than 20 articles and made numerous conference presentations in the areas of accounting information systems and auditing. He is a chartered accountant, certified information systems auditor, and certified fraud examiner, and has practical experience in public and industrial accounting. A bean counter by profession and a byte counter by choice, he has also consulted with numerous organizations. He is a member of the American Accounting Association, Institute of Charted Accountants of India, Information Systems Audit and Control Association, Association of Certified Fraud Examiners, Phi Kappa Phi, and Beta Gamma Sigma. He lives in Erie with his wife and son, and enjoys Tae Kwon Do, chess, and science fiction in his spare time.

Index

B

C

F

G

H

I

J

K

P

Q

R

S

T

U